Milton and Monotheism

Medieval & Renaissance Literary Studies

General Editor:
Albert C. Labriola

Advisory Editor:
Foster Provost

Editorial Board:
Judith H. Anderson
Diana Treviño Benet
Donald Cheney
Ann Baynes Coiro
Mary T. Crane
Patrick Cullen
A. C. Hamilton
Margaret P. Hannay
A. Kent Hieatt
Michael Lieb
Thomas P. Roche Jr.
Mary Beth Rose
John T. Shawcross
John M. Steadman
Humphrey Tonkin
Susanne Woods

Milton and Monotheism

Abraham Stoll

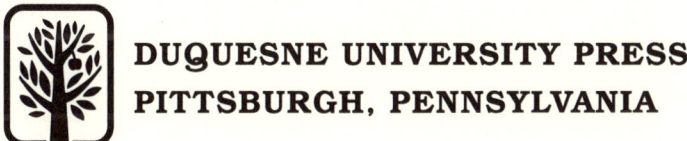

DUQUESNE UNIVERSITY PRESS
PITTSBURGH, PENNSYLVANIA

Copyright © 2009 Duquesne University Press
All rights reserved

Published in the United States of America by:
DUQUESNE UNIVERSITY PRESS
600 Forbes Avenue
Pittsburgh, Pennsylvania 15282

No part of this book may be used or reproduced,
in any manner or form whatsoever,
without written permission from the publisher,
except in the case of short quotations
in critical articles or reviews.

Library of Congress Cataloging-in-Publication Data

Stoll, Abraham Dylan, 1969–
  Milton and monotheism / Abraham Stoll.
    p. cm.—(Medieval & renaissance literary studies)
  Based on the author's doctoral thesis, presented to Princeton University, 2000.
  Includes bibliographical references and index.
  Summary: "Examining Milton's poetry in the context of many debates swirling around polytheism and monotheism, this study demonstrates the profound differences between doctrinal discourse and narrative poetry and how neither is, individually, able to fully represent Milton's monotheism—or, as Abraham Stoll says, 'a God of flickering subjectivity' "—Provided by publisher.
  ISBN 978-0-8207-0410-4 (cloth : alk. paper)
  1. Milton, John, 1608–1674—Religion. 2. Monotheism in literature. 3. Milton, John, 1608–1674. Paradise lost. 4. Milton, John, 1608–1674. Samson Agonistes. 5. Religion and poetry. 6. God in literature. 7. Christianity and literature—Great Britain—History—17th century. 8. Religion and literature—Great Britain—History—17th century. I. Title.
  PR3592.R4S68 2009
  821'.4—dc22

                                                      2008048678

∞ Printed on acid-free paper.

For Ella and Marion, and LeAnne

Contents

	Citations and Abbreviations	ix
	Acknowledgments	xi
	Introduction	1
One	Polytheism and "truest Poesie"	25
Two	Occult Monotheism and the Abstract Godhead: The Discourse of Monotheism	73
Three	God and Genesis 18 in *Paradise Lost*	101
Four	The War in Heaven and Deism	143
Five	Socinianism and Deism: The Discourse of Monotheism	183
Six	The Son after the Trinity	216
Seven	Revelation and Samson's Sense of Heaven's Desertion	264
	Afterword: Monotheism, the Sublime, and Allegory	309
	Notes	320
	Index	367

CITATIONS AND ABBREVIATIONS

All quotations of Milton's poetry are taken from *Paradise Lost*, ed. Alastair Fowler (London: Longman, 1971) and *The Complete Shorter Poems*, ed. John Carey (London: Longman, 1971). References to Milton's prose are to *The Complete Prose Works of John Milton*, 8 vols. in 10, gen. ed. Don M. Wolfe et al. (New Haven: Yale University Press, 1953–82), cited in the text as YP. All biblical citations are from the King James Version, unless otherwise noted. The following abbreviations are used in parenthetical citations and endnotes.

Bolingbroke	Henry St. John, Viscount Bolingbroke, *The Works*, 4 vols. (1844; repr., London: Frank Cass, 1967).
Dennis	John Dennis, *The Advancement and Reformation of Modern Poetry*, in *The Critical Works of John Dennis*, 2 vols., ed. Edward Niles Hooker (Baltimore: Johns Hopkins University Press, 1939).
De religione	Edward, Lord Herbert of Cherbury, *De religione gentilium*, trans. John Anthony Butler as *Pagan Religion* (Binghamton, N.Y.: Medieval & Renaissance Texts & Studies, 1996).
De veritate	Edward, Lord Herbert of Cherbury, *De veritate*, trans. Meyrick H. Carré (Bristol: J. W. Arrowsmith, 1937).
GMG	Henry More, *An Explanation of the Grand Mystery of Godliness* (London, 1660).
MM	Sigmund Freud, *Moses and Monotheism*, trans. Katherine Jones (New York: Vintage Books, 1939).

Racovian   *The Racovian Catechisme* (Amsterledam [London], 1652).

Selden   John Selden, *Opera omnia*, 3 vols. ed. David Wilkins (London, 1726).

Acknowledgments

This book has been supported by several faculty research grants from the University of San Diego. The Folger Shakespeare Library and the Huntington Library have contributed fellowships, and their collections. I thank those institutions, as well as Firestone Library in Princeton, Copley Library in San Diego, the Hebrew University and National Libraries in Jerusalem, and the British Library. A year as a fellow at the Princeton University Center for Human Values was essential to completing this study's earlier form, as a dissertation. And a year visiting Hebrew University enabled me to complete its final form, as a book.

A version of chapter 4 was published previously as "Discontinuous Wound: Milton and Deism," by Abraham Stoll, from Milton Studies 44, edited by Albert C. Labriola, © 2005. Reprinted by permission of the University of Pittsburgh Press. A version of chapter 7 appeared as "Milton Stages Cherbury: Revelation and Polytheism in *Samson Agonistes*," in *Altering Eyes: New Perspectives on Samson Agonistes*, edited by Mark R. Kelley and Joseph Wittreich (Newark: University of Delaware Press, 2002). I thank these publishers for permission to use this material.

It is an even greater pleasure to thank the people who have influenced my research and writing. Victoria Kahn has been a brilliant reader and advisor over many years. I have benefited greatly from the ideas of Jonathan Lamb, Jason Rosenblatt, Joseph Wittreich, Nigel Smith, Suzanne Keen, and the late Earl Miner. Among my fellows, I thank Erik Gray, Denise Gigante, Christopher Rovee, Joseph Jeon, and Peter Kanelos. And I thank the readers at Duquesne University Press. This page acknowledges my gratitude, but every page testifies to the generosity of these scholars.

Introduction

Paradise Lost is about the angelic rebellion and the Fall from Eden. But both of these, Milton's language implies, are part of a struggle between polytheism and monotheism. Waking up in hell, Satan depicts his revolt as an immortal battle between gods: "since by fate the strength of gods / And this empyreal substance cannot fail" (1.116–17). Beelzebub answers in kind: "and all this mighty host / In horrible destruction laid thus low, / As far as gods and heavenly essences / Can perish" (1.136–39). Satan and Beelzebub, in just the first two of 15 similar instances of the word in book 1, believe that in substance and in essence they are "gods." These polytheistic hopes are presumably delusional, yet the poetry also kindles the opposite conclusion. The word "gods" demands that apostate claims for deity, which are assertions of a polytheistic universe, be reconciled with the truth of monotheism. Such reconciliation comes only after an ontological calculation: faced with these beings, the reader must ask, are they gods? or not?

In Eve's dream, Satan so caresses the word "gods," and it is so intertwined with the fruit and its potential, that the act of disobedience reads as an assertion of polytheism:

> O fruit divine,
> Sweet of thy self, but much more sweet thus cropt,
> Forbidden here, it seems, as only fit
> For *gods*, yet able to makes *gods* of men:
> And why not *gods* of men, since good, the more

> Communicated, more abundant grows,
> The author not impaired, but honoured more?
>
> (5.67–73; italics mine)

And in the actual temptation, Satan cannot leave the word alone:

> and ye shall be as *gods*,
> Knowing both good and evil as they know.
> That ye should be as *gods*, since I as man,
> Internal man, is but proportion meet,
> I of brute human, ye of human *gods*.
> So ye shall die perhaps, by putting off
> Human, to put on *gods*, death to be wished,
> Though threatened, which no worse than this can bring.
> And what are *gods* that man may not become
> As they, participating *godlike* food?
> The *gods* are first, and that advantage use
> On our belief, that all from them proceeds;
> I question it.   (9.708–20; italics mine)

From within Satan's unyielding syntax, the insistent repetition of "gods" takes on an incantational force. Not only is it the temptation, but "gods" also names the consequence of rebellion, as well as its real danger: polytheism. The goal and the threat are the effort to be gods, or as Satan conjures it, to "put on gods." Even more than the arbitrary symbol of the apple, resistance to Satan becomes a matter of resisting the word "gods."[1]

No amount of rebellion can change the apostates' ontological status—in Satan's mouth "gods" is a vain attempt at performative utterance. But "gods" becomes more complicated when spoken by voices that are less parodied. The poet is fond of using the term in simile, as with Eve: "With goddess-like demeanour forth she went" (8.59). And he also, more dangerously, uses it in book 1 to describe the apostates: "godlike shapes and forms / Excelling human, princely dignities, / And powers that erst in heaven sat on thrones" (1.358–60). The poet is by no means calling them gods, which is protected against by the simile. But coming amid the apostates' own frequent assertions of deity, the line rings a subversive note. The word "forms," with its Platonic possibilities, suggests that some essence, one more fundamental than shape, can be understood in terms of polytheism. This clashes with the use of the word 50 lines earlier, when Satan's legions are "angel forms, who lay entranced / Thick as autumnal leaves" (1.301–02), and the clash insists that we slow down to consider these forms—whether they are angels, implying monotheism, or gods, implying polytheism. True religion asks that we calculate just what kind of beings these opening books of the poem have put in front of us.

But Milton does not make this easy. In book 2 Satan describes the heavenly council at which God announced the Creation: "so was his will / Pronounced among the gods, and by an oath, / That shook heaven's whole circumference, confirmed" (2.351–53). Again "gods" challenges the rule of God and the monotheism of the cosmos. Scholarship does ameliorate the situation with the fact that Satan is using the term in appropriate accordance with Scripture: the Hebrew *elohim* literally means gods, but is frequently used to describe angels, as Milton explains in *De doctrina Christiana* (YP 6:233–34). This word, however, is laden with another difficult association. Immediately after discussing *elohim* as angels, *De doctrina* goes on to explain that it is a plural form that is commonly read as the name of the one God (YP 6:234).[2] God's pronouncement "among the gods" accentuates this peculiarity in God's name particularly because it appears while Milton is reenacting the creation of Adam, as told in Genesis 1:26, "And God said, Let us make man in our image." In this famous passage *elohim* is matched by a plural verb, either creating the subversive sense that God is plural, or, equally polytheistic, that *elohim* says "let us" because the speech is in council. The Hebrew Bible, even on the level of its vocabulary and grammar, shuttles between the competing possibilities of one and many gods. The very effort to name the one God, to put God into language, produces contradiction and creates in the narrative a sense of negotiation. As the most literal translation of the biblical *elohim*, Milton's "gods" calls forth this monotheistic negotiation.[3]

Milton introduces an even more provocative use of "gods" in book 3, when God tells the Son that, after his Second Coming,

> Then thou thy regal sceptre shalt lay by,
> For regal sceptre then no more shall need,
> God shall be all in all. But all ye gods,
> Adore him, who to compass all this dies,
> Adore the Son, and honour him as me. (3.339–43)

Here it is not Satan speaking, but God. God must mean "angels," but his use of "gods" seems quite deliberately to increase the sense of polytheistic council. As Sister M. Christopher Pecheux has shown, Milton departs from his source text, Hebrews 1:6, by changing "angels" to "gods."[4] This ontology problem not only comes from God's mouth, but it appears at an especially crucial moment. He addresses "all ye gods" just after "God shall be all in all": the unstable distinction between gods and angels raises the sense that the distinction between such a totalizing God and his creation may be equally difficult to determine. The ontological calculation extends, therefore, to the distinction between God and angels.[5] Plus, God's larger goal in this passage is to introduce the Son to the angels. God's command to honor him "as me" attracts the same kind of doubt as "gods": as the intricacies of Milton's Antitrinitarianism show, there is also a great need for distinction between Father and Son. The ontological exercises multiply and expand until they encompass nearly all of the beings of the poem's story world: we are brought to calculate the differences between Son and God, God and angel, angel and gods, and gods and humans.

These calculations are the way in which monotheism defines itself as other than polytheism, and they are the work that constructs monotheistic narrative. They are, this book argues, a central quality of Milton's great religious poetry. Readers have long felt that Milton's late poetry is shaken by ontological instability, as in Samuel Johnson's critique of *Paradise Lost*:

> Another inconvenience of Milton's design is that it requires the description of what cannot be described, the agency of spirits.

> He saw that immateriality supplied no images, and that he could not show angels acting but by instruments of action; he therefore invested them with form and matter. This being necessary was therefore defensible; and he should have secured the consistency of his system by keeping immateriality out of sight, and enticing his reader to drop it from his thoughts. But he has unhappily perplexed his poetry with his philosophy. His infernal and celestial powers are sometimes pure spirit and sometimes animated body.⁶

Johnson complains that Milton situates his poem in the inconsistent space between pure materiality and pure immateriality, leaving the reader to endless calculations, unable to "drop it from his thoughts." Yet rather than finding the poem's struggles with ontology an inconvenience, I suggest viewing them as an index to Milton's commitment to monotheism. Milton's "philosophy," with which "he has unhappily perplexed his poetry," is monotheism—or, to put it another way, Milton's monotheism is constituted by his perplexing poetry.⁷

The Discourse of Monotheism

In *De doctrina Christiana*, Milton repeatedly makes it clear that he conceives of the godhead in terms of the singleness of monotheism. For example: "The numerical significance of 'one' and 'two' must be unalterable and the same for God as for man. It would have been a waste of time for God to thunder forth so repeatedly that first commandment which said that he was the one and only God, if it could nevertheless be maintained that another God existed as well, who ought to be thought of as the only God" (YP 6:212). Discussing the Son, Milton turns away from the Trinity to the Hebraic injunction for monotheism and to a description of God based on that quality of being one. Similarly focused on number, Adam declares: "No need that thou / Shouldst propagate, already infinite; / And through all numbers absolute, though one" (8.419–21). Here and in many other ways, Milton rearticulates God and religion to be understood by means of the concept of monotheism.

Perhaps to announce that Milton was a monotheist is to court a shrug: what Christian wasn't? Yet the concept of monotheism can be studied not just as an ideal adherence to the first commandment, but also as a historically particular version of God and Christianity. Monotheism is a topic discussed by many important thinkers in Milton's England. One marker of this importance is that, although the concept of a single God is older than the Hebrew Bible and although it was central to church theologians since the inception of Christianity, it appears to have acquired a name only in 1660. In that year, in the midst of Milton's composition of *Paradise Lost* and from Christ's College, the Cambridge Platonist Henry More coined, out of existing Greek roots, the term "monotheisme." Comparing his version of the Christian God to a more abstract and pantheistic version attributed to the Egyptians, More argues, "But thus to make the *World* God, is to make no God at all; and therefore this kind of *Monotheisme* of the Heathen is as rank *Atheisme* as the *Polytheisme* was proved to be before" (*GMG* 62).

This is the first textual trace of the word "monotheism."[8] The clear articulation of the concept became necessary to the language, it can be inferred, because of the particular attention that monotheism received. Indeed, More's coining, and his theological positions during that coining, stand at the center of a discourse of monotheism, a web of theological and philosophical texts stretching through the seventeenth to the early eighteenth centuries that examine religion through the distinction between monotheism and its implied opposite, polytheism.

The main source for More, and the watershed text for the study of monotheism in England, was John Selden's *De diis Syris syntagmata* (1617). *De diis* and its related text, Samuel Purchas's *Purchas His Pilgrimage* (1613), form a front end of the discourse as I capture it. And this study takes as its tail end Lord Bolingbroke, the deist whose essay "Farther Reflections on the Rise and Progress of Monotheism" (1745) is the first extended treatment of monotheism per se.[9] Selden is the leading voice of a group of seventeenth century scholars attempting to describe the pagan gods with new historical detail. Purchas, Selden, Gerardus Vossius, Herbert of Cherbury, and others bring their languages and an antiquarian approach to creating an account of polytheism that draws near to one historian's definition of comparative religion: "the study, in the round, of the religious traditions of the world...as phenomena to be observed, rather than as creeds to be followed."[10] From Selden's anthropological study of the gods in Scripture, the discourse arrives at the skeptical appraisal of the Christian revelation by Bolingbroke and English deism. From Renaissance humanism to deism, the discourse traces a route through seventeenth century rational religion, involving philosophers and theologians in debates about reason and miracle, revealed and natural religion, religious toleration and the imperative to define what true religion is. In articulating Christianity as a monotheistic religion, the discourse negotiates between the orthodoxies of revealed religion and the emerging skepticism of rational religion, telling us about the seventeenth century's movement toward deism and the Enlightenment reevaluation of religion.

In *Paradise Lost* Milton relies extensively on the seventeenth century study of polytheism, turning especially to Selden, who becomes chief mythographer of the gods in book 1. Milton also takes part in this transreligious perspective in *De doctrina* when he describes worship as either internal or external. "Internal worship means, in the first place, acknowledgment of the one true God and devout affection for him," he asserts, and cites Deuteronomy 6:5, "*hear, Israel, Jehova our God is one Jehova.*" Then he goes on: "Opposed to this is atheism.... And polytheism, which means acknowledgment of more than one God" (YP 6:656).[11] Matching his conception of God in numerical terms, Milton organizes the kinds of worship around quantity. Worship may be called "polytheism" or "atheism" or monotheism. Writing in the 1650s, all Milton lacks is what More will soon historically provide: the actual word. Meanwhile, he resembles Selden, Purchas, and others in the discourse who frequently make use of "polytheism" instead of "pagan" or "heathen." Whereas the more common terms dismiss other gods as simply false, "polytheism" and "monotheism" provide a quantitative and comparative distinction between the competing religions and Christianity.

Tracing monotheism in the seventeenth century, however, does not produce a Whiggish march to the Enlightenment. On the contrary, the issue of monotheism frequently becomes a site in which the advance of rational religion is challenged by efforts to maintain more orthodox conceptions of revealed Christianity. Most centrally, Henry More coins the word within an argument against radical positions that would find monotheistic worship even among pagans. As described in chapter 2, emerging from Selden's comparative work is a proto-deist position that threatens to marginalize the revealed specifics of Christianity by finding an occult monotheism within polytheism. Pagans could intuit monotheism, the argument goes, and so Christianity is not essential to true religion. In a conservative response, More defines monotheism as necessarily partaking of the Judeo-Christian revelation, and so unavailable to pagans, thus protecting revealed Christianity as the only truly monotheistic faith.

More's study of polytheism and monotheism is part of a book that defends the Trinity, and seventeenth century debates surrounding Antitrinitarian heresies represent another important place in which monotheism forces a rearticulation of orthodox Christian faith. The loudest claims against the Trinity regularly use the threat of idolatry and the numerical rhetoric of the single God to assert the basic point that the Trinity undermines monotheism. Those thinkers who take on the problem of the divinity of the Son, particularly the English Socinians of the 1650s, may be grouped as important contributors to the discourse of monotheism. Milton's Antitrinitarian positions have been increasingly acknowledged in scholarly criticism, although what label to attach to his theology remains contentious. Rather than Socinianism or Arianism, I propose the more structural and descriptive "monotheism." It is in chapter 5, "Of the Son," that *De doctrina*'s most forceful assertions of monotheism can be found, and in *Paradise Regained* the effects of Milton's monotheism are felt in Milton's Son even more than in Milton's God or gods.

It is also in the concept of monotheism that the period's two most radical heresies, Socinianism and deism, overlap. Socinianism removes the Son from the godhead in order to preserve a rational conception of the one God. It rejects mystery, but insists on Scripture as the sole revelation. Deism goes further along the skeptical trajectory, doubting all revelation, and marginalizing the Son as well as the Bible. As Charles Blount and Charles Gildon make clear, deism does so in the name of monotheism: "The Jew and the Mahometan accuse the Christian of Idolatry, the Reform'd Churches, the Roman, the Socinian the other Reformed Churches, the Deists the Socinian, for his *Deus factus*; but none can accuse the Deist of Idolatry, for he only acknowledges one Supream, Everlasting God, and thinks magnificently of him."[12]

Beginning with the second commandment, monotheism asserts itself by opposing all other gods and all forms of idolatry, and so the monotheistic drive toward true religion is a drive toward the absence of representation. Monotheism has a structural tendency toward silence and erasure—an endpoint that is sometimes called aniconism for the total absence of representability in the divine economy.[13] The violent semiotics of iconoclasm is a separate thing, one that has received considerable attention.[14] This study attempts to describe the monotheistic ideal of aniconism, and how, by pushing toward an extreme minimalism in representation and ontology, it shapes the seventeenth century religious imagination.[15] It is in the extreme position of deism that aniconism finds its clearest expression, for the deist rejection of all forms of revelation, from the miraculous revelation of angels to the entire Judeo-Christian revelation of the Bible, constructs a natural religion that is utterly aniconic. Deism offers the silent and invisible religious economy of an extreme monotheism. Although many of the most important deist texts were published after Milton's death, they are included in this study because they articulate forces that are inherent in the structure of all seventeenth century monotheism. The aniconic endpoint of deism demonstrates a quality that is present earlier: that in its very structure and in the historical articulations of it across the seventeenth century, monotheism pushes toward a rational and skeptical extreme.

The progression from More's "monotheisme," through Antitrinitarianism, to the full expression of English deism, will be described in chapter 5. This is one of two chapters, along with the second, devoted primarily to discussing the philosophers, historians, and theologians who make up the discourse of monotheism. This arrangement is largely rhetorical. It is an attempt to avoid, on the one hand, a first chapter that lays out the entire historical argument, but which is unwieldy and segregated from the remaining readings of the poetry. And on the other hand, it is an attempt to avoid burying historical claims within literary analysis by taking them on bit by bit in each chapter. Surprisingly, a history of the concept of monotheism in the seventeenth century has not been written; the emergence of what is one of comparative religion's most basic terms has largely been taken for granted. *Milton and Monotheism* begins to fill this gap, but it merely outlines what deserves a full treatment. Such a book would fall under the category of the history of ideas, and might be led well beyond the scope of this study into the German Enlightenment, Christian Hebraism, patristic writings, and the religions of the ancient Near East. In this book my instincts are more literary, and my subject is, ultimately, Milton's poetry. I do not make the most assertive of historical claims about the discourse of monotheism—that it causes Enlightenment ideas, or that rational religion causes it; that the seventeenth century is unlike every other century in its handling of monotheism; or that we can be certain that each text directly influenced Milton. Rather, I see the seventeenth century discourse of monotheism as an ongoing conversation that is an important part of this transitional period. I assume that as we become familiar with the elements of the conversation we will understand a great deal more about Milton's late poetry. The connections lie not in the proofs of the historian, but in the conceptual congruencies between poetry and theology that emerge in the study of Milton's narratives. These chapters argue that seventeenth century monotheism had a deep and structural effect on how Milton told his stories. The concept of a single God creates a number of problems for narrative, in the Bible as well as in *Paradise Lost, Paradise Regained*, and *Samson Agonistes*.

The Narrative Problems of Monotheism

This book's title alludes to Freud's *Moses and Monotheism*, which may be surprising. *Paradise Lost* would not seem to have much in common with the thoroughgoing atheism that informs Freud's text. But while *Moses and Monotheism* is the furthest thing from theodicy, it does offer a version of God, and this version will introduce, in magnified terms, the problems that confront Milton as he attempts to narrate God and his ways.

Following history and his own mythological constructions, Freud asserts that there were not one but two different men named Moses, and not one but two different gods for the Hebrews. The first Moses is a nobleman from the Egyptian court and a priest of the purely abstract and universal god, Aton. The second Moses is the son-in-law of the Midianite priest Jethro, and mediator to the Hebrews of a volcano god, Jahve. In their wandering in the desert, Freud supposes, the two men and the two gods each became one (*MM* 43). Central to Freud's myth is the way in which the single God of received monotheism splinters into two: Freud uncovers a fundamental "duality" behind monotheism. Explicitly transferring the language and structures of psychoanalysis onto historical process, Freud finds that in monotheism, like the recurrence of a traumatic memory, duality insistently breaks in upon singleness.

The monotheistic God splinters over the problem of abstraction. Freud's Aton is pure abstraction and absolute value: "a single God who embraces the whole world, one as all-loving as he was all-powerful, who, averse to all ceremonial and magic, set humanity as its highest aim a life of truth and justice" (*MM* 61). But his Jahve, the demon and volcano god, is neither abstract nor ideal, and is therefore not purely monotheistic:

> A rude, narrow-minded local god, violent and blood-thirsty, he had promised his adherents to give them "a land flowing with milk and honey" and he encouraged them to rid the country of its present inhabitants "with the edge of the sword."...It is not even sure that his religion was a true monotheism, that it denied the character of God to other divinities. It probably sufficed that one's own god was more powerful than all strange gods. (*MM* 61)

Freud rewrites the foundational myth of monotheism, the exodus from Egypt, to embody the insight that the monotheistic God must simultaneously contain both of these contradictory gods. Aton, in his perfect abstraction, is associated with spiritual and intellectual progress, the subordination of the senses to abstract thinking, and with pure monotheism. He is the pure oneness promised by the concept. But Aton alone cannot win the race for survival: first his monotheism fails in Egypt, and then it fails in the desert. Freud describes Aton and the first Moses as "uncompromising," and makes the remarkable assertion that the Hebrews killed Moses as a tyrant (*MM* 28, 43). The biblical trace of this conflict is the story of the golden calf, where the Hebrews demand of Moses a god that can be seen—the kind of god, like Freud's Jahve, that is not entirely abstract. For it is the ban on images, the impossibility of representing Aton, that Moses' people find so unsatisfactory. There is a psychological need for the concrete, and the monotheistic God only survives by encompassing the limited, material, and potentially polytheistic qualities of Jahve. The monotheistic God's survival depends upon the ability to simultaneously, and paradoxically, be both the abstract Aton and the representable Jahve.

This tension between pure abstraction and the need for concrete divinity is the central disruption felt in monotheistic narrative. The absolute transcendence implied by the concept of the single God, embodied by Freud's Aton, resists representation. So the second commandment, "Thou shalt not make unto thee any graven image" is often read, both grammatically and logically, as a necessary part of the first, "Thou shalt have no other gods before me."[16] The abstraction of the monotheistic God, however, is not only threatened by images, but also by concrete language and its tendency to anthropomorphize or limit God. So Maimonides, who is often held up as an exemplar of pure monotheism, devotes the first 40 chapters of *The Guide for the Perplexed* to refuting literal readings of biblical passages that portray God as corporeal. The inability of human language to adequately portray God leads Maimonides to insist that we cannot assign positive, especially human, attributes to God. The demanding conception of God's unity splinters in language: "Those who believe that God is One, and that He has many attributes, declare the unity with their lips, and assume plurality in their thoughts."[17] As Aryeh Botwinick explains, this negative theology quickly becomes a linguistic matter, as monotheism "emphasizes on both religious and philosophical grounds how none of the adjectives, adverbs, and verbs monotheistic theological texts ascribe to God can be construed literally."[18]

The abstract godhead of monotheism, then, represents an ideal that cannot be realized in language. As Raphael explains, "Immediate are the acts of God, more swift / Than time or motion, but to human ears / Cannot without process of speech be told" (7.176–78). The failure of language to express the godhead, when expanded into an entire story world, becomes a failure in narrative. A figure that resists embodiment in language will also resist the spatial and temporal limitations of a plot, denying the godhead the ability to be present in the narrative. The foundation of these problems is the representation of God. But narrative problems extend also to God's omniscience and omnipotence; the presence in the story world of polytheistic gods; the ontology and actions of angels and the Son; and the possibility of supernatural events such as miracles and revelations. In all of these is found a fundamental disjunction between the monotheistic God and narrative.

However, if monotheism resists narrative, it is also dependent upon it—the Judeo-Christian revelation, after all, is scriptural. The abstraction of monotheism threatens to make God utterly absent from narrative, but such an absence would stifle the narrative's ability to assert monotheism. A purely monotheistic narrative would be utterly silent, and monotheism would have no means of reproduction. In order to tell itself, therefore, monotheism must admit, for the sake of the narrative, that which it excludes doctrinally. Structurally, monotheism tends toward an extreme aniconism, or a position utterly denying the representability of the divine economy. But the abstraction of the monotheistic God is an ideal that cannot survive in the praxis of narrative: monotheism must compromise its tendency toward abstraction in order to make narrative possible. Such compromises are negotiations of what I describe in this study as the narrative problems of monotheism.

In Freud's analysis, the tension between Aton and Jahve is legible in the complexities and contradictions of the narrative. Freud associates the unification of Aton and Jahve with the unification of biblical narrative from its various sources, the Jahwist, the Elohist, and so on (*MM* 50–54). Attending to source criticism, Freud notices exactly the narratological characteristics that critics such as Erich Auerbach and Robert Alter, also thoughtful about modern biblical criticism, emphasize: "Thus almost everywhere there can be found striking omissions, disturbing repetitions, palpable contradictions, signs of things the communication of which was never intended" (*MM* 52). The distorted fabric of biblical narrative, sometimes depicting God as utterly abstract, and sometimes, in direct contradiction, depicting him as a volcano god, is precisely what reveals the violence of unification, and the construction of monotheism. Similarly, Auerbach argues that the abstraction of the monotheistic God inflects biblical narrative with "background." When God's disembodied voice calls to Abraham during the binding of Isaac, Auerbach says,

> Even this opening startles us when we come to it from Homer. Where are the two speakers? We are not told. The reader, however, knows that they are not normally to be found together in one place on earth, that one of them, God, in order to speak to Abraham, must come from somewhere, must enter the earthly realm from some unknown heights or depths. Whence does he come, whence does he call to Abraham? We are not told. He does not come, like Zeus or Poseidon, from Aethiopians, where he has been enjoying a sacrificial feast. Nor are we told anything of his reasons for tempting Abraham so terribly. He has not, like Zeus, discussed them in set speeches with other gods gathered in council.[19]

Zeus can announce his intentions in council, just as the motives of Athena as she micromanages Odysseus's life are made crystal clear by Homer's foregrounding. But the monotheistic God is so abstract that he cannot participate in council, cannot be present, or foregrounded, in narrative. The resulting gaps and contradictions, which are noticed by Freud, Auerbach, and Alter, can be read as the markers of the Bible's monotheistic narrative.[20]

Monotheistic narrative, however, cannot be pure background: to have only the elisions and the sense of absence that the abstract godhead creates would be to have no narrative at all. Even a backgrounded narrative needs a certain amount of foreground, as Auerbach's definition of background concedes: "the externalization of only so much of the phenomena as is necessary for the purpose of the narrative."[21] Narrative's minimal requirements—some form of characters, some form of a story world, and some form of plot—call for a foregrounding that the monotheistic godhead, in its abstraction, must resist. Just as Freud's Israelites call for a volcano god instead of the pure abstraction of Aton, narrative demands a God that can be present and concrete.

Monotheistic narrative is not identifiable, therefore, because it adheres strictly to the aniconic demands of the second commandment, but because it visibly negotiates the disjunction between narrative and monotheism. In Milton, such negotiation takes place most compactly in the kind of narrative aporia that Stanley Fish emphasizes. So, for example, Milton describes Adam and Eve's bower by comparing it to the pastoral settings of classical literature:

> In shady bower
> More sacred and sequestered, though but feigned,
> Pan or Silvanus never slept, nor nymph
> Nor Faunus haunted. (PL 4.705–08)

The moods and literary associations—the foreground—that gather around these bowers are vast, and Milton takes advantage of them for the sake of his poetry and narrative. But these bowers also have lurking in them polytheistic gods, and these must simultaneously be rejected: "though but feigned" precedes Pan and Silvanus as if to mark them off from the bowers, as if to put them in the background. The repeated "nor" then seems to shift the implication of the phrase from a positive statement about bowers to a denial of polytheistic gods, as if the imperative to reject polytheism finally must outweigh the attractions of the bower. Importantly, Milton does not ignore Pan and the rest. The gods have a presence in the narrative. But they do not have an unchallenged presence, as the poet lands upon the contradictory solution of both allowing and disallowing the polytheism. To be purely monotheistic would be to have little or no narrative at all—without the polytheistic associations, the bower would fade out of the poetry. So Milton negotiates the problem by first allowing the narrative to become polytheistic, and then returning to the doctrinal demands of monotheism. He garners the rich foreground of the gods, and then contains their religious implications by rejecting them as false.

This passage represents in miniature a pattern of transgression and recovery that structures much of Milton's late poetry. The narratives are not monotheistic *despite* the transgressive moments of polytheism, but rather *because* of them. For example, Milton surprisingly begins *Paradise Lost* with rich and detailed descriptions of the gods, pushing the poetry toward the polytheism of epic council. But, as chapter 1 argues, the narrative simultaneously recovers a doctrinal conformity to monotheism by developing the comparative and historical perspectives of the discourse of monotheism, in particular Selden's *De diis*. The important work done by this flirtation with the gods in book 1 is the demarcation of the border between polytheism and monotheism. Forcing the reader into making an ontological distinction between gods and angels and between truth and falsehood, the infernal council puts at the center of the poem's concerns the question of where monotheism leaves off and polytheism begins.

Such a concern with sorting out ontologies is fundamental to the concept of monotheism itself. Monotheism cannot abide a second God, or a representation of God that is not sufficiently abstract. Confronted with a potentially divine being, therefore, it necessarily launches into ontological calculation. In the face not only of the gods, but also angels, exalted men, representations of God, idols, and even allegorical figures, monotheism's claims for a single God depend upon the rejection of their divinity. The wrong answer in each case leads to the same place as the wrong sense of Milton's "gods": to polytheism. Monotheism, therefore, must be jealous of deity, and must forever patrol its borders—against all forms of the supernatural—to keep polytheism out.

The Egyptologist Jan Assmann gives a name to monotheism's border: the "Mosaic distinction." In *Moses the Egyptian*, Assmann emphasizes the Mosaic distinction as the essential characteristic of monotheism, and describes it as the foundation of all truth statements: "the distinction between true and false in religion that underlies more specific distinctions such as Jews and gentiles, Christians and pagans, Muslims and unbelievers." Transgression, and the notion of true religion itself, depends upon the Mosaic distinction. And so too does the definition of monotheism, for monotheism is a "counter-religion" that asserts itself only through the repeated dismissing of idols and gods.[22] The skeptical rejection of false or transgressive forms of deity becomes a positive theological statement of monotheism.

In narrative, the dynamic of the counter-religion takes the form of a contradictory inclusion and rejection of polytheism—a pattern of transgression and recovery. Existing always in the process of calculation, which the pattern calls forth, monotheism dwells in a destabilized space, a world that demands skepticism but also faith. And so monotheistic narrative is similarly unstable: vexed by the disjunction between monotheism and narrative, it unfolds through the often contradictory negotiations of that disjunction.[23] Reading Milton's monotheistic narratives, these pages uncover some of the complex ways in which the poet maneuvers between polytheism and monotheism. These often transgressive and contradictory moves are themselves what make his poetry monotheistic, for they work to define the borders of monotheism, and they place the narrative's gaze on the Mosaic distinction.

Theology and Narrative

The discourse of monotheism is of historical importance not because it asserts the concept of a single God for the first time, but rather because it represents a moment when English theologians and philosophers studied the concept with deep attention and care. The nascent comparative perspective that informs such concern with monotheism per se tempers the more ideological pursuit of doctrinal truth. As a result, polytheism gains some toleration, or at least a greater degree of intellectual respectability. In these conditions, the one God cannot be a matter of course, and so undergoes redefinition, for example in debates over the Trinity. Belief in the monotheistic God and monotheistic religion is set off against the comparative construction of polytheism, and the border between polytheism and monotheism increasingly goes up for grabs. In this way, the discourse conceives of monotheism by means of an active engagement with what Assmann calls the Mosaic distinction.[24] This focus on the Mosaic distinction is the conceptual point of contact between the discourse of monotheism and the concerns I outline within monotheistic narrative. The ontological calculations that Milton initiates with the word "gods," and his poetry's further negotiation of the narrative problems of monotheism, become a main expression of Milton's engagement with the discourse of monotheism.

And yet philosophy and poetry do tend to treat monotheism differently. The transgressive quality in monotheistic narrative is not often noticed by the philosophers or theologians who theorize about monotheism. Monotheism conceived in abstraction, rather than in the praxis of narrative, can maintain the abstract godhead, and can therefore distinguish clearly between monotheism and polytheism without the former threatening to slip into the latter. The Mosaic distinction, as Assmann describes its history, is entirely abstract and geometrical: "'Draw a distinction. Call it the first distinction. Call the space in which it is drawn the space severed or cloven by the distinction.' It seems as if George Spencer Brown's 'first law of construction' does not apply solely to the space of logical and mathematical construction. It also applies surprisingly well to the space of cultural constructions and distinction."[25] For the philosophers and theologians considering monotheism, a distinction drawn as cleanly as a line in geometry makes a remarkably precise tool for inquiry. But such disciplines tend not to ask how narrative, unlike a philosophical or theological tract, must have recourse to the other side of the Mosaic distinction. They ignore the problem of representation. Drawn in ink or lead, any line must fall short of geometric perfection. When the Mosaic distinction is carved out in language—in the histories and arguments of theologians as well as the stories of the Bible or Milton's poetry—it becomes particularly jagged. The Mosaic distinction is recognizable in narrative not as a simple dismissal of polytheism, but as a complex negotiation between polytheism and monotheism that continually crosses and recrosses the idealized line of the Mosaic distinction. As the zigs and zags become smaller they approach a geometrically perfect line—but never arrive at it.

Another recent theorist of monotheism, the philosopher Lenn Evan Goodman, explicitly finds no use for narrative:

> I am convinced that it is not because we are incapable of thinking conceptually that the true God eludes our grosser attempts to capture, bottle (or purvey!)—Him, for we think conceptually quite regularly in mathematics and even occasionally in the physical sciences. Rather, I suspect, we are unused to applying conceptual thought in the sphere of religion. The God we miss was the God of Sunday school and Bible tales, and we have not often enough aroused the mind to ponder theology beyond the level of Sunday school images or to study the Bible as other than a collection of tales.[26]

Goodman's work provides brilliant insight into monotheism, and this study especially owes him, and Jan Assmann, a deep intellectual debt. But Goodman, like many philosophers dating back to the deists, marginalizes the telling of tales as mere Sunday school packaging, and so emphasizes idealized categories within monotheism, such as doctrine and belief. Literary critics tend to make the same mistake in reverse, paying attention to the literary qualities of the Bible without enough emphasis on the effects of religious belief. Meir Sternberg registers this complaint against literary readers of the Bible, suggesting that they are "children of the New Criticism," in that they read the Bible as they would any other fictional text, emphasizing a direct encounter with the literary aspects of the text to the exclusion of the text's professions of religious faith. Sternberg instead studies narratological elements that link aesthetics and faith, combining formal poetics with religious belief, as in his suggestive argument for the omniscient narrator of the Bible as a necessary part of the text's monotheism.[27] The concept of monotheistic narrative will, I hope, connect aesthetics and belief in a similar way. Attention to the many demands that narrative makes on our conceptions of God will enable us to steer clear of purely philosophical approaches to monotheism that too often fail to recognize the power of stories. At the same time, monotheism implies a set of intensely felt beliefs that must have an effect on how we tell and interpret religious stories. Monotheism offers a way to describe how religious belief is itself a structuring principal of religious narrative.

Freud uncovers how the most complex workings of monotheism take place precisely in the movement from concept (Aton) to representation (Jahve), and by building on Freud to focus on the role of narrative in constituting monotheism I hope to contribute to what is an increasingly active discussion about monotheism today.[28] Monotheistic narrative, with its potential to combine aesthetics and belief, also seems to be a valuable approach to Milton's late poetry. By rewriting biblical stories, *Paradise Lost*, *Paradise Regained*, and *Samson Agonistes* bring the reader to the difficult place where religious belief and doctrine intersect with poetics and narrative. Miltonists often read to one side of this place or the other, pursuing Milton's religious beliefs separate from his poetic imagination. This split is felt especially in the longstanding debate about whether *De doctrina Christiana* should be read as a gloss on *Paradise Lost*. Monotheistic narrative offers a means of answering this in the affirmative, and adding that *Paradise Lost* can in turn gloss *De doctrina*.[29]

Monotheistic narrative, however, places Milton in a uniquely subversive position, for even the most monotheistic of texts struggles over, rather than simply draws, the Mosaic distinction. Indeed, Milton draws the Mosaic distinction by transgressing it, which may suggest why Freud lists *Paradise Lost* as one of his favorite books. Milton attempts theodicy and Freud something opposite (Assmann calls Freud "the most outspoken destroyer of the Mosaic distinction").[30] But even as Milton ultimately does demarcate true monotheistic religion, he and Freud resemble each other in that both cross and recross, both hover around, the Mosaic distinction.[31] While it may be understood as necessary to both monotheism and narrative, Milton's tendency to transgress the Mosaic distinction nevertheless brings him very near to Freud, as well as to the radical subversion of Christianity that emerges with English deism and the Enlightenment.[32] Chapter 4 describes how *Paradise Lost* was often received as a deist text by the early eighteenth century, while chapters 6 and 7 read *Paradise Regained* and *Samson Agonistes* as bound up in the Antitrinitarian debates over the divinity of the Son, and in the deist debates over the efficacy of revelation. These later chapters describe the poet as deeply engaged with the issues that matter most to the rational religion of Socinians and deists. They locate Milton within the larger clash between skepticism and faith, and in this way *Milton and Monotheism* contributes to the current critical effort to understand Milton's eclectic, often heretical religious views.[33] But it should be stressed that Milton's proximity to deism does not imply conclusive agreement: on the contrary, Milton crosses the Mosaic distinction but always returns to the side of Christian truth as revealed in Scripture; his moments of subversion are ultimately contained.

Nevertheless, "monotheism" serves as a name for a set of dynamic positions between skepticism and faith. Botwinick, in a comparison of Maimonides and Hobbes, suggests that skepticism "has at least two 'runs' in Western intellectual history: first as monotheism and then, more explicitly, and self-consciously, as skepticism."[34] The discourse of monotheism may be seen as a subset of the larger and more familiar "run" associated with Descartes and Hobbes, a discourse in which the critical methods of seventeenth century skepticism are applied to theology and the problem of one God.[35] Milton's self-conscious articulation of monotheism invests his narratives with such skepticism. With Milton caught in these forces, we might find Botwinick's description of a Maimonides torn between skepticism and faith to be a fitting description of Milton as well: "I think it makes the most sense to see Maimonides not as an atheist or rejecter of religion, but as someone who desperately wants to believe, who wants to preserve the autonomy and distinctness of revelation in contrast to philosophy, and who in all honesty needs to affirm that philosophy achieves a nearly total overtaking of revelation."[36] This struggle between philosophy and revelation in Maimonides is paradigmatic monotheism. It is precisely such a struggle that Samuel Johnson noticed in Milton.

ONE

Polytheism and "truest Poesie"

As the action in *Paradise Lost* begins, the only physical detail present is that of Satan's eyes: "round he throws his baleful eyes" to view "No light, but rather darkness visible" (*PL* 1.56, 63). These eyes construct a being who is present and observing but disembodied, like the nearly immaterial hell around him. Satan is there in the world of the story, but only barely there. Tellingly, God enters book 3 with the same minimal presence of gazing eyes: in almost identical position, at line 58 rather than 56, the Father "bent down his eye, / His own works and their works at once to view." With their reluctance to become fully present, these parallel entrances can be recognized as typically monotheistic. They resemble how Deutero-Isaiah, one of the most ideologically monotheistic books of the Hebrew Bible, introduces a council of gods only to dissolve it into total impossibility. The pagan gods are invited to prophesize and to prove their existence by doing "something, either good or evil" (Isa. 41:23). The gods' apparent presence in council suggests that we are in a storyworld in which other gods have existence. But then the gods never speak or act, as Yahweh instead declares, "I looked, and there was no one; and of these there was none to give counsel / That I should ask them and they should answer. / See, all of them are nothing, and their works are nothing; / Wind and emptiness are their images" (41:28–29).[1] In the final analysis the gods are nothing: unable to speak or do works, they have no agency or existence. The important feature of this passage, however, is not the final analysis, but the narrative's move from presence to total absence. This melting away of the gods enacts in narrative the exclusion of polytheism, a dynamic clearly absent from Homer's or Virgil's councils. The minimal presence of Satan's eyes begins the action of *Paradise Lost* within this process of monotheistic exclusion. Marginally there, Satan awakens the aniconic sense that it would be transgressive if he were fully there. This first moment installs in the story a background awareness that Satan should not have narrative presence.

Soon after Satan's eyes, however, appears his "head uplift above the wave" (1.193). Then emerges an inert but massy body, "extended…many a rood" (1.195–96). Then Satan unfurls his body, as "with expanded wings he steers his flight" (1.225), before attaining heroic stature on the shore of the burning lake, complete with shield "massy, large and round" (1.285) and spear to which the tallest pine "were but a wand" (1.294). If book 1 begins with a monotheistic anxiety about Satan's narrative presence, it goes on to exacerbate that anxiety thoroughly. The action gathers momentum with the emergence of Satan's body, and the sublime presence of Satan is fearful not only because we, like the Romantics, may feel attracted to the devil, but because in its rich presence Satan's body threatens to transgress monotheism.

Milton highlights this monotheistic anxiety when he supplements Satan's "extended" body with the simile of the Leviathan:

> Thus Satan talking to his nearest mate
> With head uplift above the wave, and eyes
> That sparkling blazed, his other parts besides
> Prone on the flood, extended long and large
> Lay floating many a rood, in bulk as huge
> As whom the fables name of monstrous size,
> Titanian, or Earth-born, that warred on Jove,
> Briareos or Typhon, whom the den

> By ancient Tarsus held, or that sea-beast
> Leviathan, which God of all his works
> Created hugest that swim the ocean stream:
> Him haply slumbering on the Norway foam
> The pilot of some small night-foundered skiff,
> Deeming some island, oft, as seamen tell,
> With fixed anchor in his scaly rind
> Moors by his side under the lea, while night
> Invests the sea, and wished morn delays.   (1.192–208)

The simile first expands Satan's physical presence, as he suddenly balloons from head and eyes and "other parts besides," to "monstrous size" and Titanic proportions. The poetry echoes this expansion: first "eyes" and "besides" form a couplet, remembered three lines later by "size," creating a sense of containment and bondage. Then the blank verse opens up with names of mythology, with Jove, Briareos, Typhon, and Tarsus. A feeling of liberty in the multiplicity and spaciousness of these sounds coincides with the inscription of Satan in the polytheism of classical myth. As the simile moves Satan away from monotheism, the transgressiveness of his body diminishes—polytheism easily admits material divinity, and for the moment the poem partakes of the familiar poetic fictions of Greece and Rome.

But for a Christian poet, a theological danger lurks within this feeling of sensuousness. The simile next wavers between the Greek gods and the beast of the Bible: "or," Milton says, Satan may be like "that sea-beast / Leviathan, which God of all his works / Created hugest." Satan is now shifted into the monotheistic world created by the Judeo-Christian God. Monotheistic anxiety rushes back in—not in merely being compared to Leviathan, but in the movement from polytheistic to monotheistic contexts. Importantly, Milton's "or" does not decide between the two systems, but rather establishes an impasse between polytheism and monotheism. Although much is at stake in the distinction between the two sides of the "or," neither the polytheistic nor the monotheistic comparison is given a stated priority. Then, while we are left struggling to understand Satan's looming presence, Milton holds up a mirror to allow us to see ourselves in the pilot of the skiff. In choosing between pagan and biblical monsters the reader has been trying to fix Satan's body in the imagination, just as the pilot would fix his anchor into solid ground. The pilot's task as he peers through the night, like the reader's, is ontological calculation—the need to determine what exactly is before him. And the consequences of a mistaken interpretation are potentially devastating. Waiting for dawn, the pilot never realizes his mistake, as the simile ends with the arousal of the whale and its Melvillean consequences imminent.

The serious work demanded of the reader of this simile is the delineation of what Jan Assmann calls the Mosaic distinction—the border between the true religion of monotheism and the falsehood of polytheism. This is an ontological calculation, one that seeks to determine whether Satan is a figure from the polytheistic world of classical myth, or the world of the Bible. That the calculation is so weighted with the anxiety of possible disaster, and that it is finally unresolved by Milton's "or," is perfectly representative of monotheistic narrative. For as in Isaiah, the text asserts monotheism not in the absence of gods, but by narrating their exclusion. This necessity of knowing whether a given figure is a threat to monotheism, of distinguishing between true and false religion, is a main project of book 1. Beginning with the aniconic image of Satan's eyes and leading to the "Synod of gods" (2.391) in book 2, book 1 confronts the reader with the fundamental monotheistic challenge: policing the borders of religion against incursions from other gods. As with Satan's body and the Leviathan simile, the monotheistic work of book 1 depends upon the sense of polytheistic transgression, and unfolds within the necessity for ontological calculation.

Book 1's monotheism, in other words, is built upon its polytheism. And so, having materialized from eyes to a fully extended body with shield and spear, Satan strides ashore from the burning lake and immediately calls to the apostates. They spring up like locusts from "the potent rod / Of Amram's son in Egypt's evil day" (1.338–39), which simile brings in the specter of Egypt, that hotbed of polytheism and sorcery. This same multitude, gathering together, is then described as "godlike shapes and forms" (1.358)—Milton has brought us to a situation that offers one of the greatest challenges to a monotheistic storyworld, that of council. If Isaiah finds that "there was none to give counsel" among the other gods, *Paradise Lost* comes to the opposite conclusion, richly depicting gods assembling for council in the catalogue of gods.

The catalogue is full of foreboding over polytheism, such as Ezekiel's vision of Judah worshipping Thammuz:

> the love-tale
> Infected Sion's daughters with like heat,
> Whose wanton passions in the sacred porch
> Ezekiel saw, when, by the vision led
> His eye surveyed the dark idolatries
> Of alienated Judah.   (1.452–57)

So common sense might ask: if the polytheism is so dark and so horrid, why not simply leave it out? If idolatry so offends, might not it have been better contained—and not been made the prominent subject of book 1? As a first approach to Milton's monotheism, this chapter gives attention to this common sense reaction, asking why Milton begins *Paradise Lost* with such a blazing display of polytheism.

The catalogue, of course, may duck the problem of monotheism, since Milton's gods are actually angels. Just after the multitude of "godlike shapes and forms," the claim that the fallen angels later became "known to men by various names, / And various idols through the heathen world" (1.374–75) establishes the apostates' angelic ontology. Apparently this removes the threat of polytheism. Indeed, the idea of an angelic origin for the polytheistic gods has been useful to syncretism dating back to Philo, and was common in Milton's period, as A. W. Verity explains.[2] But Milton is aware, in the high-stakes game of monotheistic ontology, how ticklish the distinction between god and angel is. His discussion of the many meanings of *elohim* in *De doctrina Christiana* (YP 6:233–36) shows his attention to the semantic indefinition between angel, gods, and even God. Throughout book 1 he plays upon this thin but essential distinction in the apostates' frequent claims to be, in their word, "gods." The angelic origin of the gods, like their equivocal use of "gods," may determine the narrative's conformity to monotheism. But the instability of naming as a means of making this ontological distinction suggests that simply labeling the apostates as angels may not be enough.[3]

The apostates begin in the narrative as "angel forms" entranced on the lake of fire (1.301). Eventually they will be "known to men by various names, / And various idols through the heathen world" (1.374–75). But in the following line, the poet instructs the muse proleptically to say "their names then known" in the pagan world (1.376), giving them presence in the narrative not as "forms" or beings that exist, but as "names." From the point of view of narrative, "names" is advantageous, for it allows the poet freedom to give a sensual and material presence to polytheism, while insisting, on an ontological level, that we are hearing about angels. And yet narrative has a way of drifting in the direction of nominalism—toward the sense that names are all we can know. The problem with the beings of the catalogue is that we know only what is proleptic, and nothing that is associated with their true angelic ontologies. We do not know how they looked or acted as angels, nor do we even know their true names:

> Though of their names in heavenly records now
> Be no memorial blotted out and razed
> By their rebellion, from the books of life.
> Nor had they yet among the sons of Eve
> Got them new names.[4] (1.361–5)

What to call these beings, and how to imagine them, are beyond the poet and the reader. As the catalogue is filled out with its proleptic details, the apostates have very little existence as angels beyond that single word "forms." And so their "new names" rush in to fill the void. Doctrinally it is clear that the council is angelic, but imaginatively and conceptually—on the level of the poetry and narrative—the catalogue feels like polytheism.

Prolepsis exerts a strong pull to forget the angelic ontology and to let the immediate terms of the narrative control our reading. From the outset these terms are remarkably visceral and forceful. For example,

> First Moloch, horrid king besmeared with blood
> Of human sacrifice, and parents' tears,
> Though for the noise of drums and timbrels loud
> Their children's cries unheard, that passed through fire
> To his grim idol. (1.392–96)

The more vivid the polytheistic detail, and the more its presence is felt in the narrative, the more it overshadows the angelic "forms." The idols of the catalogue become the physical and psychological beings in council. The experience in *Paradise Lost* of finding names that fail to describe their referents is familiar from the problem of fallen language. The disconcerting instability of such words as "error" and "wanton" pulls the text toward transgressiveness as the name moves from unfallen to fallen meanings. The prolepsis of the catalogue operates in the same way. Only rather than impugning Eve, the shift to the fallen world explicitly transgresses the line between monotheism and polytheism. Here the text itself is under fire, as it crosses to the wrong side of the Mosaic distinction.

The prominent polytheism of book 1 is but the most obvious example of a habit—perhaps it does not overstate the case to say an obsession—in Milton's poetry. From the Nativity ode to *Paradise Lost*, *Paradise Regained*, and *Samson Agonistes*, Milton's poetic imagination turns frequently and vividly to the gods. And not the gods familiar from the classical tradition, but the polytheistic gods of the Bible, which are far more threatening than the Cupids and Apollos of most Renaissance poetry. Thus treading the line of the Mosaic distinction, Milton's polytheism should be viewed as part of a larger issue in the poetics of Christian poetry.

Nearly every poet in Milton's England made use of the gods. But as an increasing number attempted to write poetry that was not an affront to Christianity, they began to struggle with a tradition which, developed in polytheistic Greece, made lavish use of deities. Focusing on such important predecessors to Milton as Tasso, William Davenant, and Abraham Cowley, this chapter will begin by elaborating the way the narrative presence of polytheism became a point of anxiety in seventeenth century Christian poetry.[5]

Christian poetry's interest in the gods also parallels the theological and historical discourse that studies polytheism and its opposite, monotheism. A key text in the discourse is John Selden's *De diis Syris*, as will be taken up in chapter 2. This chapter, however, first shows Selden's research to be a locus in which the comparative discourse of monotheism overlaps with the movement for Christian poetry. Selden mediates between poetry and comparative inquiry, creating a uniquely skeptical and monotheistic poetics. At the same time, Selden is a fertile source for Milton's polytheism. Each time Milton returns to the polytheistic gods, they are drawn with anthropological detail that is identifiably from *De diis*. *On the Morning of Christ's Nativity* likely borrows its pagan deities from *De diis*—as Douglas Bush notes, the ode was written in the same year (1629) in which the second edition of *De diis* was published, and so may mark the beginning of Milton's familiarity with the text.[6] *Paradise Regained* enumerates the pagan deities in a manner resembling *De diis*. Much of the detail of *Samson Agonsites*, with its Dagonalia and its development of sea imagery associated with Dagon, could be traced back to Selden, who argues for the derivation of Dagon from the Hebrew word for fish, *dag* (Selden 2:356).

And, most prominently, the material descriptions in the catalogue of gods come from *De diis*. Each detail describing Moloch, for example, is found there—that Moloch means king (Selden 2:314–15); that he is vividly soaked in blood (2:313); and that the noise of drums was used to cover the children's cries (2:313). Patrick

Hume first associates the infernal council with Selden, glossing Milton's verse with several references to *De diis*, and using details and citations, such as those attached to Moloch, which themselves are clearly taken from Selden.[7] But it is Gibbon who, in a footnote, most famously sums up Milton's use of Selden's research into polytheism: "For the enumeration of the Syrian and Arabian deities, it may be observed, that Milton has comprised, in one hundred and thirty very beautiful lines, the two learned syntagmas, which Selden had composed on that abstruse subject."[8]

Although Selden has long been named as a source for the catalogue, there has been little effort to articulate what it means that Milton brings Selden into his verse. Book 1 reveals not only that Selden was a source, but that there is an affinity between Milton's poetry and Selden's influential approach to the comparative treatment of polytheism and monotheism. In *Areopagitica* Selden is "the chief of learned men reputed" in England (YP 2:513), and he is, in Jason Rosenblatt's words, "Milton's Chief Rabbi."[9] But while Selden's legal research appears often in the prose, in the poetry it is *De diis* that consistently shows up (even in the poem's first line). Indeed, Selden is not just Milton's chief rabbi; he also seems to be his chief mythographer. While many seventeenth century poets attempt poetry that conforms to Christian truth, Milton's efforts are unique in their extensive and successful use of Selden's kind of comparative treatment of the polytheistic gods. In the catalogue of gods, *Paradise Lost* begins to consider—and transgress—monotheism precisely as it enters into seventeenth century discourse about monotheism. The close ties between *De diis* and *Paradise Lost* suggest that Selden's research sparks Milton's poetic imagination and meets the needs of his poetics.

Christian Poetry and the Presence of Gods

What I term "narrative presence" is meant to describe a quality of particular importance to seventeenth century efforts at Christian poetry. Any character, of course, is present in a narrative. But more than just a humanlike character can have presence—consider narratological elements that are only partially identifiable with anthropomorphic representation, such as an allegorical figure or God. The difficult presence of God in biblical theophany, as when Yahweh materializes and seeks to kill Moses and then just as suddenly disappears (Exod. 4:24), illustrates the partial way in which a figure can become present in a narrative. Milton's Death, with a "shape, / If shape it might be called that shape had none" (*PL* 2.666–67), has narrative presence, but neither the bodily nor the fully psychological presence we expect in a rounded character.

With a similar goal of arousing an inclusive sense of narrative presence, the narratologist Seymour Chatman places "character" within the larger category of "existents," which captures an expanded set of possible presences, including the mere objects of setting.[10] "Existents" expands critical attention beyond character to consider what Chatman calls "story-space." "Existent" implies that there is an ontology at work within the boundaries of the story-space, so that each narrative creates, at least imaginatively, a world in which characters and other figures are present. A term often used for this sense of world-building in narrative is "storyworld."[11] Importantly, a figure may be false according to real-world ontology, but its presence within a narrative implies that it is not false according to the ontology of the storyworld. In this sense every existent is truthful, and narrative presence is an ontological assertion: it asserts that a figure really exists within the ontology of the narrative. But there is a catch. If the narrative involves the presence of a figure that is clearly false, narrative presence implies that the storyworld itself is less than truthful. Narrative presence, then, defines the terms of the narrative and has the power to cast a narrative itself out of the bounds of what is truthful.[12]

Polytheism challenges Christian poets with just such an ontological assertion. If a god is too present, the implication is that the storyworld is making an ontological assertion. This is one of William Prynne's arguments, in *Histriomastix* (1633):

> Christians should not admit of the Names, and Histories, (much lesse of the imprecations, and abominable practices,) of Heathen Gods. First, because God himselfe, with all these Fathers, doe thus inhibit them. Secondly, because the second Commandement, as Philo Iudaeus well observes; doeth not only prohibit the Images, and Pictures, but even the Histories, and Fables of the Marriages, Birthes, and casualites of Heathen Gods. Thirdly, because the recital of their Names and Histories, by way of approbation, or delight, doeth give a tacite or secret allowance of them to be Gods.[13]

Even in approbation, Prynne concludes, the mere naming of a god implies its existence. Prynne goes on to argue against invocations in plays or poems, and then anticipates the excuses of his opponents. These are two: that the gods are "Invocated" or named "in sport, and merriment onely; not seriously, or in earnest"; and that "they are uttered by way of Proxie, or representation onely."[14] Prynne rejects these appeals, but they nevertheless show the position poets and critics were often forced into taking. The pressure exerted by gods in the story is relieved by the simple but significant position that the narrative itself makes no claims to be anything but fiction. It nothing affirmeth. The narrative presence of polytheism thus implies that the poem is constructing a storyworld that is false—and the poem loses its truthfulness.

And so for poets concerned about writing Christian poetry, a storyworld that is truthful according to Christian doctrine becomes an essential goal. Abraham Cowley comes nearest to articulating a creed for seventeenth century Christian poets in the opening of the *Davideis:*

> Too long the *Muses-Lands* have *Heathen* bin;
> Their *Gods* too long were *Dev'ils,* and *Vertues Sin;*
> But *Thou, Eternal Word,* hast call'ed forth *Mee*
> Th' *Apostle,* to convert that *World* to *Thee;*
> T' unbind the charms that in slight *Fables* lie,
> And teach that *Truth* is *truest Poesie.*[15]

Resembling the narratological sense of storyworld, the metaphor of the "Muses-Land," portrays Cowley as an apostle converting worlds of poetry to Christianity. This conversion hinges on the cleansing of false religion, and the harrowing of gods—Christian poets, Cowley announces, must worry over the narrative presence of polytheism. The seventeenth century's effort at "truest Poesie" in this way largely depends on the monotheism of its texts.

Neoclassical criticism approaches this same problem of the narrative presence of polytheism through the verisimilar and the marvelous. The epic, according to many of the Italian critics, must strike a balance between what is marvelous, or supernatural, and what resembles nature and is truthful. Both are necessary to poetry: the verisimilar encourages belief while the marvelous heightens wonder and emotion. They receive so much attention, however, because, while both terms are necessary, they are also contradictory.[16] Tasso in particular, in his effort to write Christian epic, repeatedly bumps up against the conflicting demands of the verisimilar and the marvelous, the latter often threatening because it is polytheistic. In his *Discorsi dell'arte poetica*, Tasso rejects classical subjects because their polytheism, though marvelous, cannot be true: "I do not think the deeds of the Gentiles offer us a subject suitable to make into a perfect epic because, in such poems, we sometimes want to refer to the deities worshipped by the Gentiles, or we do not want to. If we do not make such reference, the poem will lack wonder; if we do, it will lack verisimilitude in that part."[17] Tasso voices a basic frustration of monotheistic narrative: strict conformity to doctrine often results in uninteresting, unpoetic narrative. And good narrative, which is moving and which uses the resources of the best poets, is often dubiously monotheistic.[18]

Tasso begins to find a way out of the problem. The perfect epic, he says, should use a Christian subject: since miracles stemming from God can be truthful, "one and the same action can be both wondrous and verisimilar."[19] Here the authority of God expressed in miracle offers the Christian poet both wonder and truth. As

Bernard Weinberg glosses this passage, "verisimilitude accompanies those actions which display the operation of (natural) laws, and the marvelous is present when the same laws are violated. But add the ingredient of faith, which transforms a supernatural into a natural cause, and the same basis of credibility will be found in both."[20] At this point combining Christianity with poetry seems a perfect solution to epic's difficulty with verisimilitude and the marvelous.

But Tasso goes on to uncover another problem. The absolute truth-claims of scriptural subjects severely limit the poet:

> The epic poet, thus, must take his theme from the history of a religion held true by us. But either such histories are so sacred and venerable that it is impiety to change them (the establishment of our Faith being based upon them), or they are not so holy as to contain an article of faith within them.... The theme of an epic, therefore, should be taken from chronicles of true religion but not of such great authority as to be unalterable.[21]

The authority of God makes the supernatural truthful. But it also imposes serious restrictions on the poet, who must give up authority in the face of Scriptures that cannot be altered. These restrictions lead Tasso, in the *Gerusalemme liberata*, to construct a story that is Christian but not biblical.

But even his Crusade narrative cannot separate itself completely from the problem of verisimilitude, as each instance of the marvelous still must be reconciled with religious truth. For as soon as the poet departs from the Bible, leaving behind the express authority of God's revelation, such reconciliation is not automatic. Each supernatural event must be measured against the rigorous standards of religious truth. And Tasso makes extensive use of the supernatural in the *Gerusalemme*. This explicitly Christian epic manages to give an active role to the Furies (8.1–4), and a moment to Beelzebub (7.99). And of most importance to this discussion, Tasso develops his famous council of infernal powers in canto 4, in which he depicts Pluto, as well as an array of monsters and petty gods (4.1–18).

Mindele Anne Treip argues that Tasso relieves the pressure of Christianity's demands for truth by means of an idiosyncratic use of the term "verisimilar." In the *Discorsi del poema eroico,* which sought to justify the *Gerusalemme,* Tasso so expands the borders of truthfulness as to liberate the poet from the realism of neo-Aristotelianism: he "allows almost everything that lies within the province of the poet's imagination."[22] He does so by defining the verisimilar not as conformity to realism in the storyworld, but conformity to ideological truth that lies outside of the storyworld: Tasso "justifies marvels by reference to a realigned concept of 'verisimilitude' (understood by him as in certain contexts equivalent to inner truth, as opposed to outward realism)."[23] The marvelous can still be verisimilar if it figures forth inner truth that resides not visibly in the poem's storyworld, but beyond it. Such a loose conception of truth in the storyworld gives Tasso sufficient creative freedom, while allowing the poem to remain within the doctrinal boundaries of religion. Splitting truth off from the storyworld justifies even the apparent polytheism of Tasso's council.

The separation of the storyworld from ontological claims for truth is a strategy that resembles allegory, by means of which Spenser makes Mammon, Diana, Jove, and many other gods part of a Christian poem. So even as Spenser is widely celebrated for his religious poetry, he also could be described by Henry Reynolds as having created "an exact body of the Ethnicke (i.e. pagan) doctrine."[24] In this way allegory represents a particularly powerful solution to the problem of the narrative presence of polytheism. Phineas Fletcher's *Apollyonists* (1627) offers an infernal council that anticipates *Paradise Lost*. But it avoids the problem of polytheism with allegorical figures in the tradition of Spenser.

An alternative among English Christian poets in the first half of the seventeenth century was to follow Guillaume Du Bartas, translated by Joshua Sylvester, in retelling biblical stories. This tradition is essentially nonallegorical, as it speaks directly of biblical characters and events. And without the allegorical solution, this strand of Christian poetry shows an increased concern over the presence of gods. Du Bartas includes gods of nature such as Neptune, Aeolus, and Phoebus, although they can be read as mere figures. In a more extended fashion, on the fourth day of Creation, describing the firmament, Du Bartas rather equivocally turns the planets and celestial bodies into an opportunity to include stories about Saturn, Jupiter, Mars, and the other gods.[25] Whether or not these appearances of gods are transgressive depends on whether a critic feels it necessary to be as rigid as Prynne. But Du Bartas also typically includes asides that bring the problem of polytheism into view, as in his account of the miracles and prodigies of nature in the second day. These are full of the actions of Erebus, Pluto, and Apollo, until Du Bartas pulls back and reminds us that it is God who "many waies dooth give / To deadest things (instantly) soules to live" (1.2.791–92). And in concluding the second day, he worries aloud, "I feare some Criticke will not sticke to say, / My babbling Muse did saile with everie gale, / And mingled yarne to length her web withall" (1.2.1110–12). Defending himself against such criticism, Du Bartas claims that his yarns come from biblical, not classical authority:

> So doo I more the sacred tongue esteeme,
> Though plaine and rural it doo rather seeme,
> Then school'd *Athenian*; and Divinitie,
> For onely varnish, have but Veritie.   (1.2.1137–40)

Du Bartas hardly confronts the gods head-on, but does betray a discomfort with their appearances in the traditional poetic conceits. Others in the Du Bartas tradition show varying degrees of concern over the inclusion of gods: Michael Drayton in *Noah's Flood* (1630) mentions Neptune, while Thomas Fuller in *David's Hainous Sinne, Heartie Repentance, Heavie Punishment* (1631), includes nothing of the supernatural or gods, but does not explicitly reject them either.

But for nearly all Christian poets of the period invocations prove to be very difficult. As John Dennis later puts it, "Invocation is

Adoration, and whatever is ador'd, must, during the action, by the Adorer, be esteem'd a Deity" (Dennis 1:250).[26] The presence of polytheism is made especially risky by invocation's prominence, and by its close association to the poet's own craft. These risks, however, are also strengths—if invocation suggests that poetry itself is pagan, then rewriting invocation becomes a powerful way to realign poetry with Christianity. Du Bartas first addresses the problem in his *L'Uranie* (1574), where Urania, the muse previously associated with astronomy, becomes an advocate of biblical poetry.[27] As Lily Campbell demonstrates, Du Bartas's Urania enjoys an extended vogue as a specifically Christian muse, invoked by, among others, Drummond of Hawthornden, Samuel Austin, and Milton in book 7.[28]

However, Milton's careful qualification, "The meaning, not the name I call" (*PL* 7.5), shows a continuing dissatisfaction with Urania, for even if she espouses biblical authority she is still a daughter of Zeus. In *The Divine Weeks*, Du Bartas instead calls upon a strange "Devinely-humane" muse:

> My heedful *Muse*, trayned in true Religion,
> Devinely-humane keepes the middle Region:
> Least, if she should too-high a pitch presume,
> Heav'ns glowing flame should melt her waxen plume.
>
> (1.1.135–38)

What, ontologically, this divine and human being might be is unclear. But Du Bartas is anxious to make sure that, with her training in "true Religion," the muse is not merely one of the gods. The threat the poet must avoid is that his muse, like Icarus, will soar too high by presuming to become a god. Drayton, meanwhile, shows a restlessness in his invocations, suggesting how difficult the trope is. In his early poem, *Moses His Birth and Miracles* (1603), Drayton unapologetically invokes a god explicitly descended from Jove. But later, in *Noah's Flood*, he turns to supernatural beings authorized by Scripture, invoking an angel sent from Jehova. In *David and Goliah* (1630), he audaciously—but in view of the second commandment, safely—invokes God himself.[29]

And between *Moses His Birth* and *Noah's Flood,* Drayton takes part in one of the most complex and creative invocations of the period. Perhaps influencing his changed approach to the invocation, Drayton teams with John Selden to construct and simultaneously undo an invocation to the *Poly-Olbion* (1613). This collaboration dramatizes the key issues raised by the presence of polytheism in poetry. In addition, Selden's anti-invocation, in the form of a footnote, helps to characterize Selden's own writings and the way they interact with poetry, leading this chapter's argument toward Selden's role in Milton's poetics.

Selden's Anti-Invocation

The first 18 songs of Drayton's *Poly-Olbion* are accompanied by "Illustrations," or footnotes, by Selden. Drayton begins the first song with an invocation, calling on the "Genius of the place" to direct his course. This invocation is marked with an asterisk leading to the poem's end, where Selden announces that his "Illustrations," unlike Drayton's poetry, will not allow the invoking of a genius loci. Coming at the head of his "Illustrations," this dismissal of invocations functions as an anti-invocation. Structurally parallel to Drayton's, it launches Selden's portion of the *Poly-Olbion:*

> If in Prose and religion it were as iustifiable, as in Poetry and Fiction, to invoke a Locall power (for anciently both Iewes, Gentiles, and Christians have supposed to every Countrey a singular Genius) I would therin ioyne with the Author. Howsoever, in this and all ἐχ διὸς ἀρχόμεθα (God afore): and so I begin to you.³⁰

At the heart of this prominent disagreement is a polytheistic god: Drayton's "Genius," or what Selden calls a "Locall power." Drayton follows poetic tradition, which according to Selden is universal, when he invokes a deity to assist his endeavor. In a typically circuitous argument, Selden supports the tradition of invocation even as he puts himself above it. For in the prose of his "Illustrations" religion cannot be ignored, and God may not be put behind.

Despite Selden's correction, however, Drayton is not making an unknowing mistake. He was an accomplished historian himself, and yet fills the *Poly-Olbion* with myths and claims that are clearly untrue. Most obviously, Drayton traces the origin of England back to Brute, a myth that Drayton's mentor, William Camden, had exploded in his *Brittania* (1586).[31] Selden calls the Brute myth as "warrantable" as Ariosto, and attaches an illustration rejecting Drayton's use of it. But Drayton is not naive and has clearly chosen to include the myth. Indeed, taking the *Poly-Olbion* as a collaborative production, it becomes clear that Drayton and Selden are playing two distinct roles for the sake of a single text. Drayton supplies the poetry, which easily wanders into myth and polytheism—its organizing trope is the deification of the English rivers. And Selden supplies the rigorously historical correctives. Selden explicitly defines the differing standards for truth that the poet and the historian adopt when he comments at one point that "sufficient iustification of making a Poem, may be from tradition, which the author here uses."[32] Drayton surely follows poetic tradition rather than truth in his opening invocation and in his frequent use of polytheistic gods—a decision that is best understood as part of the multivocal project comprising both Drayton's poetry and Selden's notes.

The *Poly-Olbion's* invocation and anti-invocation together form an original solution to the problem of the narrative presence of polytheism. Whereas poets such as Du Bartas work to make the invocation truthful, Drayton and Selden allow a specifically untruthful invocation, but follow with a doctrinal rejection of the poetry in the "Illustrations." This allows for the creation of traditional poetry, with all the pleasures of marvelous invocation. And at the same time it marks the invocation as false, realigning the reader with true religion. The invocation to the *Poly-Olbion* is in fact a negotiation of the disjunction between narrative and monotheism, cleverly meeting the demands of each: the text both makes polytheism present and maintains a claim to be truthful. That this negotiation takes place by means of a slide from verse to the prose of the footnote injects the invocation with a uniquely rational poetics. The reader must suspend judgment, leave the music of the verse to follow the physical trail of the footnote through the book, and then evaluate the invocation with a perspective infused with historical and theological additions. This strategy of attaching historical footnote to verse is one Selden practices elsewhere, and one that will be central to understanding Milton's use of Selden's scholarship in his polytheistic council.

But if Drayton and Selden offer a creative solution, the obvious condescension in the anti-invocation has damaging implications for poetry. Selden draws a sharp line and places on one side of it prose and religion, and on the other side poetry and fiction, "If in Prose and religion it were as iustifiable, as in Poetry and Fiction, to invoke a Locall power." Poetry and prose can be delineated, and religion can be opposed to fiction—both without objection. But absolutely partitioned in this rigid scheme are poetry and religion: these two, Selden's formulation implies, cannot come together. Drayton's participation in the collaboration, with its cheerful embrace of polytheism, is a willing admission of poetry's fictiveness. And the first thing Selden does is to point out that this disqualifies poetry from handling religion. Tasso stretches verisimilitude in order to allow poetry to be both marvelous and true—in effect, to straddle Selden's line, including within it both fiction and religion. But Selden, whose rigorous brand of scientific history is in evidence throughout his "Illustrations," will allow no such loosening of truth. His whole project, in the *Poly-Olbion* and his other scholarship, is to ascertain truth, separating it from traditional fictions. Accordingly, he will allow no fictions on his side of the line—and poetry is shut out from Christianity.

Champion of rigorous historical truth is precisely the reputation Selden has earned. Selden has been seen as a figure for the beginnings of the modern study of history in English: David Sandler Berkowitz says that "Selden found history fable and left it fact—a reformation that he accomplished by regarding history as a science and endowing it with a scientific mind."[33] Selden's learning is evident throughout the "Illustrations," and even in his parenthetical history lesson in the anti-invocation: "(for anciently both Iewes, Gentiles, and Christians have supposed to every Countrey a singular Genius)." At the same time, clearly as part of his insistence on fact over fable, Selden is deeply dismissive of poetry for being uncongenial toward historical truth. In *Table Talk* he says,

> 'Tis a fine thing for children to learn to make Verse; but when they come to be Men, they must speak like other Men, or else they will be laughed at. 'Tis ridiculous to speak, or write, or preach in Verse. As 'tis good to learn to dance, a man may learn his Leg, learn to go handsomely; but 'tis ridiculous for him to dance when he should go.

And he seems to explain why verse is so childish with another comment: "Verse proves nothing but the quantity of Syllables; they are not meant for Logic."[34]

But Selden has a relationship to poetry more complex than mere dismissal. He even occasionally tried his hand at the childish endeavor—although the strange results only demonstrate that his more natural position is in the margins of verse. In his Latin verses commending Arthur Hopton's *A Concordance of Years*, for example, Selden writes 14 lines in praise of Hopton's work. But within these 14 lines he attaches 9 footnotes, comprising a full page of prose. And these footnotes themselves have 16 more footnotes providing citations (Selden 2:1717–18). The same thing happens in his commendatory verse to the first edition of *Purchas His Pilgrimage*. There the single word *prodiere* fits the meter, but, as Selden says, such verse cannot fit the needs of logic, let alone a style of historical inquiry that depends upon the gathering of every possible original source. So inserting a footnote as a kind of safety valve, Selden launches into the detailed treatment of polytheistic gods that lies behind his use of the poetic word.[35] What begins as a modest piece of verse explodes into a dense edifice of historical prose, as if Selden were simply unable to stay with the poetry. He is drawn, rather, to the margins of verse, recreating the encyclopedic space of the "Illustrations" of the *Poly-Olbion*.

The very look of Selden's poetry, in which words in meter expand into an inky wall of sentences and citations, captures the affinity his thinking has for the footnote. Selden's prose itself reads like footnotes: his extended works, in both English and Latin, are famously difficult to read, tortured as they are by difficult syntax, multiple languages, and the encyclopedic listing of evidence.[36] In its unstinting pursuit of truth, Selden's antiquarian method of compiling does not lend itself to a lively or even sustained narrative, much less the restrictions of meter, and so his verse swerves toward the apparatus that is specifically designed to break out of the limits of a text—the footnote. Even as he turns away from poetry, however, Selden develops, perhaps accidentally, a remarkable poetics. In the *Poly-Olbion* and his few attempts at verse, Selden yokes together poetry and rigorous historical inquiry. The result is a poetics deeply involved in the activities basic to reading history, as Anne Lake Prescott describes it in the *Poly-Olbion*: "Selden shows how to do good history: read and compare many national 'stories,' trust none completely, attend to archeology, remember cultural changes, deduce what you can from plausible etymology, and then learn to live with the gaps and confusions that preclude full knowledge." The unstinting pursuit of evidence, and the willingness to forgo the continuities of narrative for the compiling style of an encyclopedia, make what Prescott calls a "melée at the poetry's edge."[37] Selden's strong antiquarian discourse, well known in his prose works, also uniquely inhabits the margins of poetry, where, far from a second tier of commentary, it inserts itself into and transforms the poetry.

This effort at a more rational poetics is a version of Tasso's concern with verisimilitude, and related to later neoclassical positions. It emerges most dramatically in a group of midcentury texts by fellow exiles in Paris: Davenant's *Gondibert* (1653), Cowley's *Davideis* (1656), the critical prefaces to these poems, and Hobbes's "Answer." These texts argue for a poetry that is free from fable and superstition, and which conforms to emerging standards of historical and scientific truth. And as with Selden's anti-invocation, the call for truth in poetry generally centers on religious truth. As Davenant and Cowley strive to write what Cowley calls "truest Poesie," the presence of polytheism emerges as a primary threat. Accordingly, Davenant will admit nothing that resembles a god into his narrative. Cowley, however, determined to match classical precedent, develops a complex, in many ways contradictory, strategy for creating a monotheistic poem.

Davenant's Skeptical Extreme

Selden's anti-invocation shows poetry embattled by its association with fiction, separated from both religious and historical truth. The obvious strategy for restoring poetry to relevance would be to eschew both the marvelous and its specifically religious form, polytheism. That is, to put aside Tasso's sense of verisimilitude, and to make poetry match Selden's, and monotheism's, rigorous skepticism. Davenant wishes to recuperate poetry in just this way, attempting in *Gondibert* to reform heroic poetry to be invulnerable to charges of untruthfulness. Davenant's "The Author's Preface," which preceded *Gondibert* in print by three years, appeared with Hobbes's "The Answer of Mr. Hobbes to Sir Will. D'Avenant's Preface Before Gondibert" and commendatory poems by Cowley and Edmund Waller. The front matter in particular, but also the poem itself, represents the period's most concerted and polemical argument for poetry that is strictly rational and rigorously monotheistic.

As he surveys the major heroic poets in the "Author's Preface," Davenant repeatedly laments the presence in their works of angels, devils, ghosts, fairies, and monsters. Of Spenser's "Argument," for example,

> wee must observe with others, that his noble and most artfull hands deservd to be employ'd upon matter of a more naturall, and therefore

of a more usefull kinde. His allegoricall Story (by many held defective in the connexion) resembling (methinks) a continuance of extraordinary Dreames; such as excellent Poets, and Painters, by being overstudious may have in the beginning of Feavers.[38]

That he addresses the "Author's Preface" to the century's most notorious materialist should give an indication of the kind of skepticism Davenant wants to bring to heroic verse. Hobbes's "Answer" buttresses Davenant's call for exacting verisimilitude:

> There are some that are not pleased with fiction, unlesse it be bold; not onely to exceed the *worke,* but also the *possibility* of nature, they would have impenetrable Armors, Inchanted Castles, invulnerable bodies, Iron men, flying Horses, and a thousand other such thinges, which are easily fayned by them that dare. Against such I defend you (without assenting to those that condemne either *Homer* or *Virgil*) by dissenting onely from those that thinke the Beauty of a Poeme consisteth in the exorbitancy of the fiction. For as truth is the bound of Historicall, so the Resemblance of truth is the utmost limit of Poeticall Liberty. In old time amongst the Heathen such strange fictions, and Metamorphoses, were not so remote from the Articles of their faith, as they are now from ours, and therefore were not so unpleasant.[39]

Hobbes will not permit poetry to range beyond the limits of verisimilitude or "the Resemblance of truth." And because modern poets are Christian and not heathen, their faith is far beyond the "strange fictions" of classical myth.

Davenant's adherence to this skeptical poetics is largely motivated by a desire to refute what he terms the "enemies of poesy," who, he believes, object first of all on the grounds of religion.[40] He is concerned to refute those critics who, like Selden, view poetry as mere pagan fiction, and therefore insufficiently historical or Christian. So, in describing his own poetics, Davenant censures Tasso for his use of the marvelous not just because he will not admit a looser sense of the verisimilar, but also because the *Gerusalemme* threatens monotheism with its councils or "courts":

> Yet a Christian Poet (whose Religion little needs the aydes of invention) hath lesse occasion to imitate such Fables, as meanly

illustrate a probable Heaven, by the fashion, and dignity of Courts; and make a resemblance of Hell, out of the Dreames of frighted Women; by which they continue and increase the melancholy mistakes of the People. (Davenant, "Author's Preface," 6)

In a survey from Homer to Spenser, Homer, Virgil, and the other classical poets are censured but excused for their superstition and polytheism. But the Christian poets are not: with Tasso, Davenant is particularly unforgiving because "his errors which are deriv'd from the Ancients, when examin'd, grow in a great degree excusable in them, and by being his, admit no pardon" (ibid., 6). The burden on the Christian poet is decisive.

Accordingly, Davenant is especially concerned in *Gondibert* to purge his verse of gods. In the beginning of the poem, in place of an invocation, Davenant turns to history rather than a muse:

> Of all the Lombards, by their Trophies knowne,
> Who sought Fame soon, and had her favor long,
> King Aribert best seem'd to fill the Throne;
> And bred most bus'nesse for Heroick Song.   (1.1.1–4)

In the fourth line Davenant reflects on the poetic process, the "bus'nesse" of song. This introduces the poet's subject and launches the poem from the same self-conscious position that an invocation provides. But it turns to the stuff of history, trophies and fame, as the source for his poetry, and makes no recourse to a muse. History, in fact, becomes an important conceit for Davenant, who frequently reminds the reader of his claim that he is telling genuine history. In this vein he begins canto 4 by avoiding an obvious moment for an invocation with the conceit that he is examining old historical documents:

> By what bold passion am I rudely led,
> Like Fame's too curious and officious Spie,
> Where I these Rolls in her dark Closet read,
> Where Worthies wrapp'd in Time's disguises lie?   (1.4.1–4)

Once again the poet consults fame. But in addition, he has the benefit of ancient and hidden documents, the "Rolls" that reveal to antiquarians genuine history.

In *Gondibert,* furthermore, Davenant not only reforms invocation, but also carefully denies the presence of polytheistic gods in the narrative. There are no divine councils or epic machinery. Nor are there borderline supernatural figures that might be taken as impinging upon the second commandment, such as allegorical figures or angels in revelation. In the "Author's Preface," Davenant cites criticism of the classical poets for "conversations" involving the gods: Homer "often interrogates his Muse, not as his rational Spirit, but as a Familiar, separated from his body, so her replys bring him where he spends time in immortal conversation" ("Author's Preface," 3–4); Virgil "hath so often led him into Heaven and Hell, till by conversation with Gods and Ghosts he sometimes deprives us of those natural probabilities in Story which are instructive to humane life" (ibid., 4). The poet's address to a god in invocation or elsewhere may imply belief on the part of the poet. But if the gods answer, if the gods engage in conversation, then it implies that they really exist in the storyworld. A conversation gives the gods presence in the narrative, making an ontological assertion of the existence of polytheism. Such polytheistic conversations, and their formal version, councils, threaten the entire storyworld's veracity. The narrative presence of gods, in conversation and council, would render Davenant's project both historically and religiously untrue.

So, while Davenant's main subject is love, and while poetic convention often brings him very near to mentioning Cupid, Davenant ostentatiously sidesteps his presence. When beauty in the form of a virgin maid passed by the soldiers in Gondibert's camp,

> They vayl'd their Ensignes as it by did move,
> Whilst inward (as from Native Conscience) all
> Worship'd the Poets Darling Godhead, Love,
> Which grave Philophers did Nature call.   (1.1.68–71)

At the same time that Gondibert's men decorously restrain themselves from outward shows of love, the poet decorously resists an outward depiction of the god of love. Cupid is perhaps the most common of polytheistic gods in poetry—as Sidney puts it in Sonnet 5, Cupid "An image is, which for ourselves we carve."[41] Davenant reminds us of the problem of polytheism with "the Poets Darling Godhead." And then, rather than describing or even naming Cupid, he describes an "inward" worship, which is an act that can have no external or visible signs. In a good example of the metaphysical wit he occasionally displays, Davenant supplies an aniconic image to replace Cupid's overly material darts: inwardness is said to resemble conscience, which itself is often described as operating through darts or pricks. The prick of Cupid's arrow thus becomes a wholly internal and mental process, like the prick of conscience.

De doctrina Christiana opposes polytheism to "internal worship," which means "acknowledgment of the one true God and devout affection for him" (YP 6:656). Polytheism constructs an external religious economy, and the turn inward is a characteristic of monotheism. Davenant's refusal to give Cupid narrative presence, his denial of presence to all polytheism, thus takes the form of a skepticism toward outward shows of religion, and an insistence on religion and poetry that function inwardly. With the support of Hobbes, Davenant has created a heroic poem that, in allowing nothing even remotely near to polytheism, has completely jettisoned all forms of the supernatural. This rejection brings *Gondibert* near to the skepticism of deism, as David Gladish notices in his introduction: "In omitting the supernatural as an operative, causative, and reciprocating agent, Davenant presents a realistic, or at least a Deistic, world" (*Gondibert,* xi). Davenant's poetics, furthermore, results in some of the period's most clearly phrased accounts of natural religion. Without the supernatural economy of revealed religion, God withdraws, leaving nature as "the Vice-regent of God" ("Author's Preface," 15). *Gondibert*, in fact, although written well before the emergence of public deism, is probably the most deistic of seventeenth century narratives—a quality rarely noticed, but fully in keeping with Davenant's collaboration with Hobbes.

A key outgrowth of the seventeenth century's increased attention to monotheism is the rational religion of deism. The rejection of all revelation is identifiable as an attempt to meet monotheism's vigilance against other gods. Deism, as this study asserts in several ways, can be seen as an extreme point of monotheism's aniconism. Davenant's anticipation of deism thus places him at the far end of the aniconic spectrum. The skepticism that the second commandment levels against other gods issues into the total denial of all external forms of religion—into what I call the skeptical extreme.

This extreme position of Christian skepticism is precisely what Cowley emphasizes in his commendatory poem to *Gondibert*. He begins by praising Davenant's elimination of all supernatural beings:

> Methinks Heroick Poesy till now,
> Like some fantastique Fairy-land did show;
> Gods, Devils, Nymphs, Witches, and Giants race,
> And all but Man, in Man's best work had place.

And he then associates the truth that Davenant produces specifically with religion, praising the poet's rejection of both ancient and Catholic Rome:

> Some men their fancies like their Faiths derive,
> And count all ill but that which Rome does give;
> The marks of Old and Catholick would finde;
> To the same Chair would Truth and Fiction binde.
>
> (*Gondibert*, 270–71)

The inclusion of Catholic Rome makes Davenant representative of Protestantism, which reformed Catholicism in much the same way that Davenant seeks to reform poetry, eschewing external forms of religion for inwardness. But this same process also constitutes a rejection of old Rome and the polytheism of the classical world. Cowley here makes the familiar move of associating Catholicism with idolatry and polytheism. Both mistakes blend truth and fiction, and Cowley praises Davenant's skeptical protection of truth.

Cowley's Return from the Skeptical Extreme

Cowley is lavish in his approval of Davenant's extreme skepticism. But, as Dryden noticed, Cowley's own heroic verse, the *Davideis*, clearly contradicts such praise: "Neither am I much concerned at Mr. Cowley's verses before *Gondibert* (though his authority is almost sacred to me): 'tis true he has resembled the old epic poetry to a fantastic fairy land; but he has contradicted himself by his own example."[42] Indeed, the *Davideis* not only allows the supernatural, it gives presence to a multitude of polytheistic gods, such as Baal, Moloch, and Dagon. Cowley was companion to both Davenant and Hobbes in their Paris exile, and the *Davideis* was published as part of his *Poems* in 1656, shortly after *Gondibert*. And so the *Davideis* and Cowley's preface can be read as a response to Davenant, one more willing to disagree than the commendatory poem. If Davenant's storyworld upholds an extreme verisimilitude, then Cowley's has turned back toward Tasso, as well as Virgil and Homer.

And yet Cowley's turn toward polytheism, as Dryden recognizes, is deeply contradictory, especially given Cowley's simultaneous claims to be writing Christian poetry. Both in his "Author's Preface" and in the *Davideis*, Cowley argues for Christian poetry in terms more forceful than Davenant's. In his "Author's Preface" he declares,

> Amongst all holy and consecrated things which the *Devil* ever stole and alienated from the service of the *Deity*; as *Altars, Temples, Sacrifices, Prayers*, and the like; there is none that he so universally, and so long usurpt, as *Poetry*. It is time to recover it out of the *Tyrants* hands, and to restore it to the *Kingdom* of *God*, who is the *Father* of it. (Cowley, *Davideis*, b2r–v)

Poetry has been corrupted even more than true worship. And the way to rescue it from debasement is to recover poetry from the trappings of polytheism: the altars, temples, and sacrifices. Cowley goes on to identify the threat to poetry even more clearly:

> Besides, though those mad stories of the *Gods* and *Heroes*, seem in themselves so ridiculous; yet they were then the *whole Body* (or rather *Chaos*) of the *Theologie* of those times.... There was no other *Religion*, and therefore *that* was better then *none at all*. But to us who have no need of them, to us who deride their *folly*, and are wearied with their *impertinencies*, they ought to appear no better arguments for *Verse*, then those of their worthy *Successors*, the *Knights Errant*. (b2v–b3r)

If, after the strong polemic of Davenant and Hobbes, Cowley loosens up his poetics to admit the presence of polytheistic gods, he is not practicing mere license. Somehow Cowley is forging a Christian poetry that includes the gods.

That Cowley is conscious of his task is clear from his insistence on polytheistic presence in the invocation. While poets in the line of Du Bartas tend to Christianize the muse, and while Davenant forgoes invocation altogether, Cowley insists on upholding its traditional form. Moreover, he explicitly argues for his decision in the first of the notes he attaches to the poem:

> The custom of beginning all *Poems*, with a *Proposition* of the whole work, and an *Invocation* of some God for his assistance to go through with it, is so Solemnly and religiously observed by all the ancient *Poets*, that though I could have found out a better way, I should not (I think) have ventured upon it. But there can be, I believe, none better; and that part, of the *Invocation*, if it became a *Heathen*, is no less *Necessary* for a *Christian Poet*. (24n1)

Cowley calls the muse "some God," and associates him with "Heathen" religion, showing his awareness of the threat invocation offers to monotheism. As Cowley argues the point, however, the force of poetic custom—Cowley's committed neoclassicism—overwhelms such concerns. He knows the problem with invocations, but announces the necessity of finding a way to make them a part of Christian poetry.

And in the narrative that follows, Cowley is insistent in his use of the supernatural and the gods. After a brief portrayal of Saul, the *Davideis* begins in hell, with Lucifer addressing the Furies.

Lucifer is described with intimate physical detail: "Thrice did he knock his Iron teeth, thrice howl, / And into frowns his wrathful forehead rowl" (Cowlely, *Davideis,* 6). He is answered by Envy, an allegorical figure described in Spenserian detail, who is also identified as a fiend and a fury. Envy's speech fills out Cowley's portrait of an actual council:

> She spoke; all star'ed at first, and made a pause;
> But strait the general murmur of applause
> Ran through Deaths Courts; she frown'd still, and begun
> To *envy* at the praise *herself* had won.
> Great *Belzebub* starts from his burning throne
> To'embrace the *Fiend,* but she now furious grown
> To act her part; thrice bow'd, and thence she fled;
> The *Snakes* all hist, the *Fiends* all murmured.
>
> (Cowley, *Davideis,* 8)

As the participants converse, react to each other, and move around, the scene develops the spatial complexity of a storyworld, and the rich materiality of gods present in council. Over the course of the poem Cowley brings in a list of gods familiar to readers of *Paradise Lost:* Beelzebub, Moloch, Astarte, Baal, and Dagon.

Cowley's departure from Davenant is a return to Tasso (the two are often compared), and to classical examples.[43] His inclusion of the gods is part of Cowley's commitment to neoclassicism, as is evident in his note to the invocation, where he appeals to custom and the ancient poets, and elsewhere in the notes where he regularly cites Virgil and Homer. The imitation of epic, as René Le Bossu asserts, may depend upon the presence of gods: "He therefore that would be a Poet, must leave Historians to write, that a Fleet was shattered by a storm and cast upon a strange coast: And must say with Virgil, that Juno went to Aeolus, and that this God upon her instance unkennel'd the wind against Aeneas."[44] Neoclassicism, after all, imitates models developed in polytheistic Greece. Davenant, on the other hand, rejects the authority of the classical predecessors precisely for their use of gods, and he declares Tasso's councils unfit for Christian poetry. Davenant's

"Author's Preface" has been called "the manifesto of neo-classicism" by Edmund Gosse, and it, Hobbes's "Answer to Davenant," and Cowley's work should all certainly be taken as cornerstones of seventeenth century neoclassicism. Cowley and Davenant's disagreement over polytheism, then, represents a debate over how best to handle a fundamental problem within neoclassicism: whether Christian poets should imitate the ancients even in their use of gods. A focus on polytheism, and on these midcentury authors, reveals how two important modes of seventeenth century poetry, neoclassicism and Christian poetry, both compete and come together. Indeed, as will be discussed in chapter 4, polytheism continues to bedevil poets and critics of the epic later in the century. How to reconcile Christian poetry and neoclassicism takes the form of debates over epic machinery among figures such as Boileau, Dryden, and John Dennis.

The problem of whether to include the gods in poetry has more behind it than a neoclassical desire to imitate rules. In Tasso's terms, the inclusion of polytheism is what makes a poem marvelous, or, more simply, what makes a story exciting. Cowley's turn to the gods, in opposition to Davenant, is most of all an attempt at interesting narrative, which, especially for the seventeenth century, is conditioned by classical precedents. Cowley recognizes the significant pull or "charms" that the ancients exert when he calls for truthful poetry "T' unbind the charms that in slight *Fables* lie, / And teach that *Truth* is *truest Poesie*." If Cowley is to teach truest "Poesie," if he is to move the reader sufficiently to "unbind" the seductions of pagan poetry, he must legitimately compete with them. The total exclusion of the gods would be an exemplary kind of monotheism, but it may not make for sufficiently interesting, and therefore effective, narrative. So in Cowley's call for biblical subjects, he asserts the necessity of supernatural action and argues for the Bible precisely because it has more of the marvelous than classical subjects: "Are the obsolete threadbare tales of *Thebes* and *Troy,* half so stored with great, heroical, and supernatural actions (since *Verse* will needs *finde* or *make* such) as the wars of *Joshua*, of the *Judges*, of *David*, and divers others?" (Cowley, *Davideis*, b3r).

In *Gondibert*, moreover, Cowley may have recognized the pitfalls of thoroughgoing skepticism. He likely wished to avoid the problem so often felt by readers of *Gondibert:* that it is boring. As Dryden later argues regarding epic in "The Art of Poetry," narrative is strengthened by the presence and visibility of gods, which he calls "ornaments":

> Without these Ornaments before our Eyes,
> Th' unsinew'd Poem languishes, and dyes:
> Your Poet in his art will always fail,
> And tell you but a dull insipid Tale.[45]

Dryden, translating Boileau, takes a strong position against the "mistaken Authors" who had attempted to write polytheistic gods out of their narratives—against authors in the movement for Christian poetry such as Davenant. And the problem with the extreme verisimilitude of these mistakers is nothing other than a boring story, as Davenant, consciously and polemically striving for verisimilitude, finally suspects. In his postscript, printed at the end of the completed half of the unfinished *Gondibert*, he murmurs: "And perhaps if my POEM were not so severe a representation of Vertue (undressing Truth even out of those disguises which have been most in fashion throughout the World) it might arrive at fair entertainment" (Davenant, *Gondibert*, 251). Austerely rendering a naked truth, without fashion or ornament, Davenant sees, is likely to leave readers dissatisfied.

And less than polite entertainment is exactly what *Gondibert* received in the years between it and the *Davideis*. Davenant's severity and seriousness made him a perfect target for the humor of a satirical pamphlet, *Certain Verses Written by Several of the Author's Friends; to Be Reprinted with the Second Edition of Gondibert* (1653). Davenant's "friends" tease him about a range of things, most mercilessly about his syphilitic nose (references to Ovid are frequent) and his polemical seriousness. But there is also a real critical reaction to Davenant's extreme verisimilitude. In "Upon the Continuation of Gondibert," the anonymous poet objects to the lack of gods and any form of the supernatural:

> This 'tis, to be severe to us,
> For naming Gods and Pegasus.
> Couldst thou but such a horse have shap't,
> Thou hadst with gallant Massie scap't,
> Or Couldst thou but frame Gyges Ring,
> Long since (poor Will) th'hadst been a Wing,
> Thou liest not there for any plot,
> But cause a Poet thou art not. (*Gondibert*, 276)

Here the poet recycles Davenant's description of himself as "severe," but claims that the author is being severe not in his representation of truth, but to his reader. This is in part a reaction to Davenant's polemic, which would clearly be an unwelcome lecture to any reader who enjoys the presence of gods and ghosts. But the last couplet quoted also makes the same point as Dryden's "dull insipid Tale." Were Davenant to waver from the truth, it would be for the sake of plot; and by inference, his refusal to lie harms the plot. Davenant's project is to show that a poet should and can tell a rigorous truth, but the satirical poet's response is that Davenant's refusal to embellish truth with the gods merely demonstrates that "a Poet thou art not."

This midcentury grappling over the presence of gods in poetry is an important chapter in the seventeenth century debate over monotheistic narrative. It outlines the tension between monotheism and narrative, a tension at the heart of Milton's late poetry: while monotheism pushes toward complete aniconism, the demands of narrative for interesting story—or any story at all—pull away from that extreme position. Such contradictory impulses mark monotheistic narrative especially in its relationship to polytheism. For polytheism must be rejected, but, as the case of *Gondibert* shows, it must not be too thoroughly rejected. Cowley's return from Davenant's skeptical extreme negotiates this narratological problem, making the gods present while simultaneously protecting claims to be "truest Poesie." Cowley's return from the skeptical extreme rests upon an innovation crucial to the movement for Christian poetry as a whole, and to *Paradise Lost* in particular. In his handling of the polytheism of the *Davideis*, Cowley turns to John Selden's research in *De diis*. Selden's comparative and historical detail enables Cowley to maintain his claim for "truest Poesie," and in reconciling polytheism with Christianity, it anticipates Milton's catalogue of gods.

Truth and the Margins

Not surprisingly, Cowley brings Selden's scholarship into the *Davideis* in the form of footnotes. When Envy finishes her speech, and "the general murmur of applause / Ran through Deaths Courts," when the narrative panorama opens up to reveal a council in hell with supernatural and polytheistic beings present, Cowley introduces Belzebub, who "starts from his burning Throne" (Cowley, *Davideis*, 8). At this first mention of the god, Cowley supplies a note that reads very much like Selden's entry on Belzebub in *De diis*. Following Selden's method, Cowley begins with a list of references in Scripture, and then turns to classical literature, demonstrating that "one evil Spirit presided over the others." He then explains Belzebub's name as "Lord of Flies," and adds that "some think" the name was given in scorn by the Jews because sacrifices to Beelzebub were infested by flies while sacrifices in the temple at Jerusalem were not (Cowley, *Davideis*, 30n18). These details, and even some of the same language, can be found in *De diis* (Selden 2:375).[46] Although he does not cite Selden, Cowley almost certainly wrote this note with the help of *De diis*.

Cowley's treatment of Moloch displays a similarly obvious but unacknowledged debt: all the evidence appears in *De diis*, including a discussion of whether or not "passing through the fire" signified actual child sacrifice (they both agree it did), and the detail that drums and other instruments were used to drown out the cries of the victims (Cowley, *Davideis*, 72n47; Selden 2:322–23). Then in his note to Dagon, Cowley explicitly cites Selden (80n83). The note traces Dagon's etymology to the Hebrew *dag*, meaning fish, rejecting a competing notion that "Dagon" derives from corn. Cowley then briefly recounts Selden's argument relating Dagon to Atergatis, Derceto, and Oannes, concluding, "From whence our learned Selden fetches Dagon, whom see at large upon this matter" (Cowley, *Davideis*, 80n83). Cowley also refers directly to Selden in a discussion of the derivation of the name "Hebrews" (44n64). And, in a note on Baal-Phegor, Cowley reluctantly meets with "the opposition of a great person, even our Selden" (146n1). Numerous other places likely derive from *De diis*, although it is not always demonstrable that Cowley is reading Selden rather than a shared source. At least two others also influenced Cowley, Thomas Fuller, and Gerardus Vossius. But as they worked from Selden and continued his use of disparate and original sources, it is best to say that Cowley's notes, both in content and method, follow in the discourse stemming from Selden's influential study of polytheism.

By means of his footnotes, then, Cowley has tucked Selden's discourse into the *Davideis*. What such a move offers is quite simply the opportunity to write and think about polytheistic gods. Cowley has declared his intent to show that "Truth is truest Poesie." But when that poetry, even with a tone of rejection, dwells upon such details as the "Fires of Moloch" and "The double Dagon" (Cowley, *Davideis*, 59), truthfulness depends not on the verisimilitude of the narrative, but on the Seldenian detail of the footnotes. Taking the *Davideis* not simply as verse but as a project made up of both the verse and the notes, Cowley produces a text with two discernible gestures. The first, the inclusion of a god in the poetry, transgresses monotheism but provides it with the marvelous detail that is essential to a narrative. And the second gesture, the prose of the footnote, adds nothing to the plot but does the necessary work of recouping the narrative's transgression of truth. Moments of such double gesture gather around the polythestic gods: Cowley's catalogue of idols in book 2 is virtually two concurrent texts, as 14 lines of verse garner eight separate notes. As each idol is described in the verse, a footnote opens into historical prose.

If Cowley's verse seems doctrinally sound, it is because, in the sense of simultaneity fostered by such footnotes, a sleight of hand is practiced. A metonymic slide takes place within the word "truth," where truth according to religion bows out momentarily to truth according to history. When the verse clearly fails to measure up to religious truth, it immediately turns the reader's attention to the kind of truth Selden developed—which may be a different kind of truth, but is truth nonetheless.

Selden offers the poet a text that, in its rigorous historicity, seems to transform the gods. Although to some the mere mention of gods appears transgressive, Selden's method met no such hesitation: Fuller remarks that "Clergymen like best his book 'de Dis Syris,' and worst his 'History of Tithes.'"[47] Selden himself will not have an invocation in the *Poly-Olbion*, which borders on an assertion of a polytheistic ontology, but he does write and publish *De diis*. If the narrative presence of polytheism undermines Christian poetry, the kind of textual presence Selden offers does not. Part of the transformative quality of Selden's method is an insistence on objectivity, as the unbiased reporting of historical fact clearly avoids assertions of ontological truth. Selden can discuss how Moloch was worshipped according to historical records—giving him textual presence—without ever appearing to claim that Moloch actually exists. Ironically, the onus of truth concerning polytheism proves less weighty to the historian than to the Christian poet, who, as even Cowley asserts, must be wary about the mere presence of polytheism.

Not only does Cowley use Selden's research, but also his notes match Selden's construction of a complex textual space between verse and footnote in the *Poly-Olbion*. In collaboration with Drayton, Selden self-consciously moves the reader from the fictions of poetry to the rigorous truths of historical inquiry. His

"Illustrations" construct a reading process in which the reader breaks away from the flow of the poem, looks back upon the contested moment, and develops a critical and historical perspective on the assertions of narrative. One can speculate that Selden's unique poetics inspired Cowley, for such discursivity is precisely the effect of Cowley's notes. When he names, for example, "Eight hundred" as the number of years between Benjamin and Saul, his footnote quibbles with the imprecision: "not exactly: but this is the next *whole number,* and *Poetry* will not admit of *broken ones*" (Cowley, *Davideis,* 32n23). Here Cowley chooses a whole number because it will maintain the metrical flow of the verse. But while "Eight hundred" keeps the narrative moving, its imprecision must be addressed. So the note works the poetry back toward truth by interrupting the narrative and moving the eye (as it does in the first edition) to another page. In the next note, attached to a couplet on the harmony of the spheres, Cowley expresses his scientific doubt, beginning: "In this, and some like places, I would not have the Reader judge of my opinion by what I say; no more then before in divers expressions about *Hell,* the *Devil,* and *Envy*" (32n24). Fittingly hidden in the footnotes, Cowley states clearly what his notes attached to the gods imply: that the truthfulness of his "truest Poesie" depends not on the immediate and persuasive effect of the verse, but on a judgment influenced by the historicity of his notes. Cowley capitalizes on the poetics of the footnote to import the conviction of truth into the *Davideis.*

The movement of the reader's eye from the verse to the notes not only delineates the discursive approach of Selden's history, but also works to undo the immediacy of the narrative, and to deconstruct the sense of narrative presence. If the presence of polytheistic gods in the narrative represents a central threat to Christian poetry, Cowley's notes respond to the gods by offering a uniquely attenuated version of narrative presence. Scholarly footnotes are not usually read as part of the poem, but rather as a commentary on it—they are by other authors and written after the fact, and so are clearly extradiegetical. But in the case of the *Poly-Olbion* and the *Davideis*, footnotes are much nearer to the narrative. Since Selden collaborated with Drayton and published his "Illustrations" in the first edition, they are in some way an element of the diegesis and not simply an external apparatus. Even more so since he wrote them himself, Cowley's notes are clearly part of how the story of the *Davideis* is narrated. But if they are integral, the notes are part of a diegesis that is split and decentered. In a different physical place in the book and running concurrently with the story itself, they undermine the coherence of the storyworld. And so when Moloch, Dagon, and the other gods appear in the verse and *then* with Seldenian detail in the notes, they are present in the narrative in a highly fractured and self-critical way. Such narrative presence brings the gods into an unstable and aniconic narrative space much like Satan's eyes at the beginning of book 1. This space is near to what Gerard Genette identifies with mimesis in the subjunctive mood. While Chatman's "existents" imply an ontological assertion that would be in the indicative, Cowley's annotated gods reflect Genette's observation that "there are differences between degrees of affirmation."[48] In the subjunctive, the narrative presence of polytheism poses less of a threat.

Cowley's innovation in the history of Christian poetry is to return from the skeptical extreme by making use of Selden's gods in his notes. But Cowley brings *De diis* only as far as the notes. In the consummate hands of Milton, Selden is brought out of the margins and into the poetry—and the discourse of monotheism gains a full place in Christian poetry.

Selden's Prominent Place

Cowley was one of Milton's favorite poets, and a resemblance to Cowley is clear in their mutual admiration of Tasso and Tasso's divine councils.[49] But Milton's proximity to Cowley is most obvious in the use of Selden's research within those councils. Both

Cowley and Milton are acutely aware of the difficulty infernal councils make for the Christian poet, and they negotiate this difficulty by turning to *De diis*. What separates Milton and Cowley from Tasso, it could be claimed, and part of what gives the monotheistic narrative of the seventeenth century its unique flavor, is the use of Selden as mythographer.⁵⁰

As Gibbon puts it, "For the enumeration of the Syrian and Arabian deities, it may be observed, that Milton has comprised, in one hundred and thirty very beautiful lines, the two learned syntagmas, which Selden had composed on that abstruse subject." I would add that Milton had the assistance of the discourse stemming from Selden, especially the innovative blend of scholarship and poetry developed by Cowley. In composing the catalogue of the gods, Milton appears to have worked from the *Davideis*. Selden's prose on each god sprawls over many pages, but Cowley's notes condense the prolixity into a package that can be very similar to Milton's catalogue. On Moloch, Milton's lines include: "and made his grove / The pleasant vally of Hinnom, Tophet thence / And black Gehenna called, the type of hell" (*PL* 1.403–05). Cowley's note, meanwhile, reads: "*Hinnon*, a valley full of Trees close by *Jerusalem*, where *Moloch* was worshipped in this execrable manner, called *Gehinnon*, from whence the word *Gehenna* comes for *Hell*; it was called likewise *Tophet*" (78n70). It should be noted, however, that in turning to Selden for poetic detail, Cowley could himself be following Milton's lead. *On the Morning of Christ's Nativity* was published in 1645, 11 years before the *Davideis*. And it was brought out by Humphrey Mosley, who also published the *Davideis* in Cowley's *Poems*. If priority is muddled, so is the idea of direct literary debt: it is difficult to be sure that Milton took any one detail from Cowley or Selden, since Milton could have gone to the sources himself.⁵¹ The genealogy does not trace merely to Selden, but also to Cowley and the discourse of monotheism.

What this discourse gives Milton, most of all, is an engagement with the historicity and objectivity of Selden's nascent comparative religion. Even as the catalogue appalls a faithful Christian with the monstrous detail of pagan religion, it also sets up a perspective that is antiquarian in its historical interest, and potentially tolerant in its engagement with the gods. As J. B. Broadbent recognizes, the underlying feeling of empirical truth creates a liberating poetic texture, pushing the catalogue into Genette's subjunctive mood: "Milton proves his control over the devils by sophisticated anthropological manipulation, and invites us to stand back from them without necessity of belief."[52] The anthropologist, unlike the Christian theologian or the believer, can face the gods without a sense of transgression. Milton's control over the historical manifestations of the devils contains the threat they pose, as the inclusion of Selden pushes the catalogue toward the freedom of comparative religion.[53]

As the catalogue opens itself to Selden's comparative perspective, it takes on the cadence of *De diis*. Selden patiently moves from source to source, rarely editorializing, and showing more interest in getting the facts out than in entertaining the reader. Similarly, in listing possible variations without giving either priority, Milton's tone becomes both ponderous in its foreign sounds and encyclopedic in its quality of compiling. Milton takes the time, for example, to locate with specificity Dagon's temple, "Reared in Azotus, dreaded through the coast / Of Palestine, in Gath and Ascalon / And Accaron and Gaza's frontier bounds" (*PL* 1.464–66; Selden 2:356, 358, 361). Cowley is so determined to keep such unnarratable language out of his verse that he admits inaccuracy rather than include something as prosaic as broken numbers. His recovery of truthfulness takes place only in the notes. But Milton, incorporating even Selden's style into the catalogue, makes comparative and leisurely antiquarian compiling into part of his poetics.

It is this embedding of the footnote amid the gods that, as Broadbent puts it, "invites us to stand back from them without necessity of belief." Selden's prefatory "Illustration" to the *Poly-Olbion*, in moving the reader from Drayton's invocation to a historian's dismissal of the muse, constructs the margin as the particular space of anthropology, or comparative religion.[54] Cowley makes innovative use of the way that footnotes substitute an alternative discourse, in what I have called the double gesture of his council. Whenever the council threatens to transgress monotheism, Cowley attaches a note full of Seldenian detail, and, metonymically, the historical truth of footnote replaces the endangered religious truth of the poetry. Milton, in turn, makes use of Cowley's double gesture. Only, with Selden brought into the verse, he attains a simultaneity which, like a sleight of hand, blurs the two gestures. While the reader of the *Davideis* must notice the number in the margin indicating a note and then turn to the end of the book to read the information, in Milton's infernal council there is no need to leave the page or even the verse. Selden is so woven into the poetic presentation of the gods that their presence—which is what threatens the text's truthfulness—cannot be separated from the historical detail that invokes the full weight of Selden's rigorous pursuit of truth. Milton's reader is confronted by the rich material presence of Moloch and the other gods, and at the same time relieved by the historical perspective this same detail offers.

In this way the catalogue of gods represents a triumphant solution to the problem of polytheism haunting Christian poets. In comprising *De diis* with such virtuosity, making transcendent poetry out of footnotes, Milton allows the gods narrative presence, but at the same time he pulls the reader away from what Davenant fears, that such presence will be taken as an assertion of the truth of their existence. As the double gesture becomes nearly simultaneous, the negotiation of the conflicting demands of monotheism and epic narrative becomes nearly seamless. The result is a convincing claim for Milton having written the "truest Poesie."

The prominence of Selden in Milton's Christian poetry, moreover, pulls *Paradise Lost* into a theologically fluid space. At the center of Selden's project is the comparative effort to connect the many names by which a single god was known. Dagon, for example, was also Oannes, Atergatis, and Derceto (Selden 2:358). By linking disparate gods as varying names for the same thing, Selden takes part in an ancient polytheistic practice Jan Assmann calls "translation." Polytheistic translation considers all religions to be continuous, rather than divided between a single true religion and the excluded others. While, Assmann says, monotheism draws the Mosaic distinction in order to separate the one true religion from pagan falsehoods, translation sets up a comparative perspective that is directly opposite to the monotheism's exclusiveness:

> The cultures, languages, and customs may have been as different as ever: the religions always had a common ground. Thus they functioned as a means of intercultural translatability. The gods were international because they were cosmic. The different peoples worshipped different gods, but nobody contested the reality of foreign gods and the legitimacy of foreign forms of worship. The distinction I am speaking of simply did not exist in the world of polytheistic religions.[55]

Milton engages in such translation when to Chemos he adds, "Peor his other name" (*PL* 1.412), and when he lists "Astoreth, whom the Phoenicians called / Astarte" (1.438–39). Such compiling of alternatives implies a continuity between the religions of the world, which places Milton, along with Selden and the discourse of monotheism, within nascent comparative religion.

The fluidity of names in *De diis* and *Paradise Lost* is matched by a fluidity of attributes—a sense of the interrelatedness of the symbols and rites. As Milton continues with Astoreth, comparative insight extends even to the level of poetic conceit:

> With these in troop
> Came Astoreth, whom the Phoenicians called
> Astarte, queen of heaven, with crescent horns;
> To whose bright image nightly by the moon
> Sidonian virgins paid their vows and songs.   (1.437–41)

Selden explains the variation in name, Astoreth or Astarte, at the beginning of the fairly long entry. But the remaining details above can be found in a single passage, as dense as Milton's verse:

> This goddess is said to have placed a bull's head upon her own head, as the insignia of royalty, and at last, after wandering the earth, to have found a star fallen from the air...which, afterwards, she consecrated in Tyrus, her sacred island. It is by no means evident which star this may be: you may connect it with what we say regarding Remphan or Ciun. But after she had assumed the bull's head, it looked as if flames curved from her forehead, and she carried the image of the moon before her.[56]

Selden's insignia of royalty becomes Milton's "queen." The bull's head becomes "crescent horns." And the curved flames, which are the image of the moon, become a "bright image," "by the moon." Aside from the close proximity of all these details, there is a complex bit of imaginative work, which Selden accomplishes and Milton repeats. Astoreth is in some places associated with a bull and in other places with the moon. With insight worthy of a metaphysical poet, Selden suggests just how these associations might have fit together: the bull horns, if glowing, would resemble the curve of the moon. Milton first captures the conceit by modifying "horns" with an adjective usually associated in English with the moon, "crescent." And he furthers the association with the ambiguity of "by the moon," which could mean either under a moon, or by means of a moon—indicating that they worshipped Astarte's horns via the moon. Fuller cites Selden and explains his insight in simpler terms, that the idol had "the head of a bull, where the horns erected resembled the crescent moon," from which Milton likely took the word "crescent."[57]

The comparative perspective of translation and the fluidity of divine beings, however, extend only so far as the religions are pagan. At the same time that he entertains a comparatist's approach, Milton, as I have argued, forges "truest Poesie," and works to emphasize the Mosaic distinction that establishes monotheism as the one truth. Indeed, in his use of Selden, Milton seems to be asserting both the monotheistic truth of Christianity and the relativism of comparative religion. And so it must be asked, does Milton's engagement with Selden signal a loosening of Milton's conviction of the truth of the one God, or a tightening?

The answer is that both things are taking place, for Milton is engaging with monotheism precisely to the extent that he is also genuinely engaging with polytheism. Monotheism emerges as a focus of theological interest within Selden's study of polytheism, and the seventeenth century discourse of monotheism is a discourse that both asserts the truth of monotheism and, to a remarkable extent, admits polytheism into legitimate consideration. This is so because monotheism is, in Assmann's words, a "counter-religion." Defining itself by the rejection of other religions, it can only assert the truth of one God by the dismissal of other gods.[58] The example of Davenant shows how the counter-religion plays out in narrative: *Gondibert's* skeptical extreme, in banishing all vestiges of polytheism, produces a story that "languishes and dyes." In the name of monotheism, aniconism undermines narrative itself. A monotheistic narrative, then, depends upon the presence of polytheism: the gods are required for narrative and rejected within it, appearing so that they can be excluded. With the help of Selden's gods, Milton and Cowley return from Davenant's skeptical extreme, making the prominent polytheism of book 1 a mark of Milton's interest in asserting monotheism.

What Milton and the discourse of monotheism share most of all is a deep involvement in the Mosaic distinction—transgressing and thereby delineating it. In his anti-invocation, when Selden doubts that "in Prose and religion it were as iustifiable, as in Poetry and Fiction, to invoke a Locall power," he draws a stark line between what is true and what is false. On one side of the line goes true religion, which has no room for invocation, and with it goes the prose of the historian's footnote. On the other side of the line goes what is false: poetry and fiction. But

Drayton's verse transgresses Selden's line—in combination with Selden's "Illustrations," the text subverts and sets up the line of the Mosaic distinction. Likewise, when Cowley uses Selden in the *Davideis*, he creates the distinction between true and false religion, and in the movement between verse and notes he constantly transgresses that distinction. The text swings from one side of the line, in which it includes other gods, to the other side of the line, where the text snaps back into acceptability by distancing itself from belief in the anthropology of *De diis*. Cowley's double gesture reads as first false then true, alternately polytheistic and in conformity with the demands of monotheism, as it crosses and recrosses the Mosaic distinction.

When Milton uses Selden in the catalogue, the Mosaic distinction may be less obvious than in the *Poly-Olbion* and the *Davideis*, for the separate spaces of poem and footnote make the line of the Mosaic distinction easily recognizable. But even as Selden migrates out of the margins and into the verse, the dynamics of Cowley's double gesture, with the crossing and recrossing of the Mosaic distinction, are, in a greatly condensed manner, still at play. Broadbent's sense of freedom in the anthropology does not erase but coexists with the contradictory conviction that the "dark idolatries / Of alienated Judah" are horrid. Hovering around the Mosaic distinction, the catalogue of gods does not put to rest, but rather exacerbates, the shock that the polytheism of infernal council is so prominent in *Paradise Lost*. It is monotheistic narrative precisely in the theologically challenging and sublime way it forces us to feel both attraction and repulsion, both piety and transgression.

The intensified awareness of the Mosaic distinction, which characterizes the discourse of monotheism, is best exemplified by Selden's general project in *De diis* of describing the gods found in the Bible rather than those of the classical world. Selden does make extensive use of classical sources, even poets, but these always come after sacred sources and are directed at explaining the gods of the Bible. In *De diis*, the relative unfamiliarity of Tammuz, Rimmon, and the others gives those figures a jarring effect, reminding us that these are possibly gods and of much more consequence than mere poetic tropes, as such figures as Apollo and Diana have become through overuse. Unlike the classical gods with their many creative and romantic adventures, the biblical gods carry with them associations that are deeply threatening and subversive of true religion since mostly they are only present in the Bible as abominations to be rejected. And the biblical gods' very presence within sacred Scripture raises the stakes. Selden's discipline is not comparative literature, but comparative religion, and so he must be very careful to be truthful, in both the historical and theological senses of the word. The student of biblical polytheism feels the burden of explicating what must be historical and sacred truth, rather than the mere fancies of pagan poetry. Dagon is more threatening and subversive of true religion, but also, by virtue of his place in sacred Scripture, somehow more real than Cupid.

With Selden as mythographer, the anxious mode of Milton's catalogue of gods follows the method of beginning with sacred texts and working down to include classical sources. Milton's gods are at first those of the Bible, and only after Moloch, Astarte, and the rest troop by does he slide the classical gods into the catalogue. And they are a decided afterthought: "These were the prime in order and in might; / The rest were long to tell, though far renowned, / The Ionian gods, of Javan's issue" (*PL* 1.506–08). The poet then cursorily runs through a genealogy of the Titans and Olympians, but offers little of the materiality and detail found in the rest of the catalogue. By giving the classical gods such small notice, Milton, like Selden, relegates them to an inferior and derivative position—not "prime in order." This raises the prestige of the Bible over pagan literature, which matches the common claim of the Christian poets that the Bible offers better material for the poet. And the recasting of the council as biblical rather than classical gods also situates the poem within the discourses of polytheism, and has the effect of keeping the poem focused on the Mosaic distinction.

So the single extended passage from classical mythology in the catalogue, the carefully wrought fall of Mulciber, concludes Milton's portrayal of polytheism by bringing out into the open the real danger of transgressing the Mosaic distinction. The architect is introduced as "known / In heaven" (1.732–33), establishing his angelic ontology. But then Milton rehearses the ontological distinction between angel and god that lies beneath much of the tension in the catalogue: "Nor was his name unheard, or unadored / In ancient Greece" (1.738–39). As with the difficulty of proleptically portraying the apostates as idols, the rich and anachronistic detail of the god begins to push out the angelic ontology when Mulciber falls:

> and how he fell
> From heaven, they fabled, thrown by angry Jove
> Sheer o'er the crystal battlements; from morn
> To noon he fell, from noon to dewy eve,
> A summer's day; and with the setting sun
> Dropped from the zenith like a falling star,
> On Lemnos the Aegaean isle.   (*PL* 1.740–46)

The slow-motion loveliness of this fall, Milton's "counterplot," pulls the poetry into the sensuousness of the classical myths, ultimately landing the reader softly in the Greek isles.[59] The poetic possibilities of polytheism, which permits detail and, in Erich Auerbach's terms, foreground, clearly enrich the narrative. Mulciber's fall is also palpably different from "Moloch, horrid king besmeared with blood"—there is little of the anxiety and tension of the catalogue. This relaxed and luxuriant mood surfaces because, as it leaves behind biblical polytheism for classical, the threat of transgressing the Mosaic distinction recedes.

Mulciber's fall stands at the end of the catalogue as an advertisement of what Milton has specifically left behind. This kind of narrative, or counterplot, becomes attractive in its use of a polytheism that is naive toward the anxieties of monotheism, and the reader may feel why so many believers fall off from monotheism. Of course it is just after this reemergence of genuinely polytheistic narrative that Milton famously snaps back into monotheism: "thus they relate, / Erring; for he with this rebellious rout / Fell long before" (*PL* 1.746–48). If in its proleptic detail the narrative has drifted away from the angelic ontology, here it crosses back over the Mosaic distinction and insists upon inscribing Mulciber within a monotheistic cosmos. This is not so much a case of Milton tempting the reader as it is a prime example of how, in monotheistic fashion, *Paradise Lost* crosses and recrosses the Mosaic distinction. What Stanley Fish views as Milton's harassment of the reader may be seen as the textual equivocation necessary to monotheistic narrative.[60]

For the presence in book 1 of Selden, and of the kind of historical discourse he brings to the study of polytheism, leads to no firm ontological or poetic ground: it allows the presence of polytheistic gods, but at the same time reminds the reader, in a way Tasso does not, that these beings are false idols. They are clearly to be rejected—but here they are, in attractively rich detail. Selden's detail at once introduces skepticism toward gods and supplies the very material about which we must be skeptical, demanding a reading of the gods that is acutely aware of the poem's own contradictions. Wavering between the heroic pitch of Homer and the sterility of *Gondibert*'s aniconism, between the engaging sublimity of a council narrative and the distancing of historical prose, book 1 hovers around, and draws the Mosaic distinction between, polytheism and monotheism.

Two

Occult Monotheism and the Abstract Godhead

The Discourse of Monotheism

When Milton weaves *De diis Syris* into the fabric of *Paradise Lost*, he is aligning his poetry with a watershed text in the discourse of monotheism. John Selden's *De diis* is a source of material, as well as an example in methodology, for a number of seventeenth century texts that give a central place to the idea of monotheism. Common to all of these texts are detailed descriptions of polytheism that adopt the historical and comparative approach developed by Selden. This anthropological view of the gods is a fertile one for theological matters, just as in the last chapter it was shown to be fertile to Christian poets. It leads the philosophers and theologians of the discourse of monotheism to pursue the broader question of Christianity as a monotheistic religion, not only how it evolved historically, but the even more important issue of what a genuinely monotheistic Christianity looks like. As the discourse moves from the purely historical compiling of syntagmata to strong assertions of doctrine, it leaves Selden's uniquely pursued objectivity and becomes polemical. Following the influence of *De diis*, one discovers how its neutral scholarship is eventually used for divergent theological ends in the writings of Edward, Lord Herbert of Cherbury, and Henry More.

Cherbury's *De religione gentilium* and More's *An Explanation of the Grand Mystery of Godliness* disagree over whether or not a true monotheism can be discerned behind pagan polytheism. Or, as Thomas Fuller states the theory, "the most knowing and rational amongst heathens, adored not the very material image, but in, under, through, and beyond the same worshipped the true god of heaven and earth."[1] This comparative question of an occult monotheism casts doubt on the necessity of accepting God in the terms handed down by the Judeo-Christian revelation—occult monotheism implies that true religion is available without the stories of the Bible and without the doctrines of Christianity. More and Cherbury's differing interpretations of polytheism become essential to their versions of the monotheistic godhead. Defining monotheism, they struggle over the inherent problem, whether God is to be conceived of as a revealed and personal being, or as a thoroughly abstract force.

Selden's Influence

The influence of *De diis* actually begins before its publication, with *Purchas His Pilgrimage* (1613). *De diis* was published in 1617 but written in 1605 (Selden 2:210), and in that interim Selden worked with Samuel Purchas, and in some capacity (possibly writing the marginal notes), assisted in producing *His Pilgrimage*.[2] Unlike the rewritten 1625 edition, Purchas's first two editions devote considerable space to a study of polytheism that resembles Selden's at many points. *De diis*, in fact, looms over the first edition, in the form of Selden's footnote to his commendatory poem, which launches into a dense display of learning on a number of the gods from *De diis*. This specter is removed in the second edition of 1614, when Selden's poem is reprinted without the footnote. But the two texts are clearly intertwined.[3]

Purchas His Pilgrimage was itself an admired work, and alongside *De diis* is cited often in subsequent studies of the gods. It also has the distinction, according to the *Oxford English Dictionary*, of being the first text to use the word "polytheism" in English. This is not a coining like More's, however, but a translation from a Greek word with a long history.[4] Furthermore, polytheism (πολυθεότητος), appears prominently in the prolegomena to *De diis* (Selden 2:225), making Selden a likely source for Purchas's translation. (Also making Selden a source for both key words, "polytheism" and "monotheism.") In a consideration of the evolution of religion in Europe, Purchas turns a Protestant eye on the Catholic Church, and, concerning Jesuit conversions of infidels, warns that "upon that golden foundation they build afterward their owne *Hay and Stubble*, with their racke of *Confession*, and rabble of *Ceremonies*, and (the most dangerous to new Converts) an exchanged Polytheisme in worshipping of Saints, Images, and the *Host*."[5]

Purchas here takes part in the commonplace polemic against the idolatry of Rome. But his use of "Polytheisme" rather than, say, "paganism," shifts the discourse toward the comparative and historical approach of his friend Selden. The concept of polytheism, with its description of structure, is the point at which the religion of the infidels is comparable to the religion of the Catholics. While Purchas's clear rejection of both non-Protestant religions falls short of the tolerance of developed comparative religion, the effort to compare is still essential to his larger project of a complete history of world religion. In scope, Purchas is far more ambitious than Selden, as he takes on the religions of the whole world and makes use of the social data of travel writers to fill in such places as India, Africa, and the Americas. In design, too, he assembles not the modest compilations of syntagmata, but a narrative of religious development from the Creation to the present. The first book, however, on the ancient Near East, in many places reads like *De diis* with its accounts of Baal, Nisroch, Astarte, and the rest of the pantheon.[6] Also like Selden, Purchas is conscious of his effort to provide a more rigorously historical study of the gods than what is found in the poets. And so, in a gesture like Selden's in the *Poly-Olbion* of the year before, he begins by separating himself from the poetic practice of invocation:

> The Poets were wont to lay the foundations and first beginnings of their poeticall Fabrikes, with invocation of their Gods and Muses, although those works were sutable to such workmen, who according to their names were *Makers,* of those both Poems and Gods. I, as far short of their learning, as beyond them, in the scope of my desires, would so farre imitate their manner, in this matter which I intend; that, although I envie not to some their foolish claime of that Poeticall (not propheticall) inheritance, *to make my Maker:* and my matter, as in a Historie (not a Poeme) must bee made to my hands.[7]

As does Selden, Purchas claims for his historical discourse a superiority over poetry, specifically in that it does not transgress monotheistic rules against idolatry. As part of the emerging discourse, both Purchas and Selden promise a new perspective on the pagan gods.

Following Purchas and Selden in comparative accounts of world religion and gods is Sir Thomas Herbert, who in 1638 uses "politheisme" to describe the religion of Patania in his *A Relation of Some Years Travel*.[8] Next, of great importance, is Gerardus Vossius, whose *De theologia gentili et physiologia Christiana: Sive de origine ac progressu idolotriae* (1641) is a monumental work in the study of polytheism. Vossius ranges much further than Selden's study of the gods of the Bible (as D. C. Allen puts it, "there is little about shellfish that he can be told by those who fear and pray to the oyster"),[9] but Vossius cites Selden in several places,[10] and a letter from Selden records their acquaintance (Selden 2:1709). Vossius is in turn quoted often by subsequent scholars, as the texts in the discourse overlap repeatedly. Fuller's *A Pisgah-Sight of Palestine* (1650), in describing the "politheisme" of the idols of the Near East, cites Vossius frequently, but credits Selden as his main source on the gods: from Selden he borrowed "the tools and timber, wherewith the structure of this our *Jewish Pantheon* is erected."[11] Abraham Cowley refers to Vossius as well as Selden in the *Davideis,* while probably using Fuller in his representation of Dagon. And yet, demonstrating the intertwining of these texts, Fuller himself acknowledges Selden as his primary source for Dagon.[12] Two other publications that make extensive use of the research of Selden and Vossius are Alexander Ross, *Pansebia; or, A View of all Religions in the World* (1658), and Theophilus Gale, *The Court of the Gentiles* (1669).

Selden and Vossius are also main sources for the two texts that are the focus of the rest of this chapter, Edward, Lord Herbert of Cherbury's *De religione gentilium* (1663), and Henry More's *An Explanation of the Grand Mystery of Godliness* (1660). *De religione* was finished by 1645 and was to be published by Gerardus Vossius, but was brought out posthumously by his son Isaac.[13] Cherbury also had a close friendship with Selden—a warm letter from Selden remains (Selden 2:1706–07), and Selden served as Cherbury's executor. More's *Grand Mystery of Godliness,* meanwhile, is the text in the discourse in which Selden's influence is felt most directly and overtly. It is here that More coins "monotheisme."

Occult Monotheism and Cherbury

A perspective implicit to the study of monotheism and polytheism is that the pagan religions are, in some way, continuous with Christianity. This is particularly evident in Selden's method, where his willingness to use the Koran, for example, to gloss Genesis takes the significant step of reading sacred Scripture as continuous with profane writings. Similarly, Selden advances a historical model that traces religious development not through sudden changes wrought by revelation, but through historical process. The third chapter of Selden's prolegomena to *De diis* is "On the Origin and Progress of Polytheistic Gods, or the Multitude of Gods" (Selden 2:225). Selden describes a process in which humans fell from faith in the one God, beginning with a worship of the sun and the heavens (2:226–27).[14] Worship evolved into the symbolic and incorporeal and came to include daemons and dead heroes, giving rise to the beginnings of idolatry (2:237–38). Then, he says, celestial and daemonic worship eventually began to merge, creating the innumerable deities of the fables (2:242–3). The distinction between pagan religion and Christianity is drawn in Selden's prolegomena, but it is a distinction located in the evolutions of history, not in the beliefs of doctrine.

The notion of development in history, or a progression from monotheism to polytheism, becomes a structuring principle in the discourse. And, as Bernhard Lang suggests, it is central to the study of comparative religion.[15] Vossius's subtitle is *De origine ac progressu idolotriae*, and he largely reproduces Selden's story of a movement from celestial bodies to daemons, as do Fuller, Cherbury, and others.[16] The process usually found out is of mankind falling into polytheism from the monotheism revealed to the Israelites.[17] But on the far side of the discourse, Lord Bolingbroke's essay, "On the Rise and Progress of Monotheism," offers a subversive variation when he suggests that all revealed religions, both pagan and Judaic, are corruptions of an original monotheism. The story of this process receives yet another twist when David Hume argues in *The Natural History of Religion* (1757) that monotheism evolved from an original polytheism, implying that the belief in many gods, not one God, is part of the state of nature.[18] How this historical relationship between monotheism and polytheism is described will clearly exert a strong influence over theology. The portrayal of polytheism as a devolution from Hebraic monotheism reinforces the orthodox dismissal of pagan religion as fallen. Bolingbroke's version pointedly includes the Bible in the fall, insisting on a natural monotheism the Judeo-Christian revelation has failed to fulfill. Hume in turn dismisses deism's picture of natural religion by insisting that humankind is not likely to have been monotheistic in nature. Each version, however, takes part in the larger comparative project of describing the boundaries between monotheism and polytheism.

In the discourse of monotheism of the seventeenth century, debate over this historical process regularly confronted the common claim that behind the polytheism of the best pagan philosophers lies an occult monotheism—in Fuller's words again, that "the most knowing and rational amongst heathens, adored not the very material image, but in, under, through, and beyond the same worshipped the true god of heaven and earth." The fate of the souls of pagans has worried Christians all the way back to Paul, in Romans 2:14–15, and was an important subject for Ficino and the Neoplatonic philosophers who tended toward inclusiveness.[19] Calvin, on the other hand, articulates an orthodox rejection of occult monotheism, admitting that there is a "seed of religion" in everyone, but that "scarcely one man in a hundred is met with who fosters" it.[20] In the seventeenth century discourse of monotheism, writers such as Purchas, Vossius, Fuller, and Alexander Ross give particular attention to the polytheistic gods, and they all confront whether pagan religion worshipped a hidden monotheism.[21] As they uncover the details of polytheistic rites, and trace the historical processes between monotheism and polytheism, these studies are in position to investigate whether specific polytheistic rites somehow stand in for an occult monotheism. In his prolegomena, Selden develops both sides of this issue, but recognizes that the Greeks, Latins, and Egyptians inclined toward a theology, hidden from the vulgar, in which they "discerned no more than one supreme God."[22]

It is Selden's friend Herbert of Cherbury who reveals the radical implications of occult monotheism, making it the backbone of his proto-deist theology. In the opening of *De religione gentilium*, Cherbury announces his tolerance toward pagan religion: "I found that several Fathers of the Church not only held the ancient public religion of the pagans up to ridicule, but absolutely condemned it, and that theologians in the centuries following were no more lenient about anything which occurred outside their own agenda, so much so that for a long time the greater part of humanity seemed doomed to a sentence of eternal punishment" (51). Winning pagan religion back from ridicule and damnation is the main task that follows. In the tradition of Selden, Cherbury develops extensive historical data to establish a comparison between the religions of the world. But Cherbury uses the evidence to assert that their religious rituals do not fundamentally separate pagans and Christians, since monotheism is an ideal held universally—"neither educated nor ignorant people ever questioned that there was always, and is now, one supreme God" (*De religione* 276).

Like Selden, Cherbury finds a process in which worship was first directed at heavenly bodies, and then evolved onto the elements and onto humans. Cherbury uses original sources, but cites Selden several times (*De religione* 110, 115, 174) and clearly depends on Vossius as a main source.[23] But, in a significant departure from Vossius, Cherbury's survey of pagan worship is everywhere pointed at demonstrating occult monotheism. Discussing worship of the stars, for example, he claims, "As religion advanced in complexity, the pagans began to ask whether there might be any God or Deity which presided over the Stars themselves, and when they observed not only different, but contradictory effects in the Star, they were soon convinced, and acknowledged one Supreme Power who governed all things and to whom they believed the profoundest adoration was due" (58–59). A key strategy in the argument is to insist that pagan worship was merely symbolic, and therefore actually directed at the one God: "Thus, although the Hebrews worshipped a deity superior to the Sun under the same name, the pagans did not mean the Sun or any other deity...but only worshipped the Supreme God himself. I am more inclined, therefore, to believe that almost all ancient religion was symbolic, and that they do not worship one thing in another, but one thing out of another" (80). Cherbury makes use of a distinction Vossius draws between *cultus proprius* and *symbolicus*.²⁴ Vossius's point, however, is that pagans were guilty of idolatry because they worshipped material objects in themselves rather than symbolically. As John Anthony Butler points out, Cherbury switches around Vossius's distinction in order to preserve the validity of pagan worship.²⁵ With this one reinterpretation, Cherbury largely reverses the orthodox dismissal of pagan religion as idolatrous—pagan rites are transformed from polytheistic to monotheistic.

Cherbury regularly explains occult monotheism through condemnations of priesthood. Pagans naturally worshipped the one God, and the absurdities of polytheism were foisted upon them by priestcraft: "Ceremonies and rites were simply an invention of the priests, and for that reason not the common people, who just listened to what they were told, but the priests themselves must shoulder the blame. The priests, in fact, may be criticised as having themselves introduced superstition and idolatry" (*De religone* 52). Cherbury is so insistent on blaming priestcraft that his polemical intentions become obvious—written in the 1640s, *De religione* is no doubt a contribution to the anticlerical debates of the time. But Cherbury is also picking up on a recurrent theme in the discourse of monotheism, that, as Purchas puts it, idolatry was often spread through "the gainefull Collusion of their Priests."²⁶ Cherbury's polemic against priestcraft becomes commonplace among deists, as for instance in Charles Blount's *Religio laici*, where priests, both ancient and modern, are the prime villains in the imposition of revealed religion on the masses.²⁷ J. A. I. Champion's *The Pillars of Priestcraft Shaken* details this strain of anticlericalism in the later seventeenth century, revealing one of the clearest political manifestations of the discourse of monotheism.²⁸

These radical politics match Cherbury's radical theology. In numerous ways, Cherbury's version of occult monotheism pushes into the territory he bequeathed to the deists.²⁹ For occult monotheism, by insisting on the continuity of pagan religion and Christianity in the worship of one God, carries with it the implication that the traditions of the Judeo-Christian revelation may not be necessary. Historical worship and the activities of the clergy may be only so many unnecessary, even damaging, details. In this way, through Cherbury, monotheism leads to deism and its rejection of revealed religion.

For Selden's successors other than Cherbury, the study of pagan religion generally leads to conservative conclusions about revelation. Vossius argues for the typical position that the fundamentals of religion were first known through divine revelation, and that polytheism evolved in the absence of it, which leads him to value a comparative look at the gods for the way it makes clear the exclusive truth of Christianity. Or, as Ross explains in his "Preface to the Christian Reader," "the end wherefore these different opinions in Religion are brought into light, is, not that we should embrace them, but that we may see their deformity and avoid them."[30] And yet, to arrive at Cherbury's deistic subversion of revelation is to follow implications already present in *De diis*.

It is often thought that Selden, author of *History of Tythes* and leading Erastian in the Westminster Assembly, harbored more radical views than his scholarship admits.[31] Although delivered objectively, Selden gives considerable attention to occult monotheism in his prolegomena. More importantly, Selden's historical method, by bringing Christianity into a continuous relationship with paganism, has within it the liberal seeds of Cherbury's position. As Jason Rosenblatt argues, "Selden's comparatist historico-philological method aims for an aesthetic of utmost inclusiveness."[32] Historical process and continuity loosen the grip of revelation, which asserts religious truth outside of time and with total confidence. The comparative approach begins to replaces the believer's concern for the distinction between true and false made by revelation. Discussing Cherbury, Basil Willey summarizes this movement:

> It must be remembered that the old simple situation, in which Christendom pictured itself as the world, with only the foul paynim outside and the semi-tolerated Jews within the gates, had

passed away forever. Exploration and commerce had widened the horizon, and in many writers of the century one can see that the religions of the East, however imperfectly known, were beginning to press upon the European consciousness. It was a pioneer-interest in these religions, together with the customary preoccupation of Renaissance scholars with the mythologies of classical antiquity, which led Lord Herbert to seek a common denominator for all religions, and thus provide, as he hoped, the much-needed eirenicon for seventeenth century disputes.[33]

It is Cherbury's uncovering of a common denominator among Christians and pagans, what he calls the five Religious Common Notions, which brings into focus his radical version of monotheism. *De religione*, with its accounts of the gods and its arguments for occult monotheism, explicitly aims at demonstrating the validity of the Religious Common Notions. While he says that he discovered them from an intensive study of pagan religion (*De religione* 339), Cherbury first proposes them, as well as a full system of epistemology, in his earlier work, *De veritate* (1624). Religious Common Notions are innate ideas that form the essential elements of religion and are universally available through reason to all humans:

> The true Catholic Church is not supported on the inextricable confusion of oral and written tradition to which men have given their allegiance. Still less is it that which fights beneath any one particular standard, or is comprised in one organisation so as to embrace only a restricted portion of the earth, or a single period of history. The only catholic and uniform church is the doctrine of Common Notions which comprehends all places and all men. (*De veritate* 303)

Common Notions radically recast true religion, stripping it of the specific details found in the oral and written traditions, and insisting that it is more universal than any one religious organization. Considering them to be part of the "confusion" of tradition, the Common Notions push aside sacred beings such as gods and angels, as Cherbury explains in defense of the second Religious Common Notion, that the "sovereign deity ought to be worshipped": "While there is no general agreement concerning the worship of Gods, sacred beings, saints, and angels, yet the Common Notion or Universal Consent tells us that adoration ought to be reserved for the one God. Hence divine religion—and no race, however savage, has existed without some expression of it—is found established among all nations" (*De veritate* 293–94). Under the force of this skepticism, banished is the whole economy of religious beings, as well as the written tradition of sacred Scripture. True religion, as defined by the Religious Common Notions, no longer depends upon such things as the stories of the Bible, the doctrines developed by theologians, or the traditions of worship in any church.

If Cherbury's pared-down religion does not look much like revealed Christianity, however, it would do nicely to describe it as monotheism. The Religious Common Notions are essentially a more detailed account of occult monotheism, and one that places the concept of the one God at the center of theology. For the first of the religious essentials is the monotheistic certainty that "There is a supreme God": "No general agreement exists concerning the gods, but there is universal recognition of God. Every religion in the past has acknowledged, every religion in the future will acknowledge, some sovereign deity among the Gods" (*De veritate* 291). Two of the five Religious Common Notions assert monotheism: that there is one God, and that "adoration ought to be reserved for the one God."[34]

As monotheism becomes the defining concept for true religion, an important tendency emerges: true religion loses the details accrued by revealed religion. These go together, for skepticism toward revelation is a structural part of monotheism itself, as the rejection of other gods demands a position of sharp doubt toward all supernatural beings. Monotheism asks us to question the truth of each claim for deity—a skepticism encoded most of all in the aniconism of the second commandment. Monotheism, taken to a skeptical extreme such as that seen in the storyworld of Davenant's *Gondibert*, has within it the urge to disbelieve all forms of the supernatural, and so all revelation. In this way the skeptical tendencies built into monotheism lead into deism. As Cherbury's theological system sheds the trappings of revealed religion, the idea of monotheism comes to dominate.

Monotheism's inherent skepticism toward revealed detail is directed not only at other gods, but also at God: aniconism levels against anthropomorphism and other debasements of the perfectly abstract godhead. Indeed, as Aryeh Botwinick explains, monotheism pushes God beyond what is knowable: "The utterance of the word 'God' initiates a process of endless displacement that finds no resting place. All we can ever do by way of assigning a content and pinpointing a reference for 'God' is to continually assert that God is not literally to be construed in this way or that, and that he is not to be found in a humanly cognizable sense anywhere."[35] And so as Cherbury's skeptical theology strips religion of all the details of revelation, it does the same to the godhead. Cherbury's God has no excess: "For what is sufficient is due to God; excess is due to us. Why, then, as I have said elsewhere following the law of common reason, can we not apply the same rule of the perfect sphere of the religion of God that we apply to any circle? If anything is added to it, or taken away from it, its shape is destroyed, its perfection ruined" (*De veritate* 121). This is a God radically resistant to representation or even to an imaginative effort at conception. Conceived of as an abstraction as perfect and rational as a geometric figure, such a God lacks not only personality but also any sense of personal coherence at all. There is no place in which to imagine such a diffuse God, no mental concatenation upon which to hang a personality, no perceivable continuity in time that would allow humans to interact with God or represent him. In short, the energies that make up such a geometric God do not coalesce into what we would call a subject. Similarly, Richard Tuck describes how Cherbury's friend Hobbes depersonalized God into mere event: "God, on his account, was like a modern 'big bang' at the start of the universe."[36]

This utterly abstract, geometric God is a necessary product of Cherbury's comparative instincts and his belief in occult monotheism. In *De veritate* Cherbury includes a wide array of possible versions of the godhead: Romans, Greeks, Jews, Muslims, and Indians, in fact all religions, he says, worship "some sovereign deity among the Gods." And "that which is everywhere accepted as the supreme manifestation of deity, by whatever name it may be called, I term God" (*De veritate* 291). In order to make the enormous diversity of religious worship fit into the "true catholic church," Cherbury conceives of God as separate from revealed specifics. Names and manifestations are unimportant and excessive, and so the worship of the one true God can be found universally. The austerity of Cherbury's picture of the one God is later maintained by most deists, such as Lord Bolingbroke:

> But they who compare the ideas and notions concerning the Supreme Being that reason collects from the phenomena of nature, physical and moral, which we know to be the works of God, with those that the books of the Old Testament, which we suppose to be his word, give us, will be apt...to conclude that the God of Abraham, Isaac, and Jacob cannot be that glorious Supreme all-perfect Being whom reason showed them, and whom they discerned with their naked eyes. (Bolingbroke 3:363)

For Cherbury and the English deism that develops out of his seminal work, the monotheistic God is conceived of in total isolation from the details of revealed religion.

In this way a particular version of the monotheistic godhead emerges out of the comparative discourse of Selden's *De diis*. The study of polytheism, which is essentially a comparative project, develops into the radically comparative position that Christianity shares with pagan religion the same truthful elements—foremost, the belief in one God. Cherbury's Common Notions, however, represent but one trajectory which the discourse takes as it develops from Selden. Cherbury expresses a liberal impulse within the discourse of monotheism that meets an orthodox counter in Henry More. Combating the extreme implications of occult monotheism, More defines "monotheisme" as specifically dependent on the Judeo-Christian revelation, and so brings the monotheistic God back from total abstraction.

More's Monotheisme

In book 3 of *An Explanation of the Grand Mystery of Godliness*, More devotes considerable attention to the polytheistic gods, studying them in the tradition of the discourse of monotheism. Indeed, he makes numerous explicit references to Purchas and Selden, and the majority of these pages are clearly derived from Selden (see *GMG* 61, 81, 83–86, 88, 89). More's participation in the comparative discourse, along with his reputation as a latitudinarian and rational theologian, suggests that in the larger spectrum of seventeenth century theology he holds a liberal position. But as More takes part in the study of polytheism, he is determined to reassert an orthodox rejection of pagan religion. He departs from Selden's objectivity and everywhere asserts the monstrousness of polytheism—"But enough and too much of the foulness of the Pagan Superstition" is the kind of cry echoing throughout (*GMG* 84). Like Vossius, More uses the detailed anthropology of Selden's research as a way of defending the sole truth of the Judeo-Christian revelation. And so pagan religion, More announces at the beginning of book 3, cannot be monotheistic: "The crime they are accused of here is *Polytheism*, which necessarily includes in it *Atheism*. For to say There are more Gods then one, is to assert There is none at all; the notion of God, in the strictest sense thereof, being incompatible to any more then One. Wherefore the Heathen being *Polytheists* in profession, by undeniable consequence are found *Atheists*" (*GMG* 57).

For More, the dismissal of pagan religion depends upon rejecting the period's frequent arguments for occult monotheism. He describes, he says,

> sundry Superstitions of *Paganisme*, wherein, though by their subtil Apoligies they could clear themselves from *Atheism* and the worser sort of *Idolatry*, and could make it good that it was *One Eternal Deity*, be he never so Philosophically defined, that was the Chief and Ultimate Object of their Worship; yet it is hereby apparent that the best of them exceeds not the *Animal* bounds, for as much as they worshipped God in these rude Religions only out of

the sense of the gratifications of the *Animal life:* And if I have more copiously set down how foully and sordidly they have done it, my pains therein I hope may by interpreted to very good purpose, it being manifest thereby how just a victory *Christianity* had over *Paganisme.* (*GMG* x)

The basic polemic of book 3, in fact, is against interpreting the pagan worship as occult monotheism. More first rejects the claim that pagan worship of the sun was monotheistic, and then argues against the more cautious claim "in general That the *various rites* done to *Particular Deities* were meant to *One Supreme Cause of all things,* though they have the discretion not to venture to name him" (*GMG* 61).

More calls his opponents the "Apologizers for Paganisme," and argues briefly against Macrobius and Philostratus. But his polemic has more urgency than a quarrel with the ancients. He is surely responding to the debates about occult monotheism in his own period—and, although he does not name him, More could well have Cherbury in mind. While *De religione* was published in 1663, it was completed by 1645. It certainly became known to Ralph Cudworth, who later refers to "that controversy lately agitated concerning idolatry" wherein some asserted "that none could possible be guilty of idolatry, in the Scripture sense, who believed one God the creator of the whole world."[37] No other texts in the period state the case for occult monotheism with the force of *De religione* and *De veritate*—for Cudworth and More, Cherbury is probably the most obvious "apologizer" for paganism.

More's familiarity with, and his sympathy for, Cherbury's Common Notions is clear in his *Antidote to Atheism,* and was common among the Cambridge Platonists.[38] In *The Grand Mystery of Godliness,* however, More seeks to contain the Common Notions as specifically not sufficient for an understanding of true religion. Describing what he calls the "Middle life," which is a realm of rational inquiry, he calls reason "a power or Facultie of the Soul, whereby either from her Innate Ideas or Common Notions, or else from the assurance of her own Senses, or upon the Relation or Tradition of another, she unravels a further clew of Knowledge, enlarging her sphere of Intellectual light" (*GMG* 51). Common Notions, along with the study of nature through the senses and through other sources, hold great promise. But the middle life, which is the sphere made available by the Common Notions, is not, in More's system, the highest. It lies between "Animal life," which is the material, fallen world, and "Divine life," which is the spiritual world. The middle life of reason strives to close the gap between the animal and the divine, just as Cherbury's natural religion moves from the observation of nature to knowledge of the one God. Fully aware of the growing persuasiveness of such approaches, More recognizes that the middle life can seem to be dazzlingly high: "And now I have advanced the *Animal life* so high, by adding the *Middle Nature* to it, that you may perhaps marvail upon what I shall pitch that may seem more precious and desirable" (*GMG* 52). But this sarcastic aside reins in those who would extend reason into such transcendent matters as the godhead. For knowledge of God, More insists, cannot be through rational and skeptical methods alone, but depends upon a superrational intervention by the divine life. Divine life is found "taking possession of the *Middle life* or Rational powers," and it is "both the *Light* and the *Purification* of the Eye of the Mind, whereby Reason becomes truly illuminated in all Divine and Moral concernments" (*GMG* 55).

And so Cherbury's natural religion, which is described by the category of the middle life, is contained. Reason and the Common Notions go far, but to fully understand what concerns the one God requires the divine life. Possession, as More puts it, by an outside force—the divine—is the element missing from the middle way. This sense of possession reinstates what the Common Notions are designed to replace: what More calls mystery. More's text, after all, is *An Explanation of the Grand Mystery of Godliness*, and his larger goal, to which book 3 contributes, is the assertion of mystery. In the opening chapter he makes mystery the key to the divine life: "The scope or aim of all Religious Mysteries is the bringing back faln man into his pristine condition of Happiness, and to lead him again to that high station which he then first forsook when he preferr'd his own Will and the pleasure of the Animal life before the Will of God and that Life and Sense which is truly Divine" (*GMG* 2). The Common Notions make possible a system in which individuals can understand true religion through reason alone, and without things mysterious such as miracles, revelations, and revealed teachings. Cherbury's occult monotheism is based upon this natural religion, and More rejects it for its lack of mystery.

And it is precisely the necessity of the divine life, with its mystery and revelation, which More is building into the idea of monotheism. In the middle of his book 3 argument against occult monotheism, More considers the Egyptians, "a people more infamous for *Polytheism* and variety in Religions then any nation under the cope of Heaven." And he notes, "their Priests are observed more compendiously to do their Ceremonies to certain Spheres or round Globes, whereof there was one in every temple, but kept very close from the sight of the vulgar; the Priests reserving the knowledge of the Unity of the Object of their worship as an *Arcanum* only belonging to themselves" (*GMG* 61). More then disputes that such worship actually referred to the true God, arguing that it was the world itself being worshipped: "But that *This One Object of Worship* was not the true God, but the *Material World,* the very figure they make use of does most naturally intimate" (*GMG* 61). The Egyptian worship, then, remains in the animal world and does not symbolize the divine world. Indeed, all polytheism, for More, founders on its failure to worship the mysteries of the divine world, instead remaining in "the visible or sensible world" of the animal life (*GMG* 57). It is while he is asserting the inability of polytheism to transcend the visible and sensible world that More coins the term "monotheisme." Continuing to discuss the "Arcanum" of the Egyptian priests, he declares, "But thus to make the *World* God, is to make no God at all; and therefore this Kind of *Monotheisme* of the Heathen is as rank *Atheisme* as their *Polytheism* was proved to be before" (*GMG* 62). Whereas Cherbury moves by way of symbolic worship from the polytheistic rites to a pagan belief in monotheism, More insists that the sphere does not move upward to the divine, but instead represents the world. And so any monotheism that might be found among the heathens is no better than polytheism—in other words, it is not monotheism as More wants to understand the term.

In giving a name to the concept, More asserts what he thinks the idea of one God should be—his "Kind of monotheisme," in opposition to the kind put forward by the apologizers for paganism. As with Cherbury's geometric God, arguments for occult monotheism and natural religion require a godhead significantly abstracted from the orthodox God of Christianity. A God who could be properly worshipped by Egyptian rites would have to shed any specificity accrued in Scripture—such as his role in biblical stories, anthropomorphic descriptions, and his incarnation in Christ—and remain an intellectual abstraction outside of history. This is the kind of God More associates with the rational theology of the middle life, and then rejects as insufficient. After a typical argument from design in book 2, discussing how nature proves the existence of God, More admits the "Innate Notion we have of God," and describes the kind of God these Cherburian ideas arrive at:

> But seeing things so framed in Nature as they are they could not but affirm That they came from an *Intellectual Principle,* which is *God;* allowing him an ineffable happiness in contemplating of Himself and His own *Wisdome* in forming of the World, and the various kinds of Creatures therein; but phansying him withall so *fatally* affixed to his own seat, that he cannot bow himself to look so low as to take notice of any Particular or Personal carriages of men, nor stretch forth his arm either to *reward* or *punish* them. An Opinion that seems either to arise out of a desperate inability of giving a Reason of sundry accidents that happen to particular Creatures in the world, or else out of a tender regard to their own Interest; they being afraid of any other God then such as they have

> promised themselves will act nothing above or contrary to the ordinary and known course of Nature, which, as they think, is very certain assurance of future Impunity. (*GMG* 33)

Like Cherbury's geometric God, the God More pictures at the heart of natural religion is an "intellectual principle." As is typical of the fully abstract God of deism, this God has created the world, but is "fatally affixed to his own seat" and so does not "stretch forth his arm" to become involved in the affairs of humankind. A God thus removed from human action, finally, results in a religion devoid of anything miraculous: he will not act "above or contrary" to nature.[39]

The insufficiency of such a conception of God, for More, is its removal from the mysteries of Christianity. Book 2 moves immediately from its rejection of the totally abstract godhead to conceive of Christianity in terms overflowing with the mysterious and the miraculous. The main mystery of Christianity is the movement from animal to divine: "Christianity is that Period of the Wisdome of God and his Providence, wherein the Animal life is remarkably insulted or triumphed over by the Divine" (*GMG* 43). God's wisdom involves the mystery of what More calls the "exteriour Oeconomy of Christianity" (*GMG* ix). Over several chapters of book 2, More argues for the existence of "particular spirits," both fallen and unfallen, and for organized polities of good and bad angels. Christianity will eventually arrive at an overthrow of the "Dark Kingdome" "by a powerful miraculous appearance" of the good powers (*GMG* 39). And the deliverance of humanity, More insists repeatedly, will be "sensible and palpable" and "visible" (*GMG* 41). More's exterior economy of Christianity is real and miraculous, full of angels and devils and the promise of the literal fulfillment of revelation. This insistence on mystery repopulates Christianity with the spirits and supernatural events that natural religion had elided.

The first textual presence of the word "monotheism" is a moment of definition. But this definition must be understood not simply as a belief in mystery, and an assertion of the familiar God of revelation. As the concepts of monotheism and polytheism become central to seventeenth century theology, the radical possibility of Cherbury's natural religion is always present. More insists on mystery and the miraculous external economy in response to occult monotheism and the threat of the totally abstract godhead. More's monotheism can be characterized as both recognizing and attempting to move back from the skeptical extreme of Cherbury's monotheism. More's coining itself demonstrates this complex quality.

One of the fascinating things about More's articulation of "monotheisme" is that the actual construction of the word is so legible. Although the concept of one God is itself very old, this first textual trace reveals the historically local forces behind the concept. In one sentence More brings in two familiar words, atheism and polytheism, and using these as examples produces the term that is already implied by them. The construction of monotheism out of its opposite, polytheism, reveals a genealogy going back to Selden's *De diis Syris,* which uses polytheism prominently in Greek, and *Purchas His Pilgrimage,* which offers the first English translation. The word, furthermore, runs as a leitmotif throughout the seventeenth century study of the gods, serving as a marker for a comparative approach to religions. As part of More's own contribution to this discourse, book 3 presents a survey of various polytheistic rites. But he does so in a fairly polemical fashion, and in a moment when he is particularly concerned to demonstrate the inferiority of pagan religion to Christianity, he moves from polytheism to his new word, "monotheisme."

The genealogy is even clearer: when he constructs the term, More is working directly from *De diis.* His argument against apologizers who claim that polytheistic rites were "meant to One Supreme Cause of all things" quotes inscriptions from Selden's prolegomena (Selden 2:248). And his account of Egyptian priests doing "their Ceremonies to certain Spheres" all the while "reserving the knowledge of the Unity of the Object of their worship as an *Arcanum* only belonging to themselves," comes directly from the end of Selden's prolegomena. This is the primary place in which Selden asserts an occult monotheism, which he calls a "hidden theology," among the Egyptians. Selden describes how Egyptian priests secretly maintained spheres as hidden symbols of a unified and single God. These priests were initiated into monotheism, but kept it secret from the masses so that only the wisest philosophers could see through the common rites and comprehend the occult monotheism:

> Neither did they make public the hidden and near-truthful theology, nor did they keep it entirely for themselves; but in those rites which were in use for the common people, they instituted sacred mysteries, from which it was not difficult for the more rational people to seize the opportunity of unearthing the occult truth. Not so sane, in my opinion, are the prophets of the Egyptians. But even for these it was a very arcane symbol of unity. (Selden 2:249)[40]

Selden dismisses the "ridiculous figures" and the "superstition" of the polytheistic rites that the priests foisted upon the Egyptian masses. But he says that the priests "kept to themselves other mysteries, enclosed in sacred shrines, that is, certain spheres...each of which were kept very secret from the sight of the profane, and were symbols, among individual sane thinkers, as it seems, of the sole governor of the universal sphere" (Selden 2:249–50).[41]

With some exceptions, in *De diis* Selden remains objective: he reports the possibility of occult monotheism in the Egyptian priests with very little rhetoric. But at this later point in the discourse of monotheism, such objectivity has been swept aside. In Cherbury's hands, Selden's research develops into a polemical assertion of occult monotheism that nears the abstraction of deism. Henry More reaches back to the same body of research and is quite respectful of Selden as his clear authority. But he puts Selden's research to his own polemical use, staking out a position opposite to Cherbury's. In moving from Selden's polytheism to an articulation of true religion, More reasserts the necessity of mystery and revelation to monotheism. Coming out of Selden, the discourse of monotheism provides a too firm, and an increasingly too wide, foundation for rational and skeptical conceptions of religion and God. As a rational theologian himself, More traverses the same territory as the likes of Cherbury. But, determined to preserve the fundamentals of revelation, he works to turn back expanding reason with the force of revelation and mystery.

It is this quality of allowing considerable latitude toward the skeptical extreme of Cherbury, but then turning back to reassert a religion built upon the mysterious and miraculous economies of revelation, which epitomizes More's monotheism. His is a dynamic position, one which understands and contributes to the expanding rational theology, but which simultaneously attempts to contain its excesses. The possibility of contradiction in More's position may be felt in his later claim that *Grand Mystery of Godliness* is actually a proof of rational theology: "For I conceive Christian Religion rational throughout, and I think I have proved it to be so in my *Mystery of Godliness.*"[42] In fact, as we have seen, More makes considerable space for the "middle life" of reason and innate ideas. In his account, though, mystery is required to complete the rational proofs of religion. Mystery names the gap between the middle life and the divine life, but also the promise that such a gap can be traversed. More begins *Grand Mystery of Godliness* by defining mystery as

> a piece of Divine knowledge *measurably Abstruse*, whereby it becomes *more Venerable*, but yet *Intelligible* that it may be *Communicable*, and *True* and *Certain* that it may win *firm Assent*, and lastly *very Usefull* and *Effectual* for the *perfecting* of the Souls of men, and restoring them to that *Happiness* which they anciently had faln from; that so near a Concernment may as well gain upon their *Affections* as the Evidence of *Truth* engage their *Understandings.* (GMG 2)

More's mystery may resist a skeptical dissection, but it enables rational methods by offering two essential qualities that rational religion cannot produce. Far more than the abstractions of theological reasoning, mystery is "communicable" and it therefore has the potential to gain the believer's affections. More describes a God conceived of in fully rational terms: He is merely an "intellectual principle," and is so "fatally affixed to his own seat" that he cannot "stretch forth his arm" to take part in the historical events of mankind. Such a God may be described in theology, but he would hardly be communicable in more poetic terms, which "may as well gain upon their *Affections* as the Evidence of *Truth* engage their *Understandings*." How, after all, would such an affixed principle be represented to the imagination or narrated in a story? This God unable to stretch out his hand would lack the familiar avenues of miracle and direct revelation, either through theophany or by means of an angel. As mere intellectual principle, this unmysterious God would have lost all of the persuasive force of revelation.

Cherbury's geometric God and the austere natural religion of the Common Notions run the same risk. How would "the perfect sphere of the religion of God" enter a storyworld? Or, how could a poet narrate Hobbes's God, who is like the Big Bang? In his polemic against deism, John Dennis later encapsulates the problem with eliding the miracles and revelations of Christianity: "Thus the Proofs of Christianity are short and plain, and its Doctrine that leads to Felicity, admirably short and unperplexed, whereas the Proofs of Deism are abstruse (I mean to the People they are abstruse, and we have shewn, that the True Religion must be designed for all) and the Method that it takes to make us Happy, tedious and vexatious" (Dennis 1:261). And so More reaffirms the mysterious proofs of Christianity: he insists upon the Trinity (a key issue in seventeenth century monotheism), and he insists at length upon the miraculous role of angels in the "exteriour Oeconomy of Christianity." In this way mystery does not supplant rational inquiry but rather supplements it by taking over the theological work where rational conceptions fail.

More produces the first textual trace of the word "monotheism"—that is, he works to construct and define the concept of one God—within this struggle with mystery and revelation. More's complex position could even be said to have created the word. For in the concept of monotheism, the rational force of aniconism necessarily competes with revelation, as Freud shows in his myth of Aton and Jahve. There the monotheistic God is formed out of a paradoxical combining of the personal, revealed volcano god Jahve and the abstract, universal, and incommunicable god Aton. This same tension between aniconism and the basic needs of narrative for the sake of communication is felt in the disjunctions of monotheistic narrative. More's clear understanding of Cherbury's theology and his turn back toward orthodox revelation follows the same path as Cowley's return from Davenant's skeptical extreme. In both cases the dynamic is one of oscillation between the silence of aniconism and the communicability of mysterious revelation.

Toward Milton's God

As chapter 5 will show, More's monotheism anticipates the public and politicized theologies of Socinianism and deism. Before pursuing that thread further, however, this study will turn to the heart of the matter: the problems of narrating God himself. Since C. S. Lewis's *Preface to* Paradise Lost, it has been standard to compare Milton's digesting, blushing, and fighting angels to More's.[43] *An Explanation of the Grand Mystery of Godliness* suggests that much more is involved in More's position than the habits of angels—even the nature of the monotheistic godhead. Chapter 3 expands the affinity between Milton and More to the godhead, showing how the dynamics of seventeenth century monotheism can help us understand the complexity of Milton's God. Then chapter 4 continues to examine how revelation can express the monotheistic God by reading the war in heaven in terms of monotheism.

Milton is deeply argumentative about these matters, much like More. For his conception of the monotheistic God in *Paradise Lost* can be compared to the way in which More conceives of the godhead at the moment in which he coins the word "monotheisme." More's monotheism is an outgrowth of Selden's *De diis* and the discourse of monotheism. Similarly, when God enters the narrative in book 3, his way has been prepared by the infernal council, which was built on the comparative research of Selden. Both Milton's and More's monotheisms are responses to the polytheism in *De diis,* and so to the rational perspectives *De diis* engenders. Just as More is fully aware of the skeptical extreme that would cut out revelation and so silence persuasive communication, Milton builds his God, and his economy of heavenly beings, within a perspective made unstable by its own skepticism.

One familiar measure of this instability is the notoriously complicated matter of kingship in Milton's God. The political stakes of More's construction of monotheism can perhaps be glimpsed by the interesting fact that the word is coined in 1660, with his "Letter to the Reader" dated June 12, mere days after Charles's return to London. James Henry Breasted, in *The Dawn of Conscience,* which was the main historical source for Freud's *Moses and Monotheism,* explicitly associates Aton with Egyptian national politics, and so monotheism with kingship. He argues that the revolutionary appearance of Atonism in Egypt was a result of an ascendant monarchy, as the expansion of state power and national life enabled the conception of a single, universal God—"Monotheism was but imperialism in religion."[44] Monotheism, by stressing a single, unified divinity, may go with the ideals of monarchy. The royalist leanings of Hobbes, Davenant, and Cowley further suggest that the moment's attempts at a conceiving of God are also attempts at conceiving the king.

We can wonder whether kingship is reaffirmed by a God represented by the Aton-like aniconism of Hobbes and Davenant, or by the reinsertion of mystery and revelation by Cowley and More. Milton's readers similarly have been concerned whether a throne for God and the trappings of a kingly personality lend authority to kingship, or, as is also often supposed, whether the trappings of kingship tarnish the image of God. Attention to the debates over monotheism at midcentury suggests that Milton's kingly God can instead be understood as lodged precariously between textual presence and absence. Kingly imagery gives God a revealed presence that speaks of authority, but it also, from the perspective of aniconism, involves the threat of polytheism. The abstraction and unity of monotheism inculcate a unified poetics that may serve the purpose of a single monarch. But that monarch simultaneously relies heavily on a cult of his own personality, such as Charles does in *Eikon Basilica*, which text certainly looked like idolatry to Milton, for whom the ideology of republicanism appears less iconic. These dynamics may support David Norbrook's sense that a republican sublime infuses Milton's God.[45]

These political ramifications, suggested here only speculatively, serve to introduce the profound discomfiture that God's personal presence exerts on *Paradise Lost*. A kingly, enthroned God is a personal God, and one who, to many readers, is challenging because he feels too Olympian. Milton's God, the next chapter argues, is built upon such personality—and simultaneously strives against it, creating a sublime God that flickers in and out of the narrative. This problem of personality is a fundamental monotheistic problem: the difficulties of narrating the one God have traditionally been ascribed to the question of personality. As Lenn Evan Goodman explains, it is theologically necessary to narrate God, but impossible to narrate him accurately:

> Compelled by the urgency of their prophetic need to communicate the direction in which true divinity lies, prophets by a kind of poetic license of their own (as Maimonides explained) apply to God these notions and that of personality—which creates a dramatic theater for the expression of all sorts of values and ideas to which humans can relate. But to imagine we are properly describing the divine by such terms as these would be, as Rabbi Haninah put it, like praising a king who possessed millions in gold for having silver. Personality and the rest are notions from our world.[46]

Driven by the second commandment, monotheism reaches for a godhead that transcends everything human. But even as monotheism pushes toward this abstract extreme, it must at times slip out of such pure abstraction in order to narrate itself. This is a movement from Cherbury's geometric godhead back to the God of personality revealed in Scripture. And so personality may be seen as a mystery, in More's sense of the word: "measurably abstruse...but yet intelligible that it may be communicable." That is, personality allows God to be narrated. It is to this dynamic question of personality in Milton's God that the next chapter turns.

THREE

God and Genesis 18 in *Paradise Lost*

Milton's readers have long had problems with God's personality. Some have considered God, in Irene Samuel's words, "a wooden bore." Others, in a contrary position, have accused him of tyranny and viciousness. Pope's famous couplet portrays both of these qualities: "In Quibbles, Angel and Archangel join, / And God the Father turns a School-Divine." The school divine, at once a characterless figure and a familiar version of a dominating will, captures an important paradox: Milton's God both lacks personality and seems to have too much.[1]

Douglas Bush, expressing a common sentiment, believes that the narrative would be better served by a less personal God: "Artistically, no doubt, it would have been better if Milton had relied upon his power of suggestion...and had not made God a speaking character." Bush suggests an alternative to God as character, pointing to a single line to describe how Milton could have done better: he wishes Milton had written more in the vein of "Dark with excessive bright thy skirts appear" (3.380). This moment is also a favorite of C. S. Lewis, who lists it as an example of "suggestion" and "mystery." What both Bush and Lewis wish for is a version of the mysterious and sublime theophany of Exodus—they want a God obscured by, and diffused into, a pillar of smoke. The problem is that God is represented as taking part in book 3 as if he could be imagined in the form of a person, and their response, following the frequent example of theophany in the Hebrew Bible, is to undercut God's personal presence. Yet after quoting line 380, Lewis expresses regret in a way that recalls the anxieties of seventeenth century Christian poets: "Milton has failed to disentangle himself from the bad tradition...of trying to make Heaven too like Olympus." Enthroned, speaking to his heavenly council, and even, it will be shown, responding to external discipline, Milton's God is portrayed, and given a presence in the narrative, in terms of personality. Bush and Lewis, on the one hand, find Milton's God to be too personal and too present. Their readings are perceptive and represent one response courted by *Paradise Lost* as well as by monotheism in general: a skeptical longing for an abstract, unrepresentable godhead.[2]

On the other hand, J. B. Broadbent represents another common view when he argues that Milton's God is already thoroughly abstract: God lacks the attributes of personality, speaking "skeletally" and "(not) with a human tongue." Broadbent goes so far as to assert that Milton's God is as impersonal as the godhead of pantheism or deism: "Neither the 'serene and lovely God' of John Smith nor its Deistic and Pantheistic derivatives...has any more personality than a God who 'is light.'"[3] Broadbent's insightful association of Milton's God with deism recognizes the strategy that Milton uses instead of the pillar of smoke recommended by Lewis: God in *Paradise Lost* threatens to diffuse into a bundle of divine forces that lacks the coherence of an individual personality. Melting at times toward absence, Milton's God draws very near to the "Intellectual Principal" which, as described in the last chapter, was rejected by Henry More.

Such a movement toward abstraction is an essential characteristic of monotheism, as in Freud's myth of Aton. According to the philosopher Lenn Evan Goodman, the monotheistic God must not be a personality so much as a performer of fixed and knowable rules. To represent this quality, Goodman points in particular to the way Abraham engages God in debate over the fate of Sodom. After God declares his plan to judge and destroy the city, Abraham "stood yet before the Lord" and then "drew near" to ask strategically, "Wilt thou also destroy the righteous with the wicked?" (Gen. 18:22–23). Abraham wins the concession that Sodom will not be destroyed if 50 righteous are to be found—and then, remarkably, he negotiates with God, bringing the threshold down to 40, 30, 20, and finally 10 (Gen. 18:26–33). At the heart of Abraham's successful plea bargain is the obviously rhetorical question, "Shall not the Judge of all the earth do right?" (18:25). For Genesis 18:25 presupposes a God that must do right on an absolute moral scale: "Here already," says Goodman, "God is universal rather than local, and a demand is made (not a plea for mercy or refuge taking as in Islam) but a demand addressed less to God than to the (moral) logic of the concept of God." With Zeus, in contrast, the object "was to learn (if learn one could) the pleasure of the god and satisfy it at whatever cost." Abraham's question, "Shall not the Judge of all the earth do right?" would surely have drawn thunder from a Jove, but from Yahweh it draws agreement. Goodman thus argues that the primary characteristic of monotheism is an association between God and absolute value. The monotheistic God is knowable by means of the absolute morality within the concept: "For man knows what justice is and knows again what justice must be for God, if God is to be a God of universal justice.... Values are no longer subjective, so divinities may no longer make them arbitrary."[4] The key movement here is away from arbitrariness and subjectivity: for Goodman, the monotheistic God must function according to objective rules, not personal whim.[5]

Milton reads the latter half of Genesis 18 in exactly the same way as Goodman. In *The Doctrine and Discipline of Divorce* Abraham's question "Shall not the Judge of all the earth do right?" demonstrates the possibility of a clear and rational knowledge of God's law—and God's necessary conformity to that law. Milton is refuting Rivetus, who has concluded that God allowed dispensation, "but by some way to us unknown." Milton rejects such recourse to mystery, insisting upon humanity's ability to rationally ascertain law:

> But to this I oppose, that a Christian by no means ought rest himself in such an ignorance: whereby so many absurdities will strait reflect both against the purity, justice, and wisdom of God.... God indeed in some ways of his providence, is high and secret past finding out: but in the delivery and execution of his Law, especially in the managing of a duty so daily and so familiar as this is whereof we reason, has plain anough reveal'd himself.... And he hath taught us to love and to extoll his Lawes, not onely as they are his, but as they are just and good to every wise and sober understanding. Therefore Abraham, ev'n to the face of God himselfe, seem'd to doubt of divine justice, if it should swerve from that irradiation wherwith it had enlight'ned the mind of man, and bound it selfe to observe its own rule. *Wilt thou destroy the righteous with the wicked? That be far from thee; shall not the Judge of the earth doe right?* (YP 2:297–98)

Genesis 18:23 and 25 stand as Milton's first defense of the idea that "the mind of man" can rationally comprehend the Law. The sheer audacity of Abraham in arguing "ev'n to the face of God himselfe" demonstrates that divine justice cannot swerve from "its own rule." Abraham can get away with the apparent disciplining of God because, the passage demonstrates, God is supposed to conform to an absolute value of justice.

God, Milton admits, "in some ways of his providence, is high and secret past finding out." But Abraham's argument asserts man's ability to find out some of the remaining "ways of his providence"—it asserts, for Milton, the possibility of theodicy. Indeed, in justifying the ways of God in *Paradise Lost*, Milton has frequent recourse to the absolute conception of God's justice, which he finds in Genesis 18:25. It is not that God chooses to be just at such times, but that he absolutely must conform to justice. So God's frightening dictum regarding man's death, "He with his whole posterity must die, / Die he or justice must" (*PL* 3.209–10), transfers agency in the condemnation from God to the Law.

God does not personally choose the death sentence, rather the abstract value of justice demands it. And so when God dispatches Raphael to inform Adam of his freedom to fall, God's action is similarly made to be in the service of the greater rule of absolute justice: "So spake the eternal Father, and fulfilled / All justice" (*PL* 5.246–47). God's speech-act is in the service of justice, not at the discretion of his will.

But if Milton's God melts into the abstraction of a legal formula—or in More's phrase, an intellectual principle—this is only part of the dynamic that constitutes him. He is simultaneously, in Lewis's word, "Olympian." From his throne, God presides over the council in heaven, speaking, questioning, and deriding, perhaps not so far from the polytheistic tradition of Olympus. That he is both things at once—a God of personality and a God of rigorous abstraction—leads to the uniquely monotheistic problem of theophany.[6] While polytheism generally has no difficulty with the manifestation of gods, the Hebrew Bible is full of narratively complicated theophanies in which God wavers between textual presence and absence (see, for example, Exod. 4:24 and 24:10), or in which, most famously, God appears in pillars of smoke and fire. It is this obscure theophany that both Bush and Lewis reckon will solve the problem of Milton's God. But Milton does not reproduce the pillar in the poem's story, only bringing such obscurity into the narrative through the sublime language of "Dark with excessive bright thy skirts appear." What Milton turns to instead is a different, more complex and extended, theophany: that of Genesis 18. Not only does Genesis 18 construct an impersonal God that conforms to absolute justice, but it does so within a deeply complicated narrative that negotiates between God's total abstraction and his personal presence.

The beginning of Genesis 18 announces that the subject matter is theophany: "And the LORD appeared unto him in the plains of Mamre." The first Hebrew word, *Va-yera*, meaning "And he appeared," supplies the title of this portion in the Jewish tradition, so that the entire episode is referred to as a theophany, as the portion "And he appeared." Maimonides comments: "The general statement that the Lord appeared to Abraham is followed by the description in what manner that appearance of the Lord took place."[7] What follows is perhaps the most extended and complicated theophany in the Hebrew Bible. As the narrative shifts to Abraham's perspective, the Lord suddenly becomes three men: "And the LORD appeared unto him in the plains of Mamre; and he sat in the tent door in the heat of the day; And he lift up his eyes and looked, and, lo, three men stood by him: and when he saw them, he ran to meet them from the tent door, and bowed himself toward the ground" (Gen. 18:1–2). The asyndeton between the Lord and the three men does not give us their logical relationship—are they actually the Lord? Are they standing in for him? Are they his angels? Is this just how he appears to Abraham? The narrative gives no answers, but nevertheless implies that these three visitors in some manner constitute God's appearance. The three visitors form the bulk of the scene on Mamre, famously eating Abraham's food and announcing the birth of Isaac, which then leads Sarah to laugh. And here the narrative returns to the Lord: "And the LORD said unto Abraham, Wherefore did Sarah laugh, saying, Shall I of a surety bear a child, which am old?" (18:13). Once again we move, without explanation, between God and the three visitors. Then, in verse 16, the visitors reappear and set out for Sodom: "the men rose up from thence, and looked toward Sodom: and Abraham went with them to bring them on the way." Later, in Genesis 19:1 two angels come to Sodom—presumably two of Abraham's three visitors, with one staying behind. And the one left behind seems to become God: "And the men turned their faces from thence, and went toward Sodom: but Abraham stood yet before the LORD" (18:22).

It is here, standing before the Lord, that Abraham initiates his debate with God over Sodom. This second half of the chapter delivers the theophany promised by *Va-yera*—it is as if the visitation on Mamre has somehow paved the way for this face-to-face encounter between God and human. How the strange events on Mamre might enable the negotiation over Sodom is a truly difficult question, but the two parts are intertwined. Additionally, the negotiation over Sodom is what constructs the monotheistic God as necessarily conforming to absolute justice, and so pushes God into complete abstraction. Genesis 18, *Va-yera*, contains a remarkable array of characters: shifting visitors, eating angels, God in negotiations, and a God portrayed as fully abstract—a narrative of far greater complexity than the pillar of fire. Taking its two parts together, Genesis 18 seems to meditate on the difficulty of bringing a God of total abstraction into theophany—of making a God of abstraction and also of presence. The chapter is, according to John Sailhamer, "a lesson in theology" that develops "a conscious attempt to stress at one and the same time the theological relevance of the promise of God's presence along with his transcendent, sovereign power."[8]

Milton turns to the complexities of Genesis 18 with such deliberateness and persistence that the chapter deserves attention as a main building block of *Paradise Lost*. While several critics have identified instances in which Milton alludes to Genesis 18, none has observed the full extent to which the chapter controls books 3 through 8.[9] In fact, Genesis 18 is behind three of the poem's most critical exchanges: the Father and the Son in book 3, Adam and Raphael in books 5 through 8, and God and Adam in book 8. Working behind the scene as allusions do, Genesis 18 serves as a secondary narrative to the middle of *Paradise Lost*, structuring the narrative's monotheistic negotiation between an abstract God and a deeply material religious economy. The complex theophany of Genesis 18 shapes Milton's God as congruent to Henry More's: both encompassing the abstraction of intellectual principle and returning from that skeptical extreme to assert a personal, revealed God. Studying the impact of Genesis 18 on the long middle of *Paradise Lost* will help to explain the ways that Milton's narrative works to include the monotheistic godhead.

Genesis 18:25 and Paradise Lost, Book 3

Genesis 18 first enters *Paradise Lost* when the Son objects to God's stated plan to punish mankind:

> For should man finally be lost, should man
> Thy creature late so lovęd, thy youngest son
> Fall circumvented thus by fraud, though joined
> With his own folly? That be from thee far,
> That far be from thee, Father, who art judge
> Of all things made, and judgest only right.   (3.150–55)

As Thomas Newton first noticed, these lines echo Genesis 18:25: "That be far from thee to do after this manner, to slay the righteous with the wicked: and that the righteous should be as the wicked, that be far from thee: Shall not the Judge of all the earth do right?"[10]

The Son's words not only place him in Abraham's position before Yahweh, but they emphasize Milton's reading of the passage in *The Doctrine and Discipline of Divorce*. The Son adds to Abraham's words the admonition that the Father is "judge / Of all things made, and judgest only right." God is limited to operating according to rules—he judges "only" right, disallowing the unruliness of an arbitrary godhead. As Abraham challenges God's action toward Sodom in the background of allusion, and as the Son challenges his action toward Adam in the story, the necessary adherence to the abstract value of justice undercuts the sense of will in the godhead.

Milton's Arminian sense of what makes us human is worth keeping in mind. The free will to choose separates people from machines and puppets, as in *Areopagitica*: "Many there be that complain of divin Providence for suffering Adam to transgresse, foolish tongues! When God gave him reason, he gave him freedom to choose, for reason is but choosing; he had bin else a meer artificiall Adam, such an Adam as he is in the motions" (YP 2:527). The big problem with free will in book 3 is that it appears to compromise God's transcendent power, and Milton, of course, is careful to preserve God's own omniscience: "if I foreknew, / Foreknowledge had no influence on their fault" (*PL* 3.117–18). But Genesis 18:25 raises a different issue. If choosing is what separates a human Adam from a puppet Adam, then choosing is also what would separate a personal God from a mechanical God. When God seems to function according to prescription, he slips out of what Milton considers to be the hallmark of what it is to be a person. He becomes not a personality, but such a mere artificial God as is found in the motions.[11] Goodman, as quoted in the last chapter, argues that prophets apply to God notions of personality, "which creates a dramatic theater for the expression of all sorts of values and ideas to which humans can relate."[12] Personality in God marks the difference between Goodman's dramatic theater and Milton's impersonal motions. As the Son echoes Abraham in compelling God to conform to justice, he pushes him into impersonal abstraction.

By way of comparison, Milton's reading of Genesis 18:25 is in close accordance with that of Hugo Grotius. In the first chapter of *De jure belli ac pacis,* Grotius argues that the law of nature "is so unalterable that God himself cannot change it." And the precedence of natural law even over the power of God is supported first by Genesis 18:25: "Therefore God suffers himself to be judged of according to this Rule, as we may find, Gen. xviii.25."[13] So when Milton insists in *Doctrine and Discipline of Divorce* that God's justice cannot "swerve from that irradiation wherwith it had enlight'ned the mind of man," and that it "bound it selfe to observe its own rule," he is locating God within the conceptual realm of seventeenth century natural law and natural religion. This is felt particularly in the way that mystery, or the "secret" ways of Providence, stand in opposition to God's predictable justice.[14] A God who operates by secrets and dispensations, rather than the prescriptions of humanly comprehensible laws, remains mysterious and unavailable to reason.

As God in 18:25 conforms to absolute justice, his will is neutralized and the sense of personal agency is diminished. According to Goodman, this process of rational theology diminishing God's personality is the subject of Genesis 18:25: "Values are no longer subjective, so divinities may no longer make them arbitrary." Congruent with Goodman's notion of a monotheistic God, the emerging rational religion of the seventeenth century frequently reconceived of God in such impersonal terms. For Grotius, when God submits to absolute rules, God is explicitly operating without will: "The Divine voluntary Law (as may be understood from the very Name) is that which is derived only from the Will of GOD himself; whereby it is distinguished from the Natural Law."[15] What Richard Tuck calls the "minimalist Christianity" of such thinkers as Grotius, Chillingworth, and Hobbes leads to a pared-down godhead that resembles the Big Bang.[16] Cherbury's own minimalism, in the form of his "Five Religious Common Notions," by so thoroughly removing the godhead from the realm of mystery and revelation, and by constructing it according to rationally perceivable laws, necessarily reimagines God as separate from will and personality. What I call in the last chapter Cherbury's geometric God is very like the mere mechanical God constructed by Genesis 18:25. And it is like what More describes as "an *Intellectual Principle*," that, conceived as acting only in accordance with rational conceptions of nature, is "so *fatally* affixed to his own seat" that God cannot "stretch forth his arm either to *reward* or *punish*" (*GMG* 33). At least in the moment when the Son, like Abraham, ostentatiously disciplines God—"That be from thee far, / That far be from thee, Father, who art judge / Of all things made, and judgest only right"—Milton's God closely resembles the divinity that More calls an intellectual principle.

But if Genesis 18:25 constructs an abstract God outside of personality, for more orthodox readers of the period it simultaneously had the opposite effect. Exegetes pause over the strange moment leading to the debate with Abraham, when God seems to be doubtful: "And the Lord said, Shall I hide from Abraham that thing which I do" (18:17).[17] Difficulty lies in the implication that God does not already know what to do—that his omniscience and will have not lifted God into absolute certainty. He is seemingly human. Such intellectual vulnerability is deeply compounded by the debate of 18:23–33. For there, even as God transcends personality in his conformity to absolute value, he also seems to submit to Abraham's justice. Remarkably, God is discovered in a moment of haggling as though he and Abraham were in a market. And God is apparently disciplined by a mere man. So exegetes are anxious to remove from Genesis 18:25 any impression that God is being corrected. Calvin explains that "He does not here teach God His duty, as if any one should say to a judge, 'See what thy office requires, what is worthy of this place, what suits thy character;' but he reasons from the nature of God, that it is impossible for Him to intend anything unjust."[18] Calvin recognizes the passage's demonstration of our rational ability to know the nature of God, but strives to exclude what is undeniably present in the narrative: that God is being corrected by Abraham.

Milton is sensitive to this astounding possibility in 18:25 when he says that Abraham, "ev'n to the face of God himselfe, seem'd to doubt of divine justice." Abraham presumes to stand before God's face and, seemingly, to discipline him. For Milton this may demonstrate the force of the rationally knowable concept of justice. But at the same time, the very sense that such an act is presumptuous — the shock of it, recorded by such words as "ev'n" and "himselfe" — reveals a typically monotheistic anxiety that the narrative has not represented God as sufficiently transcendent and abstract. Or, as Abdiel admonishes Satan, "Shalt thou give law to God, shalt thou dispute / With him the points of liberty, who made / Thee what thou art" (*PL* 5.822–24). As Goodman would have it, God is in most circumstances not subject to such doubt, and is well beyond being disciplined by a human understanding. But, paradoxically, in Genesis 18 this assertion is made in a theophany designed around Abraham's doubt before God's anthropomorphic face.

This side of Genesis 18:25, then, pulls the God of book 3 away from the tonelessness of untouchable doctrine, making him into a thinking figure that is genuinely engaged in dialogue with the Son. With the potential to change his mind as a result of discourse, as opposed to functioning mechanically according to the laws of justice, God simultaneously takes on a surprising measure of personality. So, for John E. Parish, Milton's echo of Genesis 18:25 is central to his development of an anthropomorphic God. The fact that God is a participant in debate reduces him from a perfectly abstract being to one with human faults: at this moment, as Parish rather exaggeratedly puts it, God is "evidently glad to be warned against an error" and is shown to be a "slower witted but not intractable god."[19]

God's answer to the Son, however, is constructed precisely to put to rest such doubts as Parish and Calvin express. After the apparent disciplining of God, Milton adds reassurance not present in Genesis 18: "My word, my wisdom, and effectual might, / All hast thou spoken as my thoughts are, all / As my eternal purpose hath decreed" (*PL* 3.170–72). What the Son has just said—the challenge of Genesis 18:25—was already in God's mind, and already part of God's purpose. He was not, therefore, corrected. Moreover, it is the Son instead of a man entering into negotiations, and it could make a difference that the being most near to God offers the potential discipline. Indeed, in one of the moments that challenges Antitrinitarian interpretation, the distinction between the two speakers of the dialogue is blurred: the Son is God's word and wisdom. This detail makes what has passed no dialogue at all, but an externalization of a properly internal and self-referential meditation. To a certain extent, then, the Son could be said to solve the problem of Genesis 18:25, just as Christ may be Christianity's truly innovative solution to the narrative problems of monotheism.[20]

And yet, Milton did not have to make the Son's words echo Abraham's. That he does invoke Abraham's argument right here—the first moment that God is answered and therefore the outset of divine dialogue—suggests that he is rather trying to complicate God's relationship to the Son and their role in council.

Plus, at the end of the Son's speech Milton turns to the related moment in Numbers 14:15–16, where Moses challenges God by claiming that God's reputation is at risk in the eyes of the Egyptians. The Son asks,

> Or wilt thou thy self
> Abolish thy creation, and unmake,
> For him, what for thy glory thou hast made?
> So should thy goodness and thy greatness both
> Be questioned and blasphemed without defence. (*PL* 3.162–66)

Arguing, like Moses, that God should act in order to head off the accusations of others, the Son again puts the godhead under the sway of created beings. Merritt Hughes describes at this moment "the shock of the exposure of God's vulnerability to the Son's suasion by means of his image in the eyes of the angels."[21] Milton in fact magnifies God's vulnerability by multiplying the disciplining gaze from an individual (Abraham or the Son) to the multitude of fallen angels.

By alluding to Genesis 18 at the beginning of God's dialogue, then, Milton places God equivocally between pure abstraction and personality. The limits placed on the godhead by law make God something other than a being of personality. And the limits of discipline pull in the opposite direction, making God too much like a person. Oscillating between these positions, Milton's God becomes an unstable ontological being, perhaps looking most like the deconstructed subject familiar from literary theory.[22] Such a God is a reaction typical of monotheistic narrative. A philosophical approach to the monotheistic godhead, such as Goodman's or that described by More as an intellectual principle, can attain the conceptual abstraction found in mathematics, and in this sphere God need not—in fact cannot—have the attributes of personality. But as Goodman's reliance on Genesis 18:25 demonstrates, our conception of those terms still depends upon story. We learn that God operates by the absolute value of justice, but we learn it in a dialogue, even an argument, between God and Abraham. Subjectivity in the godhead, the name "God" as it is predicated by a subject, names the possibility of God being narrated. Subjectivity enables narrative even as it is degraded as insufficiently abstract for monotheism. This radical paradox at the heart of Genesis 18:25 produces in book 3 a God of flickering subjectivity.

As criticism grapples with "Milton's God," such deeply unstable subjectivity has left its mark: the critics themselves have oscillated between Broadbent's God who "is light" and Lewis's Olympian God. That Milton's God is at once too mechanical and too personal also makes sense of the ongoing debate over God's goodness. William Empson consistently evaluates God as a personality: as a tyrant his deep inhumanity is his shortcoming. But at the same time, Empson singles out those moments of mechanical action as especially inhuman. "Die he or justice must" is delivered, Empson says, with a "stage-villain's hiss."[23] Reading perceptively, Empson makes use of both God's Olympian personality and his necessary conformity to laws. Dennis Danielson's emphasis on God's goodness responds to Empson essentially by distancing God from personality and emphasizing his mechanical qualities. Danielson rejects voluntarism in Milton's God and argues for his conformity with the particular rules of theodicy.[24] The critics oscillate between personality and mechanical abstraction because the poem does: by placing Genesis 18:25 and its crisis of subjectivity at the outset of the heavenly council, Milton constructs just such a readerly reaction. It is a reaction brought on by the demands of monotheism.

Raphael and the Plains of Mamre

A godhead of flickering subjectivity, both terrifyingly present in, and utterly elusive from, the narrative is typically monotheistic.[25] This deconstructed character is the God that "Abraham stood yet before" in Genesis 18:22, when he initiates negotiations over Sodom. But before Abraham's face-to-face encounter with God, a great deal has gone on leading up to, and in narrative terms, enabling, the debate. Abraham confronts God in the second half of this chapter only after he has played host to the three visitors, commonly considered angels, at his tent on the plains of Mamre. The close of this scene initiates the debate over Sodom: "And the men turned their faces from thence, and went toward Sodom: but Abraham stood yet before the Lord" (Gen. 18:22). In the visitation at Mamre the angels take part in a uniquely detailed and material domestic scene in which they famously eat food. In Genesis 18 it is as if the material congress between Abraham and the angels somehow makes possible the confrontation between Abraham and God. Forming one of the most complex theophanies in the Bible, the first half of Genesis 18 establishes a polytheistic space that enables the second half. Milton makes extensive use of both parts: after 18:25 shapes the divine council of book 3, Genesis 18:1–16 takes over Milton's account of Adam and Eve and their angelic visitor Raphael, forming a secondary narrative for books 4 through 9.

Just as the second half of Genesis 18 enters at the first moment of divine dialogue, so the first half shapes the entrance of angelic visitation: Adam first spots Raphael while exactly imitating Abraham. Genesis 18:1 reads, "And the Lord appeared unto him in the plains of Mamre: and he sat in the tent door in the heat of the day." In Milton's Eden, meanwhile,

> Him through the spicy forest onward come
> Adam discerned, as in the door he sat
> Of his cool bower, while now the mounted sun
> Shot down direct his fervid rays to warm
> Earth's inmost womb, more warmth than Adam needs.
> (*PL* 5.298–302)

Adam then dispatches Eve to prepare a meal, just as Abraham sets Sarah and his household in motion to feed his guests in Genesis 18:5–8. Milton stresses Adam's eagerness to serve his "guest" (*PL* 5.313) and Eve's domestic skill and hospitality: "with dispatchful looks in haste / She turns, on hospitable thoughts intent" (5.331–32). And in so doing Milton picks up on the common gloss to Genesis 18, which considers it a model for a hospitable and well-run household.²⁶ The food Abraham and Sarah provide is the source for the feast Raphael so famously enjoys. Genesis 18:8 is the classical place in which exegetes consider angelic eating, forming the clear precedent for Milton: "And he took butter, and milk, and the calf which he had dressed, and set it before them; and he stood by them under the tree, and they did eat." The traditional scholastic interpretation is that this eating is either symbolic or takes place in a vision.²⁷ Calvin and others interpret real eating but say that before reaching the point of digestion, the food disappears—as Gervase Babington explains, the meat "did vanish in the chawing, as water doth in boiling."²⁸ Milton, of course, allows angelic digestion, and even makes a point of entering the extensive controversy surrounding Genesis 18:8: "So down they sat, / And to their viands fell, nor seemingly / The angel, nor in mist, the common gloss / Of theologians" (*PL* 5.433–36).

Then, in a fairly hidden passage, Milton has Eve eavesdropping, just as Sarah overhears Abraham's conversation and famously laughs. In Genesis 18:9 we are led to believe that Sarah is in the tent, well away from the angels when they promise Abraham that Sarah will bear a son. But Sarah "heard it in the tent door, which was behind him" (Gen. 18:10). After Raphael has left, Adam tells Eve of Satan's threat, and Eve admits, "both by thee informed I learn, / And from the parting angel overheard / As in a shady nook I stood behind" (*PL* 9.275–77).²⁹ The first half of Genesis 18 thus shadows, and authorizes, Raphael's material visit from beginning to end.

Not only is Genesis 18:1–16 a precedent for angelic eating and digestion, but it also offers Milton an imaginative and richly developed narrative space. While biblical narrative is typically spare in description and sense of place, Genesis 18:1–16 stands out as one of the most spatially detailed episodes in the Hebrew Bible. We first see Abraham in the door of his tent (18:1); then he runs to meet the three men (18:2), then hastens back to the tent to tell Sarah to bake (18:6); then he goes out to the herd (18:7); and then he goes back to the men, and we learn that he stood by them under a tree while they ate (18:8). Next Sarah's position matters: she is in the tent (18:9), and then in the door of the tent eavesdropping (18:10). Finally, after the meal, "the men rose up from thence" (18:16). So Luther wonders at the episode: "What accounts for that profusion of words in Moses? Elsewhere, even in important matters, he is very sparing of words."[30] The feeling of detail in the narrative of Mamre must have particularly appealed to Milton as he worked on Eden. Mamre's narrative space, moreover, is capable of holding both the human and the divine, and it does so in a unique way. It brings them together not in the sublime and uncanny way felt by Abraham in the binding of Isaac or by Jacob at Penuel, but in a detailed and material way—in Erich Auerbach's terms, Mamre offers the rare precedent in the Hebrew Bible of a foregrounded divine narrative.

Abraham's visitors in Genesis 18:1–16 are usually read as angels, and their visit suggests the important role of material angels in narrating monotheistic divinity. It is easy to see that material angels can more readily enter into narrative. As Samuel Johnson puts it, Milton "saw that immateriality supplied no images, and that he could not show angels acting but by instruments of action; he therefore invested them with form and matter."[31] Henry More also sees material angels as crucial to belief in the Christian God. In *The Grand Mystery of Godliness*, he uses Genesis 18 to insist that the real and material existence of spirits holds up no less than the whole edifice of Christianity. Some affirm, he argues, that angels,

> are onely Divine Imaginations in men: which can be by no means allowed, unless we should admit the Holy Patriarch Abraham to have arrived at such a measure of dotage, as to provide cakes and a fatted calf to entertain three Divine Imaginations which visited him in his test. But certainly such slight and exorbitant glosses as these can argue nothing else but a misbelief of the Text, and indeed of all Religion, and that the Interpreter is no Christian, but either Atheist or Infidel. (*GMG* 6)

The example of angels really eating serves as a test case against skepticism—anyone doubtful about Mamre is exhibiting a skepticism toward the Bible, and so doubting all of revealed Christianity. Materiality similarly shapes the storyworld of Mamre, pushing the reader to accept divine beings as thoroughly present. Eating, as Milton stresses, implies digestion and all the bodily functions; such a line of thought shoves skepticism to the remote corners of the narrative. Similarly, eavesdropping reminds us of the materiality of the dialogue—the angelic conversation does not take place in a vacuum, but, as sound waves carry, it can be overheard by those nearby. The material storyworld of verses 1–16 pry open the reader's sense of belief, creating a narrative easily inclusive of divine beings. And this influences the terms of verse 25, paving the way for Abraham's debate with God by making the presence of the divine being narratively believable.

Paradise Lost relies on the same dynamic between the abstract God and material angels. At one of God's most abstract and deistic moments, when God mechanically "fulfilled / All justice" (*PL* 5.246–47), he does so by sending Raphael to inform Adam and Eve of their free will and Satan's intent. Being fully informed, God explains to Raphael, is critical to the fairness of free will, indeed essential to theodicy. It is the angelic visit that delivers the information and upholds Milton's justification of God—God fulfills justice by means of Raphael's material visit. The God of Genesis 18:25, in other words, is made possible in *Paradise Lost* by the angels of Genesis 18:1–16. Moreover, it is during his visit, amid the materiality taken from Mamre, that Raphael narrates the monotheistic God to Adam. Raphael's materiality appears to be a way of making narratives of the abstract, monotheistic God possible.

Milton's monism, which has been the subject of several recent studies, may explain things. Monism seems to promise a solution to the narrative problems of monotheism by undoing the dualism of matter and spirit, as Stephen Fallon explains: "Instead of being trapped in an ontologically alien body, the soul is one with the body. Spirit and matter become for Milton two modes of the same substance: spirit is rarified matter, and matter is dense spirit."[32] The key to Milton's monism is the *scala natura* of book 5, where Raphael describes to Adam the smooth transition of a single matter from root to fruit to human soul to angelic intuition (*PL* 5.469–90). If there is no distinction to be made between what is corporal and what is spiritual, and if there is a seamless progression through the levels of creation, then a foregrounded narrative of divinity is possible. Moreover, the possible implication of "one first matter all" (5.472) and God's creation *ex nihilo* (7.168–73), that God himself is of the same substance as angels and humans, extends monism to the godhead, opening up the possibility of narrating God in material terms.[33]

As promising as monism seems, however, it is important to recognize that, even while monism harnesses a scientific discourse, it still functions according to the logic of narrative. Jacques Lezra has theorized the early modern discourse of atomic science and its relationship to subjectivity in a way that is useful to this examination of Genesis 18, as well as to discussion of Milton's monism. Reading Lucretius, Lezra finds within the Epicurean focus on atoms a process by which is elided the otherwise unresolvable distinction between what Lucretius calls an atom's "swerve" as property, and its swerve as event. If the swerve is a property (which implies an ontological predicate to the body), then the movement originates in that atom, paving the way for free will and the "I" of Descartes's *cogito*. If the swerve is an event external to the atom (which implies a science of materials prior to any predicate), then that body is not the originating agent of the phenomenon of the swerve. This distinction between act and event is the basis of subjectivity, and Lezra shows that its reduction to the microscopic level of atoms, the reimagining of the logically irreconcilable swerve as minimal, becomes a resolution.[34] What Lezra identifies that is germane to material angels and to that part of Milton studies which has recently paid so much attention to Milton's monism, is the strategy of moving toward minimal bodies, the atomic level, as origin in the assertion of subjectivity.

Lezra's work suggests that Milton's move to the atomic level is a strategy for consolidating angelic subjectivity. Raphael eats because "food alike those pure / Intelligential substances require, / As doth your rational" (*PL* 5.407–09). The scientific likeness at the microscopic level implies, in a swerve, likeness at a less magnified level—that of subjects, with their properties of intelligence and reason. Materiality, with its recourse to Epicurean minimal bodies, seems to substantiate in angels the quality of personality. According to Lezra, materiality demonstrates subjectivity by means of a swerve from deductive proof to novelistic suggestion. Reading Descartes's *Second Meditation,* he uncovers a shuttling between the deductive method of pure skepticism and a "novelistic" discourse. A novelistic reading makes the subject behind the *cogito* seem intuitively true, and this intuition undergirds the deductive philosophical proofs that follow: "the position taken by the philosophical subject is written already and already read *ainsi qu'un roman.*"[35] Raphael first appears to Adam as a figure of narrative, and therefore already and intuitively organized as a subject. If any skepticism about angelic subjectivity should arise—if a reader has any of the doubts of a Hobbes or a Cherbury—that skepticism is quieted by the deductive proof of subjectivity on the microscopic level. The *scala natura* convinces because it elaborates what the narrative has already led us to intuit. Milton's monism, then, appears as a narrative strategy—a means of enabling the foregrounded presence of Raphael. D. Bentley Hart has recognized the usefulness to narrative of monism: in Milton's "narrative monism," according to Hart, "all is story, all may be told."[36] The *scala natura* promises as much by positing a seamlessness between the atomic level and subjectivity, from the root to angelic intuitive discourse. This is the overwhelming effect of Raphael's lesson in ontology, as well as his own eating. It also can explain the movement in Genesis 18 from the materiality of the first half to the theophany of the second half.

Milton finds precedent for angelic materiality in Genesis 18:1–16 and makes extensive use of that foregrounded divine narrative in the middle books of *Paradise Lost*. But there is still a way in which the strategy of monism does not fully satisfy the narrative's need for coherent subjects. As Lezra points out, atomic discourse is a swerve that covers over the aporia between atom and subject, and does not instantiate the subject so much as persuade us we have intuited it. There is still a difference between the atoms of monism and the building blocks of narrative, which are not microscopic but personal. On the atomic level we expect a discourse of scientific theory and proof. But on the level of narrative, we expect beings that imitate our experience of people, and that conform to imaginative expectations of character and personality. John Guillory has made the same distinction between science and narrative, arguing that the monism of *Paradise Lost* cannot fully solve the problem of narrating divine beings: "If Milton did not distinguish between spirit and matter, except as degrees in a scale of being, there remains a point of divide beyond which representation does not reach. The ideological monism can be credited without resolving the dualistic problem at the level of representation."[37]

The logic of narrative persists even over the science of atoms, and so it makes sense to view the materiality of Genesis 18:1–16 not as a precedent for monism, but as a precedent for divine subjects in narrative. Mamre does introduce materiality, but it also works against the unifying effects of the *scala natura* and the redemptive qualities of Milton's monism. Most importantly, as we evaluate it as a biblical precedent, Mamre offers an example of deeply divided angels, beings that, like the monotheistic God, resists ontological certainty and easy narration.

There is an important qualification to be made in this discussion's account of Genesis 18:1–16, which has so far been one of narrative seamlessness. It is not at all clear that Abraham's visitors really are angels. Even as Genesis 18:1–16 portrays seemingly personal angels in a foregrounded narrative space, it builds a complex, famously ambiguous ontology that shatters the subjective coherence of the three beings. In fact, calling them angels is an interpretation I have adopted so far only for the sake of simplicity: grammar, syntax, and narrative equivocation combine in the passage to make undecidable who, and how many, Abraham's visitors really are. With this qualification in mind, the episode on Mamre must be seen as a secondary narrative that also deeply unsettles Raphael's visit. Even as Genesis 18 helps to develop the monism of material angels and even as it supplies a uniquely foregrounded divine space in the narrative, the episode on Mamre injects into *Paradise Lost* a deeply unstable ontology, coloring Raphael with the anxieties of monotheistic narrative.

The biblical narrator first announces in 18:1 that the Lord appears to Abraham, but 18:2 tells of "three men," without any attempt to reconcile the discrepancy. This conjunction of God and men naturally leads commentators to assume that the visitors are angels—but in fact the word is never used in Genesis 18. Throughout the chapter they are "men," so that in 18:16 it reads, "and the men rose up from thence," and in 18:22, "And the men turned their faces from thence, and went toward Sodom." Only in Genesis 19:1 do we get, "And the two angels came to Sodom at even." While there is no certainty that these are the same beings as the men of Genesis 18, the story does continue across the chapter divide, leading most exegetes to confer the title of angel back onto the men.[38]

Ontological ambiguity, furthermore, extends from men and angels to God and Christ. Abraham's first word to the three men, "*Adonay*" (18:3), depending on the Masoretic pointing, could mean "my lords," "my lord," in reference to a man, or "my Lord," in reference to the deity. Is Abraham talking to a man, to men, or to God?[39] Calvin adds the fourth possibility, that Abraham is addressing Christ: "For we know that angels often appeared with Christ their Head; here, therefore, among the three angels, Moses points out one, as the Chief of the embassy."[40] The grammar of Abraham's subsequent speech also confuses the number of beings.

In Genesis 18:3 Abraham speaks in the second person singular to the visitor(s), while in 18:4–5 he uses the plural. In 18:10, it is a first person singular that promises Sarah a son. These sudden shifts in number have perplexed both Jewish and Christian commentators, and they resist consensus, as Willet's gloss shows:

> Abraham seeth three men, but speaketh as to one: 1. whereby, neither a threefold knowledge of God is shadowed forth of his nature, by his benefits, by his iudgements, as Philo. 2. Nor yet hereby is signified the mysterie of the Trinitie, that one God in three persons is to be worshipped, as Rupertus. 3. Neither did Abraham speak unto every one of them particularly, as Ramban. 4. But Abraham saluteth the third person as more excellent, either for the dignitie of this person, or for some respect, which the other two had unto him.[41]

As the explanations become more torturous, it becomes clear how narratively illogical and rigorously defiant of a unified conception of the being(s) the text is. Sarah and Abraham may be in a richly spatial narrative, but their visitors flicker in and out of the foreground, resisting ontological certainty. Mamre may provide a material and foregrounded account of angels, but we still cannot know these angels as discrete beings, nor can we distinguish them from God.[42]

Initially there is very little of such ambiguity in the appearance of Raphael, whom Adam immediately identifies as an angel. Raphael is also clearly one being: Milton contains the equivocation between three and one. But the persistent echoes of Genesis 18:1–16 can be felt to haunt Raphael's visit. Behind the unambiguous presence of the angel is the antipresence of the passage's ontologically unstable beings. Whatever the presence is on Mamre, whether man or angel or God or Christ, whether one or three, it flickers not only in the Bible's narrative, but also in Milton's.

And while the ontological instability of Genesis 18:1–16 has so far haunted Raphael's visit through allusion only, in Milton's last reference to Genesis 18 instability comes crashing into the voice of the narrator. Adam and Eve have been quite assured of

Raphael's ontology as they "entertain our angel guest" (*PL* 5.328). But the narrator's announcement of the Fall disallows for the reader, in terms clearer than previous allusions do, ontological certainty:

> No more of talk where God or angel guest
> With man, as with his friend, familiar used
> To sit indulgent, and with him partake
> Rural repast, permitting him the while
> Venial discourse unblamed.   (*PL* 9.1–5)

"God or angel" suggests that, however certain were Adam and Eve, it may actually have been God that was hosted. Jonathan Richardson glosses the line by suggesting that God was present in the angel, and this need for such exegetical gymnastics indicates that we have indeed been tossed back upon the difficult ontology of the plains of Mamre.[43] This one sly reference picks up on the ghostly doubt of allusion and casts all of books 5 through 8, Raphael's entire visit, into the ontological ambiguity of Genesis 18.

Venial Discourse Unblamed

However, even as the book 9 invocation destabilizes the middle books, there is nostalgia for the language that was available there. The "God or angel" who ate with Adam afforded a special opportunity for discourse: "permitting him the while / Venial discourse unblamed." "Discourse unblamed" in the book 9 invocation hearkens back to the invocation to book 3, where the poet nervously asks of light, standing in for God, "May I express thee unblamed?" (*PL* 3.3). This is the controlling anxiety of book 3, whether the poet can give God a presence in the narrative, whether he can express God poetically, without incurring blame for misrepresenting him. As Milton's use of Genesis 18:25 shows, the question is never adequately answered. God's narrative presence is unstable throughout, and the poet claims no assurance that his choice to put God in narrative is venial. Indeed, if any consensus has been reached by Milton's critics, Milton *is* to be blamed for book 3. But in books 5 through 8, we are now told, the heavenly guest—Raphael—has been able to relate his narrative. He has reported on God's actions in book 5, the war in heaven, and the Creation, all without incurring any blame. Whatever difficulties the poet has been encountering in portraying God and angels, Raphael has not felt them. And whatever ontological instability Mamre has conferred on Raphael, from within that instability there is still the possibility of authoritative discourse.

Raphael does worry about the lawfulness of his task, like the poet in book 3. But unlike the poet, he is confident in his solution. Giving materiality to spiritual forms will "express them best":

> how last unfold
> The secrets of another world, perhaps
> Not lawful to reveal? Yet for thy good
> This is dispensed, and what surmounts the reach
> Of human sense, I shall delineate so,
> By likening spiritual to corporal forms,
> As may express them best.   (PL 5.568–74)

Raphael is here covering much of the same territory that the *scala natura* promises to cover, uniting heavenly things with the material, narratable world. But rather than atoms, Raphael makes use of a divine poetics. This is Raphael's well-known claim to be speaking to Adam according to the doctrine of accommodation, as articulated in *De doctrina Christiana*. In the chapter "Of God," Milton devotes considerable attention to accommodation, which solves the narratological problems that gather specifically around the monotheistic godhead. Accommodation emerges as Milton considers the problem of conceiving of an abstract godhead: "When we talk about knowing God, it must be understood in terms of man's limited powers of comprehension. God, as he really is, is far beyond man's imagination, let alone his understanding" (YP 6:133). A true understanding must depend on Scripture, and we can be confident that representations of God in the Bible are acceptable because the Bible has been accommodated by divine authority: "Let there be no question about it: they understand best what God is like who adjust their understanding to the word of God, for he has adjusted his word to our understandings, and has shown what kind of an idea of him he wishes us to have" (YP 6:136). The key word here is "to adjust" (Latin: *accommodare*). When Raphael says he is "likening spiritual to corporal forms," he is claiming that he is adjusting his narrative in just this way. If Raphael's discourse can be unblamed it is because, as a messenger from God, he can authoritatively perform the necessary adjustments.

Understood in Raphael's terms, the doctrine of accommodation solves many of the problems of theophany and of narrating a monotheistic God. It allows his presence in the temporal and spatial confines of narrative while simultaneously protecting his absolute transcendence. It allows the monotheistic God to take on attributes that are personal, but that still cannot be taken as literal assertions. Accommodation, as Michael Lieb's work on anthropopathy shows, is largely a process of separating God from literal language.[44] The anthropopathetic tradition responds to those moments in the Bible when God is said to feel emotion. When God repents, or grieves, or rests after the Creation, these details seem to diminish him, making him more human than the omnipotent and omniscient God of monotheism should be. In order to protect against such diminishment, the anthropopathetic tradition argues that God does not literally experience these feelings, but that Scripture speaks figuratively, for the sake of human understanding. As Lieb shows in tracing the tradition from Philo through Calvin, anthropopathy is regularly put forward as a primary form of accommodation. Both anthropopathy and accommodation are rhetorical, or poetic, strategies for reading the Bible, in which the space of figurative language marks the adjustments made to knowledge of God for the sake of human understanding.

The power of reconciliation within figurative readings is sweeping—anthropopathy and accommodation, like allegory, would quiet all of the challenges of theophany by simply calling the narrative details rhetorical. But Milton explicitly rejects this course of interpretation when discussing angelic eating—Adam and Raphael "to their viands fell, nor seemingly" (*PL* 5.434). And he will not allow figural reading in his version of accommodation. In *De doctrina* Milton puts forward his doctrine of accommodation as a response to the problem of God's feelings, and makes explicit reference to anthropopathy. Milton, however, rejects the tradition: "In my opinion, then, theologians do not need to employ anthropopathy, or the ascription of human feelings to God. This is a rhetorical device thought up by grammarians to explain the nonsense poets write about Jove" (YP 6:134). As Lieb shows, Milton is not arguing against feelings in God, but against the practice of reading those feelings as rhetorical rather than literal. Milton's accommodation is in fact quite challenging and innovative in its rejection of anthropopathy: he insists that we accept the Bible's representation of a feeling God without recourse to the wiggle room offered by figurative language. No matter how shocking the depiction of God may be in biblical narrative, "We ought not to imagine that God would have said anything or caused anything to be written about himself unless he intended that it should be a part of our conception of him" (YP 6:134).[45] This is an approach to the Bible that, in its literalness, is remarkably willing to accept interpretive difficulties and even apparent transgressions of monotheistic abstraction. In Genesis 18:25, it would be wrong to explain away Abraham's correction of God as a figurative scene—we must accept it for what it is. In fact, as we have seen, Milton emphasizes the transgressive elements of 18:25 in *Paradise Lost*.

Without figural language, Milton's approach to reading the Bible pushes the process of accommodation behind the language, so to speak, into the realm of authority. Figurative readings find room to negotiate narrative problems within metaphor, allegory, and other rhetorical forms that are at least initially a part of the language on the page. The adjustments of accommodation are legible. In contrast, Milton's insistence on literality leaves the language of the narrative, with its contradictions and transgressions, unaccommodated. The adjustments that solve these narrative problems instead come to be located in the work done by the author, within the process of authoring the text, and prior to the language on the page. Accommodation issues from God, who "has adjusted his word to our understandings, and has shown what kind of an idea of him he wishes us to have" (YP 6:136). Milton's doctrine of accommodation puts particular focus on authorship, as all interpretation must go through the process of authoring and adjusting. This becomes most apparent when Milton himself turns from the theology of *De doctrina* to the descriptive poetry of *Paradise Lost*, which, under the pressure of Milton's version of accommodation, becomes highly self-conscious about the narrative process.

That the doctrine of accommodation comes from the mouth of Raphael, who is narrating the middle books, underlines this critical process of authoring. Raphael, moreover, frequently reminds us that he must accommodate his language (*PL* 5.568–74, 6.297–301, 7.176–79). Each reference pulls the reader, and Adam, out of Raphael's narrative and forces consideration of the adjustments that are necessary prior to the language itself. These moments would be equivalent to Milton's discussion of accommodation in *De doctrina*; that is, they would be mere assertions of the necessity of accommodated language — except for the fact that Raphael is a character in a poem. *De doctrina* refers to sacred Scripture. But inevitably in *Paradise Lost* every reader must understand that Raphael, being just a character, can only speaks words created by Milton himself. Raphael claims the beautiful power of accommodation, of adjusting his narrative to create venial discourse unblamed. But each claim is undercut by the knowledge that the words are not his, and that no authorized adjustment can possibly have been made. The angel becomes an embodiment of the process of accommodation, but even as he calls to our attention what would be successful narrative, Raphael ironically marks the narrative's insufficiency.

Many readers have viewed the doctrine of accommodation as explanatory of the poetics of *Paradise Lost*.[46] But whatever Raphael's claims for his own method of narration, and whatever the poet's claims for Raphael's "venial discourse," the angel is himself a product of Milton's human language. Unless Milton can perform the divine adjustments of accommodation on his own, then Raphael's discourse is only *fictionally* unblamed. As William Madsen persuasively argues, "It is therefore difficult to understand what it means to say that Milton uses the *method* of accommodation in *Paradise Lost,* since he would hardly arrogate to himself a mode of understanding and expression that he denies to the human authors of the Bible and reserves to God alone."[47] The key distinction in accommodation is that between divine and human narrative—what is in Scripture and therefore authorized by the process of accommodation, and what is a mere invention of men. Anthropopathy, Milton says, "is a rhetorical device thought up by the grammarians to explain the nonsense poets write about Jove"; we therefore should not consider God in anthropopathetic terms because "to do so would be to follow the example of men, who are always inventing more and more subtle theories about him" (YP 6:134). With Milton's thinking in *De doctrina* so attuned to poetic invention—"the nonsense poets write"—it is not creditable that he would fail to recognize the distinction in *Paradise Lost*. None of *Paradise Lost* can be considered truly accommodated.

It could be argued that accommodation has a place in *Paradise Lost* to the extent that Milton's own language transcends the human—that is, to the extent that Milton himself is divinely inspired. James Holly Hanford and others have argued that Milton truly thought himself prophetic.[48] Milton's narrator pleads for inspiration in the first three invocations: whether the "spirit" of book 1 or Urania of book 7, the narrator's muses imply a heavenly source for his inventions and therefore an assurance that his poem has been accommodated. Yet in the final invocation, in book 9,

Milton destabilizes these assurances by introducing the possibility that *Paradise Lost* is not an inspired text, but a product of the narrator's mind alone. The invocation first asserts a vatic poet:

> If answerable style I can obtain
> Of my celestial patroness, who deigns
> Her nightly visitation unimplored,
> And dictates to me slumbering, or inspires
> Easy my unpremeditated verse. (*PL* 9.20–24)

Milton's "answerable style" betrays the same anxiety of "May I express thee unblamed?" but the direct connection to a celestial patroness seems to be an assurance that such style is to be found. For Hanford these lines are evidence that Milton truly thought himself possessed.[49] But these lines significantly begin with an "if"—Milton is not sure of his inspiration. And a mere 21 lines later, he turns to another "if":

> Me of these
> Nor skilled not studious, higher argument
> Remains, sufficient of it self to raise
> That name, unless an age too late, or cold
> Climate, or years damp my intended wing
> Depressed, and much they may, if all be mine,
> Not hers who brings it nightly to my ear. (*PL* 9.41–47)

The second possibility, that the narrator is not inspired but writing on his own, makes all the difference to his success. The poet feels inspired—something "brings it nightly to my ear." But however much he celebrates that something in the poem's several invocations, he must finally admit, displaying a skepticism toward revelation that is both deistic and monotheistic, that he cannot be sure. The implication of blameful discourse spreads across *Paradise Lost* just as nature, at Eve's transgression, "from her seat / Sighing through all her works gave signs of woe" (9.782–83).

The book 9 invocation sets up the poet as merely human, and so distances him from the possibility of creating accommodated language. It makes sense that the same invocation includes the nostalgia for Raphael's "venial discourse unblamed." The poet's loss of authority would naturally coincide with a celebration of a more exalted angelic discourse, and both the poet's loss and the nostalgia pave the way for the Fall, which is to be narrated in book 9. But the simultaneity of the poet's "if all be mine" and his nostalgia for Raphael's discourse has about it a deep irony. For when the poet's purely human discourse surfaces, it also disallows Raphael's accommodated narrative—it clinches the fact that no part of the poem can be truly accommodated, and so even Raphael's language is human and therefore insufficient. The celebration of Raphael's unblamed discourse is immediately subverted, as we become more certain than ever that the thing the poet longs for, accommodated narrative, is unattainable. Further, with the possibility of accommodated language subverted by the narrator's equivocal inspiration, all of Raphael's own claims for accommodation are similarly ironized. Raphael's repeated suggestions that he is accommodating his language name exactly how the poem's narrator fails. And, the implication that follows from this, they name exactly how Raphael's narrations themselves therefore fail, since the poet's humanity disallows Raphael the character's accommodation. Even as he calls to our attention what would be successful narrative, Raphael ironically marks Milton's, and his own, failure.

Raphael's claims for accommodation are moments of radical self-consciousness in *Paradise Lost*, when the poet announces the impossibility of narrating monotheism unblamed. Raphael's discourse is, after all, a narrative within a narrative. Shlomith Rimmon-Kenan describes such metatextuality in terms that capture the fallen mood of book 9: "The despair that arises from confronting the incapacity of language to 'reach' the world is sometimes counteracted by a search for a metalinguistic place from which to speak of the limitations of language and literature. This results in metatexts, self-conscious or self-referential literature, works that interrogate or dramatize their own difficulties in representing reality."[50] Deeply aware of the impossibility of creating accommodated language, Milton turns to the strategy of pointing out this impossibility.

We are far from discourse unblamed. But this ironic and deconstructive impasse is not, in Milton's poem, as despairing as our modern sensibilities might assume. For Milton is telling a monotheistic narrative, which is a kind of narrative not defeated by indeterminacy. Rather, it holds onto a faith in God precisely because of its thoroughgoing skepticism. Monotheistic narrative tells of God through its inability to tell of God, and unfolds by means of a self-consciousness of its own blameful expression. Genesis 18 has so far stood behind much of this sense of narratological defeat, a secondary narrative that haunts *Paradise Lost* with the impossibility of its project. But Milton returns to Genesis 18 one more time, expanding the poem's self-consciousness when in book 8 Adam tells of his debate with God in terms very like Genesis 18:25. And this second version makes use of the impossibility of narrating God in order to forge a remarkable monotheistic narrative.

Abraham's Presumption, Version Two

Raphael's narrative in books 5 through 8 is long and engrossing, and it calls forth in Adam the desire to become a narrator himself. He begs for the chance to "relate / My story" (*PL* 8.204–05). Adam's story, of course, predates the Bible and indeed all human literature and storytelling. In his relation of his remarkable meeting with God, we are witnessing what may be seen as history's first attempt at describing theophany. As usual, Eve has quietly been there first, telling, back in book 4, of her encounter with the invisible voice. But Adam encounters more than a mere voice. His story is rich with narrative detail and has a remarkable ease and fullness such as Milton might envy: Adam stands before the "presence divine" (8.314), within the foregrounded space of the garden, and engages in direct dialogue with God. Adam's is truly the world's first monotheistic narrative. With this episode, Milton returns to Genesis 18, as Adam dares, like Abraham, to debate with his Creator.

Milton's return to Genesis 18:25 dismantles the structure of the chapter as a whole, upending the movement from Mamre to Abraham's debate, and replacing it with a recursive or chiasmic structure: debate-Mamre-debate. While Genesis 18 moves in a progressive fashion, seemingly paving the way for the debate by means of the materiality of Mamre, *Paradise Lost* does not build in a single direction. The chiasmic structure returns the poem inexorably to the problem of God's personality, so that we approach Genesis 18:25 both with a greater awareness of its importance, and with less of a sense that its problems can be solved. Chiasmus turns back on itself and is a highly self-conscious figure. The recursiveness of Milton's allusions to Genesis 18 similarly builds a self-consciousness into our understanding of its theophany and the efforts at theophany in *Paradise Lost*.

Matching this effect, in Milton's return to Genesis 18:25, the problems of theophany are even more pronounced than they were in book 3. Book 3 may tone down Genesis 18 by having the Son, rather than Abraham, argue with God. But Milton's second version of 18:25 returns the story to the high-stakes scenario of a man debating with God. Every beast but Adam has a mate, so Adam dares to question God: "I found not what me thought I wanted still; / And to the heavenly vision thus presumed" (*PL* 8.355–56). Adam characterizes his speech as "presumptuous" again (8.367), accentuating the sense of shock created by a man challenging God. For Adam's argument stems from a sense of incompleteness in Creation, as if God had erred and fallen short of perfection. Such imperfection had been absent from Raphael's account of Creation, particularly his representation of the creation of Eve: "Male he created thee, but thy consort / Female for race" (7.529–30). Adam adds the challenging possibility that the Creator can be told where he has not been sufficiently thorough.

Spurring Adam's presumption is the apparent fact that the ways of God can be understood by man, and that God's actions can therefore be corrected. Milton takes this surprising possibility from Genesis 18: Adam's plea, "Let not my words offend thee, heavenly power, / My maker, be propitious while I speak" (8.379–80), evokes Abraham's formula, repeated in Genesis 18:30 and 32, "Oh let not the Lord be angry, and I will speak." Adam is trying out his powers of reason and pursues the course taken by Abraham, as described by Milton in the *Doctrine and Discipline of Divorce:* "Therefore Abraham, ev'n to the face of God himselfe, seem'd to doubt of divine justice, if it should swerve from that irradiation wherwith it had enlight'ned the mind of man, and bound it selfe to observe its own rule."

Abraham's debate with God, as has been argued, is paradigmatic of the universalizing tendency of monotheism. As Goodman and Milton both assert, Genesis 18 shows the necessary conformity to absolute values of the monotheistic God. And so it is not surprising that Milton's return to Genesis 18 is immediately followed by the most explicit statement of monotheism in *Paradise Lost*. With Adam taking on the position of Abraham and daring to question Creation, Milton's God answers:

> A nice and subtle happiness I see
> Thou to thy self proposest, in the choice
> Of thy associates, Adam, and wilt taste
> No pleasure, though in pleasure, solitary.
> What think'st thou then of me, and this my state,
> Seem I to thee sufficiently possessed
> Of happiness, or not? Who am alone
> From all eternity, for none I know
> Second to me or like, equal much less.   (8.399–407)

From the fact of Adam's human solitude, Milton's God moves to his own: he is alone, with none equal to him, and none second to him or like him. He is pure singularity. This passage finds a strong echo in one of the most monotheistic moments of *De doctrina*, as Milton discusses the unity of God and the first commandment:

"Certainly the Israelites under the law and the prophets always understood that God was without question numerically one, and that there was no other besides him, let alone any equal to him" (YP 6:147). The Sumner translation makes the echo of *Paradise Lost* even clearer by rendering it as "besides whom there was none other, much less any equal."[51]

In keeping with this explicitly monotheistic debate between God and Adam, Milton asserts the important result: that humans can therefore understand and anticipate the ways of God. Just as Abraham can "doubt divine justice," so Adam can doubt divine creation. And just as God responds to Abraham by haggling as if in the market, so Milton's God responds with an invitation to further thought and dialogue. He asks, "What think'st thou then of me, and this my state?" God's question confronts Adam with the task of using his own powers to comprehend the divine—that is, he invites Adam to conceive of the monotheistic God.

In the move from the prose treatise to the imaginative poem there is a slide from "law" to "state": in *The Doctrine and Discipline of Divorce,* Milton argues that Genesis 18 demonstrates that "God indeed in some ways of his providence, is high and secret past finding out: but in the delivery and execution of his Law, especially in the managing of a duty so daily and so familiar as this is whereof we reason, has plain enough reveal'd himself"; in book 8 it is not the revealed law but God's "state" which Adam is invited to theorize. "State" could imply something close to law, since it is the state of oneness that is under discussion, and that oneness is revealed in the first commandment. But the word does seem to introduce an avenue of inquiry beyond the Law, implying that Adam should try to figure out God's condition, his manner of existence, and his government of creation. Indeed, what he is really invited to do is to conceive of God in his oneness, and with the full implications of his monotheism. Milton's rewriting of Genesis 18 matches his commentary on it by universalizing the specific issue of righteous souls in Sodom into the greater theological issue: whether humans can know the monotheistic God.

As with Raphael's task of "likening spiritual to corporal forms" and the poet's relationship to accommodation, the moment of God's question is textured with self-conscious poetic anxiety. In order to insert Adam's imaginative and theological challenge, Milton has deliberately and prominently departed from the Genesis account of Adam's awakening and Eve's creation. In Genesis 2:18 it is God who understands that "It is not good that the man should be alone." But Milton gives that moment of rethinking to Adam—into this central moment of both *Paradise Lost* and the Bible, Milton inserts the debate of Genesis 18. By shifting from God to Adam the intellectual work of discovering the need for Eve, Milton not only stresses the human reason he associates with Genesis 18:25, but he introduces the shock generated by the human disciplining of God. This resonates with a parallel shock at Milton's own bold rewriting, which threatens to be taken as the kind of human invention that has no claim to accommodation. "If all be mine" Milton worries, and this episode certainly is all Milton's. Filling out the layers of anxiety in Milton's use of Genesis 18, we can notice the appropriateness of the poet intervening in sacred Scripture by turning to a text that explores the anxiety of intervening with God.

So when God asks "What think'st thou then of me, and this my state?" the question finds Adam in a position remarkably near to Milton's. Just as Milton in book 3 must theorize God's state, so must Adam. Just as Milton worries, "May I express thee unblamed?" so Adam worries at the outset that he is being presumptuous. And in book 8, Adam's presumption is simultaneously Milton's presumption, for both seek to add to what God has wrought: Adam by finding Creation imperfect, Milton by rewriting the accommodated Scripture. Adam's lines, "Let not my words offend thee, heavenly power, / My maker, be propitious while I speak," not only bring us back to Abraham, but could very well be the ventriloquized prayer of the poet himself. If Adam is the first human charged with conceiving of the monotheistic godhead, and if he is the first human to narrate this conception (to Raphael no less), then Milton has staged in the second version of Abraham's presumption an idealization of his own poetic task.

And in the face of Raphael's ironic insufficiency, Adam makes considerable strides toward narrating God. The second version of Abraham's presumption is met by the most delightfully obliging and friendly God of the epic. Adam's initial request for a mate draws from God a smile (*PL* 8.368). Then Adam continues to press his point, explicitly echoing Genesis 18, and God answers "not displeased" (8.398). When God turns the question back onto Adam, with "What think'st thou then of me, and this my state," Adam's response "acceptance found" from "the gracious voice divine" (8.435-36). Adam's answer—his attempt at conceiving of the monotheistic God—receives explicit approval. God concludes by saying that the entire exchange has been a trial of Adam's powers of reason, "To see how thou couldst judge of fit and meet" (8.448). This test turns on the problem of conceiving of God's "state," the greatest challenge to human reason, as well as the key problem of monotheistic narrative.

Adam's answer is fully aware of God's oneness, and of the complexities that issue from it:

> He ceased, I lowly answered. To attain
> The highth and depth of thy eternal ways
> All human thoughts come short, supreme of things;
> Thou in thy self art perfect, and in thee
> Is no deficience found; not so is man,
> But in degree, the cause of his desire
> By conversation with his like to help,
> Or solace his defects. No need that thou
> Shouldst propagate, already infinite;
> And through all numbers absolute, though one;
> But man by number is to manifest
> His single imperfection, and beget
> Like of his like, his image multiplied,
> In unity defective, which requires
> Collateral love, and dearest amity.   (*PL* 8.412-26)

Adam begins with a keen sense of his own insufficiency, admitting that "To attain / The highth and depth of thy eternal ways / All human thoughts come short." His language echoes the book 1 invocation, which asks,

> what in me is dark
> Illumine, what is low raise and support;
> That to the highth of this great argument
> I may assert eternal providence,
> And justify the ways of God to men. (1.22–26)

These verbal echoes again draw the parallel between Adam's task at this moment and Milton's task in writing *Paradise Lost*. But where the poet is bold, Adam is humble concerning his own powers of understanding. Even before Raphael had admonished him to "be lowly wise," Adam has "lowly answered"—an instinctive theologian, he arrives at an answer that, in its humility, is wise. Adam's statement of the limits of human reason could be read as an admission of Milton's own poetic failure, clipping the wings of the book 1 invocation and throwing us back into the anxiety of book 3. But this is only the beginning of Adam's answer. The inability to conceive of the monotheistic God does not disallow discourse, but in this remarkable passage actually forms the possibility of successful speech. Conceptual shortcomings become a purposive and creative part of Adam's narrative. Faced with the extreme transcendence and aniconism of monotheism, accommodation attempts to substitute knowable and visible things for the unknowable and spiritual. As this repeatedly falls short, Adam's monotheistic narrative surfaces in *Paradise Lost* with a radically different strategy: Adam makes use of his conceptual shortcomings in order to forge his narrative. Adam's poetics depend on the explanatory power of the negative—on an approach similar to the broad tradition of negative theology.

Adam is able to say a great deal about God, but not through positive statement. Instead, he describes God negatively by noting the ways he is different from a man. A man needs a mate to "solace his defects," but in God "Is no deficience found." Man needs a partner to multiply, but "No need that thou / Shouldst propagate, already infinite." God is perfect, but "not so is man." With its abundance of negatives, Adam's answer proceeds by way of negative theology, in which the transcendent God is only understood by means of statements that say what he is not. Discussing Maimonides, Aryeh Botwinick explains that in negative theology, "The utterance of the word 'God' initiates a process of endless displacement that finds no resting place. All we can ever do by way of assigning a content and pinpointing a reference for 'God' is to continually assert that God is not literally to be construed in this way or that, and that he is not to be found in a humanly cognizable sense anywhere."[52] Adam's negative theology closes the gap between human thought and the most inaccessible concepts of the divine. God is "perfect"—but what exactly does it mean to be perfect? How might that be conceived of and expressed? A beginning is made by the negative: perfection is *not* the condition of requiring another being to make up for defects. God is also "infinite," and this concept can be in some manner understood as *not* the state of needing to multiply or propagate.

The first step in Adam's negative theology is an understanding of his own limitations, and Adam's humility shines again at the close of the sentence. He knows his "imperfection" and that he is "defective" (*PL* 8.422, 424). In the verse and conceptually, these shortcomings hinge around procreation, as Adam's lack is of a partner with whom to beget others. Adam's use of "his like, his image" draws attention to the *imago dei,* and so recognizes the profound distinction between human and divine creation. Adam's language clearly refers to Genesis 5:1–3, which is about Adam's parenting of Seth—a more limited kind than God's creation of Adam in Genesis 1:26, where God said, "Let us make man in our image, after our likeness."[53] Adam's procreation is a far humbler thing, making likenesses and images that are far humbler. And appropriately, unlike God, through these offspring Adam will be plural, "multiplied."

The allusion to the *imago dei* marks not only the difference between human procreation and divine creation, it also marks the difference between human and divine creativity—the difference between God as creator and Adam as a speaker and user of language. Genesis 1:26 is a place where human intellect is often considered, where humanists take pride, as well as where Calvin expounds upon the difference between Adam's intelligence and our fallen minds infected by sin.[54] In *De doctrina* Milton argues that "traces of the divine image still remain in us," not extinguished by the Fall. And "These traces remain in our intellect" (YP 6:396). Milton's proof-texts demonstrate how humans can understand divine law and can grasp "the invisible things"—so the *imago dei* marks an optimism about human intellect and the possibility of understanding God (see also YP 6:324). This must be tempered by Michael, who seems to allow "divine similitude / In part" after the Fall, but insists that the image is severely disfigured, defaced, and perverted (*PL* 11.511–25). In book 8, however, Adam has not yet fallen, so Michael's glum correction does not yet pertain—in fact, the *imago dei* reminds us how much more capable of conceiving of God's "state" Adam must be. And yet even in this prelapsarian condition, when he is much closer to being the image of God, Adam's monotheistic narrative does not capitalize on optimistic understandings of "image," but rather takes place by means of negative language. Adam's imperfection is that he is not able to be perfect when alone, that he is imperfect at being single—unlike God. And similarly, his defect is in unity, in the fact that when alone he is not also unified and complete—again unlike God. Both name oneness as the distinguishing mark between Adam and God. And so Adam will be multiplied while God remains "through all numbers absolute, though one."

Monotheistic language must be negative, must be what Botwinick calls "the *nots* of monotheistic theology": "In monotheistic theology, 'God' as a conceptually vacant term gets perpetually filled in with a human content. The *nots* of monotheistic theology

(God is not this, and he is not that, as conventional religious terminology projects) are consistently oriented toward what we are capable of articulating and experiencing."[55] Adam's negative theology, matching Botwinick's claims, is a linguistic strategy for understanding the specifically monotheistic God. As monotheism tends toward a completely abstract God, perfect and infinite, the only way of thinking through and expressing God is by making a positive statement that is subsequently rejected because it falls short of divine truth. When God is "through all numbers absolute, though one," he is geometrically and abstractly perfect. Therefore, God actually depends upon false conceptions of him in order to be present to humans. Adam's solitude is in human terms and is accessible to human thought, and its rejection fills out our conception of God's solitude—that is, his oneness or monotheistic state. Here the logic behind Milton's combining Genesis 18 and Genesis 2:18 becomes clear. Genesis 18 brings Milton to the thoroughly abstract God of monotheism, and so to the necessity of negative theology. Genesis 2:18, the moment when Adam is discovered as imperfect in his solitude, offers Milton the ideal opposite of that solitude, and by negative example enables the description of the monotheistic God.

But even if it wins God's approval, negative theology puts Adam the narrator in a complex intellectual space: his answer shuttles between human-centered conceptions of God and their subsequent rejection as inadequate. Adam's thoughts dwell upon a God with the personality to be lonely—and then he rejects that state. This is a discourse with a great deal of instability, as can be felt in the difficult shifts in Adam's speech. A God narrated through the "*nots* of monotheistic theology," such as we see Adam perform, is very unlike a God narrated through accommodation. In accommodation the adjustment between the incorporeal and the corporeal has happened already, prior to the narrative. And the adjustment allows us to be confident that Scripture literally supplies ideas about God that "he wishes us to have." But in the negative language of monotheism, adjustments are performed within the language, and as part of the reader's experience. This is by means of the knowledge that our received language is *not* what is to be wished for. Narrative must undercut itself by making a show of its own failings, and must lack the sense of a fully authoritative author. Taken together, Adam's negative constructions present a God who is at one moment a personal God present in the narrative, and at the next moment a thoroughly abstract God, utterly removed from human comprehension. Such a God flickers in and out of Adam's narrative, just as God does in Genesis 18:25 and in *Paradise Lost* as a whole.

Adam's narrative of God, the very first monotheistic narrative, explicates Milton's own monotheistic narrative—even as Milton's contains Adam's within the self-consciousness of the poem's secondary narrative of Genesis 18. The self-deprecating mode of Adam's narrative, occasioned by Genesis 18:25, matches the poet's anxiety in book 3, and then makes use of that anxiety through negative theology. Milton's allusions to Genesis 18 construct this web of ironic and self-conscious narration, which ultimately creates a God of flickering subjectivity—now wholly abstract, now wholly personal. Adam's negative language about the godhead finds its extension in the rest of the language of *Paradise Lost*, in the ironic accommodation of Raphael, and in the self-conscious narration of the poet of monotheism.

Four

The War in Heaven and Deism

Theophany is at the heart of the narrative problems of monotheism. But while the godhead is the epicenter, shocks of narrative instability are also felt in the appearance of angels, as Genesis 18 demonstrates. The visitors on Mamre flicker, shift, and contradict their own presence, and, as with the problem of God's presence, this flickering serves as a marker of participation in monotheism. This is to map the destabilizing dynamics of theophany onto the larger economy of divine beings, and will lead to an investigation of how monotheism shapes not only the godhead of *Paradise Lost*, but the poem's entire storyworld. The outward expansion of instability brings the inquiry from consideration of how Milton represents or conceives of God, to consideration of what effect the monotheistic God has on the key element of narrative that connects him to other characters—that is, what effect Milton's monotheism has on plot.

The monotheistic godhead threatens narrative with the dwindling of personality, as God becomes less of a person and more of an intellectual principal. Parallel to this tendency, just as character diminishes under monotheism, so plot dwindles toward its minimal limits. Plot becomes nearly inconsequential, approaching what can be called the minimal requirements of narrative. This chapter examines how the absoluteness of the monotheistic

God—his omniscience and omnipotence—affects the possibility and quality of action in the war in heaven. As a result of monotheism, the poetry expresses the urge to strip away narrative detail and to operate without an economy of divine beings. Plot then dwindles, and the poem confronts an absolute silence, the impossibility of story in a monotheistic storyworld.

In this way the war in heaven approaches the aniconic silence of deism, with its rejection of religious revelation. As the latter parts of this chapter will show, the early reception of the war in heaven was deeply involved in debates over deism. Milton's angels appeared to many readers to challenge the possibility of Christian machinery in an epic poem, and so book 6 seemed to question revealed religion itself. *Paradise Lost* was received not infrequently as a deist text—and just as well was read as proof against deism. The connection between Milton and deism is surprising and has been largely ignored since the early reception. Recovering his proximity to the problems raised by deism should remind us of the truly radical possibilities of Milton's religious imagination. And it also begins to fill out our understanding of the crucial endpoint of seventeenth century monotheism, in deism and its skeptical reevaluation of revealed religion. Milton was not a deist, but his war in heaven, by virtue of its thoroughgoing monotheism, moves toward this deist endpoint, and so had the potential to be read as a deist document.

Local Forgetting

Book 6 begins with little Abdiel's heroic flight "Through heaven's wide champaign" to report Satan's plans for war to God. He is the lone just angel to emerge from Satan's book 5 colloquy, and his flight carries both the doctrinal weight of free will and the dramatic import of the commencement of the war in heaven. Flying all night, "till morn, / Waked by the circling hours, with rosy hand / Unbarred the gates of light" (*PL* 6.2–4), Abdiel's journey appears to be a rousing opening scene. But when he arrives, he suddenly gets a view of the angelic troops: "War he perceived, war in procinct, and found / Already known what he for news had thought / To have reported" (6.19–21). The narrative suddenly grinds to a bathetic halt, with Abdiel's heroism laid bare as entirely unnecessary. Abdiel's report is not needed because, of course, God is omniscient.

The sophisticated play between the words "known" and "news" points out the disjunction between omniscience and narrative that underlies this passage. News is knowledge, but knowledge that must be new — news is knowledge that has a position in time and, given Abdiel's flight, also in space. But omniscience, in its infinite abstraction, must transcend time and space. It has an always-already logic that resists such things as a messenger and a messenger's flight. Knowledge may travel fast during Abdiel's flight, but nowhere near as fast as it does in God's mind, for when knowledge pertains to an omniscient God it has nothing to do with time or space, and so nothing to do with narrative. God's omniscience collides with narrative's basic need for the space and time of plot, and the result is a moment of narratological strangeness at the outset of the war in heaven.

Patrick Hume is bothered by the contradiction and bathos of Abdiel's news, accounting for it by finding a shift from angelic to human language: these lines, he suggests, are said "after the manner of Men, for it is unconceivable that an Angel (a Spirit of more pure and enlighten'd Perfection than Mankind is) should be a stranger to the *Omniscience of* GOD *Almighty.*"[1] Two perspectives are present, an initial one that is unaware of the omniscience of God, and then, in a sudden shift, a perspective that fully realizes God's totality. The strangeness of this shift marks the disjunction between narrative and omniscience, and as well makes the narrative of the war in heaven possible. Abdiel's mistaken assumption that he will deliver news unknown to God is instrumental in creating the heroic press of the narrative: only if we believe that knowledge exists within time does Abdiel's flight matter, and so only under this misconception concerning God's omniscience can the narrative deliver the suspenseful unfolding of events that creates a good story. But Abdiel's flight is a serious misconception of God, and so the narrative must be interrupted, and undercut, by the reminder of God's abstracting omniscience. Milton risks dampening his heroic tone at this key moment, risks bathos and even absurdity in his narrative, but manages to preserve narrative and assert omniscience.

While the war in heaven is a piece of news, Milton struggles with God's omniscience. But as the narrative turns to action, the poet must confront another facet of God's monotheistic abstraction: his omnipotence. With the same courage that sent him flying "Through heaven's wide champaign," Abdiel steps in front of the armies to confront Satan. The narrative will offer the drama of his heroic blow, but Abdiel's words to Satan make it clear how meaningless the war is:

> fool, not to think how vain
> Against the omnipotent to rise in arms;
> Who out of smallest things could without end
> Have raised incessant armies to defeat
> Thy folly; or with solitary hand
> Reaching beyond all limit at one blow
> Unaided could have finished thee, and whelmed
> Thy legions under darkness.   (6.135–42)

God, being omnipotent, could simply eject Satan and his armies from heaven with one hand and one blow. This image of the single blow recalls the representation of God in the book 1 catalog of gods: "Jehovah, who in one night when he passed / From Egypt marching, equalled with one stroke / Both her first born and all her bleating gods" (1.487–89). In both cases Milton brings God's oneness—the solitary hand and the one blow—to the fore, stressing the connection between monotheism and the impossibility of genuine action on the part of others.

In raising the matter of omnipotence, Abdiel not only suggests the folly of Satan's attempt, but also the folly of Milton's effort in writing book 6. For the sake of the narrative, the war must have genuine consequences. But if God is omnipotent, why should the stroke Abdiel is about to level on Satan's head matter? As a plot event, how can this or any other part of the war have dramatic interest, let alone sublimity? And, since this narrative is a theodicy, how can it have religious significance? God's omnipotence threatens to overwhelm, with Satan's legions, the narrative of the war in heaven.[2]

And so, when the war begins, it is precisely God's omnipotence that must be forgotten. In the first press of battle, "each on himself relied, / As only in his arm the moment lay / Of victory" (6.238–40). Each angelic arm recalls—in order to set aside—the totalizing arm of God, and the "solitary hand" that Abdiel names. "Moment," as Fowler glosses it, primarily means the "determining influence," so that each angel fights as if he, rather than God, controlled the outcome. But the enjambment separates "moment" from "Of victory," so that we first read "moment" for its more common, temporal meaning. Then in the littleness in time that is a moment, time dwindles and the word is recast to mean "consequence." As the less obvious meaning becomes primary, we feel a forcing of perspective, a deliberate narrowing, until we are so focused on the angelic arms that they actually do seem to matter. But the poetry makes clear that before the stirring sense of consequentiality can enter, before the angels can imagine that in their actions lie the outcome, temporal limits must be erased. For each angel to fight as if victory really depended upon his arm, which is to say, for the battle narrative to matter, angelic action must expand in our attention to the point that God is forgotten. To the extent that the war in heaven reads as heroic poetry, God's omnipotence is delimited and fenced out of each moment of battle. Yet that such limitations on God are patently absurd, Milton himself makes clear: the battle would

> disturb,
> Though not destroy, their happy native seat;
> Had not the eternal king omnipotent
> From his strong hold of heaven high overruled
> And limited their might. (6.225–29)

God does the limiting, and his arm is behind each angelic arm—even though it serves the purposes of narrative temporarily to forget.

These narrative problems are closely related to the representational problems discussed in the last chapter, where the monotheistic God wavers between being an intellectual principle and a personality. These are the familiar difficulties of representing God—the risk of personality, the complexity of theophany, the linguistic strategies of irony and negative theology. But the war in heaven shows that these difficulties are not only located within the godhead. The narrative instability of monotheism extends far beyond God, spreading out to the economy of beings who share a storyworld with him—to the visitors on Mamre or the angels battling in Milton's heaven. In narratological terms, monotheism initially challenges the creation of character, resulting in the complexities of God's personality. And then, emanating from the central figure of God, monotheism challenges the possibility of other characters acting, and the possibility of their actions leading to the accumulation of meaningful events in a plot. God's totalizing omnipotence and omniscience threaten to make the actions of the angels inconsequential—and so threaten to shrink the possibility of plot into nothingness. Just as the monotheistic God pushes toward absolute abstraction, so he pushes the storyworld around him toward the minimal limits of narrative.

Since Aristotle, theorists of narrative have found it effective to study its simplest form, asking what are the minimal requirements of plot. Aristotle's minimal plot depends on causality: his beginning, middle, and end are linked by "causal necessity."[3] E. M. Forster's definition of plot similarly depends on cause and effect in its distinction from story: "A plot is also a narrative of events, the emphasis falling on causality. 'The king died and then the queen died,' is a story. 'The king died, and then the queen died of grief' is a plot." Gérard Genette is willing to push even further, finding plot even in the phrases "I walk, Pierre has come." But he later explains that even these most minimalist phrases are narrative because they imply "a transformation, a transition from an earlier state to a later and resultant state."[4] In each of these examples, the most minimal possible plots still must contain events that are linked by cause and effect. A plot must at least have causality: one event must not simply be followed by another event in time; events must follow by consequence. It is exactly this crucial sense of consequence that the omniscient and omnipotent God disallows. A totalizing God in the storyworld of the war in heaven threatens to remove the possibility of consequential action. Without an element of consequence, that is, without one event causing another, the narrative dwindles, receding toward a chain of events that is only barely a plot or even no plot at all. Neither Abdiel's message nor each angelic arm matters—and so the God of monotheism, in his totalizing reach, diminishes the narrative to the point of vanishing.

And yet the war in heaven does not lack plot, and the monotheistic God of *Paradise Lost* is known to us by means of the events of the narrative. As with the other narrative problems of monotheism explored so far—the presence in the storyworld of gods and of God—monotheism pushes toward a silent narrative, but finds means to return from that extreme in order to tell itself. Logically, an omnipotent and omniscient God should be able to take care of plot and history with a snap of the fingers, as Abdiel suggests at the outset of the war. If "with solitary hand / Reaching beyond all limit at one blow," God can finish Satan, why should he limit his omnipotence and turn to the so much less effective arms of angels? Why should there be a war at all? This problem also arises in the Exodus narrative, the foundational assertion in the Hebrew Bible of the monotheistic God's power.[5] There the problem of God's omnipotence weighs heavily, for one cannot help but ask why he does not simply lift the Israelites up and place them in the desert. Why must he repeatedly harden Pharaoh's heart? God himself answers these questions:

> And the Lord said unto Moses, Go in unto Pharaoh: for I have hardened his heart, and the heart of his servants, that I might shew

these my signs before him. And that thou mayest tell in the ears of thy son, and of thy son's son, what things I have wrought in Egypt, and my signs which I have done among them; that ye may know how that I am the Lord. (Exod. 10:1-2)

God has hardened Pharaoh's heart in order to show his signs to Pharaoh and to the Israelites. His signs before Pharaoh are the plagues, but they become story when told in the ears of generations of sons. God has hardened Pharaoh's heart, then, in order to create narrative. Had he simply air-lifted the Israelites, had he exercised his full omnipotence, there would have been no signs, no plague narrative, and therefore no way to know "how that I am the Lord." Similarly, Milton's God allows the war to rage in heaven for two days in order to create the proper conditions for making the Son known. God explains to the Son that he "suffers" the battle to continue,

> that the glory may be thine
> Of ending this great war, since none but thou
> Can end it. Into thee such virtue and grace
> Immense I have transfused, that all may know
> In heaven and hell thy power above compare,
> And this perverse commotion governed thus,
> To manifest thee worthiest to be heir
> Of all things.   (6.701-08)

God has so governed the war in order to "manifest" the Son. The Son's manifestation in his chariot is most immediately for the sake of the warring angels. But just as Moses will turn the plagues into a narrative for his sons, so will Raphael turn the war into a narrative for Adam, and Milton for his readers. Whether in Exodus or *Paradise Lost*, if God's absolute transcendence—his omniscience and omnipotence—were allowed full extension over the actors and actions, there would be no battle, no manifestations or signs, and no narrative. In his absolute reach, God would silence narrative altogether. Yet if the plague cycle or the war in heaven were silenced, there would be no way of knowing "how that I am the Lord"—there would be no means of conceiving of God. The omniscience and omnipotence of the absolutely transcendent God therefore deny the possibility of narrative, but simultaneously depend upon it.

From this problem in monotheistic narrative issues the strange and contradictory episode of Abdiel's news, as well as a series of similar moments in the war in heaven that I will call "local forgetting." In these moments the transcendent God is forgotten, creating the impression that angelic action is consequential. But the forgetting is only local and temporary: the narrative, despite the obviousness of the contradiction, soon swerves back to a perspective that recalls God's omniscience and omnipotence. The forgetting is for the sake of story, as it moves the narrative away from the minimal plot and toward the excitement of heroic action. But the forgetting is also a misconception, as mistaken as Adam is about the Son and Satan when he must be told by Michael, "Dream not of their fight, / As of a duel, or the local wounds / Of head or heel" (12.386–88). So the forgetting must be localized and corrected—for the sake not only of narrative, but also of monotheistic doctrine. Local forgetting is a name for a tendency in book 6 to vacillate between a sense that local action is critically important, and that it is utterly inconsequential. Milton (1) forgets God's totalizing influence in order to give the war narrative consequence and so sublimity; and (2) punctures the sense of consequentiality and, with the bathos of local insignificance, reinserts God into the narrative.

Milton's strategy of local forgetting shapes much of the war in heaven, and becomes a primary means of considering how the monotheistic God fits into the time and space of narrative. When Abdiel finds "Already known what he for news had thought / To have reported," the narrative does risk absurdity. But for Abdiel himself the realization is glorious, and he forgoes the conventional telos of a messenger, an audience for his news, and "gladly" mixes with his friends. Abdiel's pleasure is in God's knowledge, and the entire episode can be seen as an equally happy demonstration of his omniscience. In this light Abdiel's thwarted message is itself a triumphant bit of poetry. It quickly demonstrates God's transcendence of earthly matters, but by coming *after* Abdiel's flight, it simultaneously makes room for heroic narrative. Milton both asserts God's monotheistic omniscience and allows the kind of narrative that otherwise would be silenced by that omniscience.

This negotiation of the disjunction between the monotheistic godhead and narrative depends upon a discontinuity in knowledge: God's omniscience and omnipotence are temporarily forgotten and then suddenly remembered. In this way local forgetting can be jarring and even bathetic—and yet it is precisely the jolt provided by the discontinuity, the sudden reassertion of omniscience and omnipotence, that speaks forcefully about the monotheistic God. This strategy can be felt to be a variation of "the nots of monotheistic theology," with the negation mapped onto plot events: rather than the predicate failing to describe God because it is too human, the series of narrated events fails to shape a storyworld that accurately contains God's transcendence. When the narrative feels incongruous is precisely when it is speaking most eloquently about the nature of the monotheistic God.

The Discontinuous Wound and Bathos

Omniscience and omnipotence disrupt narrative, but Milton does not therefore shy away from the problem—rather than finessing the contradictions between monotheism and narrative, Milton accentuates them. "Omniscience" and "omnipotence" and their cognates appear in the poem no less than 20 times, seven of these in and around the war in heaven. Local forgetting, furthermore, draws attention to its own reversals, resulting in a narrative that makes a show of being contradictory. This is an instance of the vexed texture of monotheistic narrative and its related tendency to be self-conscious. Clearly Milton is making a show of these difficult moments as the war unfolds.

The war narrative begins with Abdiel's news and with his confrontation with Satan, where he makes it clear how foolish a war against God really is. After this preface, when the fighting begins, our initial image is of "Millions of fierce encountering angels" (6.220)—a sublime beginning. But the narrative continues its pattern of vacillating between the heroic pitch of a war story and, what disrupts the story, God's transcendence. So we learn of the awesome power of the angels, "the least" of whom could wield the elements—and then, in the second step of local forgetting, we learn that "the eternal king omnipotent / From his strong hold of heaven high overruled / And limited their might" (6.227–29). Next, once again in direct contradiction to omnipotence, "each on himself relied, / As only in his arm the moment lay / Of victory" (6.238–40). And a few lines later, when "long time in even scale / The battle hung" (6.245–46), Michael himself seems to forget God's omnipotence. Seeing Satan, they square off, and Michael imagines that their duel might be consequential: he is "glad as hoping here to end / Intestine war in heaven" (6.258–59).

Milton then continues to present the confrontation of Michael and Satan as decisive, and so creates a narrative as dynamic and interesting as any war story. The two angels are so powerful that they are compared to gods: "for likest Gods they seemed, / Stood they or moved, in stature, motion, arms / Fit to decide the empire of great heaven" (6.301–03). Here equating Michael and Satan to gods momentarily removes them from the monotheistic system and separates them from the omnipotence of the one God. They and their arms seem capable of deciding the war in heaven. The two combatants then address each other, and again Milton emphasizes their potential for their actions to determine events: "Together both with next to almighty arm, / Uplifted imminent one stroke they aimed / That might determine" (6.316–18). The "one stroke" echoes the "one blow," which, as Abdiel points out, God might have aimed at Satan—their imminent violence seems to replace the power of God.[6] But in Michael's arm, the following lines hasten to add, is a sword that reinserts God's overwhelming power into the narrative: "but the sword / Of Michael from the armoury of God / Was given him tempered so, that neither keen / Nor solid might resist that edge" (6.320–23). In the second step of local forgetting, the narrative swings back to a perspective that includes God, remembering that the weapon, and any action Michael may take, originates in him.

We learn of Michael's sword while he and Satan face each other with arms upraised. When those arms come down and the battle actually begins, we get the most condensed—and therefore most obvious and most effective—example of the vacillations of local forgetting. When Michael lowers his arm, his sword meets,

> The sword of Satan with steep force to smite
> Descending, and in half cut sheer, nor stayed,
> But with swift wheel reverse, deep entering shared
> All his right side; then Satan first knew pain,
> And writhed him to and fro convolved; so sore
> The griding sword with discontinuous wound
> Passed through him, but the ethereal substance closed
> Not long divisible.   (6.323–30)

The battle reaches epic pitch through the immediacy and materiality of the conflict: the physical movement of Michael's sword is enacted in the enjambment of "steep force to smite / Descending"; the consequence, Satan's wound, is fleshed out by "deep entering," and "griding." This materiality boldly asks the reader to consider flesh, and to take Satan's wound as literal. With the sense of a painful, griding wound, the narrative acquires consequentiality—it really does feel that the "moment of victory" lies in Michael's arm. And yet suddenly, after only the space of a caesura, the wound heals. Just like that, it disappears. For if Satan were to be permanently injured, Michael might indeed attain victory by his own action, and such an event would mistakenly conceive of their fight "As of a duel, or the local wounds / Of head or heel." Instead of local wounds we get the discontinuous wound—which reminds us of the essentially inconsequential nature of the battle. For how can the sword fight matter if there is such a short-lived effect? Of what consequence can Michael's swordsmanship be if it leaves no lasting mark on Satan's body? And as the duel is circumscribed, and its consequences limited, the provenance of God's power is maintained. Just as Abdiel's news must be already known, so the "discontinuous wound" must not remain divided. When Michael's griding sword shears off Satan's right side, we are invited, in the heat of the narrative, to forget God's transcendent role. When Satan's wound closes, we are reminded that any lasting consequences come not from angelic arms, but from God.[7]

Local forgetting is a dizzying strategy, requiring a shift of perspective between the transcendence of the divine plane and the spatial and temporal limitations of the human plane of narrative. With the "discontinuous wound" this shift is even further condensed, so that the two perspectives obtain not consecutively but at once. Just as Milton, by means of puns, packs perspectival shifts into "news" and "moment," so he destabilizes the narrative of Satan's wound with the modifier "discontinuous." Calling the wound "discontinuous" may, on the one hand, simply describe its cleavage, emphasizing, as does "griding" the duel's materiality. On the other hand, a wound, by definition, is already a break in the flesh, and a discontinuous wound may be one that does not maintain its incision throughout. That is, Satan's wound may already be healing in places even as it is still being cut. As "discontinuous" comes first in the progression of the narrative, the wound is in fact reknitting Satan's body even as it is cutting it. Satan's discontinuous wound thus condenses the divine and narrative planes into a single place. Even the healing that takes place on the other side of the tiny temporal and spatial divide of the caesura is not close enough to meet the always-already illogic of local forgetting.

In this sense, "discontinuous" modifies not just Satan's wound, but also the entire topos of wounding. It stands for the way that the very idea of a duel, and of the war in heaven as a whole, resists narrative. For the rigorous illogic of local forgetting, here compressed into "discontinuous wound," cuts its own kind of hole in the fabric of the story, and the discontinuous wound names precisely what the monotheistic narrative of the war in heaven cannot fully attain: continuity. Local forgetting enables narrative—but with its injection of illogic, or aporia, it enables a narrative that is disrupted and discontinuous.

The discontinuous wound, like Abdiel's news, represents local forgetting in a highly condensed form. And its intense contradiction and blatant incongruity have left equally incongruous traces in the reception of the war in heaven. For the war and the wound have been received as both the highest of heroic narratives and the lowest of absurd parodies—as both sublime and bathetic. For many of Milton's early readers, book 6 was an example of the grandeur of the poem. "S. B.," presumably Samuel Barrow, praises *Paradise Lost* as a "grandia...Carmina" and spends most of his commendatory poem on the war in heaven. The fighting, in particular the confrontation between Satan and Michael, demonstrates Milton's sublimity and superiority over Homer and Virgil. The Earl of Roscommon also celebrates the war and "Michael's arm," emphasizing the heroic action. John Dennis declares that "there is something so transcendentally sublime in his first, second, and sixth Books." And asserting that sublimity is Milton's "distinguishing excellence," Addison points to the same three books: "It is impossible for the Imagination of Man to distend it self with greater Ideas, than those which he has laid together in his first, second and sixth Books."[8]

At the same time, however, an entirely different reading also emerges: the war in heaven is read as absurd. In the *Rape of the Lock*, Alexander Pope zeroes in on the discontinuous wound, and specifically on the absurdity of a wound that is so inconsequential that it does not stay open. In what Edward Le Comte calls "the most devastating comment ever made on VI," Pope teases Milton for Satan's wound:

> The Peer now spreads the glitt'ring *Forfex* wide,
> T'inclose the Lock, now joins it, to divide.
> Ev'n then, before the fatal Engine clos'd,
> A wretched *Sylph* too fondly interpos'd;
> Fate urg'd the Sheers, and cut the *Sylph* in twain,
> (But Airy Substance soon unites again).[9]   (3.147–52)

Pope's famous sylph mocks the narrative absurdity of staging a duel in which the combatants instantly heal up, as "the ethereal substance closed / Not long divisible" becomes "(But Airy Substance soon unites again)." Pope's joke is appropriate enough in the narrative of a sylph and a lock of hair. But his humor raises more serious questions about *Paradise Lost*, bringing its divine events perilously close to absurdity. For Pope's allusion is faithful—the wound instantly heals in Milton too, and is similarly ridiculous. Pope lays bare the way the discontinuous wound destroys the heroic mood of the narrative and sends the war plummeting into bathos. The wound becomes trivial and even laughable, like the coyote that goes over a cliff only to return with a Band-Aid. So in *Peri Bathous* Pope recommends Milton's devils as an aid to "the art of sinking in poetry."[10]

Samuel Johnson senses the same problem. The rigorous illogic of the discontinuous wound and of the armor and weaponry of the rest of the war in heaven leads to Johnson's famous dismissal: "The confusion of spirit and matter which pervades the whole narration of the war of heaven fills it with incongruity; and the book in which it is related is, I believe, the favourite of children, and gradually neglected as knowledge is increased."[11] Incongruity leads to a sense that the text itself is childish. Arnold Stein later reads the same features of the war as a tendency toward the burlesque. Less willing than Pope and Johnson to view Milton's war as infelicitous, Stein argues that it is intentionally absurd. So that he likens Michael's wounding of Satan to hitting "a man proud of his bearing and composure with a custard pie."[12] By blunting Michael's "griding sword" into custard, the incision and its subsequent healing are covered over. Stein saves Milton from Pope's mockery of the discontinuous wound—Milton meant to be funny. But Stein's burlesque is only reading part of the war in heaven, accentuating the cartoonish elements of book 6 while overlooking the serious and sublime parts that are also present—he sees a custard pie where the text says "griding sword."[13]

The point crucial to understanding monotheistic narrative in the war in heaven is that Milton makes it both a great war story and a burlesque. The contradictions of the discontinuous wound and of local forgetting vacillate between sublimity and bathos. The sublime emerges when the omniscience and omnipotence of God is forgotten, and we are able to read the action as consequential and therefore heroic. This is the "swift wheel reverse" and the "griding sword" of Michael. But bathos emerges with the reinsertion of the totalizing God when we are reminded that the immediacy of narrative means nothing—this is the discontinuous wound, "Not long divisible." The sudden movement between the sublime and the bathetic shuttles the narrative between the forward driving, heroic mood of a martial epic and the ironic, deeply self-aware mood of parody and satire. Neither mood beats out the other—rather, the coexistence of the two can be seen as another facet of Milton's negotiation of the narrative problems of monotheism. Monotheism, with its omniscient and omnipotent godhead, pulls the story into the self-conscious space of irony and parody, where a story cannot unfold with ease and momentum. Milton cannot but allow room for such moments in his monotheistic narrative, but they must share the road with the bluff heroism and decisive action of the war story.

Claims for the sublimity of the war in heaven, therefore, require an overlooking of the bathos. So Addison locates the sublime only by laboring against readings that have been filled with laughter: "It required great Pregnancy of Invention, and Strength of Imagination, to fill this Battel with such circumstances as should raise and astonish the mind of the Reader; and, at the same time, an Exactness of Judgement to avoid everything that might appear light or trivial."[14] Only by expunging the light and trivial can Addison portray a war that, in a sublime manner, astonishes the mind. There is great reason for eliding such laughter, which, after all, is raillery aimed at angels and the sacred history of angelic war. For by pointing to the bathetic, Pope raises a kind of laughter that sounds very much like the skeptical laughter advocated by Shaftesbury, for whom ridicule represents the best test of truth: "For nothing is ridiculous except what is deformed, nor is anything proof against raillery except what is handsome and just."[15] The contradictory presence of the sublime and the bathetic together in the deformed narrative of the discontinuous wound, like much of book 6, cannot stand up to Shaftesbury's proof. And in this susceptibility to skeptical laughter, the war in heaven has the potential to be read as a deist text.

Shaftesbury's philosophy of ridicule so neatly describes the deists' own habit of raillery that many consider him a deist. Outright deists such as Anthony Collins and Thomas Woolston regularly make strategic use of ridicule against the truths of revealed Christianity, making humor "the principal weapon employed to discredit Christian miracles."[16] Parody is a devastating weapon against revealed religion in particular, since revelations combine the potential outlandishness of miracle with a thoroughly serious insistence on authority. So as Lord Bolingbroke reads *The Rape of the Lock* in an essay addressed to Pope, mockery makes the machinery of *Paradise Lost* indistinguishable from pagan superstition:

> (Homer) meant to flatter his countrymen, by recording the feats of their ancestors, the valor of some, and the prudence of others; and he employed for the machinery of his poem the theology of his age, as Tasso and Milton have employed that of theirs. Had Arnobius, and much more such a weak philosopher as Justin, or such a warm rhetor as Tertullian, lived in our days, you would have been attacked in your turn, and have been made the father of rosycrusianism, and of all the silly doctrines about sylphs and gnomes; just as reasonably as Homer has been attacked, by the

zeal of Christian writers, for teaching polytheism and idolatry. (Bolingbroke 3:235–36)

Milton's angelic machinery is grouped with that of Homer and Pope: all such revelation is superstition and polytheism in the eyes of Bolingbroke the deist.[17] Reading Milton and Pope's machinery as identically ridiculous, Bolingbroke not only undermines the local revelations of angels, but by extension rejects the Judeo-Christian revelation, which would separate Christian angels from the mythology of Homer and Pope. The deism is explicit in Bolingbroke's reading and is implicit in Pope's parody—but it is also part of Milton's poem, for a silly war in heaven threatens to become a deist war in heaven.

Milton and Deism

When Milton weaves moments of bathos into the sublime story of the angelic revolt, he runs the risk of debasing and discrediting crucial divine events. It is just such a perceived lack of seriousness in the war which goads Charles Leslie, touching off the early reception's most virulent attack on *Paradise Lost*, *The History of Sin and Heresie* (1698). Meditating on the feast of Saint Michael, Leslie takes as his text Revelations 12:7, "There was War in Heaven," but endeavors "to give a more *Serious* Representation of that *War* in *Heaven*," than "*Milton's* Groundless Supposition."[18] What makes Milton's war heretical is that: "The Gravity and Seriousness with which the Subject ought to be treated, has not been Regarded in the Adventurous Flight of Poets, who have Dress'd Angels in Armor, and put Swords and Guns into their Hands, to Form Romantick Battles in the Plains of Heaven, a Scene of Licentious Fancy" (Leslie, *Sin and Heresie*, A2r). For Leslie the battles of romance and epic lack seriousness, as if the material attributes of literary war narratives are not sufficiently religious. From Leslie's rigorously aniconic perspective, the anxiety is that Milton's machinery has made the war in heaven too much of a spectacle, opening up the sacred event to subsequent degradation among wits: "but the Truth has been Greatly Hurt thereby, and Degraded at last, even into a Play, which was Design'd to have been Acted upon the Stage: And tho once happily Prevented, yet has Pass'd the Press, and become the Entertainment of Prophane Raillery" (Leslie, *Sin and Heresie,* A2r–A2v). The "Prophane Raillery" Leslie fears is precisely the ridicule wits such as Shaftesbury are pleased to display.

Or more immediately, wits such as John Toland. In the same year as *The History of Sin and Heresie,* in what is likely a response to Leslie in his *Life of Milton* (1698), Toland defends *Paradise Lost* against charges of heresy: "As to the choice of his Subject, or the Particulars of his Story, I shall say nothing in defence of them against those People who brand 'em with Heresy and Impiety: for to incur the Displeasure of certain ignorant and supercilious Critics, argues free thinking, accurat Writing, and a generous Profession of Truth."[19] Toland's defense is humorously disingenuous. Rather than extricating Milton from charges of heresy, Toland makes a virtue of them: that a divine such as Leslie would see *Paradise Lost* as heretical actually validates Milton's accuracy and truthfulness. For Toland, just as Leslie suspects, is in the process of claiming *Paradise Lost* and Milton for the deists. Elsewhere in *Life of Milton* Toland circumscribes Milton's thought within a decidedly deistic space:

> but in the latter part of his Life, he was not a profest Member of any particular Sect among Christians, he frequented none of their Assemblies, nor made use of their peculiar Rites in his Family. Whether this proceded from a dislike of their uncharitable and endless Disputes, and that Love of Dominion, or Inclination to Persecution, which, he said, was a piece of Popery inseparable from all Churches; or whether he thought one might be a good Man, without subscribing to any Party; and that they had all in som things corrupted the Institutions of Jesus Christ, I will by no means adventure to determin.[20]

Toland aligns Milton and deism with subtle indirection. Less subtle a pairing is Toland's sequel. When an appendix to the *Life* briefly doubted the contours of the New Testament canon, public outrage led Toland to defend his skeptical approach to Scripture at greater length. So we are left with the fascinating accident that one of the most important deist questionings of revealed authority is named *Amyntor; or, Defense of the Life of Milton* (1699).[21]

Milton's name itself had already become a marker for general impiety, and readers then and now have branded him with such heresies as mortalism, Arianism, and Socinianism.[22] But Toland names Milton a freethinker—the charge of heresy "argues free thinking"—and so directs us toward the phrase that soon becomes a synonym, even euphemism, for deism. In *A Discourse of Free Thinking* (1713), Toland's friend Anthony Collins surveys rational, and often radical, theology. Ostensibly, freethinking is merely a claim for a scientific reliance on evidence, but most of the treatise assumes revealed religion to be the main bar to freethinking, making it, despite pious protests, an entirely deistic work. And Collins, like Toland, claims Milton as a freethinker. In addition to those he treats in depth, such as Sophocles, Cicero, and Hobbes, Collins makes a list of freethinkers: "Erasmus, Father Paul, Joseph Scaliger, Cartesius, Gassendus, Grotius, Hooker, Chillingworth, Lord Falkland, Lord Herbert of Cherbury, Selden, Hales, Milton, Wilkins, Marsham, Spencer, Whitchcot, Cudworth, More, Sir W. Temple, and Locke."[23] It is an appropriate genealogy for the rise of English deism, and also a list of thinkers central to the discourse of monotheism.

Late in the deist controversy, when David Hume challenges natural religion in *The Natural History of Religion* (1757), one of his first targets is *Paradise Lost*. Arguing that mankind could not exercise sufficient reason to know God merely through the study of nature, he contests Adam's awakening in book 8:

> *Adam,* rising at once, in paradise, and in the full perfection of his faculties, would naturally, as represented by *Milton,* be astonished at the glorious appearances of nature, the heavens, the air, the earth, his own organs and members; and would be led to ask whence this wonderful scene arose. But a barbarous, necessitous animal (such

as a man is on the first origin of society), pressed by such numerous wants and passions, has no leisure to admire the regular face of nature, or make inquiries concerning the cause of objects, to which, from his infancy he has been gradually accustomed.[24]

Hume recognizes how near that passage is to dramatizing the core tenet of deism's natural religion, that God can be known from the study of nature and without specific revelation. He also seems to find it rhetorically useful, in his argument against deism, to undermine the example of Milton. Hume is working against what emerges as a clear tendency among Milton's readers to assume an affinity between his work and deist ideas—John Shawcross refers to "the continued antagonism which Toland's view of religion raised and which was usually transferred uncritically to Milton."[25]

Only a few critics have noticed this connection between Milton and deism. Joseph Frank surveys Milton's antiprelatical and divorce tracts and his late poetry, and persuasively, if cursorily, evokes Milton's "movement towards deism."[26] J. B. Broadbent suggestively finds an affinity between the God of book 3 and the abstract godhead of deism, but does not develop the insight. William Kolbrenner pursues the connection by arguing that Richard Bentley's "emendations to *Paradise Lost* represent an attempt to distinguish Milton's metaphysics from those of the free-thinkers, republicans and Deists who claimed him for their cause."[27] And Catherine Gimelli Martin has recently traced the strong influence of *Areopagitica* on the deist Charles Blount.[28]

Readers have no doubt been persuaded away from the pairing of Milton and deism by his clear statements in support of the necessity of revelation. Deism is best understood as the period's most forceful challenge to miracle and religious mystery, a challenge that centers on the subversion of revelation. As John Leland, deism's most complete chronicler, explains, deism had "one main end, viz. to set aside revelation, and to substitute mere natural religion, or, which seems to have been the intentions of some of them, no religion at all in its room."[29] And so it is clear that

Milton was not in doctrine a deist when in *De doctrina Christiana* he asserts, "No one, however, can form correct ideas about God guided by nature or reason alone, without the word or message of God" (YP 6:132). And even more dissuasive: it is very hard to imagine how the sensuous and material angels of *Paradise Lost* could be reconciled with a deist rejection of revelation.

In a reversal of expectations, however, the materiality of Milton's divine beings seems to have further contributed to the deist reception. A deist poem would seem to push toward a rational religious economy free from what Bolingbroke calls "pneumatical madness" (Bolingbroke 3:532). It would, we expect, look much more like Davenant's *Gondibert* than Milton's war in heaven. And yet Milton's antideist readers do not seek to revivify a stripped-down and austere version of religion, but rather seek to control the proliferation of Milton's machinery. Milton is received as deistic not because he has constructed a cosmos devoid of the visible Christian agents of revelation, but rather because he has so accentuated them.

It is Milton's shaping of the Christian supernatural into actual beings, with bodies, personalities, and histories, that threatens to become deism in Daniel Defoe's response to *Paradise Lost, The Political History of the Devil* (1726). Maximillian Novak has characterized Defoe's occult writings of 1726–27 as part of his long-standing aversion to such deists as Toland and Collins.[30] While Defoe praises Milton's poetic powers, he is concerned to prevent *Paradise Lost* from being read as literal theology. The problem is that Milton has given sacred history such particularity and materiality that the Bible as a whole can be questioned. Speaking of the angelic rebellion, Defoe makes *Paradise Lost* a catalyst for the rejection of the entire revelation:

> Mr. Milton here takes it upon him to give the History of it as particularly as if he had been born there, and came down hither on purpose to give us an account of it; (I hope he is better inform'd by this time;) but this he does in such a manner, as jostles with Religion, and shocks our Faith in so many points necessary to be

believ'd, that we must forbear to give up to Milton, or must set aside part of the Sacred Text, in such a manner, as will assist some people to set it aside all.³¹

Aware of the deist strategy of using local contradictions and incongruities to invalidate the entirety of Scripture, Defoe fears that the jostling of Milton's "history" assists in marginalizing the Bible. In *A Short and Easie Method with the Deists* (1697), Leslie makes the same observation about deists who believe that "if things be not as they are told in any relation, that Relation must be false. And if false in Part, we cannot Trust to it, either in whole, or in Part.... We must receive all, or Reject all. I mean in any Book that pretends to be written from the mouth of God. For in other common Histories, we may believe Part and reject part, as we see Cause."³²

Accordingly, Defoe ironizes the idea of a history of the devil, making references to the devil as "historian," "chronologist," and "antiquarian," giving ironic credit for such a personal version of Satan to Milton (Defoe, *Political History*, 12, 13, 27). Defoe also denies the devil his traditional iconography, such as the cloven foot, as well as the materiality of the Miltonic hell. The cloven foot, like all material and personal conceptions of the devil, is actually a stratagem to make Christianity seem superstitious: "he finds it his Interest to foster the cheat, and serve himself of the Consequence" (Defoe, *Political History*, 265). This diabolical consequence is disbelief in the revealed specifics of Christianity. And so, while deism skeptically strips away miracle and revelation in constructing an abstract and rational religion, paradoxically Defoe strips Milton's Satan of personality and attributes as a means of combating deism.

In *The History of Sin and Heresie* Leslie reads the profusion of literal detail in *Paradise Lost* with the same anxiety: the problem with Milton's war in heaven is that he has "Dress'd Angels in Armor, and put Swords and Guns into their Hands." Against Milton's material representation of the war, Leslie invokes mystery. Revelation 12:7 is "a Great *Mystery*," and therefore "our

Inquiries must be with Reverence and profound Humility. Why else are they Mysteries?" (Leslie, *Sin and Heresie*, 1). Mystery shuts down rational inquiry, and by inculcating reverence and humility, quiets the raillery that serves the deist cause. Mystery, furthermore, removes the war from the material space that allows for representation and extension in plot. As a corrective to *Paradise Lost*, Leslie goes on to offer his own narrative of the war in heaven. Most of Leslie's version of the war is a midrashic argument between Michael and Satan over the nature of God and the Son's incarnation. After Satan and Michael's argument, Leslie's narrative merely states that "Michael fought" and goes on to lavish praise on his victory (Leslie, *Sin and Heresie*, 11–14). Leslie's war has no armor or guns, no bodies or wounds—his more reverential and more serious representation of Revelation 12:7 is in fact no representation at all. While this may be a perfectly tenable move in a sermon, it is deeply destructive of a poem that depends upon narrative. Leslie's mystery leads to no war narrative—instead to a narratological silence that is exactly what, in monotheistic narrative, Milton must struggle against.

Invoking mystery is the period's most common defense against deism, as mystery turns away the skeptical gaze that has settled on the materiality of revelation. Leslie's insistence on the mystery of the war in heaven is repeated in remarkably similar terms by Richard Bentley, also perhaps in response to Milton. In *A Discourse of Free Thinking*, Collins turns his raillery onto the war. Demonstrating that Socrates was a freethinker, Collins lauds him because he "disbeliev'd the Gods of his Country, and the common Creeds about them, and declar'd his Dislike, when he heard Men attribute Repentance, Anger, and other Passions to the Gods, and talk of Wars and Battels in Heaven, and of the Gods getting Women with Child, and such-like fabulous and blasphemous Storys."[33] Socrates is proven a freethinker—that is, a deist—for disbelieving such superstitious details. In his *Remarks upon a Late Discourse of Free-Thinking* (1713), Bentley recognizes Collins's "talk of Wars and Battels in Heaven" as "pointed against"

Revelation 12:7, complaining, "Now where has this Writer liv'd, or what Idiot Evangelist was he bred under; not to know that This is all Vision and Allegory, and not propos'd as literal truth."[34] William Kolbrenner finds it "irresistible to speculate that Bentley was thinking here also of Milton's 'war in heaven.'"[35] Since Collins lists Milton as a freethinker, it is also possible that his "Wars and Battels in Heaven" derives from *Paradise Lost*. In that case, the "Idiot Evangelist" who Bentley says bred Collins and his deist raillery would be Milton. Once again, then, Milton's war has been recast as mysterious—"all Vision and Allegory"—in order to avoid the deist implications of materiality.

This reversal of expectations, where Milton's material angels carry the import of deism, reflects the intensely problematic nature of Milton's machinery in the war in heaven. Doctrinally, Milton may assert the centrality of revelation, but his poetry seems to assert the opposite. As has been argued, it is particularly the bathos of the war in heaven that undermines the revealed events of Christianity, and so suggests a deist position. Moreover, the bathos comes deeply intertwined with the sublime, recreating in the war in heaven a skeptical perspective very like the rational doubt of deism. When the strange narrative of the discontinuous wound shifts suddenly from the sublime heights of the griding sword to the anticlimactic bathos of the healing wound, it puts the reader in an unstable interpretive position, initiating a calculating and discursive kind of reading. It becomes difficult to know whether the events of the battle are consequential or just a performance, whether to be impressed or to laugh. Such moments of discursive doubt establish in the poetry rational and skeptical thought processes about the event and about revelation itself. And when the war in heaven puts the reader in a doubtful position relative to revelation, leading the reader to ask difficult questions about how angels could act and fight for a totalizing God, the poem has the potential to be read as deistic.

These moments of discursivity result, as the first two parts of this chapter suggest, from Milton's monotheism. The bathos of the discontinuous wound is essential to monotheistic narrative, part of Milton's negotiation between the demands of narrative and the omniscient and omnipotent God. But it is also what leads to Milton's deist reception. Milton's monotheism, then, makes *Paradise Lost* susceptible to deist readings. *De doctrina* makes it clear that Milton was not a deist. But he was a monotheist, and his commitments to the rigors of monotheism were read by Leslie, Toland, Collins, Hume, and Defoe, as well as Pope and Bolingbroke, as deist. These are not so much misreadings as responses to real dynamics in Milton's monotheistic narrative.

These dynamics are most apparent in the writings of John Dennis, who in the reception is the reader most attuned to Milton's monotheism. In several important essays, written over the opening decades of the eighteenth century, Dennis analyzes Christian poetry, paying particular attention to *Paradise Lost*. In Dennis's criticism, the problem of deism, as well as a sharp concern for monotheism, center on Milton's epic machinery.

Dennis and Milton's Christian Machinery

With *The Advancement and Reformation of Modern Poetry* (1701) John Dennis writes the first extended work of criticism on *Paradise Lost*. His central assertion is that Christianity provides better material to the modern poet than polytheism provided to classical predecessors, so that by means of Christian poetry the moderns can surpass the ancients. The main example among the moderns is Milton. Dennis's study continues the seventeenth century movement for Christian poetry, arguing, as Davenant and Cowley do, for Christian subjects. But he is especially focused on the difference between polytheism and monotheism as the crucial distinction between Christian and pagan poetry. Dennis repeatedly notes how the ancients benefit from a polytheistic multitude of revelations: "Oracles, Visions, Dreams, Apparitions: And Gods and Goddesses, Nymphs and Demi-gods, Fawns and Satyrs, were see by Imagination in every Grove" (Dennis 235).

Such polytheism in fact benefits the poet, for revelations result in "enthusiasm" and the raising of passions, which Dennis considers the most essential aim of poetry. Dennis praises the ancients precisely because they are polytheistic, even arguing against the common defense of paganism, occult monotheism: they "had neither any clear Idea of one Supreme Independent Being, nor any tolerable knowledge of the Law of Nature" (Dennis 237). Christian poetry can be as good as or better than classical if it can tap into the same kind of poetic enthusiasm—that is, if it can also make use of revelation. Dennis, however, recognizes how much more difficult revelation is for Christianity, disengaged as it is from polytheism. In arguing for Christian poetry, therefore, Dennis focuses on the possibility of Christian revelation or, in poetic terms, Christian machinery.

From within this consideration of monotheism and polytheism in poetry, Dennis bumps up against, and fends off, deism. Deism surfaces repeatedly in *The Advancement* and is the subject of a surprising and extensive polemical digression: in laying the groundwork for defense of Christian machinery, Dennis devotes 42 pages to a theological discussion against deism. Considering Milton and monotheism and the problem of his machinery, Dennis finds himself in the same treacherous waters as Leslie, Toland, Defoe, and the others. *The Advancement*, published three years after Leslie's polemic and Toland's *Life*, becomes the most thorough rebuttal of the deistic reception of Milton.[36]

Dennis struggles to assert the superiority of Milton's Christian epic over polytheistic predecessors while simultaneously fending off the potential of Milton's monotheism—and this turns out to be a very difficult thing to do. Dennis's sometimes complicated positions reflect the tensions between Milton's poetry and the period's extensive neoclassical debate over Christian machinery. Neoclassical theorists such as Le Bossu, Boileau, and Dryden devoted much thought to whether or not epic machinery, inherited from the classical tradition, is appropriate in a Christian poem. On the one hand, machinery looks very much like polytheism, and therefore must be rejected. On the other hand, machinery is essential to the epic genre, used by Homer, Virgil, and the rest of the classical models.

René Le Bossu, on one side of the debate, insists upon the necessity of machinery to epic, and appears unconcerned with the threat of polytheism in poetry: "Machines are to be made use of all over, since Homer and Virgil do nothing without them"; in fact the use of machinery actually defines a poet: "He therefore that would be a Poet, must leave Historians to write, that a Fleet was shattered by a storm and cast upon a strange coast: And must say with Virgil, that Juno went to Aeolus, and that this God upon her instance unkennel'd the wind against Aeneas." Le Bossu blithely defines machinery as the appearance of gods: "The Gods are usually express'd by the Name of Machines, because the Poets make use of such to let them down upon the Theatre; from whence the Epopéa has likewise borrowed the name." But he recovers monotheistic doctrine by insisting that all such machinery is allegorical: the poet "suits himself to our gross way of conceiving Divine things."[37] Freeing it from the literal, Le Bossu's allegory, like Leslie and Bentley's mystery, implies that true divinity exists and functions in a plane other than the world of the narrative—and that the narrative refers to this divine plane through the mystical process of allegory. Allegory, as a literary form of mystery, saves epic machinery from appearing polytheistic, and therefore makes room for it in Christian epic.

Dryden expresses a commonsensical middle ground in the debate by simply allowing angels, which are authorized by Scripture, to be epic machinery: "Christian Poets have not hitherto been acquainted with their own Strength. If they had search'd the Old Testament as they ought, they might there have found the Machines which are proper for their Work."[38] The use of machinery from Scripture appears to be a simple solution, and one Milton uses in book 1 when he insists upon the angelic, rather than polytheistic, ontology of the gods. Yet adhering to biblical precedent is not an easy matter, short of exactly rewriting

Scripture in Pierre Menard fashion. In his infernal council Milton does not represent angels within the strict parameters of biblical precedent, as the narratological demands of the council lead him to depict the fallen angels proleptically, as polytheistic gods. Similarly, Milton's poetry cannot adhere perfectly to the accommodated language of Scripture: the poet's departures from biblical precedent, for example Adam's argument with God in book 8, cannot have biblical authority. It is telling that Dryden's own original retelling of biblical narrative, "Absalom and Achitophel," has no angelic machinery. The only entrance of the divine occurs in assent to David's last speech, and takes the form of a thunderclap—a stripped-down intervention with no form or body, seemingly designed to avoid the problem of machinery.[39]

The demands of narrative, in other words, complicate for Christian poets all machinery, even if taken from the Bible. And so Nicolas Boileau insists that Christianity must not be mingled at all with the visible figures of epic poetry. In *The Advancement* Dennis translates Boileau's famous verses from *L'art poetique*, where "ornaments" should be understood as machines: "The terrible mysteries of the Christian Faith are not capable of delightful Ornaments; that the Gospel offers nothing to our View, but Repentance on the one side, and eternal Torments on the other; and that the criminal Mixture of Poetical Fictions, gave a fabulous Air even to its most Sacred Truths" (Dennis 1:252). For Boileau there is no place for epic machinery in Christianity because "the Gospel offers nothing to our View"—Christianity denies a visible economy of beings. Recalling the law of the second commandment, Boileau calls machinery in a Christian epic "criminal" and offers an aniconic version of Christianity, which in the debate over machinery is the most rigorously monotheistic.[40]

At the center of this debate is the intuitive association of epic machinery with divine revelation. The intervention of machinery significantly colors a poem's theology, so that the appearance of gods or the wrong kinds of angels can make a poem transgressive, while the proper machinery—or none at all—can preserve a poem's adherence to monotheism. Dennis makes clear the identification of machinery with the workings of revealed religion:

> Now the passages of the Ancient Poets, which seem to have most Religion in them, are either those Addresses by which Men approach'd the Gods, as Invocations, Apostrophes and the like: or those Condescensions, by which the Gods communicated themselves to Men, as Revelations, Machines, etc. the First of which are Duties that belong to universal Natural Religion, the Second to Religion which is Reveal'd, Extraordinary and Miraculous. (Dennis 1:229)

Dennis uses language that is closely engaged with the theological controversies of the later seventeenth century, aligning machinery with revelation and miracle, and opposing these to natural religion. That is, Dennis names epic machinery as a crucial way of distinguishing between a poem aligned with orthodox revealed religion and one aligned with natural religion, which is the domain of deism. But it is epic machinery that causes Dennis profound problems.

Dennis's troubles are first visible in *Remarks upon a Book Entituled Prince Arthur* (1696), his earliest statement on epic. There Dennis quotes approvingly Boileau's rejection of Christian machinery (quoted above), and says that Blackmore's machinery cannot be pleasing because "Christian Machines are quite out of Nature, and consequently cannot delight" (Dennis 1:53, 105). In contrast, "The Heathen machines are enough out of Nature to be admirable, and enough in Nature to delight" (Dennis 1:105). Dennis concludes in agreement with Boileau that materiality should be limited in machinery: "they do not appear to be the most Judicious of Writers, who are seen to be luxuriant in their Descriptions of Angels or Devils, in a Christian poem" (Dennis 1:106). Immediately after, however, he must admit that Milton's machinery could be censured for the same reason. He defends *Paradise Lost* with an argument about the fallen angels' goodness, but the defense is weakly beside the point—following Boileau gets Dennis into trouble with *Paradise Lost* (Dennis 1:106–8).

And so in *The Advancement*, Dennis changes his mind. Recommending the use of Christianity by the moderns, he immediately runs up against Boileau's objection to Christian machinery. Dennis revisits the Boileau passage, only here he hedges his statement:

> we only made use of this Passage in the foremention'd Treatise, to shew, That the Mysteries of the Christian Religion were not to be mix'd with Fiction, and consequently, that it would be a hard matter to contrive Machines for an Epick Poem, upon a Modern Christian Subject; and if Boileau means any thing more by the foremention'd Passage, I shall endeavour to shew that he is mistaken and that there may not only be most exalted Poetry upon a Christian Subject, without Machines, and without Fiction, but that the True Religion, is more favourable to Poetry than Paganism, or Philosophy or Deism. (Dennis 1:252)

Dennis wants to prove that Christianity is consistent with poetry, and this is identical with an advocacy of Milton: his argument that a Christian subject will elevate modern poetry above the ancients is largely defended with passages from *Paradise Lost*. The main clog, though, is machinery, and Dennis captures perfectly the narratological difficulty that permeates the war in heaven when he says that contriving machinery for a Christian epic is a "hard matter."

Because of such difficulty, Dennis's justification of Christian machinery in poetry is not by positive assertion but comparative statement. Dennis does not say that true religion can use machinery, but that it is "more favourable" to poetry than other religions. The acceptability of Christian machinery therefore rests upon the rejection of the heretical extremes: whatever the difficulties it presents to machinery, Christianity is still more favorable to poetry than paganism, philosophy, and deism. In the following chapter *Paradise Lost* is compared to Virgil's pagan machinery. But before Dennis proceeds to this evidence, he gives a full 42 pages to disposing of philosophy and deism. Philosophy he takes as the general elevation of reason over passion, and uses it mostly as an entrance into his discussion of deism. Dennis's argument for Christian machinery, therefore, proceeds via deism—it is only after deism is rejected, in fact only by means of that rejection, that Christian, and specifically Milton's, machinery can be defended.[41]

Proving that Christianity is favorable to poetry, Dennis argues that passion is the true end of poetry, and that religion, whether pagan or Christian, is the most valuable subject of poetry because it raises the highest form of passion, "enthusiasm." In contrast, deism, lacking revelation, combats the passions and offers proof only to human reason. Dennis argues that the masses are incapable of understanding such purely rational proofs:

> all are capable of the Proofs of Revealed Religion: For, by proving the Divinity of the Revelation, the Doctrine is proved in course. But Miracles are Proofs of which all Men are capable, because they speak to the Passions, and appeal to the Senses. Since therefore, the True Religion must be design'd for all; and all Men are capable of the Proofs of Reveal'd Religion, whereas not one in Forty is capable of the Proofs of Deism, it follows, that a Religion that is not Reveal'd, cannot be the True Religion. (Dennis 1:259)

Deism is rejected because, in denying miracles and revelation, it cannot offer sufficiently passionate, and therefore convincing, evidence of the divine. Christian revelation is more passionate than deist argument, and it also, Dennis insists, harmonizes passion and reason. Such harmony between passion and reason, which is absent in deism, makes Christianity less open to ambiguity:

> For, after that Christianity has gain'd its Professors, by proving after the most plain and simple manner, all that is necessary to be believ'd in it; that is, by Miracles, attested by the unexceptionable Witnesses, it gains its End, which is the Happiness of its Believers, in so plain, so sure, and so short a Way, that the Way to Happiness, and the End, is but one and the same Thing. (Dennis 1:260)

There is no equivocation in revealed religion, as miracles and revelation convince totally and immediately, so that the "way" and the "end" are the same. Deism fails, in contrast, because rational argument requires a process that must engage and logically overcome potential moments of contradiction. Deism gets caught in the labyrinths of thought, of argument and counterargument, and thus proves itself in dilatory time. Without revelation and its recourse to mystery for explanation, deism offers only the kind of rational and discursive evidence of the divine that, in its lack of immediacy and passion, loses most people: "Thus the Proofs of Christianity are short and plain, and its Doctrine that leads to Felicity, admirably short and unperplexed, whereas the Proofs of Deism are abstruse" (Dennis 1:261).

It is against this sense of discursiveness and perplexity that Dennis justifies Christian machinery. Deism, and therefore deist poetry, entangles one in the mazes of ratiocination. Without revelation and its poetic equivalent, machinery, deism struggles to prove the divine, and succeeds mostly in creating a morass of discursive and rational argument. In contrast, Christianity and Christian poetry easily secure happiness through harmonizing reason and passion. Stressing the necessity of decorum, Dennis ejects "discord"—that is, the kind of perplexity and discursiveness that he has associated with deism (1:263–64). The harmony and continuity of decorous poetry, moreover, are specifically associated with Christian machinery. The key to this kind of decorum, passion, is represented as an angel: "the Passions, as it were, in a fiery Vehicle, transport the Reason above Mortality, which mounting, soars to the Heaven of Heavens" (1:261). In "fiery vehicle," Dennis uses a common term for angelic beings, aligning the success of Christian poetry with the literal functioning of angels. Dennis then provides a vision of the successful poem that is nothing less than a profusion of angelic beings and miraculous revelations: "he who is entertain'd with an accomplish'd Poem, is, for a time, at least, restored to Paradise. That happy Man converses boldly with Immortal Beings. Transported, he beholds the Gods ascending and descending, and every Passion, in its Turn, is charm'd, while his Reason is supremely satisfied" (1:264). In this vision of a supernatural cosmos, angels represent Dennis's hopes for

Christian poetry: the harmony of passion and reason, and the easy commerce between the human and heavenly worlds. Coming just after his polemic against deism, the vision secures machinery and revelation as essential to Christian poetry.

This vision, furthermore, is of *Paradise Lost*. Dennis's idea of an "accomplish'd Poem" repeatedly echoes Milton's: in a restoration to paradise (*PL* 1.5); in its "happy" man, picking up Milton's favorite modifier of the prelapsarian state (1.29, 3.66, 5.234, 12.642, and so on); in the frequent ascent and descent of angels; and in the bold conversation with immortal beings (3.13, 5.358, 8.367). Dennis makes *Paradise Lost* his main example of Christian poetry—the proof for all his arguments—and it is particularly Milton's machinery that characterizes this vision of the perfect poem. But significantly, it is only after deism is dismissed that Milton's machinery can be appreciated.

Forgetting the Discontinuous Wound

Dennis recognizes the deist potential in Milton, but fights for his country's poet by insisting on his clear distance from deism. This is in fact a reinvention of Milton, and one that depends upon a thorough misreading of *Paradise Lost*. For the "accomplish'd Poem" Dennis describes is decorously without discontinuous wounds: Dennis blinds himself to Milton's bathos in order to engage in his own local forgetting of deism. Milton's machinery is truly a hard matter, and throughout his critical writings Dennis finesses its complications.

At first his response is simply to ignore. While *The Advancement*, through its polemic against deism, establishes machinery as necessary to religious proof, when Dennis turns to *Paradise Lost* he curiously offers no examples of machinery. Rather, he focuses only on the Creation—a sublime narrative, but one that, with the total abstraction of the divine fiat as its crux, shies away from machinery. At the end Dennis gestures toward those parts of Milton's poem that do involve machinery: "I thought to have proceeded, and to have compar'd the Councils and Fights of Virgil and Milton; and above all, their Description of Hell and its Torments; in which both those great Poets seem to have exerted all their Strength. But I am afraid I have already run into Length, and there is Matter remaining for an intire Volume" (Dennis 1:278). If revealed Christianity is truly favorable to poetry, even in the hard matter of machinery, then councils, wars, and the underworld would seem to be the obvious places to prove it. Dennis dodges these, and any reading of machinery, citing lack of space. Yet in his next volume, *The Grounds of Criticism in Poetry* (1704), which is explicitly a continuation of *The Advancement,* Dennis mostly discusses the invocations and hymns in *Paradise Lost,* again avoiding machinery. His one approach to the matter of machinery is his praise of Raphael's descent (*PL* 5.266–87), a passage that, in its untroubled and evocative presentation of angelic visitation, resembles Dennis's vision of an "accomplish'd Poem."

This avoidance of Milton's machinery continues until the *Letters on Milton and Wycherley* (1721–22). There Dennis finally turns to the war in heaven, but Milton's machinery continues to perplex, creating in Dennis's criticism disturbing holes. Finally reading the machinery, Dennis simply excises the bathos. Chastising Addison for failing to exalt Milton over Homer, Dennis insists that the war in heaven, because it is so much more exalted than Homer's subject matter, must be more sublime. To prove it, Dennis quotes at length from the beginning of the battle (*PL* 6.203–23). This passage ends with Milton's flight into the heroic strain:

> Millions of fierce encountering angels fought
> On either side, the least of whom could wield
> These elements, and arm him with the force
> Of all their regions. (6.220–23)

He argues that if the least angel has so much power, then millions will have sublimely unutterable power. And then Dennis moves on to another image of angelic self-sufficiency, the familiar "each on himself relied, / As only on his arm the moment lay / Of victory" (6.238–40). In demonstrating Milton's sublimity, Dennis accentuates the power and consequence of the fighting angels. But Dennis here elides what I have suggested is the crucial quality of Milton's war, the sudden and contradictory descent from the heroic strain into the bathos created by God's omnipotence. In moving from line 223 to line 238, Dennis jumps over the detail that "the eternal king omnipotent / From his strong hold of heaven high overruled / And limited their might" (6.227–29). While Milton insists on the contradiction between God's omnipotence and the consequence—"moment"—of each angelic arm, Dennis effaces it.

Dennis goes on to quote three more times "The least of whom could wield these Elements / And arm him with the Force of all their Regions" (changing the enjambment, as if to bring it nearer to the heroic couplet) as he builds up to Michael and Satan's duel. Finally he gets to the "transcendentally Sublime" (Dennis 2:227): "Together both with next to almighty arm, / Uplifted imminent one Stroke they aimed / That might determine, and not need repeat, / As not of power, at once" (6.316–19). The heroic sense of power and of its consequentiality, the sense that the strokes that Michael and Satan aim matter, form the foundation of Dennis's argument. But having drawn our attention to this sublime moment of Christian machinery, Dennis suddenly gives up on book 6, and, to finish his letter, turns to the image of Satan adjourning the council of book 2 (2.506–09). The sublimity of the duel reminds Dennis of the sublimity of Satan, another example of machinery. But when Dennis leaves Michael and Satan with their arms upraised, he again turns away at the very height of consequentiality: just as the "moment" of victory lays in each angelic arm, so "with next to Almighty Arm" Michael and Satan aim blows that will "determine." Based upon the apparent power of the angelic combatants, the duel seems really to be consequential. Opportunistically quoting, Dennis establishes the sublimity of machinery, then runs before it is put to the Miltonic test. For in cutting away from Michael and Satan, leaving them frozen like Pyrrhus, Dennis edits out the influence of God. In the four lines after Dennis stops quoting, Milton describes Michael's sword, given "from the armoury of God"—God returns to the narrative, reminding us that the heroic and sublime pitch of the duel depended upon God's exclusion. And Dennis leaves out what necessarily follows from the reminder of God, the contradiction and bathos of Satan's discontinuous wound. Michael's sword meets Satan's "with steep force to smite / Descending," and sheers Satan's right side, cutting with "griding sword" Satan's "discontinuous wound"—"but the ethereal substance closed / Not long divisible." Milton carefully makes bathos as prominent as the sublime, a crucial reminder that true power rests not in angelic arms but in the omnipotence of the monotheistic God. But for the sake of his defense of Milton's machinery—in order to show its sublimity—Dennis studiously ignores the bathos.

According to Dennis, Christian revelation proves itself "in so plain, so sure, and so short a Way, that the Way to Happiness, and the End, is but one and the same Thing." But deism, by becoming involved in rational argument, does not convince easily or immediately. Its reliance on drawn-out, discursive proofs, its detours into ratiocination, mean that "not one in Forty is capable of the Proofs of Deism." As long as the war in heaven is read only for sublimity, as long as Michael and Satan are frozen with the "next to almighty arms," Milton and his machinery demonstrate the efficacy of Christian poetry and Christianity itself—"And thus Christianity performs in a Moment, what Philosophy and Deism have for Ages in vain attempted" (Dennis 1:261). But as soon as the arms come down, the moment, in both senses of the word, stops being single and immediate. The healing wound opens up the labyrinths of equivocation; contradiction undermines decorum; bathos threatens the efficacy of sublimity; and revelation undergoes skeptical appraisal. The reader is suddenly thrown back upon the skeptical calculation that so characterizes Milton's monotheistic narrative. And this sense of calculation not only threatens Dennis's defense of Christian machinery, but also threatens to make Milton's epic feel deistic. This determination to ignore bathos makes clear how radical a move it would be to notice it.

Dennis's last forgetting of the discontinuous wound itself reaches absurdity in its remarkable effort to ignore. In *Remarks upon Mr. Pope's Rape of the Lock* (1728), Dennis criticizes Pope for deploying inconsequential machinery: "for what he calls his machinery has no Manner of Influence upon what he calls his poem, not in the least promoting, or preventing, or retarding the Action of it" (Dennis 2:328). Pope's machines, Dennis goes on, "do not in the least influence that Action; they neither prevent the danger of Belinda, nor promote it, nor retard it, unless, perhaps, it may be said, for one Moment, which is ridiculous" (Dennis 2:337). This one "Moment" of consequentiality, of course, is Pope's version of the discontinuous wound, where "A wretched *Sylph* too fondly interpos'd; / Fate urg'd the Sheers, and cut the *Sylph* in twain, / (But Airy Substance soon unites again)." As Geoffrey Tillotson notes, Dennis often fails to realize that the poem is mock epic.[42] Absurdly, Dennis neglects the satire altogether and taxes Pope for ridiculousness that clearly originates in Milton. Dennis insists upon finding nothing funny in the war in heaven, and so preserves, however forcibly, his lasting judgment that book 6 is "transcendentally sublime."

The local forgetting of Milton's text has had its effect on Dennis's reading. His misreadings are, in a way, subtly attuned to the dynamics of Milton's monotheistic narrative, as he legibly overlooks the bathos in his celebration of the sublime. His enthusiasm for forgetting, however, does misconstrue the war as purely sublime—and this is a judgment with an orthodox motive. For the humor and raillery that can result from Milton's bathos debases Christian machinery and revelation, bringing it near, as Bolingbroke sees it, to Pope's sylphs. In *The Advancement* Dennis carefully rebuts deism, and in his reading of the discontinu-

wound he does the same, for deism is the party of bathos, and a sublime Milton is a Milton liberated from deism.

In the reception of *Paradise Lost*, Dennis is usually credited with being the critic who first develops an extended argument for Milton's sublimity, as well as "the first English critic to make sublimity the keystone of his poetics."[43] *The Letters on Milton and Wycherley*, in fact, are designed to prove that Dennis had preceded Addison in judging Milton sublime. He has "for these last Thirty Years admir'd *Milton* above them all for one thing, and that is for having carried away the Prize of Sublimity from both Ancients and Moderns" (Dennis 2:221). He then quotes from Addison's more famous *Notes upon the Twelve Books of Paradise Lost* in order show both his precedence and that he had considered Milton even more sublime than had Addison (Dennis 2:221–24). Dennis is right to say that he was first and more comprehensive. And his writings show that the impression of Milton as sublime emerged as a way to argue for Christian machinery and against a deistic rejection of revelation. Milton is sublime by means of Dennis's determined forgetting of bathos, suggesting that the sublime Milton, so familiar to centuries of readers, is a Milton engineered away from deism.

Looking back on Dennis and his argument for Christian machinery, Isaac Watts suggests that, "if his proposal of criticism had been encouraged and pursued, the nation might have been secured from the danger of deism."[44] It did not work on the eighteenth century as a whole. But Dennis's criticism, by constructing the sublime Milton, did help secure Milton's reputation from the taint of deism. The sublime Milton, furthermore, not only hides Milton's deist potential, but also hides a full understanding of Milton's monotheism and its contradictory and incongruous narrative texture. And so, as part of the recent critical effort to recover the early reception's strong sense of Milton's heretical leanings, and as part of this study's effort to articulate the impact of monotheism on Milton's poetry, we do well to return to

Dennis's opponent, Alexander Pope. His *Essay on Man,* addressed to Lord Bolingbroke, recognizes that laughter is unavoidable in Milton's theodicy: "Laugh where we must, be candid where we can; / But vindicate the ways of God to Man."[45] It is Pope's more honest, ironic, and bathetic reading of *Paradise Lost* that suggests that the poet was of the deists' party, although perhaps without knowing it.

FIVE

Socinianism and Deism
THE DISCOURSE OF MONOTHEISM

The last chapter described the war in heaven's "deist potential"—qualities that attracted a reception as deist, but are better described in terms of monotheism. Milton's monotheism could be read as deism because the seventeenth century discourse of monotheism itself cuts a path through the early stages of English deistic thought and is central to deism's emergence as a public heresy in the eighteenth century. The discourse of monotheism and deism go together in several ways: the assertion of a single God leads to the absolute abstraction of the deist godhead; the aniconism of monotheism encourages the erasure of revelation in the natural religion of the deists; and deism views itself as expressing a purer form of monotheism. So deism makes an endpoint for the discourse of monotheism in this study, and produces the most complete articulation of monotheism in the period, Lord Bolingbroke's essay "Farther Reflections on the Rise and Progress of Monotheism," which appears to be the first text to declare its subject matter to be "monotheism."[1]

A focus on the single God and a deep concern for the implications of monotheism on Christianity are in fact present in much of the rational religion of the later seventeenth century. Among latitudinarians, Henry More's associate Ralph Cudworth engages often with the perspectives of the discourse of monotheism in *The True Intellectual System of the Universe* (1678). Cudworth, for example, moderates More's position on occult monotheism, admitting that many pagans believed in one God but insisting that they were still idolatrous for their worship of other gods. In the first use of the word "monotheism" that I have found after More's, Cudworth concludes, "And thus the Pagan Theists were both Polytheists and Monotheists in different sences, they acknowledged both many Gods and One God."[2] Edward Stillingfleet's *Origines Sacrae* (1666) touches upon polytheistic religion in detail in his discussion of the defects of Phoenician, Egyptian, Chaldean, and Greek history. And John Locke's *The Reasonableness of Christianity* (1695) picks up on many of the themes familiar from the discourse of monotheism, including polytheism, the abstract single God, God's personality, mystery, miracle, and revelation.

However, the imperatives of monotheism, in particular its demand for a single, exclusionary God and its drive toward purer forms of aniconism, tend to push theologians into ever more rational positions. With latitudinarians seeking a *via media*, it is the more radical Socinians and deists who articulate the most extreme monotheistic positions. Socinians reconstruct basic Christianity in rational and monotheistic terms, to the point of denying the Trinity.[3] Deists pursue the aniconic imperative of monotheism to the point of rejecting miracles, angels, and all revelation.[4] Within the discourse of monotheism it is apparent what historians of seventeenth century rational religion have generally said about latitudinarians, that they absorbed many of the insights of rational religion, but blunted the most radical implications.[5] Socinians and deists, by contrast, were willing heretics, and pursued monotheism to transgressive conclusions.

Monotheism does seem to call forth a drive for purity.[6] The seventeenth century trajectory toward purely rational conceptions of the monotheistic God appears as a kind of arms race, which the deists think they have won. So Charles Blount and Charles Gildon, whose *Oracles of Reason* (1693) is a landmark of public English deism, celebrate the monotheism of the deist God as the culmination of a long historical progression: "The Jew and the Mahometan accuse the Christian of Idolatry, the Reform'd Churches, the Roman, the Socinian the other Reformed Churches, the Deists the Socinian, for his *Deus factus*; but none can accuse the Deist of Idolatry, for he only acknowledges one Supream, Everlasting God, and thinks magnificently of him."[7] For Blount and Gildon, deism is to be understood as a fulfillment of the logic of monotheism, the best answer to its rejection of all other idols, and the most magnificent, because most abstract, expression of God. Additionally, in the passage can be seen the breaking of the Trinity, both in the Jewish and Islamic rejection of Christianity and in the deist rejection of the Socinian Son. When removed from the godhead, the Son typically becomes a created being, which for the deists appears as a *Deus factus*, an idol. This deist sense of enlightened monotheism organizes Socinianism and deism as progressive steps in the seventeenth century effort at a pure monotheism. Both Socinian Antitrinitarianism and deist natural religion lead down the same rationalizing and monotheizing trajectory, with the deists going further.

This chapter focuses on Socinianism and deism as monotheistic theologies in the hope that their extreme positions will best articulate the discourse of monotheism in the later seventeenth century. It describes several of the ways in which Socinians and deists theorize and rely upon the concept of the single God, as well as their continuities with earlier thinkers in the discourse of monotheism. The centrality of monotheism to these two well-known schools of thought eventually will elucidate how monotheism matters to Milton's last poems, *Paradise Regained* and *Samson Agonistes*. This chapter forms the beginning of an argument for Socinianism and deism as contexts for Milton's late experiments with monotheistic poetry.[8]

Socinianism and the Trinity

Several Antitrinitarian heresies, including Arianism, can be traced from the patristic period.[9] But in the sixteenth century, within the revolutions of Reformation thought, Socinianism emerged as the most potent opposition to the Trinity, beginning with the death of Michael Servetus in 1553, burned at the stake for his arguments against the Trinity.[10] In 1565 was founded the Minor Reformed Church of Poland, in Raków, which went on, under Fausto Sozzini, to publish a great number of progressive tracts that not only argued against the Trinity, but also for religious toleration and a rational approach to Scripture. Among these is *The Racovian Catechism* (1605), which became a manifesto of Socinianism that spread through Europe. Many of these texts circulated in England in the early seventeenth century, and, according to H. John McLachlan, were of particular interest to the liberal theologians at Great Tew.[11] Antitrinitarian expressions, however, remained muted in the first half of the seventeenth century.

But an explosion of Socinian thought and publication in England occurred midcentury. The best-known Socinian was John Biddle, whose overt arguments against the Trinity in the 1640s and 1650s brought forth censorship and landed him in prison on several occasions. As a polemicist writing from both prison and exile, Biddle produced several texts that captured the debates of the moment, including *A Confession of Faith Touching the Holy Trinity* (1648) and *A Twofold Catechism* (1654).[12] A number of other Socinian texts also came onto the scene. Thomas Lushington's *Expiation of a Sinner* (1646) was a translation of the Socinian Johan Crell's commentary on Hebrews. In 1648 Milton's friend John Goodwin translated Acontius's *Satanae stratagemata*. The Latin *Racovian Catechism* was printed in London in 1651, titled *Catechesis ecclesiarum quae in Regno Poloniae*, a book apparently licensed by Milton. And an English translation, probably done by Biddle and spelled *Racovian Catechisme*, appeared the following year. *The Two Books of John Crellius* appeared anonymously translated in 1665. Of course, anti-Socinian tracts emerged too, including Francis Cheynell's *The Rise, Growth, and Danger of Socinianisme* (1643), Edmund Porter's *God Incarnate* (1655), and John Owen's *Vindiciae evangelicae* (1655).

Within these Socinian debates, opposition to the Trinity is regularly couched in claims for a purer monotheism. The orthodox godhead appears as idolatrous and polytheistic. Biddle, for example, begins his preface to *A Confession of Faith* with the full-voiced, biblical rhetoric of idolatry: "The History of the Old Covenant everywhere relateth how the Israelites went a whoring after Idols, and could by no means be held close to the Lord their God. And it had been well for us, if this Fickleness of retaining God in Knowledge had not seized Christians also." He goes on to claim that the Antitrinitarian position represents a further purification of Protestantism: "For tho Luther and Calvin deserve much Praise for the Pains they took in cleansing our Religion from sundry Idolatrous Pollutions of the Roman Antichrist, yet are the Dregs still left behind, I mean the gross Opinion touching three Persons in God" (Biddle, *A Confession*, D4r–v). Just as Blount and Gildon later claim deism is the purest expression of monotheism, so Biddle views his Antitrinitarianism as a more complete stripping away of idolatrous and polytheistic elements.[13] Appeals to the monotheism of the Hebrew Bible are particularly powerful in Antitrinitarian polemic. The first commandment is a ready support for Socinians, and a favorite of Milton's in *De doctrina*, where, for example, he points out that the Son quotes the first commandment as "the clearest possible testimony, the Father is that one true God from whom are all things" (YP 6:214).[14]

The concept of monotheism is flexible, however, and also serves the other side of the argument. Francis Cheynell finds that by making the Son human rather than divine, Socinians are guilty of their own worst charge: "None pretend to be greater enemies to Idolatry, then the *Socinians*, and yet they doe clearly maintain this Idolatrous principle, namely that *divine Honour* may be given to one whom they conceive to be a meer man, Christ blessed for ever."¹⁵ Similarly, More's second use of the word "monotheisme" argues against Antitrinitarians by claiming monotheism for the orthodox godhead: "They destroy the worship of the Son of God under an ignorant pretence of Monotheisme; whereas the more distinct knowledge of that one God does not make us less Monotheists than they."¹⁶ Everyone, of course, wants to be monotheistic. That the idea of a single God supports both sides of the Antitrinitarian debates demonstrates the urgency of the monotheistic imperative, as well as its resistance to solution. When both Antitrinitarians and their orthodox opponents can claim monotheism for their side, then it becomes clear that monotheism is not itself a determining force in the debates as much as the battleground on which the conflict takes place. Using Jan Assmann's vocabulary, we can say that in the debates over the Trinity, both sides together are at work on the Mosaic distinction, that line which distinguishes true monotheism from false polytheism. Debates over the Trinity at midcentury, taken together, articulate the concept and the consequences of a single God, and so mark an important movement in the discourse of monotheism.

Where Milton fits into these Antitrinitarian debates has engendered much scrutiny among his readers. The very fact of Milton's Antitrinitarianism has always been a contentious issue. Milton's early reception was clearly well attuned to it: John Dennis casually suggests that Milton "was a little tainted with Socinianism," and Daniel Defoe and Jonathan Richardson, among others, associate him with Arianism.¹⁷ Milton's radicalism, however, has undergone what Joseph Wittreich calls an "ambush"—in the centuries after these early readers it has been repressed and reconfigured as orthodoxy.¹⁸ The collaborative work of W. B. Hunter, C. A. Patrides, and J. H. Adamson, *Bright Essence: Studies in Milton's Theology,* is the strongest voice for an orthodox Trinity in Milton's works. And Hunter's questioning of the provenance of *De doctrina* should be regarded as a continuation of the effort of *Bright Essence:* the ejection of *De doctrina* from the canon would have disallowed, among other things, Kelley's convincing parallels between it and the doctrines of Arianism and Socinianism.[19] At this point, however, *De doctrina* has been convincingly defended. And recent criticism has begun the important work of recovering Milton's heretical positions, particularly on the Trinity, from orthodox constructions.[20] It is safe to begin from the assumption that in his later years Milton was not an orthodox Trinitarian.

Even granting Milton's Antitrinitarianism, what to call it has also been a source of debate. He has been associated with the Antitrinitarian reformers Servetus and Bernardino Ochino, with Unitarianism and Socinianism, with subordinationism, and with orthodoxy.[21] Frequently Milton has been called an Arian: Kelley, for example, calls *Paradise Lost* "an Arian document."[22] If one has to pick, Arian may be the most fitting label, given the Son's clearly divine existence prior to the Incarnation in *Paradise Lost*.[23] But it is surprising that both the authors of *Bright Essence* and Bauman give very little consideration to the more radical Antitrinitarian school of Socinianism, since in Milton's period a Socinian controversy raged, while significantly less was said publicly about the third century writer Arius. The strongest historical connection we have between Milton and Antitrinitarianism is with the key Socinian document, the *Racovian Catechism*. As secretary for foreign languages in 1651, Milton licensed a Latin edition of the *Racovian Catechism*, demonstrating his familiarity with Socinianism's central expression.[24]

Ultimately, Christopher Hill is right to dismiss the "great pother" made over how to label Milton's theology, arguing that it is too "eclectic" to fit a single heresy.[25] Here Milton will simply be called an Antitrinitarian—and a monotheist, which term has the virtue of describing structural principles in Milton's thought without having to squeeze his theology under a single proper name. Nevertheless, attention to the points of controversy within the Socinian debates of the period are helpful. Socinian texts are current and part of public controversy in the crucial period of the 1640s and 1650s, when Milton seems to have developed his Antitrinitarian views.[26] And the radicalness of Socinianism highlights the contours of Milton's Antitrinitarian theology, as is clear from the way Milton uses Socinian positions as extreme cases in *De doctrina Christiana*. There is no cause to decide that Milton was a Socinian: as will be discussed in the next chapter, he is quite clear in *De doctrina*, as well as in *Paradise Lost* and *Paradise Regained*, that he does not agree with key elements of Socinian Christology. Nevertheless, Milton's proximity to Socinian thought is palpable, and comparisons serve to delineate what is at stake when Milton rejects the Trinity. While Milton should not share the label of Socinian with Biddle and the others, they all should share the label of monotheist.

Our key text in the discourse of monotheism, *An Explanation of the Grand Mystery of Godliness*, in addition to being the text in which Henry More coins "monotheisme," is also largely involved in defending the Trinity. As More argues for the necessity of Christian mystery in general, he quickly asserts the truth of the Trinity, against what is by 1660 a widespread Antitrinitarian discourse. More's title is itself a riposte in the debates. The "Mystery of Godliness" is from 1 Timothy 3:16, a text that was commonly read as proof of the mystery of God's incarnation in the Son.[27] The *Racovian Catechism*, however, argues that the word "God" in "God was manifested in the flesh" is not in the Greek and so "nothing certain can be concluded out of this place" (*Racovian* 55). Milton makes the same case in *De doctrina*, relying on Erasmus's authority in finding the passage corrupt (YP 6:244).[28] While both *De doctrina* and the *Racovian Catechism* argue against the "Mystery of Godliness" as proof of the Son's equal divinity, More uses it as a clear scriptural proof of the Trinity.

More's overarching assertion of the centrality of mystery strikes at seventeenth century rational religion as a whole. More opposes rational religion that has been taken too far, so that mystery becomes entirely excluded (matching what was argued in chapter 2 concerning occult monotheism). Such extreme rationality was commonly deployed by Socinians against the mystery of the Trinity. Socinian discourse is full of claims such as Biddle's against the Athanasian position of three persons in one godhead: "For who is there (if at least he dare make use of Reason in his Religion) who seeth not, that this is...ridiculous" (*Confession of Faith*, D4v2–5r).[29] Klaus Scholder argues that this rationalism of the Socinians is actually of greater historical importance than their Antitrinitarianism. He views Socinianism as a center of emerging rational religion and suggests that Socinian positions inevitably led to the thoroughgoing reason of natural religion: "the socinian approach had almost of necessity to lead to a radical rationalism, all the more so, the more powerfully the rule of reason developed and extended its sway."[30]

Socinian rationalism went hand in hand with a rigorous focus on Scripture as the only source for religious truth, what McLachlan calls the Socinian "combination of scripturalism and rationalism."[31] The centrality of Scripture is evident in the premise of the *Racovian Catechism*, which begins by asserting first the "certainty" of the holy Scriptures, and then their "sufficiency" (1–9). The *Racovian Catechism*, like so many Socinian texts, founded Antitrinitarianism upon the sufficiency of Scripture, since, by many convincing accounts, there is little evidence for the Trinity in the Bible.[32] This conviction, that the Trinity was not to be found in the Bible, was furthered by the increasingly rational readings brought to bear on Scripture by humanists such as Erasmus. The most famous point of controversy was the Johannine Comma, 1 John 5:7, which had long stood as a main piece of scriptural evidence for the Trinity. Erasmus omitted it from his New Testament, considering it a Latin interpolation.[33] The *Racovian Catechism* argues similarly for its spuriousness (21, 23–24), as Erasmus came to be a significant resource for Antitrinitarian argument.[34] Arguing against the unity of three persons in the Trinity in *De doctrina*, Milton also rejects the Johannine Comma, and, just as he does with 1 Timothy 3:16, cites Erasmus (YP 6:221, 244). *De doctrina* is itself a remarkable display of the ethic of *sola scriptura*. Milton's claim in the "Epistle" that he would derive his creed "from the word of God and from that alone" (YP 6:120), announces what *De doctrina*, through copious quotation and rational exegesis, carries out with scrupulousness. Such biblicism has roots in liberal Protestantism as a whole, but has a particular affinity with the Socinian approach.

Marking his resistance to this potent combination of biblicism and rational exegesis, More explicitly rejects the recent humanist doubts concerning the Johannine Comma (*GMG* 11).[35] And he argues in several places against other key Socinian positions, such as the denial of the divinity of Christ and his death as a satisfaction for human sin (*GMG* 7–15, 504–09). Furthermore, Henry More had earlier tangled directly with Biddle over the question of mystery and its application to Scripture. In *Conjectura cabbalistica* (1653), which depends upon a mystical reading of the Bible, More says that anthropomorphic representations of God in the Bible are to be read not literally but as a "conceit" for the sake of the imaginations of the vulgar.[36] In the following year, in the preface to *A Twofold Catechism*, Biddle argues that we should trust the language of Scripture, accepting even anthropomorphic representations of God as the privileged way of conceiving of God (an argument very close to Milton's theory of accommodation). And he then names *Conjectura cabbalistica* directly, rejecting its method of reading for literary conceits and dismissing it as Platonism and mysterious religion.[37]

Along with a rational approach to language, the Socinian rejection of mystery naturally accompanies a turn to the logic of mathematics. By asserting the singleness of God in response to the Athanasian position of three persons in one godhead, monotheism undermines the numerical illogic of the Trinity. Johan Crell, for example, urges the reader, "Reckon up now those Persons, and you will have three most high Gods."[38] Biddle relies on the logical distinction between one and many to argue that three persons cannot be in a single, unified God: "If the word God, taken for the most high God, (as here it is) be predicated of three, it is an Universal (since not onely Aristotle, but common understanding, sheweth that to be an Universal, which may be predicated of many; that a Singular, which cannot so be predicated) and consequently there are three Gods" (*Confession of Faith*, D5r).³⁹ This attention to the logic of mathematics represents a basic congruence between Socinianism and monotheism. With its commandment to believe in only one God, monotheism relies on the clarity and logic of numbers, and this mathematical clarity proves very effective against the Trinity. In *Grand Mystery of Godliness*, More therefore protects his version of monotheism, which includes the Trinity, by undermining basic mathematical principles. He finds *"latitude of sense* in the word *One"* in the Athanasian Creed, and claims that "the word *Equal* is not to be understood mathematically." Then he goes on to say that "this *latitude of sense* being once admitted, which is necessarily implied, the meaning of *Athanasius* his Creed may prove such as no imputation of either *Polytheisme, Idolatry,* or unconceivable *Impossibility* can be alledged against it" (*GMG* 456). By hobbling mathematical logic, the Trinity is rescued from impossibility, idolatry, and polytheism.

This Antitrinitarian turn to the sharp logic of mathematical argument is expressed most forcefully by Milton himself, in his discussion of the Son in *De doctrina*: "The numerical significance of "one" and "two" must be unalterable and the same for God as for man. It would have been a waste of time for God to thunder forth so repeatedly that first commandment which said that he was the one and only God, if it could nevertheless be maintained that another God existed as well, who ought to be thought of as the only God" (YP 6:212).⁴⁰ Not finding mathematics a strong suit, orthodox Trinitarian thinking had over the centuries turned away from numerical distinctions in favor of the complicated vocabulary of God's essence, *ousia*, and the persons, *hypostases*, of the godhead. The logic of singleness gives Antitrinitarians an effective counter to these baroque and mysterious arguments.

Maurice Kelley recognizes the importance of logic to Milton's Antitrinitarian position by glossing chapter 5 of *De doctrina* with several references to the *Art of Logic*. The key moment of Antitrinitarianism in that text is when Milton ties the logic of numbers to essence: "For number, as Scaliger correctly says, is a property consequent on essence. Therefore, things which differ in number also differ in essence, and never do things differ in number without also differing in essence. *Here let the theologians take notice*" (YP 8:233).[41]

Milton engages with the Trinitarian distinction between essence and substance by insisting on its conformity to mathematical logic. At the heart of his argument in *De doctrina* is the rejection of the mysterious conjunction of three persons or substances in one divine essence, with the key move being the claim that there in fact is no distinction to be made between essence and substance (or person). The Athanasian Creed asserts that there are three persons in the Trinity, but one divine essence. In chapter 2 of *De doctrina*, Milton makes essence and person fundamentally identical by collapsing the two terms *ousia* and *hypostasis*, into one:

> the essence of God, since it is utterly simple, allows nothing to be compounded with it, and that the word *hypostasis*, which is variously translated *substance, subsistence,* or *person,* is nothing but that most perfect essence by which God exists from himself, in himself, and through himself....*Hypostasis*, therefore, is clearly the same as essence and in the passage cited above many translate it by the Latin word *essentia*. Therefore, just as God is an utterly simple essence, so he is an utterly simple subsistence. (YP 6:140–42)

Milton guts the subtle vocabulary of Trinitarian doctrine, insisting on simplifying the language that has been added to Scripture. Once "person" is equivalent to "essence," there cannot be three persons in one divine essence, and mathematical logic has been restored: "Anyway, no one will deny that the Son is numerically different from the Father. And the fact that things numerically different are also different in their proper essences, as logicians call it, is so obvious that no reasonable being could contradict it" (YP 6:262).

Milton's God cannot be divided into *ousia* and *hypostasis*—being one, his subjectivity cannot be parsed. Socinians repeatedly make the same argument for God's simplicity, and against our ability to discover distinctions within him. The *Racovian Catechism*, matching *De doctrina*, insists that essence and person are the same thing. It asserts that "It is very conducive hereunto to know that in the essence of God there is but one Person." And it demonstrates the assertion: "Inasmuch as the Essence of God is but one in number, there cannot be so many persons therein, since a person is nothing but an individual intelligent Essence" (18). Biddle, like Milton, insists that human language cannot parse the godhead: "were it granted that the word God taken for the most high God, is appropriated to one of the three Persons in the Godhead, yet could it at no hand be made use of to distinguish him from the other Persons. For how should a word, equally common unto three, not only be appropriated to one of them, but also be set to distinguish him from the others" (*Confession of Faith*, D6v–D7r). As with the Socinians, monotheism leads Milton to a conception of the godhead which, above all else, is irrefragable:

> Two distinct things cannot be of the same essence. God is one being, not two. One being has one essence, and also one subsistence—by which is meant simply a substantial essence. If you were to ascribe two subsistences or two persons to one essence, it would be a contradiction in terms. You would be saying that the essence was at once one and not one. If one divine essence is common to two components, then that essence or divinity will be in the position of a whole in relation to its parts, or of a genus in relation to its several species, or lastly of a common subject, in relation to its non-essential qualities. (YP 6:212)

Milton's God is monotheistic and Antitrinitarian to the extent that he is a unified and discrete subject. If the doctrine of the

Trinity attempted to reconcile the Son with monotheism by theorizing and institutionalizing the fracturing of divine subjectivity—allowing three persons in one essence—then Milton's monotheistic response is to reinstate the ideal of a single and simple godhead.

Milton's and the Socinians' emphasis on the Father's unity is a typically monotheistic gesture. That God is indivisible and totalizing is part of monotheism's insistence on God's singleness. Whether oneness leads to absolute unity, or the other way around, the two go intimately together in monotheism, in what Lenn Evan Goodman calls "the intuition of the absoluteness of being and its uncompromisability by any plurality of subjects, predicates, times, aspects, or regards."[42] In *Paradise Lost* Adam intuits the same movement toward the absolute in monotheism when he says to God, "No need that thou / Shouldst propagate, already infinite; / And through all numbers absolute, though one" (8.419–21). The negative theology of Adam's description suggests how Milton's Antitrinitarianism can also be viewed as the kind of negative description that so often follows from God's total abstraction. In *De doctrina,* Milton is most monotheistic in his treatment of the Son: it is precisely in the denial of the Trinity that Milton's God emerges in pure singleness. The rejection of Trinitarian vocabulary and Trinitarian compromises in subjectivity become in *De doctrina* a rigorous statement of monotheism.

As narratological strategies such as Adam's negative theology indicate, the indivisibility of God is only an ideal of monotheism. Once the monotheistic God enters into narrative, his absolute abstraction cannot be maintained, creating in narrative a fractured subjectivity. The ideal is compromised in praxis, as Freud captures when he splits the one Hebrew God into Aton and Jahve. Just as the monotheistic God becomes two in Freud's analysis, so it became three in the Trinity. The Christian revelation can be viewed as a fracturing of the monotheistic ideal of absolute unity: Jesus Christ doubles the monotheistic godhead, which is then trebled by the Spirit.[43] In this light, the Trinity appears as the major solution offered by Christianity to the narrative problems of monotheism. And so in the seventeenth century, when radical Christians reconsidered the Trinity, they were faced with the typically monotheistic problem of how to conceive of God. Reconceiving the tripartite godhead in monotheistic terms, they become caught in the structuring dialectic between intellectual principle and personality.

This is a structural problem inherent to all monotheism, and so it is legible also in Socinianism. One manifestation of this monotheistic problem of personality appears famously in Biddle's insistence upon a literally visible God. In typically blunt fashion, Biddle faced the monotheistic problem of God's personality head-on — and created both a stir among opponents and embarrassment among allies. His insistence on a literal interpretation of Scripture in *A Twofold Catechism* — against More's claim that the Bible uses "conceit" and mystery — leads Biddle to conclude that God must have a visible body, very like humans. The catechism asks, "Is God in the Scripture said to have any likeness, image, similitude, person, and shape?" and Biddle's listing of the numerous scriptural passages, beginning with Genesis 1:26, forms an affirmative answer. Biddle goes on to argue that God has personal emotions, such as anger and repentance (*Twofold Catechism*, 11–14).[44] Biddle's *A Twofold Catechism* led to his imprisonment, and to John Owen's scathing response the following year, *Vindiciae evangelicae,* where Owen argues at length against Biddle's visible God, accusing him of idolatry for his anthropomorphic conceptions.[45] And not just the orthodox objected to Biddle's personal God — it became an embarrassment for later Unitarians, so that Stephen Nye, in *A Brief History of the Unitarians,* explicitly rejects Biddle's anthropomorphism as absurd and impossible.[46]

Few could agree with Biddle's assertion that God really has a visible body and a personality capable of passion. But even as both Trinitarians and Antitrinitarians shied away from the eccentricity of Biddle's conception of God, Milton seems to have held very similar views. Biddle's explicit assertions in *A Twofold Catechism* closely resemble the claims Milton makes in chapter 2 of *De doctrina*. Biddle rejects the notion that the Bible communicates in poetic conceits, insisting instead on a literal interpretation of passages that give God a physical presence and a personality. Milton argues, at the beginning of his passage on accommodation, that "theologians do not need to employ anthropopathy, or the ascription of human feelings to God. That is a rhetorical device thought up by grammarians to explain the nonsense poets write about Jove" (YP 6:134). As Michael Lieb has shown, Milton is not here rejecting passions in God, but rather the reading of those passions nonliterally, as rhetorical figures.[47] This challenging bit of heterodoxy is one of the strongest points of contact between Milton and Socinianism—as well as the point at which Biddle and Milton emerge as thoroughly monotheistic.

It is crucial to recognize, however, that Biddle and Milton are not monotheistic because they believe in a visible or literally personal God, nor because they rely upon the mathematical logic of one God. They are monotheistic because their theology brings them right to the contradictory and unstable position between personality and abstraction. More than most thinkers in the period, Milton and Biddle are enmeshed in the intractable problem of the monotheistic God. By the same token, seventeenth century debates over the Trinity are a crucial part of the discourse of monotheism because they assemble themselves upon the deeply unstable conceptual terrain of the one God. Or, in Jan Assmann's terms, debates over the Trinity are monotheistic for the way they draw and redraw the Mosaic distinction between monotheism and polytheism.

In its handling of God the Father, Antitrinitarianism displays significant continuity with earlier conceptions of God in the discourse of monotheism. But it also adds a deeply vexing element to our consideration: the Son. If the Son is no longer a part of the divine Trinity, the monotheist must question what exactly he is. Monotheism challenges Milton and the Socinians to reject the Trinity—and simultaneously challenges them to account somehow for the being who is left over, who looks suspiciously like a polytheistic extra.[48] Broken off from the Trinity, the Son becomes extremely important to the definition of monotheism—he becomes a major place in which the Mosaic distinction is drawn. As a result, a great deal of the ontological instability that we have so far found gathering around the monotheistic godhead migrates onto the Son. The next chapter will pick up Milton's Antitrinitarianism at this point, describing Milton's conceptions of the Son once he has been separated from the Father and the Trinity. In particular it will stress the important differences between the Son in *Paradise Lost* and the Son in *Paradise Regained* as a way to show how these two very different products of Milton's poetic imagination are shaped by the imperatives of monotheism. In this chapter, the discussion continues by locating deism within the discourse of monotheism.

Deism and Revelation

At midcentury, in the midst of the public emergence of English Socinianism, Thomas Edwards offered a vignette in *Gangraena* about the inexorable expansion of skepticism that must follow from Antitrinitarianism. It may seem paranoid, but proves to be a prescient vision of the course of seventeenth century rational religion. Referring to the trial of the Socinian Paul Best, he describes a conversation outside Westminster Hall:

> the discourse was as follows, *That hee would be loth the Parliament should bring* Paul Bests *bloud upon them for his denying the Trinitie.* Whereupon this Gentleman answered him, that hee could prove cleerly out of the Scriptures a Trinitie of Persons. Unto whom this Sectarie replyed, *How will you prove the Scriptures to be the word of God?* and this Sectarie reasoned against them, saying there were twenty severall Scriptures, as many as Translations; and Translations are not true; for so the Priests will tell us, that this is not rightly translated: and for the Originals there are divers Copies; besides, I cannot understand them, neither is it my fault that I doe not: In summe, the man reasoned there was no Religion

at all in the Kingdome, but all Religion that hee knew of was, *To doe justly, and be mercifull.* Unto which the Gentleman replyed, The Heathen they were just and mercifull, and therein did as much as you. This Sectarie rejoyned, *For ought hee knew, the Heathens were saved as well as any now.*[49]

It is a quick progression from the denial of the Trinity to the denial of Scripture. The Sectarian then replaces both Trinity and Scripture with natural religion, naming two major tenets, that religion can be reduced to essentials separate from revelation, such as justice and mercy, and that heathens could be saved without access to Christianity. Edwards describes the very trajectory of radical religion in the latter part of the century, as it evolves from Socinianism to deism.

As the two most visible heresies in the late seventeenth century, Socinianism and deism are often lumped together in polemics. Within this discussion of the discourse of monotheism, we are in a position to recognize just how related they are — for Socinianism and deism most of all share a concern with monotheism; their points of contact are also points central to the discourse of monotheism. This analysis pays attention to the continuity between Socinianism and deism as a way of clarifying the landscape of rational religion, and pointing out the centrality of monotheism to the period's theology. And, by explaining how deism departs from Socinianism, it will demonstrate the ways that deism and its ideas serve as a logical endpoint to the discourse of monotheism.

The 1670s and 1680s saw a rapid expansion of Socinian ideas, so that, as Andrew Marvell recounts in *The Rehearsal Transpros'd* (1672), "Socinian books are tolerated, and sell as openly as the Bible."[50] By the 1690s, a wave of Socinian publications, from figures such as Stephen Nye and Thomas Firmin, began to effect the transition to Unitarianism. Biddle's writings were republished at this time in a high-quality folio, *The Faith of One God* (1691), probably by Firmin and Nye. And this and subsequent collections spurred vigorous opposition by latitudinarians such as John Tillotson and Edward Stillingfleet. These expanding public debates coincide with the emergence of deism as a public controversy. Charles Blount begins his career as the first polemical and public deist with *Anima mundi* (1679). And he explicitly styles himself as Herbert of Cherbury's disciple with *Religio laici* (1683). Blount's collaboration with Charles Gildon in a collection of new and past works, *Oracles of Reason* (1693), appears as notable companion, in size and retrospective aims, to *The Faith of One God*.

With both deism and Socinianism—or Unitarianism as it was now often called—circulating simultaneously, orthodox polemicists often took aim at both heresies, either indiscriminately or with the conviction that they were together scheming to undo Christianity.[51] Stillingfleet's *Discourse in Vindication of the Doctrine of the Trinity* (1697) elaborates their overlap most fully, as its preface compares Socinians and deists at length. "I cannot but observe," he says, "that in the late *Socinian* Pamphlets, there is too strong a bias towards Deism."[52] In Stillingfleet's view, Socinians are merely deist puppets: "And thus we find our Unitarians serving the Deists in all their methods of overthrowing Revealed Religion and advancing Deism among us."[53] Stillingfleet's *Vindication* is largely a response to Stephen Nye's *A Brief History of the Unitarians*, which was published in 1687, but reprinted in *Faith of One God*. Stillingfleet ranges broadly through Nye's arguments, but at the end shifts from Nye to the deist John Toland, offering a lengthy refutation of his *Christianity Not Mysterious* (1696). Often using Locke's *Essay*, he argues point for point against Toland's notion of reason, and his claim that nothing in the Gospel is above reason.[54] Stillingfleet refutes Toland's text as if there were no need to make a distinction between the Unitarians and what is probably the most famous contribution to deist literature. *Christianity Not Mysterious* is rightly known as a deist landmark, but, published in the midst of these Antitrinitarian controversies, it was initially read as a Socinian text.[55] Nye responded to Stillingfleet immediately, professing to be puzzled by his attention to Toland: "But suppose the Bishop had disarmed the Gentleman; what is that to us?"[56] Nye is eager to distance himself and

Unitarians from Toland and from deists in general. His *A Discourse Concerning Natural and Revealed Religion* (1696), published the same year as *Christianity Not Mysterious*, attempts "a Vindication of Natural Religion, against Atheists and Scepticks; an assertion of Revealed Religion, against Deists."[57] With deism emerging as an even more radical heresy, Antitrinitarians felt the urgent need to separate themselves from it—and no doubt orthodox polemicists found it useful to elide the two parties.

The most obvious affinity between Socinianism and deism, which both also share with the discourse of monotheism, is resistance to mystery. On the title page to *Christianity Not Mysterious*, Toland famously announces, "There is nothing in the Gospel contrary to Reason, nor above it; and that no Christian Doctrine can be properly called a Mystery." Similarly, the Socinian *An Impartial Account of the Word Mystery* makes the same claim that "God never uses any Term to teach us his Mysteries, but what we have a clear and distinct Idea of."[58] (The Lockean language of clear and distinct ideas circulates throughout these debates over mystery, and was a part of suspicions about Locke's beliefs on the Trinity.)[59] Toland argues that the authority given to divine revelation has led Christians to believe things that contradict reason, and "to adore what we cannot comprehend." And he calls this irrationality "the undoubted Source of all the *Absurdities* that ever were seriously vented among *Christians*."[60] This conviction that mystery has overwhelmed the best parts of Christian religion and led to corruption in the church is also repeatedly asserted in *An Impartial Account*, which argues, "Mystery is a Supplement ready at hand, when we fall short of Reason. In a word, Mystery is a Salve for all Diseases, It dazles the Eyes of simple Men, or rather betwitches them in as great a measure, that by seeing they perceive not the Ridiculousness of the Opinions imposed upon their Belief, and it makes wise Men willingly to shut them."[61]

But while Toland acknowledges the Socinian rejection of mystery, he works to separate his position from theirs in a crucial way.

Speaking of the orthodox reliance on mystery, he says, "And tho the *Socinians* disown this Practice, I am mistaken if either they or the *Arians* can make their Notions of a *dignifi'd and Creature-God capable of Divine Worship*, appear more reasonable than the Extravagancies of other Sects touching the Article of the *Trinity*."[62] While Socinians rightly, in Toland's eyes, reject the mystery of the Trinity, they do not reject mystery sufficiently. What remains when the Socinians break up the Trinity is still highly unreasonable: a created God and a god that, while not the one God, nevertheless deserves divine worship. Toland's sentiment matches that of Blount and Gildon, quoted at the beginning of this chapter, when they chastise Socinians for a *deus factus*. The created Son looks like mystery and superstition and is pushed aside by the deist in order to avoid the irrationality of idolatry. The deist has no room for the Son because, as Blount and Gildon say, the deist "only acknowledges one Supream, Everlasting God, and thinks magnificently of him."

Around the figure of the Son, deism separates itself from Socinianism, and the goal in this rationalizing trajectory is a purer monotheism. It was a common complaint that deism neglected the Son. Richard Baxter's *More Reasons for the Christian Religion* (1672) includes a lengthy answer to Herbert of Cherbury's *De veritate* that begins with the way that Cherbury excludes the Son from the process of repentance.[63] Deist deemphasis of the Son takes many forms, emerging most spectacularly later in the outright dismissal of Christ's miracles.[64] More covertly, Blount's 1680 translation, with annotations, of Philostratus's life of Apollonius Tyaneus, offers a subtle but potentially debilitating parallel between the pagan worker of miracles and Christ. Henry More also discusses Apollonius at length in the *Grand Mystery of Godliness*, but draws the parallel between him and Christ, "that the *Gravitie and Divinitie of the one* and the *Ridiculousness and Carnality of the other* may the better be discerned" (*GMG* 102). In contrast, Blount is significantly more equivocal, as he claims to give Christ preeminence over Apollonius, but nevertheless articulates a highly rational and comparative approach, as Christ is to be studied alongside Apollonius, and Christianity is to be studied as one among many religions.[65]

Ultimately, deism's rejection of religious revelation not only reduces the authority of the Son, it actually makes him inessential. Deism tended to reduce Christianity to a set of moral rules—the Common Notions of natural religion. This simple moral code replaces the role of the Son as mediator, for the religious essentials are available without the specific intervention of the Son. In *Religio laici* Blount follows Cherbury's Common Notions in listing five "Catholick or Universal Principles." As these principles replace the specifics of atonement and satisfaction in Christianity, the Son is left out of the process: "Man can do no more on his part, for the satisfying of Divine Justice, than to be heartily sorry and repent him of his Sins."[66] The Son becomes excess, a revealed being who is outside of the minimal requirements of natural religion—and so he appears as an idolatrous threat to the singleness of pure monotheism. Blount and Gildon, in *Oracles of Reason*, see the Son as an unnecessary complication, and liken his mediatorial office to idolatry: "A Mediator derogates from the infinite mercy of God, equally as an Image doth from his Spiritualitie and Infinitie."[67] Bolingbroke most explicitly declares the incompatibility of monotheism with the Son:

> The expectation of the Messiah did not clash with monotheism. But they (the Jews) might imagine, that the belief of God the son, and God the holy Ghost did so very manifestly; the trinity not having been early reconciled to the unity of God. Other nations seemed to be better prepared by philosophy, by that of Plato in particular, and by the polytheistical notions of divine natures, some in the godhead, and some out of it, for the reception of the gospel, or of the theology which the preachers of the gospel taught. (Bolingbroke 3:369)

The Son and the Trinity push the godhead away from monotheism, which Bolingbroke cuttingly suggests is why Christianity historically had better success among polytheistic cultures than among the Jews. Platonism, which for Bolingbroke means a profusion of revelations and revealed beings, "prepared" the way for the Gospel and its three gods. And yet even the Jews were not monotheistic enough for Bolingbroke's rigorous deism. In his articulation of an abstract God that is entirely removed from revealed detail, Bolingbroke declares that even the God of the Hebrew Bible cannot meet the proper conception of the godhead:

> But they who compare the ideas and notions concerning the Supreme Being that reason collects from the phenomena of nature, physical and moral, which we know to be the works of God, with those that the books of the Old Testament, which we suppose to be his word, give us, will be apt...to conclude that the God of Abraham, Isaac, and Jacob cannot be that glorious Supreme all-perfect Being whom reason showed them, and whom they discerned with their naked eyes. (Bolingbroke 3:363)

The details of the Hebrew Bible place God within revealed history, evoked by the biblical synecdoche "Abraham, Isaac and Jacob." These particulars cannot be reconciled with the purely monotheistic God that reason collects from nature. Bolingbroke's deistic God cannot be found anywhere in Scripture because it is too purely monotheistic.

Not only does the biblical God fall short of the monotheism of the deists, but so does the Bible itself. Despite the deists' rhetorical strategies of coyness and irony, opponents saw clearly the true stakes of natural religion. In *An Account of the Growth of Deism in England* (1696), William Stephens describes what separates deists from latitudinarians: "their desire to lay aside scriptural revelation as rationally incomprehensible and thus useless, or even detrimental, to human society and to religion."[68] This is also a key point that distinguishes deists from Socinians: whereas Socinians based their radical positions on the authority of Scripture, championing the Protestant call for *sola scriptura*, deists specifically cut Scripture out of religion. Scholder describes how Socinianism expanded its rational approach to religion, but attempted to maintain the authority of revealed Scripture. Reason, he says, inevitably clashed with the Bible, and Socinianism gave way to deism and its marginalization of revealed Scripture: "they could not prevent reason making itself increasingly independent of scripture. The more formally the scripture principle was used on the one side, and the greater the self-awareness of reason on the other, the more inexorably conflict developed which by the nature of things necessarily led to criticism of scripture."[69]

As deism pushes scriptural revelation aside, it also pushes aside the particular details revealed in the Bible. These go together, of course: as the authority of Scripture diminishes, so do the importance of the stories. So the Son recedes from divinity, angels and miracles are discredited, and, as in Bolingbroke's objection to the God of Abraham, Isaac, and Jacob, God himself is separated from the events narrated in the Hebrew Bible, becoming totally impersonal and unnarratable. In sum, the entire economy of divine revelations is purged: deism wants little to do with the agents and events of the biblical stories.

This stripping away of the divine economy, which the last chapter traced in the neoclassical and deist response to Christian machinery, articulates a rational rejection of the Christian supernatural. This is the defining gesture of deism, and is recognizable, to offer an example, in the shift from John Locke's claims for reason to John Toland's. Locke, in the *Reasonableness of Christianity*, celebrates the use of reason up to the point where it might deny revealed religion, and then he very pointedly insists upon the necessity of supernatural revelation:

> Hence we see that *Reason*, speaking never so clearly to the Wise and Vertuous, had never Authority enough to prevail on the Multitude; and to perswade the Societies of Men, that there was but One God, that alone was to be owned and worshipped. The Belief and Worship of One God, was the National Religion of the *Israelites* alone: And if we will consider it, it was introduced and supported amongst that People by *Revelation*.[70]

Locke's basic argument is visible here, that knowledge of the one God may be available through reason to the wisest philosophers, but it is not available to the multitudes without revelation. But Toland, who positioned himself as a disciple of Locke, pushes rational critique into the domain of revelation. Published a year after Locke's *Reasonableness*, Toland's deist manifesto *Christianity Not Mysterious* argues that nothing in the Bible is contrary to reason. And while he does not reject revelation outright, he does claim as much efficacy in reason as revelation. While Locke makes the common antideist assertion that the exercise of reason does not bring natural religion to the masses, Toland says that true religion is easily comprehensible in nature: "what is reveal'd in Religion, as it is most useful and necessary, so it must and may be as easily comprehended, and found as consistent with our common Notions, as what we know of Wood or Stone, or Air, of Water, or the like."[71] Toland here adopts Cherbury's vocabulary of Common Notions, asserting that the basic elements of nature, perceived by a reasoning mind, are as good as the supernaturalism of revelation.[72] Bolingbroke, as usual, is even more forthright: "the knowledge of one Supreme Being is to be acquired by reason, without the necessity of any revelation" (Bolingbroke 3:364).

We have seen the Son and God stripped of revealed detail. But in this movement to a purely rational religious economy the two supernatural elements most frequently challenged are miracles and angels. Deists often do not reject the possibility of miracles outright, but put severe limits upon them. Toland argues that miracles cannot exceed the bounds of reason: "No *Miracle* then is contrary to Reason, for the Action must be intelligible, and the Performance of it appear most easy to the Author of *Nature*." He does not deny them, but insists that God is "not prodigal of miracles."[73] Deism regularly limited the authority of miracles by emphasizing a skepticism toward the witness of the miracle. Cherbury emphasizes that "the truth of revelation depends upon the authority of him who reveals it" (*De veritate* 308). And, speaking specifically of "reports of marvellous and extraordinary events," he insists that their veracity hinges upon the historian or author who saw them and reported on them: "All belief, though corrupted in the course of centuries, must in the last resource rest on the knowledge or understanding of the author from whom the belief originated" (314–15).[74] The witness of miracles is regularly debased by the deists by aligning it with the common figure of the wicked priest. Miracle becomes an imposition of priestcraft—a means of tricking the masses away from natural religion.[75] In Bolingbroke's extreme expression of deism, the absence of miracle is the precondition for a rational and monotheistic, natural religion: as the one God is known "by reason, without the necessity of any revelation, or of any miracles to impose it" (Bolingbroke 3:364). And so deism's opponents understood that miracles were crucial to turning the tide away from natural religion and back toward revealed orthodoxy. Locke, arguing for the necessity of revelation, discusses at length the Son's miracles, which prove to be the key to the masses' belief: "we see the People justified their *believing in him, i.e.* their believing him to be the *Messiah*, because of the Miracles he did."[76]

If revelation in the New Testament brings deists to consider Christ's miracles, in the Hebrew Bible their opposition to revelation focuses on angels. As Cherbury puts it, "revelations are most frequently made with the medium of spirits which have been recognized in all ages as a special order of beings, invisible, impalpable, free of physical substance, endowed with rapid movement, and variously called angels, demons, intelligences and geniuses" (*De veritate* 309). The Common Notions, by excluding revelation, render these beings superfluous. Hobbes submits biblical angels to a materialist interpretation that denies their real presence: "But if we consider the places of the Old Testament where angels are mentioned, we shall find, that in most of them, there can nothing else be understood by the word *angel*, but some image raised, supernaturally, in the fancy."[77] The fourth part of *Leviathan*, on the "Kingdome of Darknesse," degrades spirits, daemons, and angels, making them examples of superstition and largely denying the external economy of revealed religion. Hobbes argues that the Judeo-Christian tradition adopted its belief in angels and other spirits from pagan philosophers, an argument Bolingbroke makes frequently in his essays, describing what he calls the "pneumatical madness" of Christianity and all revealed religion (Bolingbroke 3:532). Bolingbroke views belief in spirits as one of the most shocking corruptions of monotheism:

> All I mean to observe is, that an intellectual world of subordinate and of created gods, of demons, of souls, and other spiritual inhabitants, being once assumed, as it was together with the unity of God...the philosophers did much the same thing in a metaphysical, as they and the priests had done in a mythological way. They made as many spiritual beings as they wanted, and they generated them as they could....It is impossible to consider without astonishment, how these spiritual beings were multiplied from age to age, by Pythagorician and Platonic philosophers, by Jewish Cabbalists, and by Christian divines both orthodox and heretical. (3:290)

Spiritual beings such as angels become, in Bolingbroke's view, impositions upon monotheism, the remnants of polytheism unfortunately foisted upon the Judeo-Christian tradition.

As revealed Christianity is grouped with polytheism, both debased by a superstitious acceptance of miracles and angels, the uniqueness of the Judeo-Christian revelation itself is questioned. This makes apparent a basic pattern in deistic thought: skepticism toward personal revelation leads to skepticism toward revelation as a whole. Deism rejects revelation in both of its senses—as a local phenomenon such as an angel, and as the Judeo-Christian revelation itself. Locke's *Reasonableness of Christianity* makes a concerted effort to break this pattern by asserting both the clear persuasiveness of miracle and the unique truth of the Judeo-Christian revelation. Locke's extended discussion of reason within faith is aimed primarily at proving the necessity of revelation, demonstrating throughout most of the treatise the efficacy of Christ's miracles. It also pays frequent attention to the status of the Jews, and in its latter pages argues that the Israelites alone, unlike pagan cultures that lacked God's revelation, had access to true religion. Locke in the last part of *Reasonableness* asserts the uniqueness of the chosen people in the face of the assumptions of natural religion and the arguments for occult monotheism. He accepts, as does the argument for occult monotheism, that reason can discover the one God. But he says that, in practice, it rarely did—in pagan religion, dominated by priestcraft, superstition ruled:

> In this state of Darkness and Ignorance of the true God, Vice and Superstition held the World. Nor could any help be had or hoped for from *Reason;* which could not be heard, and was judged to have nothing to do in the case: The Priests every where, to secure their Empire, having excluded Reason from having any thing to do in Religion. And in the croud of wrong Notions and invented Rites, the World had almost lost the sight of the One only True God. The Rational and thinking part of Mankind, 'tis true, when they sought after him, found the One, Supream, Invisible God: But if they acknowledged and worshipped him, it was only in their own minds.[78]

Locke concedes the deist positions on reason and priestcraft, and perhaps even nods at Cherbury's Common Notions (which he rejects in his *Essay*). But he argues that all of the insights of natural religion remained hidden among a few philosophers, and were not available to the masses. And so in practice, he goes on, the Jews alone were monotheistic. This monotheism was due to revelation: "The Belief and Worship of One God, was the National religion of the *Israelites* alone: And if we will consider it, it was introduced and supported amongst that People by *Revelation*."[79] Natural religion is admitted only up to the point that it would elide revelation. Natural religion's assertion of occult monotheism undoes the Judeo-Christian revelation by blending it with paganism, and in response Locke insists on the uniqueness of Jewish monotheism, and so the necessity of revelation.

Locke's insistence on the uniqueness of Jewish monotheism serves as the impetus for Bolingbroke's essay on monotheism. Bolingbroke begins by declaring, "there was something in Mr. Locke's discourse concerning the reasonableness of christianity, very repugnant to what I have advanced about the knowledge of the one true God" (Bolingbroke 3:331). And he goes on to argue against Locke's propositions "that all the heathen were in a state of darkness, and ignorance of the true God, and consequently that the belief and worship of one God was the national religion of the Israelites alone" (3:334). Bolingbroke asserts the presence of occult monotheism among the Greeks, Egyptians, and even the Chinese, which defeats Locke's claims of uniqueness. But he goes further, arguing that the Israelites themselves actually were not sufficiently monotheistic, that the one true God "will be found inconsistent with the tenor of the mosaical history" (3:348). Bolingbroke considers Locke's monotheism—and the monotheism reflected in the Bible—too material and too inflected by the accidents of history and personality. He says that Locke "uses these two expressions, the true God, and one God, as if they were exactly synonymous; whereas they are not really so.... It is not unity alone that constitutes the complex idea, or notion of the true God. There is, there can be but one such Being, and yet a monotheist may be as far from the knowledge of the true God, as the rankest, and most superstitious polytheist" (Bolingbroke 3:334). The true God, for Bolingbroke, is one separated from "the very worst of human imperfections" (3:335)—that is, removed from the personality and revealed history of the Judeo-Christian tradition. Bolingbroke's monotheism extends beyond the mere criterion of singleness to depend upon God's total abstraction from revelation, so that even the Israelites in the Bible look like superstitious polytheists. The Israelites of the Bible not only have the wrong conception of God, but they also represent a degradation of true monotheism rather than, as Locke claims, its unique apotheosis.

Taking aim at the distinction between an ideal monotheism and that of the Israelites, Bolingbroke goes on to picture "an inhabitant of Thebes in Egypt" who, he says, may be either an outright monotheist or a polytheist with an understanding of occult monotheism. And he imagines this Egyptian "was not less scandalised when he saw this Being, of whom he had the sublimest conceptions that the mind of man can frame, degraded into the rank of a local tutelary divinity, the God of Abraham, of Isaac, and of Jacob, the God of one family, and one nation" (3:368). One important move here is in locating monotheism in Egypt. Egypt, in the Hebrew Bible as well as Christian tradition, is widely viewed as a sink of polytheism. Assmann traces the matter of Egyptian monotheism in *Moses the Egyptian*, identifying it as a primary way of undermining the Mosaic distinction between true Judaic and false Egyptian religion.[80] It is precisely this tradition, with its exclusionary rejection of false religion, that the spectacle of Bolingbroke's more assiduously monotheistic Egyptian subverts. Furthermore, when Bolingbroke's Egyptian monotheist is "scandalised" by the God of Abraham, Isaac, and Jacob, he looks very much like an English deist. Prevailing conceptions of monotheism are not rigorous enough, debasing the true, fully abstract God into "a local tutelary divinity." Bolingbroke is rejecting the same divine qualities that Freud associates with Jahve, the volcano God who is "A rude, narrow-minded local god, violent and bloodthirsty." In contrast, Aton represents a "more spiritual conception of God, a single God who embraces the whole world"—he is entirely abstract and universal (*MM* 61). Aton comes from Egypt, and one way to view Bolingbroke's monotheism, and that of the deists, is that it becomes purely Atonistic.[81]

Aton is removed from all connections to myth. He does not reveal himself in miracle or theophany, but rather remains too rationalized to enter into history or to be known by revelation. Jahve, in contrast, has "the features that proved the terrific grandeur of this volcano-god, such as, for example the pillar of smoke which changed to one of fire by night, or the storm that parted the waters so that the pursuers were drowned by the returning floods of water" (*MM* 48). That is, Jahve is a God of theophany and revelation. And as a revealed god, Jahve is equipped with the specificity that can allow him to take part in the stories of myth, and that make him legible in the narratives of the Bible—with no more famous example than the pillars of smoke and fire that allow him to be present to the Israelites and present in the narrative of Exodus. As Freud argues, the concreteness and narratability of the Jahve religion were essential to its survival, as the religion of Aton, in its total abstraction, was unacceptable to the masses: "The Jewish people of Moses were quite as unable to bear such a highly spiritualized religion, to find in what it offered satisfaction for their needs, as were the Egyptians of the Eighteenth Dynasty" (*MM* 57–58). The Israelites' constant return to the golden calf captures this dynamic in the biblical story, reflecting the human need for revelation and concrete religious particulars. Monotheism itself, driven by the unifying principal of oneness and its skepticism toward the supernatural, tends toward the philosophical and ethical religion of Aton. But it cannot survive when it passes beyond revelation, becoming too abstract to forge a relation with the more poetic realm of religious imagination.

Monotheism in the seventeenth and eighteenth centuries arrives at the Atonistic endpoint: Bolingbroke and deism as a whole move toward the aniconic extreme, a God entirely removed from revelation. Opponents of deism were fearful of this endpoint, arguing repeatedly that deism might satisfy the educated by appealing purely to reason, but that it cannot satisfy the masses, who need miracle and revelation. As John Dennis, explaining the "folly of deism," puts it, "all men are capable of the proofs of Revealed Religion, whereas not one in Forty is capable of the Proofs of Deism, it follows, that a Religion that is not Reveal'd cannot be the True Religion."[82] By denying revelation, deism loses its ability to communicate. Setting monotheism up outside of biblical revelation means imagining religion without its detail: God is stripped of theophany and revelation, disallowing his presence in history; religious events are stripped of miracles, which create the sublimity that moves the masses; the religious economy as a whole is stripped of the personalities and agencies of angels and other divine beings (such as the Son) who are crucial to the events of unfolding religious history. Ultimately, the religious imagination slips into nothingness and silence, an imaginary state that cannot meet the minimal requirements of plot, character, and storyworld. In short, monotheism taken to the extreme of seventeenth century deism removes itself from the elements of narrative. This is the basic disjunction between monotheism and narrative, and it helps us to understand the deist resistance to sacred Scripture. Deism's skepticism toward miraculous revelation, as well as its overall rejection of the Judeo-Christian revelation and the stories of the Bible that report it, are instances of monotheism pulling away from narrative.

The chapter 4 discussion of the reception of the war in heaven placed Milton in an uneasy relation to revelation. Caught between the pure aniconism of monotheism and the demands of narrative, *Paradise Lost* tends toward total abstraction, then swerves back to revelation. Similarly, Christopher Hill senses that Milton underwent a struggle with the revelation of sacred Scripture as a whole. He suggests that Milton "went as far in source criticism as one could go without asking the fundamental question—Is this the word of God? and answering it in the negative."[83] Even amid such skepticism, Milton, of course, does not reject Scripture; on the contrary, the scripturalism of *De doctrina Christiana* banishes such a supposition. Furthermore, Milton clearly states there that specific revelations are necessary to true religion: "No one, however, can form correct ideas about God guided by nature or reason alone, without the word or message of God" (YP 6:132). Scriptural revelation is the single and certain authority in *De doctrina* and obviously enables the narrative in *Paradise Lost*.

Paradise Regained and *Samson Agonistes*, however, probe further. The next two chapters read the 1671 volume as nearer to the skeptical extreme, locating it in the context of Socinianism and deism. In *Paradise Regained* is evident Milton's deep engagement with Antitrinitarianism, and chapter 6 reads the poem in relation to the Socinian conception of the Son as a mere man. In *Samson Agonistes* can be found Milton's consideration of theodicy without the assistance of revelation—chapter 7 reads it next to the natural religion and epistemology of Lord Herbert of Cherbury. In both poems Milton experiments with storyworlds free of miracle and revelation, creating religious economies that are notably more aniconic and disenchanted than in *Paradise Lost*. And in both he is led to consider the rational and freethinking possibilities of religious toleration and nascent comparative religion. In *Paradise Regained* and *Samson Agonistes,* monotheism feels toward the edge of religious skepticism.

Six

The Son after the Trinity

Adam's book 8 encounter with God was interpreted in chapter 3 as a main expression of monotheism in *Paradise Lost*. God's question, "What think'st thou then of me, and this my state, / ...Who am alone / From all eternity" (*PL* 8.403–06) both asserts an utterly monotheistic godhead and challenges Adam to conceive of it. Adam's answer—humble, wise, but also a negotiation of the problems of monotheism—dramatizes the unstable position of the adherent to monotheism, as well as the adherent who seeks to be a poet of monotheism. Importantly, in this foundational myth of monotheistic narrative, in both God's question and Adam's answer, Milton relies upon the vocabulary of Antitrinitarianism.

When God says of himself, "Who am alone / From all eternity, for none I know / Second to me or like, equal much less" (8.405–07), he rejects the orthodox defense of the Trinity based upon equality between Father and Son. The anti-Socinian polemicist Francis Cheynell, for example, commenting on Philippians 2:6, argues, "and therefore the Son counts it not robbery to be equal with the Father, because he subsists in the nature of God."[1] Commenting in *De doctrina Christiana* on the same Scripture, Milton interprets equality against the Trinity: "But if the sense of the passage is that he is an equal, it rather refutes than proves the theory that he is of one essence with God. For equality cannot exist except between two or more essences" (YP 6:274–75). That the Son and the Father do not have the same essence is the central claim in Milton's Antitrinitarianism, and one of the most important objectives of *De doctrina* itself. It is ultimately his separate essence that, contra orthodox formulations, denies the Son equality with the Father: "in these passages, as elsewhere, we are taught about the Son's divine nature as something distinct from and clearly inferior to the Father's nature" (YP 6:273).

Further, when Adam answers God in book 8, he makes the statement (apparently accepted) that God is under no necessity to propagate: "No need that thou / Shouldst propagate, already infinite; / And through all numbers absolute, though one" (*PL* 8.419–21). For Maurice Kelley and Michael Bauman, this is a decidedly Arian assertion.[2] Orthodox Trinitarian thought asserted the Son's shared essence and did so largely by maintaining that the Son was not begotten by the will of the Father, but by a necessary act. If the Son is begotten as a necessary result of the divine nature, there is less risk that Christ's sonship will imply secondariness or contingency. Such logic also served Socinians: Johan Crell argues, "either the Son is not the most high God or was begotten of the Father by necessity of nature" (Crell, *Two Books*, 276).[3] Milton, insisting on the Son's secondary status, concludes, "however the Son was begotten, it did not arise from natural necessity, as is usually maintained" (YP 6:208).[4] In book 8, as Adam works out God's monotheistic nature, he is not only arguing with God, but with those contemporaries of Milton who are debating the Trinity.

In fact, the entire presence of Genesis 18 in *Paradise Lost* can be read as a meditation on the Trinity. Many commentators, including Augustine and Luther, understand the three visitors to be a reference to the Trinity.[5] Not just the number of angels, but the deep ambiguity of persons forges the link to the Trinity, for Calvin: "The reason why Moses introduces, at one time, three speakers, while, at another, he ascribes speech to only one, is, that the three together represent the person of one God."[6] And so Socinians must take Genesis 18 into account. For example, Crell's commentary on Hebrews, translated by Thomas Lushington, moves from Hebrews 13:2 to declare, "how vainly they are mistaken, who think that the three men who were seen and invited of Abraham, Gen 18:2, were the persons of the holy Trinity."[7] In light of these debates, Milton's rewriting of Genesis 18 appears to be a strong Antitrinitarian gesture: in the figure of Raphael, he reduces the three visitors to one and defines the one figure as an angel rather than a part of the Trinity.

Conceiving of the monotheistic godhead in *Paradise Lost*, Milton and Adam slip into the language and source texts of Antitrinitarianism. No wonder: these are the theological debates of the period that most articulately deconstruct and defend the godhead. Especially with the emergence of the Socinian controversies of the 1650s, discussion of monotheism, as the last chapter showed, frequently revolved around the problem of the Trinity. By the same token, in *De doctrina* Milton articulates his monotheism most forcefully in his Antitrinitarian discussion of the Son. When Milton turns to poetic representations of the Son, he is just as deeply enmeshed in the ideas and key words of current Antitrinitarian debates. The Son of Milton's poetry therefore bears close comparison to what is said about the Son in *De doctrina*, and in the contemporary Socinian controversy. These theological contexts, as complex as they are, do not produce final answers about Milton's theology; Milton's poetry tends to work against conclusions such as whether Milton was an Arian or a Socinian. But they can help us to understand the poetic challenges Milton faces when writing about the Son in both *Paradise Lost* and *Paradise Regained*.

They reveal that, from a representational and narratological perspective, Milton faces a unique and thorny problem: what to do with a Son who has been removed from the Trinity. This is a problem of monotheistic narrative, for it is born of monotheistic objections to the Trinity and it presents familiar difficulties to the poet trying to tell divine stories. At bottom is an ontological problem, for if the Son is not God, then what exactly is he? An angel? A man? Something else? And this ontological ambiguity accompanies representational problems, as the poet must struggle over how to portray the Son and how to include him in narrative. A Son imagined after the dissolution of the Trinity must be an odd creature, so much so that Defoe later declared that Milton "made a meer je ne sçay Quoi of Jesus Christ."[8]

Paradise Lost *and the Preincarnate Son*

Detaching the Son from the tripartite godhead creates wide-ranging complications. Antitrinitarians are forced to be very particular about just what the Son is if we are to believe he is not God. Many answers emerge: a mere man, a divinely honored man, an angel, a figure above angels, a god (but not God)—in short the entire ontological spectrum, stopping short of the one God. The imperatives of Antitrinitarian thought destabilize the Son as a subject, marking for us the ontological negotiations typical of a close concern with monotheism. For example, the first thing the *Racovian Catechism* declares about the Son's essence is that he "is a true man by nature" (*Racovian* 27). But it goes on to ask, "Is the Lord Jesus then a meer man?" which draws the answer, "By no means"—the Son's miraculous birth, although not an incarnation of God, proves him to be something elevated above mere man (*Racovian* 27). And after the Resurrection, furthermore, "he became the Head of Angells and Men" (47), and so is deserving of divine honor. This kind of honor then calls forth the obvious monotheistic question: "But is not the first commandment of the decalogue altogether changed by this addition, namely, that we ought to acknowledge Christ for a God, and celebrate him with Divine honour?" (85) The catechism finds no conflict with the first commandment, precisely because the Son is not God, but "subordinate to that one God" (85). Yet in these carefully calibrated interpretations and reinterpretations, it is evident that the newly positioned Son has not put to rest monotheistic anxiety. The instability of his ontological situation rubs as uncomfortably against the first commandment as it did when the Son belonged to the Trinity.[9]

The Socinian distinction between the Son before and after the Resurrection reflects the way that many of these ontological negotiations take place around questions of timing. Just who the Son is depends upon where in the sacred history one looks. The most important distinction has to do with the Incarnation. Because it would imply a superhuman ontology, Socinians regularly deny an actual preincarnate history to the Son. The *Racovian Catechism* argues against several texts suggesting the Son's role in Creation, in particular insisting that the beginning of John does not imply that the Son was literally present at the Creation as the Word (43–48). Denials of the Son's role in Creation are accomplished by reading time figuratively in order to move the creative act to a later moment. Biddle sees the act of creation as a metaphor for the Son's regeneration of the world: "the holy Scripture, whilest it attributeth creation unto Christ, doth, what by the nature of the thing it self, what by the circumstances of the places, what by the express words, signifie that it is meant not of the first and old creation, but of the second and new, consisting in the reduction of things to a new state, condition, or order" (Biddle, *Confession of Faith*, 7). The *Racovian Catechism* goes on to refute claims that it was Christ who brought Israel out of Egypt, led them through the desert, and was seen by Isaiah (50–52). Any such role in the events of the Hebrew Bible would, of course, imply an existence prior to Jesus' time on earth as a man. And finally, what is the logical conclusion to Socinian denials of preincarnate history, the *Racovian Catechism* argues at length against the Incarnation itself—for if there was no Son beforehand, then there was no movement into the flesh (also see Biddle, *Confession of Faith*, 11).

Whether the Son has an existence prior to the Incarnation ultimately depends upon his origin. Trinitarians claim that the Son always existed, coeternal with God, and so without an identifiable beginning. Antitrinitarians, however, claim the Son was created, and seek to determine the moment of creation, the point at which he was "begotten." The *Racovian Catechism* argues against the orthodox position that "Christ was begotten out of the Essence of the Father from Eternity" (32). Similarly, Milton's first assertion about the Son in chapter 5 of *De doctrina* is that he is begotten and so not equal to the Father: "By GENERATION God begot his only Son, in accordance with his decree.... Generation must be an example of external efficiency, since the Son is a different person from the Father" (YP 6:205). If the Son is begotten willfully by God's decree, then he is not coeternal with God, and so he is both a creature and subordinate to the godhead.[10] The most frequent source text for the begetting is Psalm 2:7, "I will declare the decree: the Lord hath said unto me, Thou *art* my Son; this day have I begotten thee." In the *Racovian Catechism* this passage places the Son in time and so separates him from eternity: "for the word, [*today*,] inasmuch as it denoteth a certain time, cannot signifie eternity" (34). Similarly, Milton argues, "So God begot the Son as a result of his own decree. Therefore it took place within the bounds of time, for the decree itself must have preceded its execution (the insertion of the word *today* makes this quite clear). As for those who maintain that the Son's generation was from eternity, I cannot discover on what passage in the scriptures they ground their belief" (YP 6:209–10).

That the Son is begotten in time, as Milton claims in *De doctrina*, is a consistent preoccupation in *Paradise Lost*, and proves to be a key to Milton's Christology in the poem. It is the first thing God tells us: his opening address to the Son begins with "Only begotten Son" (*PL* 3.80). The angelic choir celebrates this quality in the Son in book 3: after the Father, "Thee next they sang of all creation first, / Begotten Son, divine similitude" (383–84). And the first event in the plot of *Paradise Lost* turns out to be the begetting itself. As Raphael reports, God announces before all the angels,

> Thrones, dominations, princedoms, virtues, powers,
> Hear my decree, which unrevoked shall stand.
> This day I have begot whom I declare
> My only Son, and on this holy hill
> Him have anointed, whom ye now behold
> At my right hand; your head I him appoint;
> And by my self have sworn to him shall bow
> All knees in heaven, and shall confess him Lord. (5.601–08)

These lines reiterate three key points from *De doctrina*: that the Son is begotten, that the begetting is by God's "decree," and that it was done on "This day," implying that the event takes place in time not eternity. As a created being, and one created not by necessity but by God's voluntary decree, the Son is both subordinate to the Father and not eternal.

The Son's begetting is an unmistakable marker of Antitrinitarianism, the clearest sign in *Paradise Lost* of Milton's rejection of the Trinity. It is a theologically contentious event in that it separates Antitrinitarianism from orthodoxy. But it also marks a point of contention between Milton and Socinianism, a place where Milton's Son emerges as idiosyncratic, a largely unprecedented figure even among Antitrinitarians. Although the Son's begetting delineates his subordinate position, it carries with it a difficulty for Socinians. For a moment of creation may be read to imply a preincarnate history, which is a position acceptable to Arians but not to Socinians, with their insistence on the Son as mere man. So the *Racovian Catechism* connects the begetting of Psalm 2 to the Resurrection, on the authority of Acts 13:33. "Begetting" for Socinians must be a real generation—but one specifically placed at the Resurrection, as Paul asserts.[11] Strangely, then, both orthodox and Socinian readings of the Son's begetting are metaphoric. Trinitarian readings loosen it from the literalness of "this day" to find the Son begotten eternally, and Socinian readings view begetting as a metaphor for the resurrection and exaltation of the Son, not the literal generation.

Whether or not to read the begetting as a metaphor has been a point of extended contention among readers of *Paradise Lost*.

Kelley summarizes the debate over the Son's begetting in book 5, between such important critics as Masson, Saurat, Fletcher, and Grierson.[12] The problem centers on the seeming contradiction between "This day I have begot whom I declare / My only Son," based on Psalm 2:7, and the moment later in book 5 when Abdiel calls him "begotten Son, by whom / As by his Word the mighty Father made / All things" (5.835–37), which is based on John 1 and implies that the Son was present at the creation of the angels, well before "this day." To avoid inconsistency in the poem, many read the begetting as metaphoric, which can be supported by *De doctrina*. But seeing the Son's begetting in *Paradise Lost* as purely metaphoric is inadequate. That position pushes Milton toward orthodoxy, with the implication that the Son is eternal. William Hunter suggests that the Father's announcement about the begetting of the Son in book 5 is to be read "as one enormous metaphor," and uses this to imply that Milton is an orthodox Trinitarian.[13] Or a purely metaphoric begetting may push Milton toward Socinianism, which transfers the generation to the Resurrection. Instead, Milton quite self-consciously positions himself between the Trinitarian and Socinian positions by insisting on the begetting as both literal and metaphoric.

The most salient part of Milton's reading of the begetting is that it is not only metaphoric, but also literal. Milton asserts the literalness of the begetting, first against orthodox theologians who metaphorize it into eternity, and, immediately after, against "modern scholars" (that is, Socinians) who deny the begetting a place in preincarnate history:

> In scripture there are two senses in which the father is said to have begotten the Son: one literal, with reference to production; the other metaphorical, with reference to exaltation. Many commentators have cited those passages which allude to the exaltation of the Son, and to his function as mediator, as evidence of his generation from eternity. As a matter of fact they have some excuse, if there is any room for excuse at all, because not a scrap of real evidence for the eternal generation of the Son can be found in the whole of scripture. Whatever certain modern scholars may say to the

> contrary, it is certain that the Son existed in the beginning, under the title of the Word or Logos, that he was the first of created things, and that through him all other things, both in heaven and earth, were afterwards made. (YP 6:206)

Milton then gathers his scriptural evidence, commencing with the beginning of John, and concludes, "All these passages prove that the Son existed before the creation of the World, but not that his generation was from eternity. The other texts which are cited indicate only metaphorical generation, that resurrection from the dead or appointment to the functions of mediator, according to St. Paul's own interpretation of the second Psalm" (YP 6:206). Milton readily concedes Paul's metaphoric reading in Acts 13:32–33, but he goes out of his way to insist upon a literal reading of Psalm 2, which, contra both Socinians and Trinitarians, locates the Son's generation as the first of created things, before the creation of the world.

Milton's belief in a Son who is really generated and really acting in the events of preincarnate history is repeatedly asserted by means of a rejection of both orthodox and Socinian readings and their mutual reliance, to very different ends, on metaphor. So his explanation of the Son's role in Creation is again framed as specifically not orthodox and not Socinian: "In the beginning was the Word. He was God with God, and although he was not supreme, he was the firstborn of all creation. It follows that he must have existed before his incarnation, whatever subtleties may have been invented to provide an escape from this conclusion, by those who argue that Christ was a mere man" (YP 6:419).[14] Milton's Christology steers between orthodox Trinitarianism and Socinianism to conceive of a subordinate Son existing and acting in preincarnate history. Of course, this does not solve the problem of inconsistency in book 5 of *Paradise Lost*—the Son has been literally begotten, but clearly at a time prior to the creation of the angels and outside of the poem's narrative. *De doctrina* does not solve the inconsistency of the poem, but it does show us the careful work Milton puts into delineating a non-Trinitarian Son that is also active in preincarnate history.

Confusion arises from the fact that in the poem we are not given the literal begetting as a plot event. This is surely because the Bible similarly remains silent. Insisting on the Son's literal generation, Milton concludes his discussion of begetting in *De doctrina* by declaring, "What I have quoted is all that is revealed from heaven about the generation of the Son of God. Anyone who wants to be wiser than this is really not wise at all" (YP 6:212). The original moment of the Son's preincarnate history remains shrouded in the ambiguity of the opening of John. But despite such confused beginnings, the preincarnate history is remarkably developed in the poem. While *De doctrina* on the whole says little about the Son before the Incarnation, *Paradise Lost* can be seen as a concerted effort at imagining the Son's preincarnate history. This is a period rich with theological questions and imaginative possibilities: When was the Son begotten? What did the Son do prior to the Incarnation? What was he like? Although these flights of imagination find little place in *De doctrina*, it is clear that they form a large part of *Paradise Lost*. The poem goes where the system of theology cannot, narrating the effects of the Son's begetting, his station at the right hand of God, his role in Creation and the war in heaven. As Kelley puts it, by means of the Son, "Milton makes the dry and meager bones of his theology live in the feigned image of poetry."[15]

The preincarnate Son that Milton develops in *De doctrina* is in fact most innovative in that it enables the narrated Son of *Paradise Lost*. The two texts are different at many points, but they also work in tandem: *De doctrina* argues for the Son in preincarnate history, and *Paradise Lost* imagines the consequences. The preincarnate Son matters precisely in that he is narratable: he appears, thinks, and acts within the time and space of the storyworld. Furthermore, the Son's entrance into the theological position of preincarnate history—that is, his begetting—is also the moment that generates the plot events of the narrative. The Son's begetting, in Milton's hands, leads to Satan's rebellion, which in turn leads to all of the major plot events of the poem: the war in heaven, the apostates' fall, Adam and Eve's fall, and their expulsion from the garden. The linking of Satan's rebellion to the begetting is entirely original. Despite its extensive treatment of the begetting, *De doctrina* makes no mention of it as a motive for rebellion, as Kelley points out.[16] And Hunter makes the even more stunning observation that, "Not only is there no support in the *Christian Doctrine* for this interpretation, but the exaltation of the Son has never been related to Satan in this way by any Christian tradition."[17] Kelley calls Milton's invention "a theological fiction introduced by Milton to give a motivating force to his epic," and MacCallum celebrates the boldness and sheer inventiveness of this innovation as "evidence of his powers as a dramatist."[18] It is a stroke of plotting genius, such as is often celebrated in Shakespeare's adjustments to his sources.

Milton's Antitrinitarianism as a whole has been recognized as a catalyst for Milton's imaginative efforts in *Paradise Lost*. Defoe laments Milton's Arianism but sees that it was born of dramatic need: "But the thing was necessary to Milton, who wanted to assign some cause or original of the Devil's rebellion."[19] Irene Samuel points out that Milton's Antitrinitarianism, by assuring a separation of persons, facilitates the council of book 3: "Doubtless Milton's Arianism made it possible for him to handle the council in Heaven as a dramatic dialogue between distinct speakers more easily, and with less conflict between what he saw as dramatically desirable and what he felt as doctrinally correct, than a Trinitarian might." William Empson is willing to go even further by suggesting that the poetic needs of *Paradise Lost* are what determined Milton's theology: "what his imagination had produced amounted to being an Arian." Poetic exigency may not trump the seriousness of *De doctrina*, but it is remarkable how well what Milton puts in place of the Trinity—his uniquely preincarnate Son—serves his poetic purposes.[20]

The dramatic benefits of Milton's preincarnate Son first emerge in the Son's plea for mercy in book 3, where he tempers the Father's anger (*PL* 3.144–84). When the Son chastises the Father with the perspective of Grace, the Father's answer shows a deep integration of their thoughts: "All hast thou spoken as my thoughts are, all / As my eternal purpose hath decreed" (3.171–72). We have an external dialogue, but the Son is actually expressing the Father's thoughts, completing the Father's combination of justice and mercy, and taking part in that essential act of a "decree." A separate being, but very nearly God, this unique thing, the preincarnate Son, offers the Father a chance at dialogue, which is to say, a chance at entering the narrative in a more complete manner.

As the Son mediates between God and narrative, he also stands in for the utterly abstract Father when it comes time to act. The Son most obviously becomes an actor for the Father in the war in heaven, engaging the apostates in a battle that an abstract godhead could not wage. *De doctrina* makes clear that the Son lacks the divine attributes, including omniscience and omnipotence (YP 6:265–66), and this separation from divinity allows for consequential action in the plot, even if the third day of the war proves a rout. Despite the narrative complexities of the war in heaven, exemplified in chapter 4 by the discontinuous wound, the war can be seen as one of the main poetic fruits of Milton's particular version of Antitrinitarianism: the Son's actions would be available neither to the orthodox Son who is equal to the Father nor to the Socinian Son who has no existence prior to the Incarnation.

After the war in heaven, the Son's second great preincarnate action is the Creation. Begotten and present in a way far more literal and material than the Word at the beginning of John, the Son is uniquely present at, and active in, Creation. Whereas the Bible offers either "the Word" or the terse formula of "God said" in Genesis 1, the Son prepares an expedition (*PL* 7.193), allowing the Father's infinite abstraction to move through the spatio-temporal limits of narrative in a chariot.[21] The Son also appears to exit the gates of heaven (7.205–09); he stops the chariot and uses the golden compasses (7.224–31); and after Creation he "arrived, and sat him down / With his great Father" (7.587–88). This coming and going and the use of technology are the most visible, material, and narratable of the creative acts, and they naturally belong to the Son.

At the outset of the Creation, it is made clear that the Son will be acting for the Father: "So spake the almighty, and to what he spake / His Word, the filial Godhead, gave effect" (*PL* 7.174–75). But this mediation is not without the well-known complexity that during the Creation itself the Son is not mentioned at all. The difficulty first appears when, seven lines after the Son uses the compasses, we are told, "Thus God the heaven created" (7.232). The creating agent is then called "God" throughout.²² With each mention of God, the Son's absence is felt, and even as the world unfolds so beautifully, there is a building sense of contradiction. Finally, after "God" has completed the six days of Creation, it is the Son who returns to heaven. At this point Milton takes the time to explain the confusion by pointing to God's transcendent power, his monotheistic resistance to narrative: "The filial power arrived, and sat him down / With his great Father (for he also went / Invisible, yet stayed such privilege / Hath omnipresence)" (7.587–90). This ambiguity between God and Son resembles the ontological instability of Genesis 18, suggesting that we are seeing the negotiations typical of monotheistic narrative.

Patrides considers the blending of God and the Son in Creation to be evidence of a Trinitarian position.²³ On the contrary, this blending elegantly resolves one of the pressing arguments against Antitrinitarianism. Genesis 1:26, "Let us make man in our image," with *elohim* for God and a plural verb, is a traditional place to defend the Trinity. So Calvin: "Christians, therefore, properly contend, from this testimony, that there exists a plurality of Persons in the Godhead."²⁴ In *Paradise Lost*, "God" has replaced the Son as creative agent through most of the sixth day, when the Son suddenly resurfaces in the narrative: "the omnipotent / Eternal Father (for where is not he / Present) thus to his Son audibly spake. / Let us make now man in our image" (7.516–19). Emphasizing the Father's infinite power and presence, these lines remind us that the real agent of creation is the Father. But simultaneously, the Son emerges on cue, practically scurrying to God's side like an amanuensis—in *Paradise Lost*, "Let us make man" is clearly spoken to a subordinate Son, not to an equal part of the Trinity.

Milton is quite clear in *De doctrina* that the Son is not the principal cause of Creation, but rather is merely instrumental: "For the Father is not only he *by* whom, but also he *from* whom, *in* whom, *through* whom, and *on account of* whom all things are, as I have shown above, inasmuch as he comprehends within himself all lesser causes. But the Son is only he *through* whom all things are, and is therefore the less principal cause" (YP 6:302). The Son's instrumentality, that creation goes *through* him, leads to the inevitable complications between God and Son in monotheistic narrative. But on the whole monotheistic instability is quite dexterously managed—the preincarnate Son generally serves the needs of the narrative. So in Milton's versions of Genesis 1:26, the Son seems to appear most of all for the sake of dialogue. In *De doctrina*, Milton glosses 1:26 by explaining that "when God is about to make man he speaks like a person giving careful consideration to something, as if to imply that this is a still greater work" (YP 6:316). In the poem the presence of the Son allows the Father to speak "audibly," which implies an auditor, a sharer in conversation. With "Let us make," God attains a narrative presence not felt in the kerygmatic utterances of the other days of Creation. And the Son becomes an integrated, rather than excessive or contradictory, part of the narrative.

The Son and the Father then blend most ineluctably at the creation of Adam. Adam is actually created by a "he," but nowhere can it be determined whether the pronoun refers to the Father or the Son (*PL* 7.526, 529, 537, 548). "God" has done the creating heretofore, making him the logical antecedent. But coming immediately after "Let us make man," there is room for doubt. Plus, after the creation of Adam, "the creator...up returned" (7.551–52) to the gates of heaven, and "the filial power arrived" at God's eternal house (7.587). Such deep ambiguity, however, is given a triumphal quality. Unlike in the invocation to book 9, where ambiguity between God and angel is part of the tragic collapse of poetic "discourse unblamed," the unknowable antecedent of "he" is surrounded by angelic song and Sabbath celebration at the end of book 7. Far from threatening the narrative, the Son's ontological instability is a constructive force in the celestial narrative of *Paradise Lost*.[25] Like God's creation, Milton's poetry unfolds *through* the Son.

Milton draws our attention to the poetic instrumentality of the preincarnate Son as an "expression" of God. The Son offers a conception of divinity that has substance and is visible, as when he enters the poem and "was seen / Most glorious, in him all his Father shone / Substantially expressed, and in his face / Divine compassion visibly appeared" (*PL* 3.138–41). This passage is based on Hebrews 1:3, which is a key text for Socinians arguing for the inequality of Son and Father.[26] As Milton repeats the word "express," the Antitrinitarian import fuses with the role that expression plays for the poet. As a visible expression of the invisible God, the Son is clearly representable in a way that the Father is not—so the Son, on the right hand of God, "all his Father manifest / Expressed" (*PL* 10.66–67).[27] This process becomes more complicated when the Son receives instruction from the Father upon leaving for war: "He said, and on his Son with rays direct / Shone full, he all his Father full expressed / Ineffably into his face received" (6.719–21). In this use of "express," the sense of giving out information melts into the sense of light shining forth, and both of these take on the ineffable valences of theophany and the conveyance of divinity—appropriate to the Son's deployment in the war. This moment also recalls the invocation to book 3: "Hail holy Light, offspring of heaven first-born, / Or of the eternal co-eternal beam / May I express thee unblamed?" where light and verbal expression are intertwined in the approach to God and in the poetic problem of theophany. The central anxiety of the invocation is one of expression: can the poet put God into his poem without blame? In *Paradise Lost*, Antitrinitarianism offers an affirmation, as the preincarnate Son becomes a narratable expression of the monotheistic Father.

The Son's Identity in Paradise Regained

If the Son facilitates narrative in *Paradise Lost*, however, he has the opposite effect in *Paradise Regained*, known from its earliest reception as Milton's boring epic. According to Edward Phillips, Milton knew that it was "generally censur'd to be much inferiour" to *Paradise Lost*, and he was vexed by his readers' disappointment. According to Defoe, *Paradise Regained* is "a Dull Thing, infinitely short of the former (*Paradise Lost*), nothing to compare with it, and not like the same Author, and this is the Universal Opinion of the Age about these two Books."[28] Such judgments have continued among modern readers, who have called the poem "cold" and the plot "indifferent."[29] This shift from the heroic narratives of celestial war and universal creation in *Paradise Lost* to the stunted, antiheroic narrative of *Paradise Regained* coincides with the fact that the Son in the latter no longer has a preincarnate history.

Paradise Regained is set after the Incarnation, so in the moment of the story the Son is human rather than the divine being of the pre-Incarnation narrative. But Milton goes further, nearly erasing all connection to the preincarnate Son. This is a connection every reader of *Paradise Lost* would expect when coming to the sequel, so right away Satan announces that the Son of *Paradise Regained* may not be the Son of *Paradise Lost*:

> His first-begot we know, and sore have felt,
> When his fierce thunder drove us to the deep;
> Who this is we must learn, for man he seems
> In all his lineaments, though in his face
> The glimpses of his father's glory shine.   (PR 1.89–93)

Satan remembers the preincarnate Son, but is not sure whether to see that figure as continuous with the human Son of God recently revealed. This ambiguity continues throughout the poem, so that

D. C. Allen recommends that readers forget *Paradise Lost* and the Son's divinity altogether.[30] *Paradise Regained* refrains from linking the pre- and postincarnate Sons until the very end, when the angelic choir reveals to the Son that Satan, "long of old / Thou didst debel, and down from heaven cast / With all his army" (*PR* 4.604–06). Ultimately, the Son of *Paradise Regained* is the Son of the war in heaven and *Paradise Lost,* but only after that identification is held in suspension—and pursued with urgency—across the length of the poem. Without a preincarnate history, the Son functions for nearly the entire poem as purely human. And with a mere man as Son, *Paradise Regained* cannot attain the heroic pitch and narrative continuity of *Paradise Lost.*

The shift away from a preincarnate Son is a shift from a generally divine to a human poetic perspective. The divine, or celestial, perspective of *Paradise Lost* enters the beginning of *Paradise Regained* with the invocation, "I who erewhile the happy garden sung" (*PR* 1.1). And our expectations for a celestial narrative are fed by the initial frame narrative, in which the divine and infernal councils, including the reprise of God's speech, angelic hymns, Satan's rhetoric, and polytheistic speeches, promise a narrative set in heaven and hell. But the entrance of the Son enacts a rapid descent to the human: "So they in heaven their odes and vigils tuned: / Meanwhile the Son of God, who yet some days / Lodged in Bethabara" (1.182–84). Although in book 2 Satan goes back to his conclave, the heavenly council and choir are replaced by the human discourse of the Apostles and Mary—and the celestial point of view is not seen again until after the pinnacle. The starkness of the shift to the human level becomes a discontinuity in the narrative, the same kind of discontinuity (in fact, modeled on it) as led modern biblical criticism to posit a separate source for the frame narrative of Job. The example of Job is instructive because if you remove the frame and read only the center, the narrative becomes radically inconclusive. So René Girard compares the frameless Job to *Oedipus Rex,* with the radical disassociation of humans from fate or divine will.[31] Indeed, without the debate between God and Satan, and without the conclusion in which God returns Job's wealth, there would be very little in the Book of Job to explain why he suffers or to what end. It is precisely the celestial narrative of the frame that elevates Job from a human, potentially tragic story to a story that demonstrates the workings of God—that is, to theodicy or to monotheistic narrative. In imitating the Book of Job, *Paradise Regained* reproduces the sense of a disjunction between the human and the divine. And, what is even more interesting, it reproduces the textual sense that the disjunction has been forcibly bridged. The kind of joints between sources such as we find in Job are also visible in *Paradise Regained*, only the disjunction is not between authors but poems. What is felt as a joint is the move from the preincarnate history of *Paradise Lost* to the merely human history of *Paradise Regained*.

In narrating a Son who is almost entirely human, *Paradise Regained* draws Milton even closer to Socinian Christology. The poem departs from the pre-Incarnation ontology that separates *Paradise Lost* from the Socinian conception of the Son as mere man, and dares to experiment with how such a Christology would unfold, how such a Son would think and act. The dominant humanity of the Son has led John Rogers to ask whether *Paradise Regained* is a Socinian text. Rogers rightly concludes that when the angelic choir announces the Son's preincarnate ontology, the poem lands upon a Christology that is specifically opposed to Socinianism. But this is a late action, one that hurriedly turns the poem against Socinianism only after an extended dalliance with it.[32] For almost the entire poem—what lies within the frame narrative—the Son, Satan, and the rest of the actors seem wholly unaware of the Son's preincarnate history. Even if Milton ultimately comes down on the side of a preincarnate Son, the poem wavers between it and the Socinian claim for a mere man. *Paradise Regained*, I would suggest, represents a serious experiment in the Socinian view—an imaginative response to the often persuasive claims of the Socinians.

The central problem in this experiment is the "identity motif," which Barbara Lewalski calls "the very substance of the dramatic action."[33] As many critics have recognized, Satan, the Son, and the reader all struggle to understand whether the Son is human or divine, and in particular what is meant by the phrase "Son of God." From its outset, the identity motif is charged with the problem of Socinian Christology. It begins with Satan's doubt, whether the "first begot" whose thunder drove him to hell is the same as the human Son now wandering the desert. That the Son is identified as "first begot" reminds us that he is the created being of Antitrinitarian Christology. Satan's confusion marks the boundary between the essentially Arian Christology of *Paradise Lost* and whatever we may have in *Paradise Regained*. Satan's "Who this is we must learn" is an exhortation to determine whether the Socinian belief that the Son is merely human pertains in the poem's present.

But with the exclusion of the celestial narrative, and from within the human-centered storyworld, the hermeneutic of the identity motif becomes skeptical and deeply anxious about knowledge. Satan pursues his course of inquiry doggedly, but repeatedly expresses doubt about how to understand the combination of the divine and human in the Incarnate Son, using careful phrases such as "If he be man" (*PR* 2.136). Frustrated by the problem of ontology, he probes the Son directly: "These godlike virtues wherefore dost thou hide?" (3.21). But solutions are not forthcoming. The problem of identity ultimately rests on the ambiguous phrase "Son of God," which, as Satan notes, is impossible to parse:

> Be not so sore offended, Son of God;
> Though Sons of God both angels are and men,
> If I to try whether in higher sort
> Than these thou bear'st that title.   (4.196–99)

The phrase "Son of God" is what initiates Satan's inquiry upon hearing it from John the Baptist. But right up to the final temptation on the pinnacle, the investigation is inconclusive:

> Thenceforth I thought thee worth my nearer view
> And narrower scrutiny, that I might learn
> In what degree or meaning thou art called
> The Son of God, which bears no single sense;
> The Son of God I also am, or was,
> And if I was, I am; relation stands;
> All men are Sons of God. (4.514–20)

Satan's puzzlement may be insincere, a rhetorical strategy that is part of his tempting.[34] But Satan's rhetorical powers are of significantly less consequence than in *Paradise Lost*. Several times Satan is bereft of his power of speech, utterly defeated as a rhetorician (*PR* 3.1–4, 3.145–49, 4.21–24). Book 4 begins with a picture of Satan totally without pretense or power to dissemble:

> Perplexed and troubled at his bad success
> The tempter stood, nor had what to reply,
> Discovered in his fraud, thrown from his hope,
> So oft, and the persuasive rhetoric
> That sleeked his tongue, and won so much on Eve,
> So little here, nay lost; but Eve was Eve,
> This far his over-match. (4.1–7)

It is with this sense of confusion that Satan in book 4 returns again and again to his deep uncertainty about the Son of God: "Sons of God both angels are and men" (197); "Then hear, O Son of David, virgin-born; / For Son of God to me is yet in doubt" (500–501); "The Son of God, which bears no single sense" (517);

> And opportunity I here have had
> To try thee, sift thee, and confess have found thee
> Proof against all temptation as a rock
> Of adamant, and as a centre, firm
> To the utmost of mere man both wise and good,
> Not more. (531–36)

Satan's obtuse repetition suggests genuine bafflement.[35]

In fact, more sincere than is in his best interests, Satan becomes a figure for the impossibility of rationally comprehending the nature of the Son. Satan gets nowhere in his research and is seen butting his head against the inaccessible mystery of the incarnate Son. Satan's attempts at understanding yield a deeply contradictory hermeneutics—knowledge in this poem is hard to come by, and information once learned does not seem to stay learned. Christopher Hill, sensing Milton's own doubt and experimental spirit in writing the poem, suggests, "Satan is not the rhetorical deceiver of *Paradise Lost*, but one half of the poet talking to the other half."[36] Satan's hermeneutic struggles are also Milton's, as he experiments with conceiving of the Son after the dissolution of the Trinity.

Being satanic, it may not be surprising that Satan is doomed to make little progress in his understanding of the Son's identity. What may be remarkable, though, is that the Son also achieves no discernible breakthrough in his self-understanding. The Son is a humble man without a significant knowledge of what it means to be the Son of God—and his search for self-identity is as ambiguous and contradictory as Satan's investigation. The Son begins by reflecting back on his baptism and the miraculous visitation of the dove, that moment of revelation when his identity may have been resolved. Whereas the accounts in Matthew, Mark, and Luke report the event in a straightforward narration, Milton rewrites it through the Son's own perspective. And with the subjective, first-person narrative comes a perspective that is far more doubtful in tone. In a jarring piece of verse, Milton compresses the syntax of predicate statement to the point of near contradiction:

>   but he
> Straight knew me, and with loudest voice proclaimed
> Me him (for it was shown him so from heaven)
> Me him whose harbinger he was.
>   . . . .
>
> And last the sum of all, my Father's voice,
> Audibly heard from heaven, pronounced me his,
> Me his beloved Son, in whom alone
> He was well pleased.   (1.274–77, 283–86)

The verb "to be," the signifier of essence, falls out of the repeated formulation, "Me him" and "Me his" as if the Son cannot understand or believe the mystery of being both me (man) and him (God). Although next to each other in the poetry, "me" and "him" seem infinitely separate, as the Son stutters or lingers over the mystery. This surprising compression is repeated four times, prominently at the head of two lines, and then across an enjambment. The strangeness of the Son's diction and Milton's versification mark the Son's struggle to understand his own identity. His hermeneutic matches Satan's: both are trying to figure out how divinity meets humanity within the Son of God.

The Son says that he knew from the Spirit "that I no more should live obscure, / But openly begin" (1.287–88). But what should be begun remains ambiguous. And as he reflects back on the scene of baptism, the Son is thinking from a position of ignorance. "And now by some strong motion I am led / Into this wilderness, to what intent / I learn not yet, perhaps I need not know" (1.290–92). He is undeniably human in the reach of his knowledge, and therefore dependent on special revelation from God for information. Remarkably, he suggests that his limited human knowledge may be sufficient: he has felt "some strong motion," but knows not how to interpret it, and may never learn. Sounding humble, but also drawing near to the rational positions of Socinians and deists, the Son considers that there may be no need for divine revelation. To regain paradise perhaps requires no more understanding than is available to any human without the clarity of special revelation. The Son prepares us for a poem that may be entirely disenchanted, with no clear miracle or revelation to instruct either the Son or us. In support of such a disenchanted, entirely human reading, Hill argues that "until the very end of the poem his consciousness of himself is that of any potential Son of God exposed to temptation." MacCallum notices that the Son lays no claim to a timeless personal existence or to a knowledge of the will of the Father, and argues that the Son's knowledge can be derived strictly from Scripture, making him a man "using right reason and the revelation of scripture to arrive at self-understanding."[37] This is the kind of rational scripturalism that underlies both *De doctrina* and Socinianism.

And yet there are moments of greater insight. It is with a sense of divine knowledge that the Son asks, "Why dost thou then suggest to me distrust, / Knowing who I am, as I know who thou art?" (*PR* 1.355–56). In such moments, the hermeneutic bumps into confusion—there is simply no way fully to understand what the Son knows, or whether he is merely human or in some manner divine. At least for the moment, the Son has extensive knowledge, comprehending both his own and Satan's understanding. But this more divine knowledge is again challenged by the Son's apparent insight into Satan when he rejects the invitation to idolatry: "Get thee behind me; plain thou now appear'st / That Evil One, Satan for ever damned" (4.193–94). The Son's "now" contradicts, or is discontinuous with, the previous statement of authoritative and divine knowledge. D. C. Allen is attuned to this sense of contradiction or fluctuation in the Son's self-knowledge: "As we read the epic, we watch him as he crosses and recrosses the boundary between the two persons, for it is out of this wandering to and fro, out of the humanly uncertain and the divinely sure that Milton gives validity to the test and extracts from it a highly dramatic conclusion."[38] As with "Me him," the poem uses bald contradiction in the hermeneutic process to resist, across the length of the poem, any conclusions to the identity motif.

The God-Man

Resolution eventually comes. The angelic choir announces that "long of old / Thou didst debel" Satan in the war in heaven, clarifying that this Son is to be identified with the preincarnate Son. Like *Paradise Lost* and *De doctrina Christiana*, *Paradise Regained* finally insists that the Son is not a mere man. But the poem is focused on indecisiveness in Christology more than conclusion, emphasizing how hard it is to know the Son's ontology. *Paradise Regained* is not a Socinian document, but it is a text that broods upon Socinianism and the many questions it raises.

The poem's recurring questioning of the name "Son of God" is itself a dramatization of one of the key ambiguities in the Socinian debate. When Satan seeks to learn "In what degree or meaning thou art called / The Son of God, which bears no single sense," he is inquiring into a topic that garners the attention of many Socinian tracts. Crell, for example, in his extended argument "That Christ is not the Most High God," draws his second argument from "the name of *The Son of God*," claiming that "by this very appellation, the Son is distinguished from God" (Crell, *Two Books*, 50–52). Crell and other Socinians argue for the name "Son" as evidence of inequality and a separate essence, as Milton does in *De doctrina:* "a real son is not of the same age as his father, still less of the same numericall essence: otherwise father and son would be one person" (YP 6:209). Crell develops a lengthy explanation of the name "Son of God," covering all the major appearances in Scripture, and explains that he has "spoken somewhat largely" on the topic in part because "that Christ is the Son of God, is commonly believed to contain the strongest argument of the contrary opinion." That is, the name "Son of God" is commonly understood to support the Trinitarian position, and so Crell has specifically given the issue his attention: "Wherefore it is to be shewn in a few words, how exceedingly men commonly err, and the true opinion be proved from the reason whereby Christ is the Son of God."[39] The possibility of multiple interpretations of "Son of God" is acknowledged in John 10:33–36, where Jesus argues against Jewish charges of blasphemy by showing that Scripture also uses the phrase for humans. Such scriptural support for a broad understanding of "Son of God" is important to Socinian arguments for a human Son, and also repeatedly serves Milton's argument for the inequality of God and the Son (YP 6:207, 219, 238; see Crell, *Two Books*, 146–47; *Racovian* 19–20). As Kelley's annotations suggest (YP 6:207, 238), the Antitrinitarian insistence on the multiple senses of "Son of God" underlies Satan's inquiries into the Son's identity. Satan, in this light, takes on the voice of a skeptical theologian, experimenting with the possibilities of a Son outside of the Trinity—and finding no clear answers.

The multiplicity of possible readings of "Son of God" is itself important to the Antitrinitarian position. The identity motif seems to position the Son now as human, and now as divine, and such a changeable and inconsistent ontology is an orthodox strategy used to support the Trinity. Socinians frequently argue against the orthodox position that in some places in Scripture the incarnate Son is speaking as human, and in others he is speaking in his divine nature. For Socinians, such a parsing of the Son—now human, now divine—appears as a way for orthodox thinkers to avoid recognizing the subordination of the Son. In *The Two Books*, Crell repeatedly rejects orthodox attempts to "evade by the distinction of Natures" the conclusion that the Son is not identical to the Father. For example, in his discussion of Matthew 11:27, he concludes that "the last, and most usual" strategy in orthodox debate "consisteth in the distinction of the Natures of Christ. For they say commonly these things are spoke of Christ, according to the humane Nature, and not according to the divine" (Crell, *Two Books*, 46–47, 106). *De doctrina* reads the same passage with the same concern: "But here, perhaps, my opponents will break in again with the same objection as before; for they use the two natures of Christ, and their conjunction in the office of mediator, as a convenient little device for evading any arguments brought against them, with the result that they are more difficult to pin down than Vertumnus" (YP 6:259–60).

Orthodox interpretations of the Son appear as changeable as the seasons, which for Milton and the Socinians is a problem with the Son's office as mediator. Milton points out that for his orthodox opponents, "whatever measure of divinity the Son attributes to the Father alone, as to one greater than himself, he should be understood to do so in his role of man or of mediator" (YP 6:225).

Established primarily in 1 Timothy 2:5, "There is one God, and one mediator between God and men: the man, Jesus Christ," the office of mediator brings together the Son with the Father, and the godhead with mankind. What Milton calls their "conjunction" allows orthodox arguments to finesse the most persuasive Antitrinitarian passages of Scripture. And it also significantly blurs what for Antitrinitarians must be a precise distinction between Father and Son. So Milton adopts a position that undermines such a conjunction of divine and human by insisting the Son is entirely human within the office of the mediator. His gloss of 1 Timothy 2:5 is typically Socinian and protects the singleness of God: "Here the whole person of the mediator is given the name 'man' (a name which really applies only to his inferior nature), rather than that he should be thought equal to the Father, when the reference is carefully and specifically to one God. Besides it is quite inconceivable that anyone could be a mediator to himself or on his own behalf" (YP 6:217–18).[40]

Against the orthodox office of the mediator, Milton insists that the Son is excluded from the divine attributes, including omniscience and dominion. This discussion leads in *De doctrina* to an extended gloss of Matthew 20:23, a passage that helps to explain why in *Paradise Regained* Milton so assiduously resists solutions to the identity motif. In Matthew, the mother of Zebedee's children asks Jesus to put her sons in a place of honor, "the one on the right hand, and the other on the left, in thy kingdom." Jesus answers that "to sit on my right hand, and on my left, is not mine to give, but it shall be given to them for whom it is prepared of my Father." The key phrase "not mine to give" apparently cedes dominion to the Father. It is the Son, moreover, who does the sitting at the right hand of God (Hebrews 1:3). Understandably, the passage is important to Socinian arguments.[41] But according to Milton it is commonly explained by Trinitarians as the Son speaking in the role of the mediator, which can be sometimes divine and sometimes human. Milton, however, will not allow interpretation to make such a distinction:

> They wanted him to grant their request to the utmost extent of his power, human or divine.... Christ answers, again, as a whole person, *it is not mine*. Moreover, he affirms that it is not in his power at all, but in the Father's alone, in case they should think, for some reason, that really it was his. To have replied only in his role of mediator would (perish the thought) have been very like playing the sophist. It would mean that he had tricked the mother and her sons with an evasion of the kind which logicians call *expositio prava*, or *aequivoca*, which is when one replies in a sense or from an angle different from that of the questioner. The same must be true of other passages of a similar kind where Christ speaks of himself. Once his two natures have coalesced hypostatically into a single person, whatever Christ says of himself he must say it (unless he makes a distinction himself) not as if he possessed one nature or the other, but as a whole person speaking about a whole person. Those who take it upon themselves to tear apart this hypostatical union, as it is called, rob Christ's speeches and replies of all their sincerity. They substitute for Christ an unknown quantity, now one person, now another, and everything it says is ambiguous and uncertain, true and false at the same time. When dealing with such opponents, one may aptly ask Horace's question: With what knot shall I hold this face-changing Proteus? (YP 6:228–29)

The Son in Matthew 20:23 must abjure omnipotence, "in case they should think, for some reason, that really it was his" in order to make clear the distinction between the Son's attributes and the Father's. Mediation introduces the slippery subjectivity of "now one person now another," and the mother and sons of Zebedee would be misled by a Son that moved so easily between God and man. To allow the line between Father and Son to be blurred, that is, to answer as an orthodox mediator, would be to play the sophist, and to trick with equivocation. Milton's concern is that the orthodox mediator would make the Son ontologically unstable and insincere. The orthodox mediator threatens to make the Son an "unknown quantity," and his words "ambiguous and uncertain, true and false at the same time."

The same charge applies to Milton's opponents, orthodox Trinitarians who, in relying upon the dual natures of the mediator, are as slippery as Proteus. These shape-shifting theologians may lie behind Satan's appearance in *Paradise Regained* as an Archimago-like "aged man in rural weeds" (*PR* 1.314). Taking on the typically deceptive guise of a hermit, and, more specifically, the Catholicism of Spenser's shape-shifter, Satan enters into dialogue with the Son in the revealing figure of a Renaissance Proteus. Satan immediately probes the identity motif, noting that "thou seem'st the man" John the Baptist called Son of God, and then tempting the Son to display his divinity: "But if thou be the Son of God, command / That out of these hard stones be made thee bread" (1.327–30, 342–43). A miracle would demonstrate the Son's divine rather than human nature, solving the identity motif with the same logic as the orthodox use in the mediator. The Son rejects the first temptation by deflecting dominion over life from himself to God, insisting that "Man lives not by bread only, but each word / Proceeding from the mouth of God" (1.349–50). Refusing to act as God and perform a miracle, the Son's answer to Satan is the same as Jesus' to the mother and sons: "it is not mine." The question of identity goes carefully unanswered, as the Son resists the temptation to make a clear distinction between his human and divine natures. This refusal immediately unmasks Proteus: "Why does thou then suggest to me distrust, / Knowing who I am, as I know who thou art?" (1.355–56). While most readings rightly interpret the Son to be saying that a miracle would demonstrate mistrust in God, a corollary meaning emerges from *De doctrina:* that a miracle would suggest distrust by asserting the divine nature of the mediator, and "To have replied only in his role of mediator would (perish the thought) have been very like playing the sophist."

The Son draws closest to Matthew 20:23 in the second temptation, when, refusing the offer of earthly glory, he tells Satan that he seeks glory for God: "I seek not mine, but his / Who sent me, and thereby witness whence I am" (*PR* 3.106–07). Echoing the "not mine" of Matthew as well as the paradoxical "Me him" of book 1, the Son's answer resolves into a deeply ambiguous blending of

Son and Father: "I am" names both the Son and Yahweh, and the claim that the Son comes from "I am" makes him both subordinate to God and self-originating. In the last temptation Satan similarly tries to establish the Son's divinity, and the Son, with exquisite care, avoids making the distinction between human and divine nature. Placing the Son on the pinnacle, Satan declares, "Now show thy progeny; if not to stand, / Cast thyself down; safely if Son of God" (4.554–55). The Son's answer, "Tempt not the Lord thy God" (4.561), is a refusal both to depend upon divine power, and to speak for it. It is unclear whether the Son's words refer to himself or the Father, but if the referent is the Father, the Son refuses to be presumptuous about divine will, and if the referent is himself, the Son refuses to act miraculously, which is to say, he refuses to assert the divine nature of the mediator. In either case, the Son is declaring that "it is not mine."

The Son in Matthew 20:23, according to *De doctrina,* takes care to speak and act "not as if he possessed one nature or the other, but as a whole person speaking about a whole person"—that is, he must keep the problem of the dual natures in the mediator unresolved. Similarly, Crell argues that "The exception concerning the humane Nature, according to which it was not his to give, whereas it was according to the divine, hath here no place, both for the simple negation, and also because he here opposeth not one Nature to another, but his own Person to the Person of the Father, and what he taketh away from himself he attributeth to him" (Crell, *Two Books,* 78). The Antitrinitarian response to the orthodox mediator is to insist on the Son not as containing two natures, but as a simple, whole person. The identity motif of *Paradise Regained* represents an extended opportunity to distinguish divine and human natures in the Son, and so to cleave the whole person of the Son into two. It is an occasion for orthodox Trinitarianism that is pursued relentlessly by Satan, making him one of those theologians that seeks to make the Son "now one person, now another." And the Son's identity is also pursued by the reader, who may be tempted into Satan's inquiry, or may resist that Protean perspective. *Paradise Regained*, no doubt, courts the hermeneutic desire to solve the identity motif—but it also courts the conclusion that the mystery cannot be solved. Until the angelic choir, the Son resists the identity motif by rejecting Satan's temptation to disclose divinity, and by being so apparently confused himself about what he knows. The ambiguity surrounding the Son's self-knowledge undermines both Satan's and the reader's detective work. As *Paradise Regained* extends through four books, up until the angelic choir, the poetry makes the same point as his gloss of Matthew: that we must be willing to accept the mystery of the Incarnation without distinguishing God from man.

Discussing the Incarnation in *De doctrina*, Milton does not say that the human and divine natures are indistinct, or, as the Socinians would argue, that there is no divine nature. Rather, he insists that both divine and human natures are within the Incarnate Son, but "We do not know how it is so, and it is best for us to be ignorant of things which God wishes to remain secret" (YP 6:424). Just as *Paradise Regained* works hard to undermine any inquiry into the way divine and human natures blend in the Son's identity, so *De doctrina*, sounding like Raphael, shuts down any line of questioning that would draw distinctions within the mediatorial office. This mysteriously incarnate Son, resistant to curiosity and hermeneutics, Milton calls the *theanthropos*, or God-man: "How much better for us, then, to know only that the Son of God, our Mediator, was made flesh and that he is called and is in fact both God and man. The Greeks express this concept very neatly by the single word *theanthropos* (God-man). As God has not revealed to us how this comes about it is much better for us to hold our tongues and be wisely ignorant" (YP 6:424).[42] Milton repeatedly makes use of this title, which emphasizes the surprising fact of the combination of human and divine in the Son, and at the same time resists prepositions that could explain how the God and the man relate. The compound word creates a sense of shock, like the asyndeton in the Son's "Me him...Me him." Both emphasize the convergence of the human and the divine natures, but also mark how that convergence cannot be explained through the grammar of a preposition. And so the incarnate Son remains unavailable to logical inquiry.

Milton's God-man cannot be parsed to reveal the border between his human and divine natures because the Incarnation itself, Milton insists, is a deep mystery. After citing 1 Timothy 3:16, the source text for Henry More's *Grand Mystery of Godliness,* Milton warns, "As this is such a great mystery, let its very magnitude put us on our guard from the outset, to prevent us from making any rash or hasty assertions or depending upon trivialities of mere philosophy" (YP 6:420–21). Milton's great objection is to an overly detailed inquiry into the Incarnate Son. Like the Socinians, Milton is suspicious of mystery, and will not accept it in the Trinity. But Milton takes his own path with the God-man, departing from the Socinians who argue for the Son as a mere man. Milton is willing to admit mystery in the God-man because of Scripture: "There is, however, not a single word in the Bible about the mystery of the Trinity, whereas the incarnation is frequently spoken of as a mystery" (YP 6:420). In Milton's Christology there is a transferral of mystery, from the relationship between God and Son in the Trinity, to the relationship between the divine and human in the God-man. Mystery slides away from the single godhead, but settles in the incarnate Son.

The shifting courses of mystery and the Son can be described in terms of Milton's monotheism. It is in the name of monotheism that Milton first rejects the Trinity, carving out a conception of God as single and completely separate from the rest of creation. Under such Antitrinitarianism, divinity, matching the monotheistic tendency toward complete abstraction in the godhead, becomes a thing utterly separate from the human world. Such an absolute distinction between God and the created Son is most visible in the preincarnate history of *Paradise Lost*. When the poetry turns to the incarnate Son of *Paradise Regained*, Milton is faced with the same need to define monotheism, only now the distinction must be drawn between the divine and human. The Socinian Son, being mere man, draws a sharp line between God and humans, and so protects the absolute abstraction of the monotheistic godhead. But Milton backs off from this most rigorously monotheistic version of the Son: unlike the Socinians, he does not see the Son as merely human. In what can be recognized as a variation of the monotheistic pattern of returning from the skeptical extreme—similar to Cowley's rejection of Davenant's aniconism—Milton turns back from the purest monotheistic distinction between the divine and human by admitting mystery. The God-man of *Paradise Regained*, by allowing mystery, is lodged in the negotiations between pure monotheism and the needs of narrative.

Milton's Christology is also monotheistic in that he recreates in the Son the tension between divinity and personality that is typical of the single God. Just as the God of monotheism wavers between absolute transcendence and the personality necessary for human thought and narrative, so the Son wavers between the expansive knowledge of God and the humble self-knowledge of man—the tensions that underlie the monotheistic God of *Paradise Lost* resurface in the identity motif of *Paradise Regained*. The identity motif draws a line between God and man, but this border, like all borders delineated in monotheistic narrative, is traced not with a single stroke, but by the to and fro of contradictions. The Son knows something now, and later seems to know it not; he has a divine perspective now, and later a human perspective. Without continuity from one moment to the next, it becomes difficult to read the Son as a unified subject. He becomes less of a well-rounded figure, the kind we find in novels who is capable of growth, and more of a partial subject, the kind that does not imitate a person but, like an allegorical figure, represents ideas or energies.[43] All the pressure between the infinite abstraction of divinity and the spatio-temporal limits of human history and narrative come to bear upon the Son, as the ontological instability of the monotheistic God slides into the unstable identity of the incarnate Son, who emerges from the identity motif with the fractured subjectivity of the God-man.

By setting up a preincarnate history in *Paradise Lost*, Milton creates a monotheistic narrative that conveys the cosmic history with relative clarity. There the Son's mediatorial office bridges the gap between the abstract godhead of monotheism and the demands of narrative, making him a solution to the narrative problems of monotheism. But in the Christology of *Paradise Regained*, Milton short-circuits mediation by imagining the Son separate from preincarnate history. This makes his mediatorial office far more disjunctive, undoing the Son's ability to negotiate between the human and divine, and breaking his subjectivity. We are left with the poem, and the Son, that so dissatisfy Defoe.

Indifferent Narrative and Miracle

Many readers have discovered a plot in *Paradise Regained* based upon the Son's growing self-knowledge. Just as the incomplete story of *Samson Agonistes* is completed by recourse to Samson's intellectual development, so *Paradise Regained* acquires a progressive plot by recourse to arguments that the Son acquires insight into his own nature. But the inexplicability of Milton's God-man, by undoing the Son's subjectivity, functions in the narrative of *Paradise Regained* as Samuel Johnson's missing middle functions in *Samson Agonistes:* it breaks the logical coherence of the plot. Without continuity of knowledge and consciousness, the God-man cannot grow as a person. The narrative of the Son's inner life does not unfold from beginning to middle to end, but rather denies any sense of learned information or conclusion. As Stanley Fish insists, nothing changes, and we arrive at the "indifferent" narrative of *Paradise Regained*.[44]

The seeming exception to indifferent narrative is the miracle of the angelic choir. It is then that the identity motif is solved and the Son and the reader learn definitively that he is the same figure we know from *Paradise Lost*. This key moment is delivered with miraculous splendor:

> straight a fiery globe
> Of angels on full sail of wing flew nigh,
> Who on their plumy vans received him soft
> From his uneasy station, and upbore
> As on a floating couch through the blithe air,
> Then in a flowery valley set him down
> On a green bank, and set before him spread
> A table of celestial food, divine,
> Ambrosial, fruits fetched from the tree of life,
> And from the fount of life ambrosial drink. (PR 4.581–90)

Milton stresses the miraculousness of the angelic intervention, with the "fiery globe of angels," the "floating couch," and the "celestial food." For the first time in an otherwise naturalistic plot, the supernatural becomes unequivocally present in the narrative. And as is the purpose of miracles, the spectacle gives authority to the important information soon to be revealed: that the Son has a preincarnate history in which he fought the war in heaven against Satan—"him long of old / Thou didst debel, and down from heaven cast / With all his army" (4.604–06). With a flourish, the chorus removes the poem from the arid irresolution of the identity motif, and closes off the Socinian Son. The angelic choir is the Jobean frame narrative that rescues the poem from human-based tragedy and delivers it into the celestial narrative of theodicy. And miracle is the plot event that defeats indifference. On the level of narrative, miracle offers what Tasso calls the marvelous and what Dennis finds in epic machinery—a stirring and heroic plot event.[45] At the same time, on a theological level, miracle pulls *Paradise Regained* back from an extreme Socinian position. The Son is not a mere man, nor is the religious economy rationalized and disenchanted.

It is worth recognizing how much miracle accomplishes in the poem. But it is even more important that miracle comes so late. *Paradise Regained* is for the most part a version of the Son without miracle, matching Christopher Hill's claim about Milton's theology in general: "Milton plays down all the miraculous elements in the Gospel story. Paradise is regained by human resistance to temptation, not by the sacrifice of a God."[46] Milton does not write extensively about miracles in *De doctrina*, but when he does it is to mark them as insignificant. He does not reject them outright, but declares: "Miracles are no more able to produce belief than, in itself, doctrine is: that is to say, they cannot produce it at all"; "They are blessed who believe without miracles" (YP 6:565).[47] Reading *Paradise Regained* within a Socinian and deist context highlights its disenchanted, unmiraculous storyworld—and suggests that it may not be outlandish to compare it to Thomas Woolston's *Discourses on the Miracles of our Saviour* (1727), the controversial deist text that denies Christ's miracles. Milton does not deny or mock miracle in *Paradise Regained*, as Woolston does. But he long defers it, so that for the length of the poem the absence of miracle and the debilitating stakes of unclear revelation are intimately felt. Miracles and revelation are not just absent, but are actively avoided. The Son's frequent refusals to act are refusals to act miraculously: he will not turn stones into bread nor command a table in the wilderness. Nor, in the last temptation, will he enact any kind of miraculous action or divine revelation. According to Stanley Fish, when Satan says "to stand upright / Will ask thee skill,"

> This comment suggests that there is a level of skill—short of miracle—that would suffice, but that Satan does not expect the Son or any other mere man to have it. That he does have it, and that it is not a skill dependent on divine intervention (whether of the Son or the Father), is evidenced by the phrase "uneasy station" (4.584), which suggests not a revealed God standing gloriously at front and center stage but a man who is doing the best that he can in a difficult situation to be true to the best that he knows. ("Things and Actions Indifferent," 180)

Miracle and divine revelation are the grandest of plot flourishes, events that cannot be indifferent. As Fish points out, Milton uses his own remarkable poetic skill to make the Son's great miracle in the Matthew and Luke accounts into a natural event. Milton is deferring miracle just a bit longer, removing it from its most obvious place on the pinnacle so as to prolong the now-overwhelming sense of its absence.

The lack of miracle most of all suspends our understanding of the Son by keeping his identity ambiguous. A miracle would demonstrate divinity, and so as readers grapple with the identity motif, attempting to understand whether or not the Son is mere man, the poem tempts us to discover miracles. Hill argues that until the end the Son is human, but his claim must be qualified in a way that captures Milton's subtlety. Hill attaches a footnote to his argument: "Except perhaps in 2.383–86, where Jesus appears to claim ability to perform miracles."[48] This is the passage in which the Son repudiates Satan's banquet: "I can at will, doubt not, as soon as thou / Command a table in the wilderness." For this brief moment, but only for a moment, the Son seems to be much more than mere man. The possibility of miraculous revelation similarly hovers over the entire poem, and for Lewalski it becomes the key to resolving the identity motif. She finds in the poem a progressive understanding of the Son's identity, but his self-knowledge depends on what she calls "special illumination" (*Milton's Brief Epic*, 163). After each temptation, she argues, the Son merits a special revelation from God that advances his self-knowledge, before reverting to human understanding. The theory of revelation thus explains the Son's discontinuous knowledge, in particular his surprising knowledge of his miraculous ability to command a table in the wilderness. For at that moment, "he seems to receive another of those divine illuminations, enabling him to assert the lordship over Nature due him as the Creator and Son of God" (*Milton's Brief Epic*, 221). And on the pinnacle, revelation finally serves to complete the Son's hermeneutic progress: "It seems reasonable to suppose that the miracle of full illumination accompanies that other miracle, and that the attribution of both the statement and the standing so unqualifiedly and forcefully to Christ indicates that he has now become again (as before in heaven) the conscious agent of the divine power in working the defeat of Satan" (*Milton's Brief Epic*, 317). Some of the most authoritative Miltonists have debated whether a miracle occurs on the pinnacle; it is hard not to think that Milton's readers are acting out the very debates over Christology that occupied Socinians and their orthodox opponents.

Milton himself introduces the possibility of the Son receiving a miraculous revelation when he has the Son announce,

> And now by some strong motion I am led
> Into this wilderness, to what intent
> I learn not yet, perhaps I need not know;
> For what concerns my knowledge God reveals.   (1.290–93)

But in these lines the Son admits that a revelation may not be necessary. Not only does the Incarnation remain mysterious to readers of Scripture, as Milton insists in *De doctrina*, but perhaps it need not be revealed to the Son either. Indeed, the key revelation of the Son's identity, the visit of the dove during his baptism, is reported in doubtful terms. The moment is repeatedly recalled, but that very repetition undermines the authority of the revelation. In book 1, the poet, Satan, and the Son all bring up John the Baptist and the dove, suggesting the explanatory potential this event has. The narrator's account of divine revelation is straightforward and seemingly authoritative: "on him baptized / Heaven opened, and in likeness of a dove / The Spirit descended, while the Father's voice / From heaven pronounced him his beloved Son" (*PR* 1.29–32). But then comes Satan's version, which includes greater doubt: "thence on his head / A perfect dove descend, whate'er it meant, / And out of heaven the sovran voice I heard, / This is my son beloved" (1.82–85). The facts are similar—the dove, the voice, the beloved son—but some details are interestingly varied. For example, for Satan the dove is "perfect," while for the narrator it is a "likeness." Subtle discrepancies in reporting suggest that we may not be receiving a wholly reliable or clear account, a skepticism encouraged by Satan's aside about the dove: "whate'er it meant." Lastly, the Son's account repeats the facts, but with a subtle sense of equivocation:

> Heaven opened her eternal doors, from whence
> The Spirit descended on me like a dove,
> And last the sum of all, my Father's voice
> Audibly heard from heaven, pronounced me his,
> Me his beloved Son. (1.281–85)

At this moment of divine revelation, when the Son learns that he is the beloved Son, the mysteriously opaque nature of sonship is marked by the inassimilable "me his, / Me his." The stuttering phrase inserts itself between "pronounced" and "beloved Son," injecting the same kind of doubt as Satan's "whate'er it meant," and seemingly a degree of personal anxiety.

As the three versions of the dove unfold in book 1, it becomes clear that revelation and miracle depend very much on witnesses. This is exactly the critique leveled by emerging rational religion. Edward, Lord Herbert of Cherbury, gives impetus to the strand of thought by framing his skepticism toward revelation as a matter of the authority of the witness. Cherbury admits that revealed truth exists, but insists that "the truth of revelation depends upon the authority of him who reveals it." We must, therefore, experience a revelation for ourselves and judge it with our own faculties so that we cannot trust a revelation reported by another. He explains, "revelation must be given directly to some person; for what is received from others as revelation must be accounted not revelation but tradition or history. And since the truth of history or of tradition depends upon him who recounts it, its foundations lie outside us, and in consequence it is, so far as we are concerned, mere possibility" (*De veritate* 308). Here we can apply Cherbury's advice to a close reading of *Paradise Regained*. Cherbury warns that "it is hardly sufficient to apprehend what is revealed except through our faculties" (308)—as readers exercising our faculties on the text of the poem, we can only apprehend a miracle by its presence in Milton's language. And despite critics' assumptions that revelations and special illuminations appear throughout the action, until the fiery couch at the end there is no language that specifically describes a miracle in the present tense of the poem. Irene Samuel argues as I do, that *Paradise Regained* pointedly eschews mystery and miracle: "What then would he have said to readings of *Paradise Regained* that make its meaning turn on sudden secret mysterious revelation from on high to the protagonist, not one of which is narrated in the gospels—his main source—and not one of which is so much as indicated by a single word in his poem?"[49] Miracle only enters the poem by the report of witnesses, as with the dove, or by the ambiguous statements of the Son. The Son's much-studied phrases, claiming that he can command a table in the wilderness or declaring on the pinnacle "Tempt not the Lord thy God," invite us to find miracles, but never allow them to be substantiated by the text.[50]

Miraculous revelation finally does enter the poem, and after long delay the identity motif is resolved and the Son separated from Socinian Christology. But even at this prominent juncture, the angelic choir expresses a strange indifference to the whole problem of the Son's ontology:

> True image of the Father whether throned
> In the bosom of bliss, and light of light
> Conceiving, or remote from heaven enshrined
> In fleshly tabernacle, and human form,
> Wandering the wilderness, whatever place,
> Habit, or state, or motion, still expressing
> The Son of God.   (*PR* 4.596–602)

Whether "throned" in the heaven of *Paradise Lost*, or "in human form," whether man or God, does not seem to make a difference. In "whatever place," no matter the distinction between humanity and divinity, he is "still expressing / The Son of God." It is as if the identity motif that has so engrossed Satan and the Son, and that has formed the central problem of the poem, does not matter. The pinnacle gives way to the angelic choir as a miraculous climax to the plot, but even miracle fades into anticlimax. The poem then ends with the Son quietly returning home, no different to the human eye from when he began:

> Thus they the Son of God our Saviour meek
> Sung victor, and from heavenly feast refreshed
> Brought on his way with joy; he unobserved
> Home to his mother's house private returned. (4.636–39)

Entering in the penultimate foot of the penultimate line, "he unobserved" begins a walk that can slip the reader's notice as easily as the Son marches past potential observers. The Son's quiet exit undermines the narratological effects of miracle, and, simultaneously, is a doctrinally important return to a human ontology. Despite the angelic choir's revelation of the Son's preincarnate history, he exits toward his mother's house rather than his Father's. This does not deny the information given by the choir. It is not a repudiation of the pre-Incarnation ontology, but a powerfully indifferent response: the plot's anticlimax deemphasizes miracle and evinces as little concern for the angelic revelation of the Son's identity as the angels themselves.

The poem's conclusion is one more moment of what Stanley Fish sees as a narrative of indifference, and a plot that resists such things as climax, development, and denouement. But indifference is in this case specifically directed at the identity motif, asserting that the solution to the extended detective work is unimportant. What the famously bland plot ultimately assures is that the distinction between the human and divine within the Son is a thing indifferent. And this indifference surfaces precisely in the absence of miraculous revelation. The angelic choir solves the identity motif at the end, and revelation would solve it earlier as well. Miracle's absence for the length of the poem instead creates a hermeneutic space that fosters theological uncertainty. And the poem's final anticlimactic subversion of the choir ensures that we do not view miraculous revelation as overly important—

matching Milton's sentiment in *De doctrina* that "Miracles are no more able to produce belief than, in itself, doctrine is: that is to say, they cannot produce it at all." The absence of revelation in *Paradise Regained* marks out the limits to human knowledge and so maintains the God-man as a thing indifferent, just as Milton characterizes him in *De doctrina:* "As God has not revealed to us how this comes about it is much better for us to hold our tongues and be wisely ignorant."

Socinian Toleration

Paradise Regained is particularly interested in framing the ontology of the Son as a thing indifferent. This indifference, an uncertainty that goes under the name of the God-man, separates Milton from a Socinian Christology since it resists the conclusion that the Son is mere man. However, this very same indifference, applied in particular to Antitrinitarian Christology, brings Milton closer to another Socinian position: that of religious tolerance.

Alongside its rejection of the Trinity, Socinianism can be characterized as one of the seventeenth century's primary articulations of religious toleration. Socinianism's tenets, according to H. John McLachlan, "regarded from one angle as a radical scheme of doctrine, seen from another constitute a plea for freedom in matters of religious faith."[51] The association of Socinianism and toleration has both a historical and structural explanation. Historically, Antitrinitarianism in the Reformation begins with Michael Servetus, whose outspoken opposition to orthodox Trinitarianism led to his death at the stake in 1553.[52] Servetus's death, defended by Calvin, led to two of the period's great statements of both religious toleration and Antitrinitarianism: Sebastien Castellio's *De haereticis* (1554) and Giacomo Acontius's *Satanae stratagemata* (1564). These liberal humanists exerted significant influence over the development of Socinianism in Poland and continued to be central to English Socinians in the seventeenth century.[53] McLachlan particularly cites Acontius, whom he calls the "direct precursor" to the Tolerationist (and perhaps Socinian) work of Hales and Chillingworth in the 1630s.[54] The close historical connection between Socinians and repression surfaces again in the 1650s, with the repeated censorship and imprisonment of John Biddle, so that Antitrinitarianism itself becomes inseparable from an expression of religious freedom.

Structurally, Socinianism has an affinity with religious toleration based upon its rejection of any doctrine that is extrabiblical. Scripturalism is the hallmark of Socinian argument, which bases its objection to the Trinity on the assertion that proof is nowhere to be found in the Bible. By definition, then, the Trinity is a thing indifferent, without positive command in Scripture. Socinians argue that the imposition of doctrine by the church impinges upon true religion, and so make a case for toleration of multiple views when it comes to things indifferent. As Acontius argues, "It is a great hindrance to us in all these things, if we judge of the nature of God and his will and every occurrence otherwise than according to that doctrine which is set forth in Holy Writ."[55] His influence is especially felt in William Chillingworth's *The Religion of Protestants* (1638), which asserts the exclusive authority of Scripture as the common ground that will lead to religious toleration.[56] This appeal to biblicism involves a return to the basic tenets of Christianity and a stripping away of accumulated tradition—a process that depends upon the identification of what is necessary for salvation and what is indifferent. Acontius, like Cherbury, attempts a set of minimal Christian truths for irenic purposes. These are propositions that do not impinge upon things indifferent, and so can be agreed upon by all Christians.[57] In one variant of book 7, Acontius, like Cherbury, goes so far as to make a numbered list of the six elements that can be abstracted from Christianity. Asserting both a monotheistic and Antitrinitarian position, the first proposition is: "1. That there is one true God and he whom he sent, Jesus Christ, and the Holy Spirit. And that it is not right to deny that the Father is one and the Son another, because Jesus Christ is truly the Son of God."[58]

The liberty to hold doctrines that are not positively commanded by Scripture becomes, for Socinians, the liberty to reject the Trinity. This was a liberty not commonly granted. In 1648, the Westminster Assembly condemned *Satanae stratagemata* as a Socinian text, for its denial of the divinity of Christ. At midcentury, particularly in the case of Biddle, the question of the ontology of the Son, the Antitrinitarian consideration of his divinity, is the most controversial of things indifferent, and therefore the most rigorous test of religious toleration. Probably in response to the Westminster Assembly's condemnation, Milton's friend John Goodwin in 1648 translated the first four books of Acontius's *Stratagemata*. Included in the front matter is a commendation by Milton's admired predecessor Pater Ramus, and a letter from John Dury to Samuel Hartlib, both associates of Milton. With his own clear commitment to Antitrinitarianism emerging at this time, Milton likely knew Acontius's work—a later Unitarian writer, within a consideration of Socinian toleration, suggests that "some of the finest passages of Milton's *Areopagitica* may be traced to Acontius."[59]

Milton, at the very least, arrives at the same nexus of Antitrinitarianism and toleration as Acontius, both in *Of True Religion* and in his preface to book 5 of *De doctrina*. Just two years after *Paradise Regained*, Milton published his treatise on religious toleration, *Of True Religion, Haeresie, Schism, Toleration* (1673). There Milton makes the concept of indifference central to religious toleration, including a toleration of Socinianism. Milton says of one who persecutes another on slight pretense, "But he is wont to say he enjoyns only things indifferent. Let them be so still; who gave him authority to change their nature by injoyning them? If by his own Principles, as is prov'd, he ought to tolerate controverted points of Doctrine not slightly grounded on Scripture, much more ought he not impose things indifferent without Scripture" (YP 8:427–28). Milton here argues against a standard Anglican doctrine by which things indifferent can be enforced by the magistrate, placing what is neither commanded nor prohibited by Scripture under the authority of the church. Keith W. F. Stavely associates the doctrine with Hooker's *Ecclesiastical Polity* and with Edward Stillingfleet's *Irenicum* (YP 8:427n44). The latter also professes toleration, but with the conservative slant of Anglican and latitudinarian support of church authority. Milton is circumspect in this pamphlet, careful to speak to rather than against orthodoxy. But in opposing Stillingfleet's use of indifference, Milton aligns himself with a more radical version of toleration, which insists that for things indifferent there should be no restrictions on religious freedom.

As he does in *De doctrina*, in *Of True Religion* Milton declares the overall necessity of revelation: "True Religion is the true Worship and Service of God, learnt and believed from the Word of God only. No Man or Angel can know how God would be worshipt and serv'd unless God reveal it" (YP 8:419). Revelation is indispensable, again separating Milton from the emerging deism. But Milton's emphasis here is on biblicism—matching the Socinian position, he will allow nothing in true religion that is not strictly from Scripture. Heresy is defined as the subversion of *sola scriptura*: "Heresie therefore is a Religion taken up and believ'd from the traditions of men and additions to the word of God." And so the greatest heretics are Catholics: "Whence also it follows clearly, that of all known Sects or pretended Religions at this day in Christendom, Popery is the only or the greatest Heresie: and he who is so forward to brand all others for Hereticks, the obstinate Papist, the only Heretick" (YP 8:421). One sticking point for modern readers is that Milton's expression of toleration in *Of True Religion* includes an eagerness to deny toleration to Catholics—"If it be askt how far they should be tolerated? I answer doubtless equally, as being all Protestants" (YP 8:426). This hardly sounds tolerant, but it can be reconciled with Christian liberty when we understand Milton's emphasis on biblicism. The greatest problem with Catholicism, what makes it heretical, is that it departs from the Bible and adds traditions to the word of God. The papist is "the only Heretick" in the sense of the arch-heretick, or the type of heresy—he embodies the primary means of being heretical. So by excluding Catholics, Milton is excluding all additions to Scripture, and protecting tolerance for any sect that is based upon Scripture.

The most consistently named Protestant sect is Socinianism—three times in *Of True Religion* Milton calls for toleration of Socinians (YP 8:423, 424–25, 437). Not only are they a group regularly denied toleration, but Socinians are also themselves exemplars of toleration, in effect opposites to the intolerant heresy of Catholicism. Milton's version of religious toleration is based upon the ethic of *sola scriptura,* and few in the liberal Protestant landscape embody the ideal as well as the Socinians, who are among the sects Milton celebrates for being "perfect and powerful in the Scriptures" (YP 8:426). The Socinian and liberal-Protestant emphasis on biblicism, moreover, constructs a tolerant attitude as part of true religion. The Bible is a clear judge that should allow Christians to "avoid and cut off many Debates and Contentions, Schisms and Persecutions" (YP 8:420). And the impressiveness of the scholarship and intentions behind such sects as Socinians should inspire a kind of gentleness or psychological tolerance: "What Protestant then who himself maintains the same Principles, and disavowes all implicit Faith, would persecute, and not rather charitably tolerate such men as these, unless he mean to abjure the Principles of his own Religion?" (YP 8:426). In particular, such charity should be exercised with things indifferent, which have no positive or negative status in Scripture, and so must be outside of censure: "What can it be but love of contention for things not necessary to be done, to molest the conscience of his Brother, who holds them necessary to be not done?" (YP 8:428).

Milton makes a similar appeal for psychological tolerance in the brief but remarkable preface to book 5 of *De doctrina*. This is the moment when Milton becomes most controversial, embarking on the Antitrinitarian doctrine of the Son. And once again, Antitrinitarianism must go hand in hand with religious tolerance.

The only preface to a book in *De doctrina*, this is a poignantly anxious passage. Milton argues for the Trinity's lack of scriptural support and the illegitimacy of extrascriptural doctrine—that it is a thing indifferent and not subject to church authority. As in *Of True Religion*, the Catholic Church marks the opposite of true religion's biblicism:

> The Roman Church demands implicit obedience on all points of faith. If I professed myself a member of it, I should be so indoctrinated, or at any rate so besotted by habit, that I should yield to its authority and to its mere decree even if it were to assert that the doctrine of the Trinity, as accepted at present, could not be proved from any passage of scripture. As it happens, however, I am one of those who recognize God's word alone as the rule of faith; so I shall state quite openly what seems to me much more clearly deducible from the text of scripture than the currently accepted doctrine. (YP 6:203)

From Protestants, Milton hopes for a more scriptural as well as a more tolerant approach—and this toleration is based upon an appeal to psychological indifference: "This one thing I beg of my reader: that he will weigh each statement and evaluate it with a mind innocent of prejudice and eager only for the truth. For I take it upon myself to refute, whenever necessary, not scriptural authority, which is inviolable, but human interpretations. That is my right, and indeed my duty as a human being" (YP 6:203–04). Kelley's notes identify Milton's themes of biblicism and toleration as obviously Socinian. Clearly anxious about how book 5 will be read, thinking perhaps of the imprisonment of Biddle and the condemnation of Acontius's book, Milton pleads not only for freedom from church tyranny, but also from tyranny that can be lodged in the individual reader.

Among Socinians, this psychology of tolerance is most clearly to be found in Acontius's *Satanae stratagemata*. Satan's main strategy, according to Acontius, is to sow discord through impetuousness and intolerant attitudes. Satan, he says, "will propogate sundry controversies, quarrels, discords, brawls, and finall enmities, that in consequence thereof they may rail at one another with abusive words."[60] The best response is to recognize when an issue is not a necessity: "And so my counsel is this, that as soon as you perceive that something false is being taught, before you set about contradicting it, you carefully consider whether it is of little or no moment."[61] That is, each Christian should refrain from debating and pursuing things indifferent. He repeatedly advises patience, humility, and a quiet mind as a way of refraining from the rash pursuit of contradiction:

> Moreover if those, with whom the matter lies, carefully weigh it with a quiet mind and an uncorrupt judgment, unless therefore the reasoning be of such a kind and the language used have the power of inducing that tranquillity of mind and what I may call healthiness of judgment in the adversaries, but rather of having an altogether contrary effect, it will not resist Satan but exceedingly favour his cause.[62]

Unfortunately, he goes on, pride generally causes disputants to lose this tranquility — and, in accordance with Satan's strategies, religion breaks into schism and violence.

It is just such a threat that, in his dogged effort to understand the ontology of the God-man, Satan poses in *Paradise Regained*. Satan's strategy, Acontius says, is to get Christians to divide themselves into schisms over nonessential matters. A lack of psychological indifference — a tendency to be too argumentative and proud — destroys toleration. One therefore resists Satan by working to avoid disagreements over the nonessentials — by being indifferent to things indifferent. The Satan of *Paradise Regained* pursues the very strategies that Acontius calls satanic:

> So Satan, whom repulse upon repulse
> Met ever; and to shameful silence brought,
> Yet gives not o'er though desperate success,
> And his vain importunity pursues.   (4.21–24)

And the Son appears as a model of Acontius's "tranquility of mind," forever "unmoved" or "unshaken," in the face of Satan's obvious rage. The Son doggedly remains indifferent, "with unaltered brow" (*PR* 1.493). It is to the psychology of toleration, what Acontius calls "tranquility of mind" and "healthiness of judgment," that Milton appeals in the indifferent narrative of *Paradise Regained*. Stanley Fish argues that *Paradise Regained* does not just represent indifference, but it also pushes its readers to themselves assume indifference. Similarly, the Son's ability to remain tranquil of mind in the face of temptation and vain challenge is itself a representation of the challenge the poem puts before the reader. Courting the desire to understand the God-man, *Paradise Regained* repeatedly denies resolution, as if seeking to exercise the reader's tranquility of mind. This attention to response, to how *Paradise Regained* will be read, how the Antitrinitarianism of *De doctrina* will be received, reflects Acontius's movement from the political toleration of religion to psychological toleration.

In *Of True Religion*, Milton declares that "the hottest disputes among Protestants calmly and charitably enquired into, will be found less than such" (YP 8:424). The basic hermeneutic problem of *Paradise Regained*, how to conceive of the Son, is just such a hot dispute—between Trinitarians and Antitrinitarians, and between Socinians and Arians. *Paradise Regained* exercises our ability for calm inquiry and our acceptance of things indifferent, even this most difficult and radical of things, the ontology of the Son. In its own indifference, it is at once a radical statement of Antitrinitarianism, and an irenic intervention in the debates over the Trinity.

Seven

Revelation and Samson's Sense of Heaven's Desertion

In the preface to book 5 of *De doctrina Christiana*, Milton insists that in contemporary debates the Trinity is defended without the support of divine revelation: "Of course, if my opponents could show that the doctrine they defend was revealed to them by a voice from heaven, he would be an impious wretch who dared to raise so much as a murmur against it, let alone a sustained protest" (YP 6:204). It is worth recognizing Milton's tone. As he imagines the kind of revelation that would give clarity to the contentious issue of the Trinity, he imagines nothing less than a voice from heaven. Rhetorically, it is clear that such an authoritative revelation, though heard on Sinai, is not likely to be heard in seventeenth century England. Direct, external revelation of doctrine feels improbable and enters *De doctrina* as a piece of irony. The preface continues: "But in fact they can lay claim to nothing more than human powers and that spiritual illumination which is common to all men" (YP 6:204). The Holy Spirit is a powerful force in Milton's doctrine, being an inward illumination necessary to interpret the Bible.[1] But it is insignificant compared to a voice from heaven, which, as an external revelation, could enforce consent beyond the individual. The voice from heaven is irresistibly powerful—but it remains unattainable, an ironic marker of how far away such doctrinal certainty is.

Paradise Regained is equally remote from such miraculous revelation. The poem's many versions of the baptism of the Son undermine the authority of the "voice" that "From heaven pronounced him his beloved Son" (*PR* 1.32). And the identity motif, with the related question of Socinian Christology, remains ambiguous in the prolonged absence of divine revelation. The companion piece to *Paradise Regained*, *Samson Agonistes*, continues the engagement with the problem of divine revelation and continues to delve into the difficulties of understanding divine will in the absence of irrefutable revelation. Milton's tragedy pushes further: while *Paradise Regained* eventually brings in angels to answer our doubts, *Samson Agonistes* never allows angelic revelation, leaving us without the full understanding that miraculous revelation can provide.

Without a voice or an angel, Samson is left with the opaque phenomenon of internal revelation. While the Son briefly feels "some strong motion" (*PR* 1.290), Samson feels a whole panoply of inward events—what the poem calls intimate impulses, divine impulses, divine instincts, and rousing motions. These stirrings in Samson, particularly the famous rousing motions, have long been an interpretive crux, providing the key, it seems to many readers, to understanding the poem. As a last chance at divine revelation, these impulses, instincts, and motions would indeed shed light on Samson's actions and God's will, if only they were as clearly interpretable as a voice from heaven or a visiting angel. But, as this chapter will suggest by comparison with the Common Notions of Lord Herbert of Cherbury, they are not. *Samson Agonistes* goes further than *Paradise Regained* by experimenting with a world entirely devoid of divine revelation, a world unhappily caught in the verisimilar conditions predicated by the natural religion of Cherbury and his successors in deism.

As an experiment in a world without revelation, *Samson Agonistes* marks the skeptical extreme of Milton's monotheism.

The chapters of this book have recorded how monotheism, with its structural need to exclude all other divine beings, and with its resistance to representations of the divine, has made Milton's poetry profoundly uncomfortable with revelation. The narrative presence of polytheistic gods, the personal presence of God, the actions of angels and the Son are all forms of revelation and all challenges to monotheistic narrative. In *Samson Agonistes*, these external revelations are eliminated, and revelation dwindles to an invisible, inaudible, inward event. Samson's impulses, instincts, and motions, like the fully abstract godhead of monotheism, cannot be narrated, and so can never be adequately interpreted.

As local revelation disappears, so does the poem's ability to narrate revelation in its greater sense, the Judeo-Christian revelation. Samson's despairing "sense of heaven's desertion" (*SA* 632) goes unremedied, and the possibility of theodicy, the poem's ability to claim with the Chorus that "Just are the ways of God, / And justifiable to men" (293–94), collapses. With the fall of theodicy, the poem opens itself, at least momentarily, to the subversion of the Mosaic distinction—to what is a surprisingly persuasive attack on the Judeo-Christian revelation itself. So the poem, in pushing to the skeptical extreme of monotheism, ends up with a raw confrontation between the monotheism of the Israelite God and the polytheism of the Philistines. With this confrontation, *Samson Agonistes* becomes both Milton's most direct meditation on monotheism, and his closest approach to the subversive theology of deism.

The Angel of Judges 13

Milton's poems are usually full of supernatural beings: *In Quintum Novembris* shows Satan's machinations; the Nativity ode gives us polytheistic gods in procession and flight; in *Lycidas* pastoral is interrupted by the voices of Phoebus and Neptune, the personified river Camus, and the shade of Saint Peter; in *A Mask*, Comus is a god and his nemesis a spirit; *Paradise Lost* and *Paradise Regained* are overcrowded with Satan, gods, God, allegorical figures, and angels. *Samson Agonistes* is alone among the major poems in portraying only humans. Milton spells out his effort at naturalism in the introductory essay, where he reworks Aristotle's distinction between intricate and explicit plot, "which is nothing indeed but such oeconomy, or disposition of the fable as may stand best with verisimilitude and decorum." By joining decorum with verisimilitude, Milton makes an aesthetic imperative out of realism. Propriety demands that the poem's characters and plot events should conform to the ontology of the real world and the creation of a disenchanted storyworld.

To attain verisimilitude Milton puts aside his habitual use of the supernatural, and while *Samson Agonistes* shows no sign of missing the presence of spirits or gods or daemons, Samson and members of the tribe of Dan name one particular being whose absence matters very much: the angel of Judges 13. Faced with the moment's disenchantment, Samson, Manoa, and the Chorus look repeatedly and nostalgically back to a time when revelation was available. Their despairing efforts at understanding their universe always return to the angel that announced Samson's birth. As he first takes a seat, Samson recalls "Times past," and his lament uses the angel as synecdoche for "what once I was":

> O wherefore was my birth from heaven foretold
> Twice by an angel, who at last in sight
> Of both my parents all in flames ascended
> From off the altar, where on offering burned,
> As in a fiery column charioting
> His godlike presence, and from some great act
> Or benefit revealed to Abraham's race?   (SA 23–29)

Manoa, upon seeing Samson's "miserable change," similarly turns to the angel, which in his thinking also stands for Samson's former glory. He asks, "For this did the angel twice descend?" (361). And the Chorus, apparently not sufficiently reassured by Samson's claim that he feels "rousing motions," calls for the angel's presence as he leaves for the temple:

> Go, and the Holy One
> Of Israel be thy guide
> To what may serve his glory best, and spread his name
> Great among the heathen round:
> Send thee the angel of thy birth, to stand
> Fast by thy side, who from thy father's field
> Rode up in flames after his message told
> Of thy conception, and be now a shield
> Of fire. (1427–35)

Joseph Wittreich has counted ten references to the angel of Judges 13, more than any other detail from the Judges story—more even than Samson's marriages.[2]

The persistent nostalgia for the angel of Judges 13 is a longing for the kind of certainty that springs from divine revelation. *Samson Agonistes* is written in a moment beset with the problems of enthusiasm, foremost among which is the difficulty Geoffrey Nuttall describes: "how men could discern God's Spirit within them from their own fancies."[3] A visit from an angel would be a welcome alternative to the Spirit. External revelation would provide a much clearer means of understanding God's will, and, because verifiable, would be far less susceptible to the excesses of enthusiasts. But the poem is not a simple rejection of enthusiasm. The longing for revelation is found among highly fallible characters and takes place within Milton's most rational story-world, suggesting that, in accordance with emerging deism, the desire for an angel could be read as a fault. The angel of Judges 13, then, is an object both of desire and of skepticism. The wish for the absent angel evokes a feeling that must have been common in the late seventeenth century as enthusiasm encroached from one side and deism and the enlightenment encroached from the other: that the problems of theology, as well as political action, were more easily handled when angels and revelations were more creditable. In *Samson Agonistes* we see Milton dramatizing a relationship to revelation that is both skeptical and nostalgic, creating a poem vexed by uncertainties about the veracity of miraculous revelations, but also by uncertainties about how to proceed without them.

As the characters of the poem recall and invoke the angel of Judges 13, the angel is repeatedly identified by the fact that he appeared twice, and that he ascended in a miraculous blaze of fire (*SA* 23, 361, 635, 1431). Both details are marks of the Book of Judges' own narrative of skepticism, the fascinating appearance of the angel before Manoa's wife and her husband, which itself questions angelic revelation. The appearance of the angel of Judges 13 is as troubled by interpretive and ontological ambiguities as the appearance of the visitors in Genesis 18. As Manoa and his wife try to interpret the angel who appears before them to announce Samson's birth, they display a skepticism toward revelation, one that embodies the ontological calculations that are fundamental to monotheism.

The narrative first enacts the kind of crisis of authority that lies at the heart of the skeptical critique of revelation: a concern for the authority of the witness of the revelation, such as Cherbury expresses. Perversely, for the masculinist culture of the Bible, the angel appears not to Manoa, but to his wife—a character graced only with the name "woman" or "wife" (both translations of the single Hebrew word *isha*). Manoa's wife immediately tells Manoa of the visit, repeating the announcement that she will bear a son and that he will be a Nazarite. Manoa's response, however, is that he must see this for himself—skeptical of the woman's authority, he prays for another visit. "God hearkened to the voice of Manoah" (Judg. 13:9) and sends the angel, but again the angel appears only to his wife. She runs and gets Manoa, and this time he sees the angel and his miraculous fiery ascent, becoming fully convinced of the authority of the revelation. But such certainty comes only after the extended uncertainty of the visits to Manoa's wife and her apparently unpersuasive account of them. Manoa's wife faces the difficulty of conveying divine revelation to one who has not witnessed it, for the authority is hers rather than the angel's. The startling detail that the angel twice comes to her, rather than to Manoa, destabilizes the narrative of revelation, for transmission of the annunciation rests in the unauthoritative report of a woman. Divine revelation seems but a hair's breadth away from being an old wives' tale.

Furthermore, Manoa's wife and Manoa both show a reticence to accept the angel as an angel, seemingly skeptical of his supernatural ontology. The narrator's voice first tells us that "the angel of the lord" appears to Manoa's wife, making it clear, on the authority of the narrator, that this is an actual angelic revelation (Judg. 13:3). But when she reports the visitation to Manoa, she cautiously says, "A man of God came unto me, and his countenance was like the countenance of an angel of God, very terrible: but I asked him not whence he was, neither told he me his name" (13:6). As the angel remains silent about his name and origin, Manoa's wife jumps to no conclusions. He looks like an angel, but she maintains a careful skepticism, calling him a man. Manoa similarly resists any enthusiastic interpretations, praying, "O my Lord, let the man of God which thou didst send come again unto us" (13:8). When the angel appears a second time, the narrator continues to call him an angel (Hebrew: *malach*): "and the angel of God came again unto the woman" (13:9). But Manoa and his wife continue to say "man" (*ish*): "Behold, the man hath appeared unto me, that came unto me the other day" (13:10). The discrepancy between the narrator's *malach* and Manoah and his wife's *ish* allows the reader, who is privy to the authority of the narrator, to look on with greater knowledge and to recognize Manoa and his wife's mistake, a situation often called tragic irony.

However, tragic irony has no place in Judges 13, since skepticism toward the angel does not prove to be a mistake. Judges 13 is quite unlike the *Bacchae*, where the audience knows that Dionysus is a god and looks on Pentheus with pity as his skepticism leads to ridicule and punishment. In the polytheism of the *Bacchae*, there is no need for human skepticism toward revelation since there is no limit on divine beings. But in monotheism, divinity must be very jealously guarded. By forbidding the worship of any god but God, monotheism makes every supernatural appearance into a moment filled with the potential for a lapse into polytheism. So when Manoa wants, like Abraham, to offer the angelic visitor food, he receives a remarkable warning: "And the angel of the LORD said unto Manoah, Though thou detain me, I will not eat of thy bread: and if thou wilt offer a burnt offering, thou must offer it unto the Lord. For Manoah knew not that he was an angel of the Lord" (Judg. 13:16). The angel helpfully steers Manoa away from the mistake of offering a sacrifice to an angel, which would be a transgression against the one God. The correct ontological interpretation is necessary to avoid polytheism, and the angel must intervene because, we are told, Manoa is at this moment still unsure of the angelic ontology.

Such uncertainty, and the monotheistic need for careful ontological calculation as a result, is the preoccupation of Judges 13, from the problem of Manoa's wife witnessing the angel, to the discrepancy between "angel of God" and "man of God," to the risk of the burnt offering.[4] But in being slow to recognize the angelic ontology of their visitor, Manoa and his wife are not punished, as is Pentheus. They are instead rewarded with a clear sign of the angel's divine mission, and with the birth of Samson. When the angel finally ascends on the flame of the altar and reveals his true heavenly nature, there is no rebuke, but rather a sense of the satisfactory conclusion to their skeptical struggle: "And Manoah and his wife looked on it, and fell on their faces on the ground. But the angel of the Lord did not more appear to Manoah and to his wife. Then Manoah knew that he was an angel of the Lord" (13:20–21). Before even the true angel of the Lord, Manoa and his wife are exemplary in their skepticism toward external revelation. Judges 13 does not preclude revelation, but rather insists, for the sake of monotheism, that it be met with rigorous circumspection.[5]

In the Book of Judges, the angel announces Samson's birth in chapter 13, and then neither appears nor is mentioned again. But with its retrospective structure, Milton brings *Samson Agonistes* repeatedly back to the angel, as if his appearance were the key to the present. References often include that the angel was "twice descending" (*SA* 635) and that he manifested himself miraculously, "As in a fiery column charioting / His godlike presence" (*SA* 27–28). The first detail recalls the skepticism of Manoa and his wife, and the second the triumphant certainty that can emerge from such skepticism. As the poem looks back with nostalgia at the angel of Judges 13, it is looking for revelation that has been tested and proven true, a kind of revelation that has been purified by skepticism and made ready to serve the needs of monotheism.

Samson, Manoa, and the Chorus all look for the angel of Judges 13, but never witness his return—and in his absence *Samson Agonistes* descends into tragedy. *Paradise Regained* also unfolds in the absence of miracle and revelation, and the two are companionable for their similarly rational and human-centered perspectives. But it is the matter of angels that ultimately distinguishes the poems. *Paradise Regained* finally returns to revelation, when the angelic chorus becomes present at the end, reinstating the celestial narrative and ensuring the comic-Christian promise of paradise regained. *Samson Agonistes*, in contrast, never brings the angel of Judges 13 into its storyworld. And without angelic revelation, it is like *Paradise Regained* without its final angelic chorus. Just as the Book of Job can be read as a tragedy if its frame narrative is removed, so *Samson Agonistes* reads very much like *Paradise Regained* without its frame of supernatural revelations. In its adherence to a pure monotheism, *Samson Agonistes* becomes tragic.

Inward Revelation and Cherbury's Common Notions

In a world without angels and miracles, in the absence of external revelation, Samson still must find a way to interpret God's will. *Samson Agonistes* offers a seemingly powerful alternative: inward revelation. Critics commonly hold Samson's inner development to be the true subject of the poem. They rightly stress that Milton has transformed the bully of the Book of Judges into a melancholy thinker, so that what matters most in the poem is Samson's mental agon. Samson's weakness, in the course of the play, stems not from his shorn hair, but from his spiritual and mental disposition—and the peripeteia of the spiritual plot, when Samson chooses to go to the temple, stems from some growth in his inner self, or some advancement of his understanding of God's will. John Steadman describes "a pattern of internal events—a spiritual plot," rather than "a sequence of causes entirely outside the mind and will of the agent."[6]

As revelation moves inward, it changes from the visible features of angels to a set of inward events—the instincts, impulses, and motions that constitute for Samson, as well as the critics, a mental agon. Just what these inward stirrings are, and whether they advance Samson's spiritual plot to the point of a redemptive ending to the poem, has been a primary source of investigation among Milton's readers.[7] Ultimately under debate is the efficacy of Samson's inward revelations—whether they really do communicate God's will. I agree with Stanley Fish and those who doubt redemptive readings, that we have no way of knowing if Samson's inward experience is not wholly solipsistic, that it cannot be shown that his rousing motions and other stirrings are really "of God."[8] In this chapter, I am less interested, however, in trying to resolve this debate than in suggesting a new context—that of Cherbury's monotheistic theology.

Inward, divine revelation clearly drives Samson in the Book of Judges. In the last verses of chapter 13, after the angel has disappeared, never to return, we learn that Samson was born, and that "the Spirit of the Lord began to move him at times in the camp of Dan between Zorah and Eshtaol" (Judg. 13:25). "Spirit of the lord" reappears several times, always as a spur to action, as before the lion, "the Spirit of the Lord came mightily upon him, and he rent him as he would have rent a kid" (14:6; also see 14:19 and 15:14). "Spirit" is an ambiguous word (Hebrew: *ruach*), as evidenced by the many possible meanings *De doctrina*

Christiana gathers (YP 6:281–86), and its controversial iterations among Quakers and Puritans. But in Judges the spirit is always identified as "of the lord" (*ruach adonay*), so that its divine origin is not in doubt. A Samson motivated by the spirit of the Lord is certainly following God. Milton, however, never uses this key phrase. The Chorus, just after calling for the angel of Judges 13 to assist Samson, also wishes for "that spirit that first rushed on thee / In the camp of Dan" (*SA* 1435–36). But like the angel, "the spirit of the lord" is not available in the present moment. Instead, Milton offers a set of phrases that feels as if it should provide greater specificity, replacing the mysterious valences of "spirit" with psychological or epistemological terminology that would seem to be more precise.

Milton reworks "spirit" into a catalog of phrases: "intimate impulse," "divine impulsion," "divine instinct," and "rousing motions." Samson, describing his marriage to the bride of Timna, echoes the biblical phrase "of the Lord," but supplements it with the term "impulse." Samson tells the Chorus that his parents

>   knew not
> That what I motioned was of God; I knew
> From *intimate impulse*, and therefore urged
> The marriage on.   (221–24; italics mine)

Manoa, recounting Samson's marriage choices from his perspective, tells Samson,

> I cannot praise thy marriage-choices, son,
> Rather approved them not; but thou didst plead
> *Divine impulsion* prompting how thou might'st
> Find some occasion to infest our foes.
> I state not that.   (420–24; italics mine)

Samson, remembering his former glory, speaks of,

>   when in strength
> All mortals I excelled, and great in hopes
> With youthful courage and magnanimous thoughts
> Of birth from heaven foretold and high exploits,
> Full of *divine instinct*.   (522–26; italics mine)

And finally, Samson resolves to go to the temple on the authority of "rousing motions":

> Be of good courage, I begin to feel
> Some *rousing motions* in me which dispose
> To something extraordinary my thoughts.
> I with this messenger will go along. (1381–84; italics mine)

A sense of technical jargon imbues these impulses, instincts, and motions, suggesting that we are given a more particular and more rational description of inspiration than Judges affords. This sense of scientific specificity, this attempt at a rational approach to revelation, is the first suggestion that *Samson Agonistes* can usefully be compared to the skeptical theology and epistemology of Lord Herbert of Cherbury.

In *De veritate*, Cherbury, as has been discussed, admits the possibility of revelation, but insists that we submit it to a skeptical evaluation of its authority. "The truth of revelation depends upon the authority of him who reveals it," he says. "We must, then, proceed with great care in discerning what actually is revealed. Since there may be false revelations, I think it is hardly sufficient to apprehend what is revealed except through our faculties" (*De veritate* 308). Just as Manoa must see the angel of Judges 13 for himself, each thoughtful person must rely on his or her own apprehension and understanding, not an outside authority, to judge the veracity of revelation. This means proceeding with "great care" in evaluating each revelation, just as Manoa and his wife do. And the necessary ontological calculations are made possible, according to Cherbury, by means of "our faculties." These faculties are Cherbury's Common Notions, innate ideas that act as the final arbiters of truth for each individual. Common Notions are within everyone, and the five Religious Common Notions guarantee that, regardless of access to specific revelation, basic religious truth can be discovered through reason. The Common Notions thus put the human mind first and marginalize revelatory events, what Mario Rossi calls a "permanent revelation."[9] It is this substitution of faculties for angelic revelation that *Samson Agonistes* shares with Cherbury's natural religion. When Milton excludes the angel of Judges 13 and replaces the "spirit of the lord" with the technical language of impulses, instincts, and motions, he draws very near to Cherbury's Common Notions.

The second reason for positing an affinity between *Samson Agonistes* and *De veritate* lies in their handling of revelation in its larger sense, the Judeo-Christian revelation. Cherbury's Religious Common Notions, as discussed in chapter 2, form the foundation of his natural theology, which asserts that true religion is available to each individual through the study of nature. The first of the Religious Common Notions, that "There is a supreme God" (*De veritate* 291), implies that the knowledge of the one God could be intuited even by pagans who lack the benefit of revelation. This occult monotheism effectively renders the specifics of the Judeo-Christian revelation unnecessary—marginalizing sacred Scripture, church authority, and local revelations in the form of miracles, voices, or angels. It is not just local revelation that is extraneous in Cherbury's system, but the entirety of revealed religion, and his skepticism toward the former enables his skepticism toward the latter. *Samson Agonistes* experiments with Cherbury's skepticism toward revelation in the local sense, and also stages the same movement to the greater sense of revelation. Seeming to trace the path of Cherbury's quickly expanding skepticism, Milton brings Samson and the poem's readers from a consideration of inward revelation to the possible marginalization of the Judeo-Christian revelation itself. So that in the figure of Dalila, Milton subverts the Mosaic distinction and expresses a surprising tolerance toward polytheism.

Although not widely read now, *De veritate* was very influential in the seventeenth century, so it seems likely that Milton would have been familiar with it. Published in Paris in 1624, it was reprinted in London several times and exerted significant influence on the Cambridge Platonists, particularly its assertion of the Common Notions.[10] Richard Baxter's *More Reasons for the*

Christian Religion, published one year after *Samson Agonistes*, includes a lengthy discussion advertised on its title page, "Some Animadversions on a Tractate *De Veritate*." In 1683, Cherbury's epistemology formed the explicit basis for Charles Blount's *Religio laici*, the first salvo of the deist controversy.[11] And in 1690 *De veritate* was named as a primary target in John Locke's *Essay*, which in its first sentence rejects "the established opinion amongst some men, that there are in the understanding certain innate principles."[12] Cherbury and Milton, moreover, share an abiding interest in the study of polytheism and monotheism and are fellow travelers in the seventeenth century discourse of monotheism. Cherbury was close friends with John Selden, and *De religione gentilium* owes a profound debt, both through direct citation and methodological influence, to Selden's *De diis Syris*. Meanwhile, Selden is Milton's "Chief Rabbi," the primary source for his Hebraic studies.[13] Like Cherbury, Milton repeatedly mined *De diis* for polytheistic detail, in *Paradise Lost* and in *Samson Agonistes*, where the representation of Dagon as a sea god can be traced to Selden. Their shared interest in oriental studies particularly converges in the 1640s. Cherbury finished *De religione* in 1645 and also republished *De veritate* in the same year, an apparent contribution to the anticlerical sentiment at that time—of which Milton and Selden were outspoken voices.[14] This is the period of Milton's work on divorce, when he clearly studied Selden closely, and when David Masson suggests that they met.[15] Milton's subsequent engagement with Socinian thought draws him even nearer to the rational religion that Cherbury inspired, so that although there is no direct reference to Cherbury in Milton's writing, I propose an affinity between their ideas. With both men working in the discourse of monotheism, and with both acquiring reputations for orientalism and liberal theology, such an affinity is not unrealistic.

Milton does closely resemble Cherbury when, in the preface to book 5 of *De doctrina*, the possibility of external revelation is embarrassingly remote: "Of course, if my opponents could show that the doctrine they defend was revealed to them by a voice from heaven, he would be an impious wretch who dared to raise so much as a murmur against it, let alone a sustained protest" (YP 6:204). Offering the most absurdly clear and distinct form of revelation, Milton's irony implies the opposite, that it is highly unlikely that revelation could proceed with such precision. Cherbury's famous encounter with an external sign, as recounted in his autobiography, makes an interesting parallel. Having received praise from Grotius for *De veritate,* Cherbury still hesitates to publish it because of its radicalness. He prays for "some sign from heaven" to show whether to publish or suppress the book. Then: "I had no sooner spoken these words, but a loud though yet gentle noise came from the heavens," and "I took my petition as granted, and that I had the sign I demanded, whereupon also I resolved to print my book."[16] This can only be ironic, in a way Cherbury would savor: a direct, external revelation authorizes *De veritate,* a book that takes aim at exactly this sort of private, unverifiable revelation. Like Milton, Cherbury feels the pressure of making heretical statements and responds with the sort of cavalier wit that inflects much of his autobiography and poetry—offering an authorizing sign that, according to the arguments of *De veritate,* can have no authority.[17] From within the seriousness of *De doctrina,* Milton's "voice from heaven" has a similarly ironic timbre. It seems nearly laughable when divine revelation is so distinctly perceived and so clearly understood.

By marginalizing external revelation, Cherbury reduces religion to the most universal of propositions, the five Religious Common Notions. These dismiss the details of Scripture, pushing theology inward and replacing the realm of external revelations that Henry More calls the "exteriour Oeconomy of Christianity" (*GMG* ix) with mental faculties. In paring the accumulated stories and traditions of revealed religion, the Religious Common Notions also create a thoroughly abstract God, one stripped of all excess. The Common Notions are powerful examples of the abstracting tendency in monotheism.[18] And they form the basis of Cherbury's inclusive theology, an occult monotheism that elides the crucial distinction between those privy to the Judeo-Christian revelation and those not—rendering unimportant the Mosaic distinction between Christianity and false religion.

To read *Samson Agonistes* alongside Cherbury is to find Milton engaging with the most radical wing of the discourse of monotheism. It is to find him thinking past even the rational theology of Socinianism and considering the ideas associated with deism, which Cherbury is widely credited with inspiring. But while it shows his deep involvement in the issues of deism, particularly the rejection of external revelation and the related claim for religious toleration, *Samson Agonistes* ultimately distances Milton from a deist position by making clear the necessity of angels, just as in *De doctrina Christiana* Milton rejects natural religion's claims for ascertaining religious truth without revelation (YP 6:132). *Samson Agonistes* is not an endorsement of Cherbury's ideas or a statement of doctrinal conviction, but rather an experimental staging of them that demonstrates a significant affinity and, simultaneously, a determined departure.

Impulses, Instincts, and Motions

The similarities between the terminology of *De veritate* and Samson's inward inspiration are striking. In detailing the Common Notions, *De veritate* has much to say about instincts, impulses, and motions, and all of these are substitutes for external revelation. Although his language of inspiration is probably more loosely used than the technical vocabulary of Cherbury's system, Milton is clearly turning toward the kind of philosophical and theological inquiry that Cherbury develops. A comparison with Cherbury's system shows that, in his description of Samson's inspiration, Milton has constructed a descending scale of certainty: we go from the untroubled veracity of "divine instinct" (*SA* 526), to the ambiguity of "impulse" (223), to the apparent unreliability of "rousing motions" (1382).

In determining the nature of Samson's impulses, instincts, and motions, the foremost question will be one of origins: is Samson's perceived inspiration truly of God? As Stanley Fish points out, if Samson's inspiration really is divine, it becomes the key to what he calls a "regenerationist" reading of the poem—a reading that finds a happy ending in Samson's internal development.[19] Genuinely divine inspiration becomes proof that in his actions, especially his final act, Samson has not been deserted by heaven. Manoa, the first of the regenerationist readers, makes it of the highest importance to a happy ending that God is with Samson in the end: "And which is best and happiest yet, all this / With God not parted from him, as was feared, / But favouring and assisting to the end" (SA 1718–20). In Judges, the "spirit" is unambiguously "of the Lord," but things are not so clear in Milton's retelling. And if it cannot be known for certain that these internal phenomena truly are of God, if there is room in the poem for skepticism toward such inspiration, then Samson's "swoonings of despair, / And sense of heaven's desertion" (631–32) may at the end be an unchanged condition.

Most of *De veritate* is occupied with answering questions of epistemology, leading in particular to how we know things divine. Cherbury lays out a complex system that focuses on the internal faculties of the mind and centers on innate knowledge, his Common Notions. He discovers four classes of faculties, and the complex workings of these faculties determine true or false perception. In descending order according to the primacy of their function, these are: natural instinct, internal apprehension, external apprehension, and discursive thought (*De veritate* 115). The first, natural instinct (*instinctus naturales*), contains the Common Notions that originate in divine Providence: "In treating of these Notions, I am defending God's cause, Who has bestowed Common Notions upon men in all ages as media of His divine universal Providence" (118). As the medium of Providence, natural instinct is that class of faculties which is both necessary to the discovery of truth and an utterly reliable means for that discovery. The second, internal apprehension (*sensus internus*), is closely allied to the Common Notions, helping to determine such abstract truths as love, hope, and conscience, and is the most important set of faculties after natural instinct (146). Yet internal apprehension is not wholly reliable. It is divided into two classes, mental and physical, and while the mental faculties operate like the Common Notions and inform us of Providence, the physical faculties do not. Error can easily arise from confusion of the mental and physical classes. Then external apprehension, which is of less importance, comprises those faculties that perceive external objects—in other words, the senses. Finally, discursive thought is the rational working of the mind—and it is the least reliable.

The kind of inspiration that proves most reliable for Samson is divine instinct. This is associated with an earlier time when Samson's life was full of miraculous feats of strength and purposive thoughts. Samson was then at his zenith,

> when in strength
> All mortals I excelled, and great in hopes
> With youthful courage and magnanimous thoughts
> Of birth from heaven foretold and high exploits,
> Full of divine instinct, after some proof
> Of acts indeed heroic, far beyond
> The sons of Anak, famous now and blazed,
> Fearless of danger, like a petty god
> I walked about admired of all and dreaded
> On hostile ground, none daring my affront. (*SA* 522–31)

Samson is near to God—"All mortals I excelled" and "like a petty god / I walked about"—for, he says, he was "full of divine instinct." Milton's choice of the word "instinct" matches Cherbury's use of it to describe the class of faculties containing the Common Notions. Neither "carelessly diffused," nor swooning from "sense of heaven's desertion," Samson swells with the kind of certainty in his execution of God's will that Cherbury's natural instinct begets. Instinct, unlike much-disparaged enthusiasm, guides us truthfully in political matters such as Samson faces:

"It is by means of this Common Notion that, as I believe, we can resolve all doubts which are apt to spring up concerning the government of the world" (*De veritate* 119). And it is through instinct that we can know with certainty God's will: "God has bestowed on us not only a representation of His form but also some portion of His divine wisdom. I make bold to say that the Creator Himself is revealed in some of these Common Notions" (126). Cherbury's assertion here that Common Notions are divine revelation sets up his later argument against revealed religion: Common Notions replace traditional revelation as a means of knowing true religion. Cherbury also strengthens the epistemological value of Common Notions by making them as authoritative as more traditional revelations, such as the appearance of an angel. Milton makes the very same analogy between revelation and instinct by grouping divine instinct with "thoughts / Of birth from heaven foretold." The certainty of Samson's status as a Nazarite is established by the angel of Judges 13, and his thoughts of that revelation are simultaneous with his divine instinct.

In the events of the story, the next form of inward inspiration is an "impulse," which Milton applies to Samson's decision to marry the bride of Timna. If "instinct" holds out the promise of genuine revelation, "impulse" proves much less certain. According to the *Oxford English Dictionary*, "impulse" in Milton's period could be used in two crucially different ways, both as an external force originating in a good or bad spirit, and as a wholly internal, psychological phenomenon.[20] At stake in these competing meanings is whether or not Samson's impulse originates in God, and so reveals God's will. This makes an enormous difference to the poem: Samson's unlawful marriage to the bride of Timna is best defended with recourse to God's will, and assurance that Samson's earlier transgression was part of God's plan provides hope that his greater indiscretion with Dalila will prove similarly provident.

The word is used twice about Samson's decision to marry the bride of Timna, but with significantly different modifiers. First,

Samson tells the Chorus that Manoa and his wife, "knew not / That what I motioned was of God; I knew / From intimate impulse, and therefore urged / The marriage on" (*SA* 221–24). Then Manoa, recounting his view of the inspiration, says to Samson, "thou didst plead / Divine impulsion prompting how thou might'st / Find some occasion to infest our foes. / I state not that" (421–24). That the impulse may be "intimate" implies only that it was felt internally, which could mean that it originated within Samson and is unconnected to God's will, or that it was sent from God but did not take the external form of an angel. If the modifier is "divine," however, it marks the impulse as genuine inspiration, originating from God. The crucial question of the impulse's origin is still unanswered. Perched between the divine and the human, Samson's impulse resembles Cherbury's equally equivocal faculty, internal apprehension.

It is the object of much of Cherbury's discussion of internal apprehension to clarify exactly this doubt about divine origin. While natural instinct is a certain arbiter of truth, internal apprehension must deal with "internal senses" that can be false. These senses "are influenced by the incongruous and contradictory character of objects. For these reasons great care must be exercised; otherwise, owing to conflicting notions, we may surrender ourselves to unworthy impulses" (*De veritate* 149). The risk of error in internal apprehension throughout *De veritate* is associated with the word "impulse" (Latin: *affectus*). Cherbury aligns the impulse with the physiological influence of the bodily humours, and with any form of violent passion. These impulses are the part of internal apprehension that is physical, and they must be repressed by the mental part. For only internal apprehension having to do with the mind can overcome the impulses and lead to "Blessedness":

> The inner forms of apprehension which I attribute to the mind are those which do not arise from objects nor their images nor from bodily humours but proceed from those faculties which are concerned with the common good, and can react upon the apprehensions

> produced by objects or by their images or by the bodily humours, with the consequence that they establish control over all kinds of evil and violent passions and reversing their impulse can overcome them and finally repress and allay them. And so at last they enjoy conformity with the objects of the Universe and embrace them only, thus giving assurance of the eternal Blessedness of the soul. (*De veritate* 155)

Samson's impulse, Cherbury alerts us, may be the wrong kind of internal apprehension. He interprets it as the right kind, declaring that his intimate impulse was "of God," and telling Manoa that the impulse was "divine." But if, as the word "impulse" suggests, the revelation is merely intimate, which is to say internal and so on the physical side of Cherbury's internal apprehension, there is a very real danger that it has proceeded not from God, but from the bodily humours or the "contradictory character of objects." Rather than repressing these impulses with his mental faculties, Samson mistakenly exalts them as divine. While Cherbury warns that "great care must be exercised" with internal apprehension, lest one submit to "unworthy impulses," Samson enthusiastically accepts his impulses as authentic. Samson's epistemological work may be distressingly naive.

So it is left to Manoa, who displays exemplary skepticism in Judges 13, to question Samson's interpretation of his impulse. Manoa says that Samson did "plead / Divine impulsion," invoking a sense of childish persuasion that is prone to exaggeration, as well as an orator's reliance on rhetoric. Speaking to the Chorus, and in retrospect, Samson calls the impulse merely "intimate." But in the moment of special pleading to his father for acceptance of his impulse to marry the bride of Timna, Samson seeks a greater sense of certainty and authority. Cherbury's critique of revelation centers upon the possibility of just this kind of rhetoric. Whereas religious truth by means of the Common Notions is a matter of individuals using their own faculties, revelation depends upon another's word—"upon the authority of him who reveals it." The person who reports the revelation may, as Samson appears to have done, distort the truth. Manoa registers the rhetorical nature of Samson's report in the word "plead," and provides a response that would warm Cherbury's heart: "I state not that." With Manoa before us as, for the moment, an exemplary skeptic, we must realize that Samson's decision to marry the bride of Timna may have no divine authority behind it, but rather may be impulsive in the modern sense of the word.

Indeed, modern, psychological uses of "impulse" and "impulsive" turn away from the sense of an external force. Returning to the *OED*, "impulse" in modern usage means exclusively an "Incitement or stimulus to action arising from some state of mind or feeling." This movement within the word "impulse" from possibly external to strictly internal, matches the movement John Guillory traces when he finds an evolution from daemon to Freud's *zwang*, or compulsion. Much as the comparison to Cherbury does, Guillory places *Samson Agonistes* within Max Weber's process of "disenchantment." In a section of the essay headed simply "Intimate Impulse," Guillory says, "Samson exhibits what Freud calls a *Schickalszwang*, a 'fate compulsion,' described in *Beyond the Pleasure Principle* as 'being pursued by a malignant fate or possessed by some "daemonic" power.'"[21] He goes on to explain that the "daemon" behind such compulsion is quickly translated into internal and analytic language that refers not to external forces, but to childhood influence. Guillory's discussion of vocation places Samson between the inward, self-prompting of impulse and the external, social pressure of the law, which is a different set of terms than my more literal and theological polarity between intimate and divine impulse. But the "psychologizing move" he identifies is the same. What is disappearing from our formulation of the workings of the mind is the appearance of spirits or angels, which for Guillory stand for law, but in my analysis stand for themselves—that is, for revelation. It is this nexus between internal mental functioning and external revelation that so recommends Cherbury as a context for *Samson Agonistes*. And Cherbury's use of impulse, as apprehension that is specifically not divine, matches perfectly Milton's stated effort to forge a "fable as may stand best with verisimilitude and decorum."

If Samson's inspiration now rests equivocally between "intimate impulse" and "divine impulsion," certain evidence of divine presence depends upon his last and greatest moment of inspiration, his "rousing motions." Any hope for a regenerationist ending, one proving that Samson finishes his life, "With God not parted from him," rests upon the certainty of a divine origin to these rousing motions. As with "impulse," "motion" can signify either a strictly internal process, or a process instigated by an external spirit. According to the *OED*, "motion" in Milton's period could mean "An inward prompting or impulse," or a desire or emotion. This sense need not be specifically carnal or impious, but was often used in the same way as the modern "impulse." So Richard Hooker is cited: "Whereas unto mens inward cogitations, unto the privie intents and motions of their hearts, religion serveth for a bridle." However, "motion" could also specifically mean "a working of God in the soul"—like impulse, its semantic field is divided between implications of divine and human origins (see "Motion," *OED*). Yet, turning again to *De veritate*, Samson's "rousing motions" appear to originate not from God, but, quite unequivocally, from Samson's body. Specifically disassociated from the Common Notions, "motions" prove to be a part of internal apprehension that is specifically not divine, and therefore specifically prone to error.

Internal apprehension operates closely with natural instinct and the Common Notions, but is divided, as we have seen, into two classes: apprehensions attributed to the mind and physical apprehensions. The former have to do with things divine, and the latter with "pleasant or unpleasant nervous sensations, such as those of lust, itching, tickling, laughter, sloth, yawning, stretching, sleep grief, irritability, rage, fear, terror, weeping nightmare and many others" (*De veritate* 165–66). And it is with these purely bodily apprehensions that "motions" are everywhere associated. The "motions of the bodily humours" (Latin: *motus*) "fill us with discomfort, producing coarse and oppressive sensations. The faculties relating to these apprehension apply to the world while those of the preceding class (mental apprehension) apply to God" (165). Because they are internal, physical apprehensions can easily be confused with mental — with the significant difficulty that "coarse and oppressive sensations" might be mistaken for divine inspiration. For this reason Cherbury warns that mental apprehensions, which are analogous with God, "produce in us a sense of tranquility and happiness.... In this they differ from the physical faculties, which produce coarse and violent feeling" (155–56).

Samson's inspiration is cast not just as motions, but as "rousing" motions: Samson appears to be experiencing the kind of coarse sensation Cherbury associates with physical apprehension, and not the kind of tranquility associated with divinely inspired mental apprehension. Indeed, his inspiration comes just after his encounter with Harapha, just after Samson has finally risen to his feet and become excited with the prospect of battle. Such excitation, such motions within the body, are causally linked by Cherbury to the rage that raises Samson in the face of Harapha's goading. When Samson threatens to swing Harapha in the air, then "dash thee down / To the hazard of thy brains" (1240–41), he is overflowing with what Cherbury calls "coarse and violent feeling." Samson's rousing motions seem to originate in mere physical excitation, not in God.

Thought and Theodicy

By replacing external revelation with internal inspiration, Milton folds all possibility of a redemptive reading into Samson's interior. The array of technical terms used to describe that interiority suggests that a rational and systematic understanding of inspiration within the human mind — such as Cherbury puts forward — will clarify Samson's relationship to divine will. And yet Samson's impulses and motions, even as they promise scientific specificity, must finally be seen as rigorously equivocal, rendering God's will opaque. Cherbury builds his whole system upon his Common Notions, which, in place of external revelation, are the certain means of knowing God's will. But in *Samson Agonistes* the Common Notions fail. Apparently not as universal as Cherbury claims, Common Notions are only available in the distant past of Samson's "divine instinct." Like the angel of Judges 13, merely the object of nostalgia, they are as seemingly remote as Eden.

If in the difficult present of *Samson Agonistes* such a pretty theory as innate ideas is disallowed, Samson and the Danites are left groping with the faculty Cherbury says is most removed from the Common Notions: that of discursive thought. Although Samson felt an impulse to marry the bride of Timna, he had none with Dalila. And in the absence of even so equivocal an inspiration as an impulse, Samson turns to his own ratiocination: "I thought it lawful from my former act, / And the same end" (231–32). Whereas he "knew" from intimate impulse that he was acting according to God, he merely "thought" his action lawful according to prior experience. According to Cherbury, such discursive thought (*discursus*) "takes the lowest place" among the faculties because it operates in the absence of analogies formed by the other faculties.[22] If there is no other way of ascertaining truth, we fall back on discursive thought, just as Samson seems to do without an impulse or instinct to guide him in the marriage of Dalila. But there is a problem: discursive thought, Cherbury announces at the beginning of his chapter on the subject, "is more liable to error than any of the other faculties" (*De veritate* 232). Indeed, "every important error is due to it" (239).

Discursus is frequently associated with the Spenserian sense of wandering: it "wanders among bypaths, often stumbling in its tracks, and when it seeks support from the yielding confusion of truths it brings to the ground its whole crazy structure of principles" (*De veritate* 232). Milton's Chorus constructs thought as similarly erring:

> Yet more there be who doubt his ways not just,
> As to his own edicts, found contradicting,
> Then give the reins to wandering thought,
> Regardless of his glory's diminution;
> Till by their own perplexities involved
> They ravel more, still less resolved
> But never find self-satisfying solution.   (*SA* 300–306)

Cherbury and Milton agree on the problem with discursive thought: it does not lead to the rarified certainty of either Common Notions or angelic revelation. Cherbury explains that it "does not of its own right have access to the analogy which exists between us and the first cause" (*De veritate* 235). Cherbury's Common Notions operate by analogy, so discursive thought is said to provide no access to the operations that enable the natural knowledge of God, remaining outside of those best Common Notions, natural instincts, which can substitute for revelation. For Milton, if we include *Paradise Lost*, *discursus* is similarly a weakened substitute for the immediate certainty of angelic intuition. Raphael explains to Adam that,

> the soul
> Reason receives, and reason is her being,
> Discursive, or intuitive; discourse
> Is oftest yours, the latter most is ours,
> Differing but in degree, of kind the same.   (*PL* 5.486–90)

Until he feels the rousing motions, Samson's "I thought it lawful from my former act, / And the same end" stands as his most recent effort at determining God's will. It is the error that has shaped the action of *Samson Agonistes*, as well as the mode that prevails throughout most of the action: Samson's despair and his dialogues with the Chorus, Manoa, and Dalila are all similar efforts at thinking through divine will. Samson's moment of extreme distance from divine instinct, which can be distilled into the single word "thought," thus controls the bulk of the poem. *Samson Agonistes* is about thought—it stages an intellectual agon—but, appropriate to the faculty's misleading character, it offers a bleak and disparaging account of it. Samson, we learn right away, struggles not with physical pain but with thought, which lingers as a Dantesque punishment for his earlier thought to marry Dalila:

> I seek
> This unfrequented place to find some ease,
> Ease to the body some, none to the mind
> From restless thoughts, that like a deadly swarm
> Of hornets armed, no sooner found alone,
> But rush upon me thronging, and present
> Times past, what once I was, and what am now. (SA 16–22)

Thought stays with Samson, still like a swarm, and so besets him that he no longer distinguishes it from physical pain:

> Thoughts my tormentors armed with deadly stings
> Mangle my apprehensive tenderest parts,
> Exasperate, exulcerate, and raise
> Dire inflammation which no cooling herb
> Or med'cinal liquor can assuage,
> Nor breath of vernal air from snowy alp. (623–28)

After each of these struggles with thought, Samson laments the absence of the angel of Judges 13—ironically naming the remedy. Of course, the angel never returns, and after so much pain it must be a balm to Samson when he announces, "I begin to feel / Some rousing motions in me which dispose / To something extraordinary my thoughts" (1381–83). Yet the successful transcendence of discursive thought at play's end depends entirely on whether or not rousing motions are legitimate. And while Manoa and the Chorus work hard to believe it is so, the ambiguity of rousing motions contradicts them. Milton's technical language, furthermore, sends us reading through the abstruse philosophy of Herbert of Cherbury, which only perpetuates discursive thought. Thought in *Samson Agonistes* becomes a forest with no escape into the open air of religious certainty.

It is perhaps the defining difference between *Paradise Lost* and *Samson Agonistes* that Samson has no Raphael, but only the unreliable "rousing motions." Like Adam, Samson once moved comfortably in the sure knowledge of God's will—although by means of innate ideas rather than an angel, he had access to divine instinct just as Adam has access to angels and their intuition. Samson remembers nostalgically how before Dalila he lived "Full of divine instinct," until, matching Adam and Eve's free choice to eat the apple, "swoll'n with pride into the snare I fell" (*SA* 532). In the moment of the drama, access to divine will is in the seemingly irrecoverable past: distanced from any guiding knowledge, Samson lives in relation to his divine instinct as fallen man lives in relation to prelapsarian Adam.

Samson's fall, however, originates not with Dalila's snare, but with Samson's moment of "thought," when he decides to marry Dalila. This has important repercussions. For when Milton leaves Samson to make his choices without an angel, or Common Notions, or any form of reliable revelation, Samson has no choice but to turn to discursive thought. This renders Samson's knowledge of God's will partial or even erroneous, and Samson is forced to make his decisions from relative ignorance. His fall, then, is not a matter of free will, as it is in *Paradise Lost,* but of knowledge, or rather ignorance. And since the absence of the angel of Judges 13 is not Samson's fault, in the final analysis he is not deserted by heaven as a result of his haircut, but rather ends up shorn as a result of heaven's desertion.

This undermines the justice of God. For in *Paradise Lost,* Milton makes knowledge the essential precondition to free will, and free will in turn the precondition to a just God. God instructs Raphael:

> advise him of his happy state,
> Happiness in his power left free to will,
> Left to his own free will, his will though free,
> Yet mutable; whence warn him to beware
> He swerve not too secure: tell him withal
> His danger, and from whom, what enemy
> Late fallen himself from heaven, is plotting now

> The fall of others from like state of bliss;
> By violence, no, for that shall be withstood,
> But by deceit and lies; this let him know,
> Lest wilfully transgressing he pretend
> Surprisal, unadmonished, unforewarned.
>   So spake the eternal Father, and fulfilled
> All justice.   (*PL* 5.234–47)

Adam, whose free will puts the whole burden of choice upon him, must be properly informed. But if Adam is told "His danger, and from whom, what enemy," Samson, with neither revelation nor access to a version of Cherbury's Common Notions, has no such clear information when faced with his marriage decision. Samson's knowledge of God's will is partial, and he must make his choices with the aid of discursive thought alone. Samson's fall is located in his descent from divine instinct to impulse to thought, and so is not a fall in the sense of fault, but in the sense of distancing from heaven. Because Samson's sense of heaven's desertion is prior to his divulging his secret to Dalila, it is not a result but the cause of his error in Dalila's lap. Samson battles such pretensions: "Yet stay, let me not rashly call in doubt / Divine prediction" (43–44). But the terms Milton chooses to describe Samson's inspiration suggest just this kind of doubt. God sends Raphael to Adam lest justice be impugned. But there is no angel, and so seems to be no justice, in Samson's fall.

Such injustice works to the disadvantage of Samson but, more crucially, also to the disadvantage of God. God's insistence upon free will in the above passage from *Paradise Lost*, strengthened by the overwhelming repetition of the term, is both linguistically and conceptually inseparable from his insistence that Adam be fully advised. And the detailed information Adam receives is necessary to God meeting the standards of the absolute value of justice—God's direction to Raphael, "fulfilled / All justice." That Samson is never warned of his danger or his enemy thus significantly threatens the justice of God. And yet this says less about the requirements of justice as an absolute value than about what is required to perceive justice from the human perspective. For

Raphael must speak with Adam not in order to improve Adam's decision making, but lest he "pretend / Surprisal, unadmonished, unforewarned." "Pretend," here, does not carry the sense of imposture but of assertion, of mere claiming: God wants no argument, wants no *discursus*, claiming that humans were unprepared for their trial. It is for the sake of justifying the ways of God to man that God insists upon revelation. That Samson, and Milton's reader, are insufficiently informed therefore threatens the project of theodicy. From within a world relying on discursive thought rather than external revelation, Samson and his tribe are in serious danger of finding themselves unable to justify the ways of God. This is why the Chorus's "Just are the ways of God / And justifiable to men," delivered in the moments after Samson's admission of "I thought it lawful," rings so hollow.

Toleration and Polytheism in Dalila's Country

The collapse of revelation, with the absence of the angel of Judges 13 and the failure of Samson's inward inspiration, leads to the collapse of theodicy. For the ways of God become less certain as Samson and the Danites lose contact with him. The Chorus doggedly asserts the truth of theodicy, but nevertheless seems aware of the alternatives. Immediately after "Just are the ways of God / And justifiable to men," the Chorus considers the possibility of atheism: "Unless there be who think not God at all" (*SA* 295). Such people walk obscure in the Chorus's view, but it is telling that atheism even comes to mind. More common, the Chorus says, are those who "doubt his ways not just," who see God as contradicting his own edicts. Such people reject theodicy, and so "give the reins to wandering thought," becoming too involved in philosophy, like the fallen angels of *Paradise Lost*, and becoming caught in "their own perplexities" (300–306). Coming to *Samson Agonistes* from the discourse of monotheism, it feels likely that Milton is calling to mind the emerging rational theology. Deism was regularly charged with atheism, and it did often suggest that the Judeo-Christian God was in danger of being too arbitrary. Additionally, the deist conception of religion, without all the stories of miracles and revelations, was often perceived as too philosophical and discursive. Perhaps giving voice to the religious uncertainty of the late seventeenth century, even the Chorus cannot help but sense what shaky ground religion is on in this verisimilar moment.

That Milton makes room for such considerations in *Samson Agonistes* should not be surprising if we take seriously his tendency toward religious toleration. In the preface to book 5 of *De doctrina*, in *Of True Religion*, and in the indifferent narrative of *Paradise Regained*, Milton's tolerant position calls for acceptance of things indifferent or unrevealed. This is an assertion of the need to admit uncertainty and tolerate diverse views in the absence of revelation. Following this line of reasoning, the collapse of revelation in *Samson Agonistes* would seem to open up a large field for religious toleration—and, indeed, Milton goes on, through Dalila, to imagine a world rich in toleration. As the poem shifts from Samson's conversations, with their failed efforts at theodicy, to the appearances of Dalila and Harapha and the final denouement, a picture of religious toleration and plenitude among the Philistines shines forth, one that contrasts starkly with the despair of the Israelites. Dalila's country beckons, though it is a place that worships many gods. Through Dalila and Harapha, the poem approaches near to the edge of polytheism, as well as to the objectivity of comparative religion.

This follows exactly Cherbury's progression from subversion of local revelation such as angels to the skeptical reevaluation of revelation in its greater sense—the Judeo-Christian revelation. Cherbury's Religious Common Notions not only replace external revelations, they also open up religious truth to those who stand outside of the Judeo-Christian revelation, allowing pagans to perceive the true God. This inclusiveness is implied by Cherbury's "true Catholic Church" in *De veritate*, but receives full expression in the later work, *De religione gentilium*. In the opening chapter, Cherbury announces his irenicism: "I sincerely wish, then, that modern theologians would be more tolerant in what they lay down concerning the souls of pagans" (*De religione* 53). And the main work of *De religione* is to establish a comparison between the religions of the world, which then allows Cherbury to argue for identity rather than difference: showing polytheists actually to have been occult monotheists. A veteran of the Thirty Years' War and a reluctant participant in England's civil war, Cherbury seeks a natural religion that would end all religious strife by obviating all major distinctions between religions.

So it is that, to a greater extent than Selden, Cherbury is lauded as one of the most important early contributors to comparative religion. In his history of comparative religion, Eric Sharpe credits Cherbury with giving coherence to deism, which "as a whole was important in the prehistory of comparative religion in that it seriously put forward a set of criteria by which religion might be judged, without calling in any kind of belief in revelation."[23] The discourse of monotheism itself can be characterized as nascent comparative religion, with Cherbury representing its most radical expression. Cherbury's and Henry More's competing conceptions of monotheism reveal that the fundamental skirmish within the discourse of monotheism is the authority of revelation. More asserts a form of monotheism specifically designed to protect orthodox revelation, while Cherbury's epistemology raises the very real question whether the Judeo-Christian revelation will maintain an exclusive claim on truth. What Cherbury brings to the discourse of monotheism is not just a liberal mapping of revelation, but the even more radical possibility of abolishing the Judeo-Christian revelation altogether.

There is major friction in the ideology at this point, a paradox surrounding revelation that structures the ending of *Samson Agonistes*. The difficulty is that while the comparative impulse issuing from the study of monotheism begins to subvert the exclusive truth claims of revealed religion, monotheism itself turns out to depend utterly on revelation. The Mosaic distinction, as Jan

Assmann theorizes it, is unique to monotheism and fundamental to its definition, being the ideological border that defines true monotheistic religion. It is also predicated entirely upon revelation: "There is no natural or evolutionary way leading from the error of idolatry to the truth of monotheism. This truth can come only from outside, by way of revelation."[24] Revelation makes claims of absolute truth that are above the flow and continuity of logic and argument. It forcefully asserts, and this superrational mode forms the very basis of monotheism's claim to have the only true God. Monotheism's loudest proponents in the seventeenth century came to suspect revealed religion, even as revelation proves to be the main pillar supporting it.

The distinction between monotheism and polytheism—the Mosaic distinction—is not merely numerical, but includes a fundamental shift in perspective from an absolutism to a religious relativism. Assmann associates religious relativism with the polytheistic practice of "translation," which is the willingness to recognize the similarities between gods and to equate, for example, one culture's sun god with another's. One divine name can be translated into another because a basic similarity, a common ground, is recognized across the borders of nations, languages and religions. And it is just such relativism that monotheism, with its division into true and false religion by the Mosaic distinction, necessarily and structurally rejects:

> The Mosaic distinction was therefore a radically new distinction which considerably changed the world in which it was drawn. The space which was "severed or cloven" by this distinction was not simply the space of religion in general, but that of a very specific kind of religion. We may call this new type of religion "counter-religion" because it rejects and repudiates everything that went before and what is outside itself as "paganism." It no longer functioned as a means of intercultural translation; on the contrary, it functioned as a means of intercultural estrangement. Whereas polytheism, or rather "cosmotheism," rendered different cultures mutually transparent and compatible, the new counter-religion blocked intercultural translatability. False gods cannot be translated.[25]

In its detailed study of polytheism, Cherbury's *De religione* expends a good deal of energy on the relativistic practice of translation. Indeed, its project of demonstrating the Religious Common Notions hinges upon translation—on the assertion that all religions share a common ground. In translating even across the Mosaic distinction, Cherbury thus radically subverts monotheism—paradoxically, following monotheism's skepticism toward revelation to its most rigorous conclusion, Cherbury's pure monotheism threatens to become polytheism.

It is this difficult and shocking endpoint to monotheistic skepticism that Milton stages in the latter half of *Samson Agonistes*. The absence of any form of local revelation in the first half threatens theodicy by leaving only logical argument—*discursus*—to do the work of justifying the ways of God. Samson receives no assertion of monotheistic truth, but instead is left with "swoonings of despair / And sense of heaven's desertion." And it is fresh from this despairing version of monotheism, essentially a deistic endpoint to monotheism's skepticism, that Milton brings Samson and his world into confrontation with a not unattractive polytheism, figured by Dalila. The fruit of relativism and toleration is dangled in front of us, as Samson, wandering in discursive thought, watches Dalila approach clothed in the nautical language of the sea god Dagon. And without revelation and its facilitation of theodicy, the confrontation with Dalila and polytheism seems more equal than one might expect.

Dalila's arguments are fairly easily disposed of until the last, which is simply never answered. In her final argument, Dalila asserts the equal legitimacy of Philistian religion, and in claiming for Dagon a fair share of truth, Dalila stakes out a relativistic perspective that brings us, at least for the moment, remarkably close to Cherbury. Stripped of the specifics of revelation by the early parts of *Samson Agonistes*, we are now put in front of nascent comparative religion. With a maddening disregard for Samson's approval, Dalila argues for the equal truthfulness of Philistian religion:

> To mix with thy concernments I desist
> Henceforth, nor too much disapprove my own.
> Fame if not double-faced is double-mouthed,
> And with contrary blast proclaims most deeds,
> On both his wings, one black, the other white,
> Bears greatest names in his wild aery flight.
> My name perhaps among the circumcised
> In Dan, in Judah, and the bordering tribes,
> To all posterity may stand defamed,
> With malediction mentioned, and the blot
> Of falsehood most unconjugal traduced.
> But in my country where I most desire,
> In Ecron, Gaza, Asdod, and in Gath
> I shall be named among the famousest
> Of women, sung at solemn festivals,
> Living and dead recorded, who to save
> Her country from a fierce destroyer, chose
> Above the faith of wedlock-bands, my tomb
> With odours visited and annual flowers.
> Not less renowned than in Mount Ephraim
> Jael, who with inhospitable guile
> Smote Sisera sleeping through the Temples nailed.   (969–90)

Samson is very concerned with his own fame, how he will be "proverbed" (203). And this long passage begins with Dalila's smart reminder that Fame is "double-mouthed," by which she means that every narrative can be retold from a different and contrary perspective—Samson's already equivocal position in history is made even more tenuous. This basic lesson in relativism challenges Samson's legacy and the play's ending by anticipating and matching Samson's tomb. As a monument to Samson's heroism, Manoa vows to build a tomb covered in evergreen and palm, and "The virgins also shall on feastful days / Visit his tomb with flowers" (1741–42). But this is little different from Dalila's "tomb / With odours visited and annual flowers." What is meant to stand for Samson's single victory, and to become a lasting index of the unique sacred history of the Jews, suddenly has a double. As the victory is over idolatry, and the sacred history is monotheistic, a second winner is utterly deflating. Dagon cannot also win.

Dalila's dismissive description of the Israelites goes on to characterize them as a people founded upon the very borders and distinctions that Assmann identifies. Assmann, as we have seen, describes the Mosaic distinction as radically altering the world, causing the space of religion to be "severed or cloven" into true and false religions. As a counter-religion, monotheism violently rejects all that is on the wrong side of the border drawn by the Mosaic distinction. Dalila says, "My name perhaps among the circumcised / In Dan, in Judah, and the bordering tribes, / To all posterity may stand defamed." She refers first to circumcision, which is a physical cleaving and distinction, and the symbol of God's covenant with the Israelites making them, and no one else, the chosen people. She then names Dan, one of the 12 tribes to be distinguished among the Jews, and Judah, the southern part of a split kingdom, before giving a name that can be well applied to all monotheists: "bordering tribes." Samson's are the people, in other words, of the Mosaic distinction.

Dalila then crosses over—"But in my country"—into the polytheistic space on the other side of the Mosaic distinction. On the other side there is no defaming, and there are no distinctions or divisions, but rather a burgeoning plenitude: "In Ecron, Gaza, Asdod, and in Gath / I shall be named among the famousest / Of women." Quite unlike Samson's divided and border-ridden country, Dalila's overflows with important cities, and her catalog fills the pentameter line as if all and more are invited. In her prophecy of fame, Dalila is not the most famous, but rather among them, as if polytheistic history itself offers a more social and congenial alternative to the solitude of the chosen people.

Of course, this vision of polytheistic peace and plenitude looks a lot like Enlightenment fantasy. And "bordering tribes" sounds very like seventeenth century England. Dalila's last plea is perhaps so surprisingly sympathetic because it holds out what many in Restoration England deeply desired: an end to sectarian strife. As Assmann explains, the cleaving of the Mosaic distinction has a ripple effect: "We start with Christians and pagans and end up with Catholics and Protestants, Calvinists and Lutherans, Socinians and Latitudinarians, and a thousand more similar denominations."[26] With Dalila we are enticed by the possibility of a religion without the violent distinctions between the many subdivisions and sects. Assmann helps us see that these divisions have their origin in the fundamental distinction between true and false, the Mosaic distinction separating monotheism and polytheism. *Samson Agonistes* brings us to this insight, as we lend a sympathetic ear to Dalila, and perhaps regret the border distinguishing Christians and pagans.

Dalila makes explicit what England, in arriving at a deist rejection of the Mosaic distinction, would leave behind, when she turns to one of the less flattering episodes in the history of the Israelites: "Not less renowned than in Mount Ephraim / Jael, who with inhospitable guile / Smote Sisera sleeping through the temples nailed." Inhospitable, graphically murderous, and, again, physically cleaving the flesh, monotheism is again portrayed as suffering under its own structural need to divide. The truly subversive force of Dalila's last lines, however, lies in their assertion of a relativism that threatens to dissolve monotheism's most important distinction: the totality of the Jewish revelation contained in the sacred Scripture. Fame's double mouth suggests a competing historical truth of the sort antiquarians and chronologists might dig up — powerful in the light it might shed upon specifics of the Bible, but not powerful enough to subvert the text itself. But when Milton has Dalila compare herself to Jael, and therefore her legacy to Scripture, he takes the truly subversive step of imagining another sacred history. For it is not just songs and tombs, the comparison implies, but a sacred text that might preserve Dalila's fame — an alternative Book of Judges; a Philistian bible.[27] By making Dalila a hero, by providing a different narrative to the same events, this other bible lays bare for those who imagine it the fact that there is no objective evidence recommending the Judeo-Christian Bible. This moment of relativism, in Assmann's terms a moment of translation between God's Bible and Dagon's bible, suggests that the only thing separating Milton's sacred Scripture from this and any other possible sacred scripture is the mere fact of the Judeo-Christian revelation.

That revelation is the only thing separating pagans is exactly Cherbury's point: his Religious Common Notions prove the fundamental common ground between even Jews and Philistines and isolate the points of difference as extraneous matters of ritual and detail grafted onto religion by revelation. That there can be no common ground whatsoever, that there is nothing relative but only things true and false, is the hard line drawn by the Mosaic distinction. And, as Assmann points out, it is specifically revelation that accomplishes this blockade of relativism: "The boundaries of intranslatability which the Jewish, the Christian and somewhat later the Islamic monotheisms erected in the name of revelation must be viewed against the background of the firm cosmotheistic belief in translatability in the name of nature."[28] Finding that Christianity rests only on revelation might elicit a shrug from an orthodoxy that assumes the centrality of the Christian revelation. But Milton offers the insight in the radical context of a poem that, as we have seen, rigorously marginalizes revelation. He introduces the relativistic insight from within a world of discursive thought, which is to say from within a world requiring reasons precisely because it is denied revelations. The lack of specific external revelation in the shape of the angel of Judges 13 has provided fertile ground for the suggestion of religious relativism: following exactly the trail blazed by Cherbury, Milton expands a skepticism toward the specific revelation of supernatural beings to a skepticism toward the total Judeo-Christian revelation.

The Dagon Agon

Of course, right after Dalila leaves, the Chorus, with Samson in agreement, wastes no time reinscribing her into the Judeo-Christian revelation: "She's gone, a manifest serpent by her sting" (*SA* 997). From the distinctionless space of religious relativism, Dalila is immediately thrust into Satan's camp, beginning a movement toward a reassertion of the Judeo-Christian revelation, with its fundamental divisions between true and false, good and evil—a movement that culminates in the Chorus's closing assertion of Providence: "All is best.... / And ever best found in the close" (1745, 1748). The Chorus ends happily certain in its convictions, but how satisfactory those convictions are to Milton or to the reader must be influenced by the blunt and decidedly violent victory that monotheism imposes. Samson's next interlocutor is Harapha, who in his pure physicality seems to provide relief, like the longed-for cooling herb, from Samson's tormenting thoughts. If Dalila in her cleverness goes unanswered, Harapha is handily put down precisely because he offers Samson the terms under which monotheism can triumph: not the relativism of equally truthful revelations, but the bald assertion of absolute and single truth that can be won through pure force. Monotheism's only hope is that God prove stronger than Dagon: Samson simply tells Harapha, "Then thou shalt see, or rather to thy sorrow / Soon feel, whose God is strongest, thine or mine" (1154–55).

Harapha makes a foray into the kind of subversive argumentation Dalila has used when he charges Samson with using black magic:

> Thou durst not thus disparage glorious arms
> Which greatest heroes have in battle worn,
> Their ornament and safety, had not spells
> And black enchantments, some magician's art,
> Armed thee or charmed thee strong, which thou from heaven
> Feign'dst at thy birth was given thee in thy hair,
> Where strength can least abide.   (*SA* 1130–36)

It is usually monotheism that cries out against witchcraft—Freud lists the rejection of magic as the first difference between monotheism and polytheism (*MM* 20). By calling Samson a practitioner of black magic, Harapha cleverly inverts the Mosaic distinction, grabbing for Dagon and polytheism the high moral ground. It is the Philistines, it appears, that worry about superstition, so how clear a distinction can monotheism make between itself and Gentiles? This is the very technique that Freud uses, with the same subversive end in mind, when he argues that Moses was Egyptian and monotheism an Egyptian invention.

But while his inversion of the Mosaic distinction resembles Dalila's, Harapha's argument is more easily rebutted because it has reduced the complex theological issue to a matter of mere strength. Samson dismisses the charge of witchcraft: "I know no spells, use no forbidden arts; / My trust is in the living God who gave me / At my nativity this strength" (1139–41). Reference to Samson's nativity recalls the distant assurances of the angel of Judges 13. But now, finally, there is a clear and distinct way to demonstrate the continued domain of that revelation. "For proof," Samson tells Harapha that he wants to

> challenge Dagon to the test,
> Offering to combat thee his champion bold,
> With the utmost of his godhead seconded:
> Then thou shalt see, or rather to thy sorrow
> Soon feel, whose God is strongest, thine or mine. (1151–55)

It is only after the Dagon agon is reduced to this simple equation that Samson succeeds in shedding his debilitating sense of heaven's desertion, announcing to Harapha:

> these evils I deserve and more,
> Acknowledge them from God inflicted on me
> Justly, yet despair not of his final pardon
> Whose ear is ever open. (1169–72)

While mired in the wanderings of discursive thought, Samson felt radically distanced from God. But with the introduction of physical action and the solid distinctions it can draw, Samson knows the proper course and—suddenly—quits despairing. God is no longer distant and unreachable but is the "living God." And with the surprising appearance of his ear, God even gains a physical presence in the text.

As Samson feels himself drawing closer to God, and as he seems to draw strength from that sense of certainty, Harapha, overgrown and flabby, perfectly represents the weakness of Dagon. Because of his parodic treatment in 1 Samuel 5, Dagon is probably the most ridiculous of polytheistic gods to appear in the Bible. As he quails before Samson's threats, Harapha brings us back to that unequal confrontation, where the presence of the ark in his temple repeatedly sends the statue of Dagon crashing to the ground. In both cases the question, "whose God is strongest, thine or mine," is rendered absurd by the overwhelming force of the monotheistic God. What begins as monolatry—both God and Dagon are real and one will prove slightly stronger—is forced into monotheism when the very idea of confrontation is parodied. God cannot fight with a god because only God is real. This leap from monolatry to monotheism is implied in the change, present in the first edition, from lowercase to uppercase *G* in Samson's earlier threat: "I once again / Defy thee to the trial of mortal fight, / By combat to decide whose god is God" (1174–76). Harapha's whipped but still boastful retreat then acknowledges that Samson's is not a god, but God: there actually can be no contest. And as Samson's strength blossoms into the omnipotence of monotheism, the utter vanity and weakness of Harapha's position unfolds from the absurdity of Dagon to the absurdity of all polytheism. As Harapha leaves he continues his boasting, but his theology expands from Dagonism. His last speeches, short and presumably spoken in full retreat, invoke a pantheon familiar to readers of Milton and to scholars of polytheism such as Cherbury and Selden: "O Baal-zebub! can my ears unused / Hear these dishonours, and not render death?" and "By Astaroth ere long thou shalt lament / These braveries in irons loaden on thee" (1231–32, 1242–43). Monotheism triumphs over Dagon, Baal-zebub, Astaroth, and over polytheism as a whole.

Yet that this triumph is forged entirely by means of a strong arm may debase it. Whatever Providence can be asserted by the end of the poem, it is asserted on the basis not of Samson's intellectual quelling of Dagonism before Dalila, but his physical domination of Dagon in Harapha—a domination reproduced on a larger scale in the catastrophe of the temple. Dalila articulates the violence of a monotheism based upon borders and distinctions, the most fundamental being the Mosaic distinction itself. And the poem's offered response is not an engagement with the theological and intellectual implications of Dalila's critique, but an even greater display of force.

That Samson is finally just a brawler seems unsettling. But more importantly, in the problem of "rousing motions" Samson's physical bullying comes to stand for an intellectual bullying, a kind of theological imposition, which is at the heart of the poem's problematic assertion of faith. When the poem's action degenerates into a merely physical agon, it suggests that the rousing motions Samson feels just after Harapha leaves are not of divine origin but, as Cherbury warns us, are from Samson's body. It seems likely that Samson is merely physically excited, and that he feels not divine inspiration but rising blood. Which is to say, even though Samson has begun to feel closer to God, and therefore more certain in his faith and his actions, we are still denied any more objective means of verifying Samson's feelings. God may be just as distant as ever, and monotheism may depend entirely upon mere strength. Samson has no doubts. But like Cherbury when he warns us, "it is hardly sufficient to apprehend what is revealed except through our faculties," and like Manoa when he abjures, "I state not that," Milton's reader must be shrewdly skeptical toward these rousing motions. Agreeing with the interpretation of rousing motions as divine inspiration, it becomes clear, we make a willful and logically unsupported jump from the physical body to intellectual or spiritual faith. When Manoa concludes that Samson died "With God not parted from him," we can only agree if we ignore the evidence of Samson's churning humours and embrace rousing motions as divine inspiration. Similarly, to believe in Providence as a result of Harapha's defeat, we must make an intellectual jump from the very same physical agitation to faith in the victory of the one God. The same churning humours that deny internal regeneration also deny the doctrinal regeneration: moving from those motions to inspiration requires the same forcing of intellect and logic as moving from Dalila's critique to acceptance of Samson's victory over Harapha.

The triumph of monotheism, then, rests upon both a reliance on brute force and a brutish forcing of the mind. This intellectual forcing is what Assmann identifies when he discusses the "cleaving" of religious space that the Mosaic distinction performs in its assertion of absolute truth. Such an absolute cannot be argued for by means of comparison or logic, but must simply be asserted. This act of intellectual forcing differs from the relativistic and comparative perspective suggested by Cherbury and Dalila, and relies entirely on the illogical authority of revelation. Thus, Milton's skeptical siege upon revelation in *Samson Agonistes* ultimately threatens the Mosaic distinction itself. When angels are replaced with internal inspiration, and inspiration subsequently reduced to discursive thought, all that is left for the assertion of truth is the mere forcing. As revelation is deconstructed into the blunt cudgel of Samson's oaken staff, the Chorus's claims that "All is best," and that "Just are the ways of God / And justifiable to men"—in other words, all redemptive and faithful interpretations of the action—are uncovered as purely wilful impositions upon the intellect.

But the poem's despairing version of monotheism need not lead us to become polytheists—or atheists or deists—any more than it leads the Chorus or Manoa after Samson's death. Their attempt at redemptive conclusion, as weak as it may seem, must finally be read as the only tenable position given the poem's verisimilar world. It is even brave to assert Providence in the face of the period's swelling rationalism. What is disallowed, however, is the possibility of explaining or adequately defending the choice to remain faithful—lost with revelation is theodicy.[29] And if the inability to justify Providence is not to lead to a rejection of God, then it must lead to a rejection of the conditions that threaten theodicy: the poem's banishment of revelation. *Samson*

Agonistes does not advocate a deistic rejection of revelation, but stages the kind of world imagined by Cherbury in order to demonstrate its greatest flaw, the inability to put into words, thoughts, actions—in sum, the inability to narrate—theodicy. *Samson Agonistes* experiments with deistic theodicy and finds it tragically impossible.

This experiment ultimately makes the case for the necessity of angels. If it is not the end of theodicy but the means to the end that fails, then Samuel Johnson's famous complaint that *Samson Agonistes* "must be allowed to want a middle, since nothing passes between the first act and the last, that either hastens or delay the death of Samson" identifies a sense of logical disjunction in the narrative that applies equally well to the project of theodicy.[30] Indeed, as Samson's life and death are this story's means of theodicy, the missing middle of the plot is identical with the missing middle of theodicy. This points out the essentially narrativistic quality of Milton's theodicies: as with Aristotle's plot, they must have a beginning, middle, and end. It also shows that Johnson's middle is the absent angel of Judges 13. In his verisimilitude, Milton loses the possibility of explicit dialogue between Samson and God by means of the angel, as well as the proof of divine command that the presence of the angel in the storyworld can offer. Dialogue and presence in the storyworld are essential elements of any narrative, and when they are dissolved into the invisible and unknowable events of internal inspiration, the narrative about Samson and God is broken in the middle.

For a demonstration of the necessity of angels to theodicy, we can turn to Joost van den Vondel's *Samson; or, Holy Revenge*, in which the angel of Judges 13 does appear—and makes God's will and Samson's role in Providence perfectly evident. Vondel actually gives the angel a name, Fadaël. At the moment of Samson's decision to go to the temple, he reports that Fadaël had previously come in answer to his prayers, and had reinstated his strength. Then, after Samson's death, Fadaël enters the play, appearing before Samson's mourners to announce that Samson was a hero in God's cause, that he will be sainted, and that he is the type of Jesus Christ.[31] Replacing the rousing motions before the temple, and unequivocally asserting that all is best afterward, Fadaël clearly justifies God's ways with Samson. Or, to further picture the necessity of angels, we can imagine *Paradise Lost* without them. The result is something not far from *Samson Agonistes:* jumping from books 1 through 3, to 9, to the end of 12, you get not only a story without a middle, but also an unjust fall and the kind of bewildered and insecure sense of heaven's desertion that no attempt at a happy ending could dispel.

This experiment in theodicy without angels is also an experiment in aniconism — in monotheistic narrative taken to the skeptical extreme. As such, *Samson Agonistes* is not the culmination of Milton's theology, as Mary Ann Radzinowicz suggests. On the contrary, it labors to carve out exactly the position that *Paradise Lost* takes as its starting point: by demonstrating how the lack of revelation disrupts theodicy, it functions as a defense of the epic's extensive use of angels and other forms of the supernatural. It operates as the negative space of *Paradise Lost,* a shaping absence demonstrating exactly what Milton chose not to do in his epic. *Samson Agonistes* stands in relation to *Paradise Lost* not as a statement of later and different theology, but as a more detailed shading of the same monotheism.

The aniconic perspective, as an extreme position of seventeenth century monotheism, is prominently included and prominently disallowed in all three late poems. The narrative struggles that issue from this aniconism, the calculations born of extreme monotheism, are the philosophy that Johnson complains "perplexed" Milton's poetry. We see them most clearly in *Samson Agonistes,* which places Milton on the threshold of the radical theology of the deists and the relativistic perspectives of nascent comparative religion. In this way it is Milton's purest expression of monotheism.

Afterword

Monotheism, the Sublime, and Allegory

In place of a conclusion, this short, speculative essay frames my argument by moving later in time, to the eighteenth century reception, and earlier in time, to Edmund Spenser. By taking a broader view, drawing back from a close historical and theoretical focus, I hope to weave Milton's monotheism into larger literary and critical conversations. To begin, I pick up a thread from chapter 4, on the war in heaven. There I argued that Milton's monotheistic narrative carries the potential to be read as deist, and that John Dennis constructs a sublime Milton in order to avoid a deist Milton. With a discourse of sublimity thus emerging from Dennis's encounter with monotheistic narrative, this essay's speculation is that the eighteenth century sublime contains the afterlife of Milton's monotheism.

As Dennis himself points out, he is the first critic fully to identify Milton as the poet of the sublime, even anticipating Joseph Addison. Dennis ignores the bathos of the war in heaven, instead presenting a *Paradise Lost* that is sublime in its use of epic machinery and revelation. Pioneering the sublime Milton, Dennis describes how, "he who is entertain'd with an accomplish'd Poem, is, for a time, at least, restored to Paradise. That happy Man converses boldly with Immortal Beings. Transported, he beholds the Gods ascending and descending, and every Passion, in its Turn, is charm'd, while his Reason is supremely satisfied" (Dennis 1:264). The easy movement and conversation of angels and gods provide passion to transport the reader, leading to poetic enthusiasm. And so in Christian poetry and *Paradise Lost*, epic machinery lifts the verse to the heights of sublimity.

Dennis's sublime uses angels, daemons, apparitions, and miracles, which can be awful and terrifying.[1] But he is still closer to the neoclassical sublime of transcendence or elevation than to the more familiar versions of Edmund Burke and Immanuel Kant. For although the content of the poetry may be mysterious and awful, the poetry itself must remain clear and unconfused. As David Morris puts it, "The phrase clear and distinct ideas (probably adapted from Locke) runs through his criticism like a leitmotif." Burke, in contrast, establishes the firm distinction between the sublime and the beautiful, and announces: "A clear idea is therefore another name for a little idea."[2] While Kant, according to Samuel Monk's paraphrase from the *Critique of Judgment*, sees the sublime as growing out of the failure of expression, "In experiencing the sublime, the imagination seeks to represent what it is powerless to represent, since the object is limitless, and thus cannot be represented. This effort and this inevitable failure of the imagination are the source of the emotions that accompany the sublime."[3]

Essential to this later sense of sublimity is the breakdown of language. Whereas Dennis carefully forgets those parts of *Paradise Lost* that challenge the clarity of the sublime, Burke celebrates them as "obscurity," locating this quality both in the subject matter and in the representation. Poets have the advantage over painters because language allows for a happy confusion in obscurity, as, for example, in Milton's description of Satan as a tower: "The mind is hurried out of itself, by a croud of great and confused images; which affect because they are crouded and confused."[4] It is this kind of linguistic confusion that the discontinuous wound introduces into the narrative of the war in heaven—in the impossible image of a wound healing even as it is cut, and in the pall of radical insignificance that the healing casts over the rest of the action. But Dennis avoids the discontinuous wound because, to create his version of the sublime, the deep sense of contradiction and bathos in the war in heaven must be forgotten. What Dennis forgets is precisely that kind of obscure language Burke comes to celebrate.

That the failure of language can be productive marks a point of convergence between later theories of the sublime and the narrative texture of monotheism. As Aryeh Botwinick describes it, the experience of monotheistic language feels very like Burke's crowded and confused images: "The utterance of the word 'God' initiates a process of endless displacement that finds no resting place. All we can ever do by way of assigning a content and pinpointing a reference for 'God' is to continually assert that God is not literally to be construed in this way or that, and that he is not to be found in a humanly cognizable sense anywhere." In monotheistic narrative, discursivity and aporia mark moments of skeptical calculation, moments when the poet negotiates the disjunction between monotheism and narrative. These negotiations carry narrative back and forth across the Mosaic distinction, each crossing of the border foregrounding the concept of the single God, and so pointing us to him. Each crossing becomes a sign of the narrative's monotheism. Monotheistic language, as Botwinick describes it, is a constant skeptical negation that is "instrumental for stating the thesis of God's otherness."[5]

With congruent insight, Kant argues that conceptual difficulty is itself taken as a key component of the sublime, forming "a feeling of displeasure that arises from the imagination's inadequacy." This displeasing failure of the imagination is purposive:

> The *quality* of the feeling of the sublime consists in its being a feeling, accompanying an object, of displeasure about our aesthetic power of judging, yet a displeasure that we present at the same time as purposive. What makes this possible is that the subject's

own inability uncovers in him the consciousness of an unlimited ability which is also his, and that the mind can judge the ability aesthetically only by that inability.

Just as the negative language of monotheism points to the monotheistic God, so obscurity carries us to sublimity. It is fitting, then, that for Kant the biblical sublime is located in the second commandment because it negates what can be felt by the senses. "Perhaps the most sublime passage in the Jewish Law is the commandment: Thou shalt not make unto thee any graven image, or any likeness of any thing that is in heaven or on earth, or under the earth, etc." With the absence of sensible images and likenesses, monotheism is "wholly negative as regards the sensible," and this explains the sublime sense of "enthusiasm" it can create.[6]

The later sublime of Burke and Kant is equipped to comprehend monotheistic narrative more nearly than the neoclassical sublime of Dennis or of Nicolas Boileau, who championed Longinus's association of the sublime with the *fiat lux*. Longinus finds sublimity not in the second commandment but in "Let there be light," which produces not fearfulness or obscurity, but "elevation."[7] The *fiat lux* offers nothing negative: its kerygmatic statement demonstrates clear authority, and its performative utterance is the height of linguistic clarity. The movement from the neoclassical sublime to the Kantian sublime can be understood in this movement from the *fiat lux* to the second commandment.

Burke's most famous reading of *Paradise Lost*, that of Milton's Death, records the same relationship between the second commandment and the sublime. Sublimity here is foremost a matter of obscurity, as Milton makes spirit and matter deeply inseparable, and the language fully contradictory:

> The other shape,
> If shape it might be called that shape had none
> Distinguishable in member, joint, or limb,
> Or substance might be called that shadow seemed,
> For each seemed either; black it stood as night,
> Fierce as ten Furies, terrible as hell,

> And shook a dreadful dart; what seemed his head
> The likeness of a kingly crown had on. (*PL* 2.666–73)

Burke sums up: "In this description all is dark, uncertain, confused, terrible, and sublime to the last degree."⁸ Like the discontinuous wound, Death is not just an obscure idea, it is constructed out of contradictory language: "shape / If shape it might be called that shape had none" throws the reader into a space of confusion and calculation. It becomes a moment of linguistic failure, which is productive of the sublime. And for Burke, this textual sense of obscurity and terror is particularly associated with polytheism. Leading up to Milton's death, Burke describes obscurity in idolatrous terms:

> Almost all the heathen temples were dark. Even in the barbarous temples of the Americans at this day, they keep their idol in a dark part of the hut, which is consecrated to his worship. For this purpose too the druids performed all their ceremonies in the bosom of the darkest woods, and in the shade of the oldest and most spreading oaks. No persons seems better to have understood the secret of heightening, or of setting terrible things, if I may use the expression, in their strongest light by the force of a judicious obscurity, than Milton. His description of Death in the second book is admirably studied.⁹

Burke takes a quick turn through the kind of comparative religion developed by Selden and the discourse of monotheism. The details of paganism, of American religion and the rites of the Druids, invoke a sense of polytheistic transgression, as Milton's Death becomes an idol in the gloomy obscurity of an American hut. Death is terrible not only because he is obscure, but also because he transgresses monotheism. Moreover, and perhaps more threatening, if heathen priests practice the art of obscurity, then England's great poet becomes pagan. Milton seems "to have understood the secret" of these priests better than anyone else—Burke's remarkable association comes near to making Milton a high priest of polytheism. With this picture of idolatry as a lead-in, Burke's reader approaches Milton's Death with a trepidation that is specifically identified as monotheistic, and with the sense that *Paradise Lost* is a poem that transgresses monotheism.

What Burke's sublime records is the precarious position Milton inhabits in the borderland between monotheism and polytheism. Drawing and redrawing the Mosaic distinction, the negotiations of monotheistic narrative frequently put *Paradise Lost* in danger of slipping into idolatry. Monotheistic narrative is structured around the continued threat of polytheism and the real terror that the narrative will transgress the commandments of monotheism. This terror is fundamental to Milton's poetry, and it becomes the sublime.

Burke is simultaneously responding to the presence of allegory, as seen through Milton's reception of Spenser. The sublime anxiety over polytheism is felt in *Paradise Lost* in the material presence of gods, the personal presence of God, the difficult ontology of the Son, and the problem of Christian machinery, but may be felt most acutely in allegory. As discussed in chapter 3, the doctrine of accommodation can only be said to authorize the poetry of *Paradise Lost* to the extent that it adheres closely to the details of Scripture. When Milton's narrative diverges from biblical precedent, the "adjustments" made by divine accommodation cease to have an effect. And among the mimetic figures of the epic, Sin and Death famously stand out as different, being pure creations of the poet's imagination. It is especially allegorical figures, so obviously built by poets, that look like idols in a monotheistic poem. So Henry Reynolds says that *The Faerie Queene* is "an exact body of the Ethnicke doctrine."[10]

The Faerie Queene does not usually have this opinion about itself: it is entirely willing to fill its storyworld with gods, including Mammon, Venus, Cupid, Diana, Proteus, Neptune, Jove, Mercury, and the entire council of the Mutabilitie Cantos. One might include the demigods as well, and, throwing open the door, nearly every fairy and personification crowding the poem. Some monotheistic anxiety does surface amid the allegory. In Isis Church, for example, Spenser blends remarkably precise polytheistic detail with a sense of Christian prayer and piety. The place itself, "Isis Church," implies syncretism, but Spenser introduces Osyris by marking the confrontation between true and false religion, announcing, "Well therefore did the antique world invent, / That Justice was a God."[11] The episode stands out for its detailed sense of exoticism and orientalism, a particularly interesting anticipation of Milton's monotheistic narrative. Duessa's descent into the underworld in book 1 is also read by Gordon Teskey as similarly inflected by the problem of the gods. This is part of Teskey's argument that allegory derives crucial energy from polytheism, but simultaneously rejects it, creating a violent situation in which "the dead gods twitch."[12]

The most sustained of polytheistic episodes in *The Faerie Queene* is the divine council of the Mutabilitie Cantos, and this also stands out as a moment when Spenser seems to be anticipating Milton. As it unfolds over two cantos, the poem seems entirely oblivious to the demands of monotheism—Titans confront Olympians with no sign of the poet's hesitation. But this untroubled narrative of polytheism is purchased, so to speak, by the fragment of canto 8. There Spenser suddenly drops the blatant polytheism and concludes by praying to "Him that is the God of Sabbaoth hight: / O! thou great Sabbaoth God, grant me that Sabaoths sight."[13] Spenser invokes the Lord of Hosts, the monotheistic God who rules all other assemblies, as if he alone should be given precedence over the previous two cantos. In the manner of monotheistic narrative, Spenser crosses the Mosaic distinction to admit polytheism in cantos 6 and 7, and then recrosses to the doctrinally proper side by reinstating monotheism. It is always tempting to read the fragment as itself a poetic effect, in which case the instability of monotheism could be said to cause the fragment. Rather like reading across the divisions between sources in the Hebrew Bible, the fragmentation of the end of the Mutabilitie Cantos could be read as a visible fault line emanating from the unstable convergence of monotheism and narrative.

The obscurity of the last two lines gives a sublime presence that seems to enable the polytheism filling the previous books and cantos.

Whether or not such a thing is persuasive, it is entirely fitting that the monotheistic God dangles at the end of *The Faerie Queene*. The fractured and marginal presence of the "great Sabbaoth God" in the Mutabilitie Cantos can stand for the presence of the monotheistic God in *The Faerie Queene* as a whole. For the great majority of the poem is easy about polytheism, allowing classical gods as well as nymphs and sprites and personifications, with little hesitation over their potential transgressiveness. Overall, it is as if the line between monotheism and polytheism were of little importance to Spenser. In contrast, Milton struggles mightily with the Mosaic distinction. This struggle corresponds to his move away from Spenserian allegory, a move that exacerbates the problem of polytheism, and so makes monotheism a focus.[14] The move from *The Faerie Queene* to *Paradise Lost* can be understood in light of this book's argument: one way to describe how Milton departs from Spenser's allegorical poetry is through monotheistic narrative. In fact, in the unstated background of much of this book's discussion of Milton's narrative has been the negative example of *The Faerie Queene*. But *Paradise Lost*, of course, does not banish allegory altogether. Unable to attain a complete aniconism, it instead works to make room for Spenser, just as it makes room for the gods and for epic machinery. As the most explicit rewriting of *The Faerie Queene*, Sin and Death in particular tell us about Milton's response to Spenserian allegory. They form a monotheistic response.

If Death's shapeless shape figures the perplexity and contradiction of Milton's monotheistic narrative, it is a radical evolution out of the shape of Death's mother. Milton's Sin explicitly recalls Spenser's Errour:

> The one seemed woman to the waist, and fair,
> But ended foul in many a scaly fold
> Voluminous and vast, a serpent armed

> With mortal sting: about her middle round
> A cry of hell hounds never ceasing barked
> With wide Cerberian mouths full loud, and rung
> A hideous peal: yet, when they list, would creep,
> If aught disturbed their noise, into her womb,
> And kennel there, yet there still barked and howled,
> Within unseen. (PL 2.650–59)

Critics often note a physical resemblance. Fowler's gloss, for example, points to the fact that both Sin and Errour are half woman and half monster, both wield a "mortal sting," and both swallow up their young. But it is not just the allegorical figures that look the same: in his description of Sin, Milton shifts into decidedly Spenserian language. The portrait of Sin is itself very near to a Spenserian stanza. If you move "Within unseen" up one line, the entire description unfolds within the nine-line form — eight in pentameter and the ninth an alexandrine, with the slight difference that Milton's alexandrine has seven feet. In this "stanza," Milton develops very Spenserian-sounding alliteration: "fair / but ended foul in many a scaly fold," and "voluminous and vast." And he excavates some typical Spenserian archaisms: "many a scaly fold" and "full loud." Both "foul" and "fold" also appear in Spenser's description.[15]

In addition, the end of Milton's alexandrine, "unseen," echoes the final sounds that dominate the Errour episode: its first seven alexandrines end with "men," "disdaine," "gone," "plaine," "glaunst," "traine," and "constraine." As the c-rhyme, which appears three times, including the ending couplet, this sound is clearly the most important of each stanza. This prominence buttresses what is probably the most perfectly emblematic alexandrine in *The Faerie Queene:* "That hand or foot to stirr he strove in vaine: / God helpe the man so wrapt in *Errours* endlesse traine."[16] The physical image of Errour's tail figures forth with satisfying precision the moral notion of an entanglement with error. And with the sense of resolution that comes from a well-made rhyme, "traine" stands out as an independent and framed emblem. As the physical image converges with the moral idea in the location of the culminating *n*-sound, Errour functions as a perfect Spenserian allegory.

Milton's alexandrine invokes this zenith of Spenserian allegory, but also severely deconstructs it. The alexandrine is, of course, broken by enjambment and is a foot too long. The stanza itself has no rhyme and is skewed by the tendency of Miltonic blank verse to continue its momentum across the enjambment. From within the roiling sea of Milton's blank verse a Spenserian stanza can be discerned, but just as quickly it is lost. Just after "Within unseen" Milton goes back to his familiar style with a vengeance: "Far less abhorred than these / Vexed Scylla bathing in the sea that parts / Calabria from the hoarse Trinacrian shore" (*PL* 2.659–61). The negative simile, the jarring use of "hoarse," the esoteric place names, and the enjambment, all signal that Spenser is in the past. Indeed, the evocation and subsequent distancing of Spenser is precisely the allegory that Sin and Death figure forth.

Victoria Kahn argues that in the Sin and Death episode Milton is deeply self-conscious about his poetics, creating an allegory of allegory.[17] Sin and Death, I would add, allegorize Milton's movement away from specifically Spenserian allegory. They tell the story of a new generation of allegory, which is also a genealogy of Milton's monotheistic narrative. When the extra two feet of "Within unseen" are attached to the Spenserian stanza, Milton's allegory melts the visible materiality of "traine" into the immaterial. Following the same descent, Sin's offspring, the next generation of allegorical figure, is a "shape / If shape it might be called that shape had none"—a figure of immateriality and perplexed ontology, matching the concerns of Milton's monotheistic narrative. In its mystical figuring of abstractions by material detail, Spenserian allegory can be seen as a solution to the narrative problems of monotheism. This kind of resolution is what Milton's skeptical allegory foregoes. Equivocating between materiality and immateriality, Death both risks becoming polytheism and works to assert monotheism. Death's impossible shape sets off rigorous ontological calculations, and drawn by these is the Mosaic distinction.

Kahn and Steven Knapp both suggest that in Sin and Death Milton develops the rhetorical ambivalence that in the eighteenth century will become sublimity. Knapp ultimately discovers a crisis in the conception of the individual, as personifications terrify because they threaten to become fanatical representations of a single ideal.[18] But Burke's handling of Milton's Death suggests a religious rather than psychological or purely rhetorical source for the century's anxiety over allegorical figures. Burke tells us that Death is to be feared in the same way that polytheism is to be feared. As Knapp shows, Milton takes Spenserian allegory and makes it sublime; from the perspective of this study, that transformation can be identified with Milton's engagement with the one God.

Sin and Death reveal a literary context for monotheistic narrative, showing how Milton reworks Spenserian allegory and how that reworking becomes the sublime. Both acknowledging its Spenserian heritage and allegorizing its Miltonic difference, the episode of Sin and Death offers a genealogy of Milton's poetics: moving from Sin to Death takes us from Spenser to Milton's monotheistic narrative; moving from Milton to Burke then takes us to the sublime, revealing in the celebration of obscurity how Death's perplexed shape tells of Milton's monotheism.

NOTES

Notes to Introduction

1. Compare Adam's words to the fallen Eve concerning the apple: "inducement strong / To us, as likely tasting to attain / Proportional ascent, which cannot be / But to be gods, or angels demi-gods" (9.934–37).

2. This in turn leads to a refutation of Trinitarian readings: "Attention should be paid to all these points to prevent anyone from being led astray by linguistic ignorance into assuming immediately that when the word Elohim is used with a singular it denotes a single essence composed of several persons" (YP 6:236). Also see YP 6:315–16 and Kelley's note 57.

3. Compare James L. Kugel, *Traditions of the Bible: A Guide to the Bible As It Was at the Start of the Common Era* (Cambridge, Mass.: Harvard University Press, 1998), 51–52. Milton's reenactment of Genesis 1:26 may respond to Rashi's commentary, which reads the plural as indicating that God is speaking to his heavenly court. Rashi says that God takes counsel with the angels so that they will not be jealous of humans—evoking a feeling of strife that is clearly present in Satan's mind. Rashi also captures the way that *elohim* wavers between monotheistic and polytheistic meanings: he admits that Genesis 1:26 provides an opportunity for the skeptic, but argues that the next verse forms a rebuttal to him, as *elohim* is repeated in 1:27 but becomes the subject of a singular verb (not visible in the English), "So God created man in his own image." First risking polytheism and then rebutting it, this passage captures the ontological negotiations that surround the one God. These negotiations are perhaps most clear in the punning of the tetragrammaton, which resists naming God in the present tense.

4. Milton is quoting Hebrews 1:6, which reads "And again, when he bringeth in the first-begotten into the world, he saith, And let all the angels of God worship him." Sister M. Christopher Pecheux, "The Council Scenes in *Paradise Lost*," in *Milton and the Scriptural Tradition*, ed. James H. Sims and Leland Ryken (Columbia: University of Missouri

Press, 1984), 82–103, shows that Milton departs from this text for Psalm 97:7, which has "worship him all ye gods."

5. This distinction is also a part of *De doctrina's* consideration of *elohim*, which notes that visiting angels are sometimes referred to as God (YP 6:234). Milton cites Judges 13, which is discussed at greater length in chapter 7.

6. Samuel Johnson, *Life of Milton*, in *Lives of the English Poets*, 3 vols., ed. George Birkbeck Hill (Oxford: Clarendon Press, 1905), 1:184.

7. According to Herbert Grierson, "A high and austere monotheism is of the innermost texture of Milton's soul." See *Encyclopedia of Religion and Ethics*, ed. James Hastings (Edinburgh: T&T Clark, 1915), vol. 8, s.v. "Milton," p. 646.

8. "Monotheism," *The Oxford English Dictionary*, 2nd ed., 1989. "Monotheismus," *Theologische Realenzyklopädie* (Berlin: Walter de Gruyter, 1994). "Monotheismus," *Historisches Wèorterbuch der Philosophie* (Basel: Schwabe, 1971–98). As late as 1736, Nathan Bailey, *Dictionarium Britannicum* (London: 1736), includes "monotheism" among a list of brand-new words in his dictionary: "The following words in some modern Authors, not occurring till the Dictionary was entirely printed, except the Preface, I chose rather to insert them here, than omit them" (preface).

9. See "Monotheismus," *Theologische Realenzyklopädie*.

10. Eric J. Sharpe, *Comparative Religion: A History* (London: Duckworth, 1975), 3.

11. Maurice Kelley shows that Milton is here following Wollebius, whose *Compendium theologiae Christianae* was published in 1626 (YP 6:656n3). The general orthodoxy of Wollebius's work does not mean that Wollebius was ignorant of developing rational conceptions of religion, as John W. Beardslee III points out in *Reformed Dogmatics* (Oxford: Oxford University Press, 1965),3–11.

12. Charles Blount and Charles Gildon, *The Oracles of Reason* (London: 1693), 91.

13. Brian Schmidt, "The Aniconic Tradition," in *The Triumph of Elohim: From Yahwisms to Judaisms*, ed. Diana V. Edelman (Kampen: Kok Pharos, 1995), 75–105.

14. Several good studies have shown the centrality of iconoclasm to English poetry, and to Milton, for example, Kenneth Gross, *Spenserian Poetics: Idolatry, Iconoclasm, and Magic* (Ithaca, N.Y.: Cornell University Press, 1985); Ernest B. Gilman, *Iconoclasm and Poetry in the English Reformation: Down Went Dagon* (Chicago: University of Chicago Press, 1986); David Lowenstein, *Milton and the Drama of History: Historical Vision, Iconoclasm, and the Literary Imagination* (Cambridge: Cambridge University Press, 1990); Lana Cable, *Carnal Rhetoric: Milton's Iconoclasm and the Poetics of Desire* (Durham, N.C.: Duke University Press, 1995).

15. It is worth recognizing similarities to Sanford Budick, *The Dividing Muse: Images of Sacred Disjunction in Milton's Poetry* (New Haven, Conn.: Yale University Press, 1985), on Milton's imagery: "Milton's journeys on the *via negativa* and the *via positiva* are continuous. In fact, the meaning of each way is only realized by combining it with its inverse. Systematically and deliberately, Milton, I believe, sets visual analogies into motion with an eye to their imminent depletion" (7).

16. Schmidt, "The Aniconic Tradition," 79–80. Jan Assmann, *Moses the Egyptian: The Memory of Egypt in Western Monotheism* (Cambridge, Mass.: Harvard University Press) 1997, says that "the second commandment is a commentary on the first" (4).

17. Moses Maimonides, *The Guide for the Perplexed*, trans. M. Friedlander (New York: Hebrew Publishing, 1881), 1:171–72; also, "Positive attributes imply polytheism" (1:208).

18. Aryeh Botwinick, *Skepticism, Belief, and the Modern: Maimonides to Nietzsche* (Ithaca, N.Y.: Cornell University Press, 1997), 4.

19. Erich Auerbach, *Mimesis: The Representation of Reality in Western Literature*, trans. Willard Trask (Garden City, N.Y.: Doubleday, 1957), 5–6.

20. Robert Alter, *The Art of Biblical Narrative* (New York: Basic Books, 1981), draws the connection between monotheism and the disjunctions of biblical narrative:

> The monotheistic revolution of biblical Israel was a continuing and disquieting one. It left little margin for neat and confident views about God, the created world, history, and man as political animal or moral agent, for it repeatedly had to make sense of the intersection of incompatibles—the relative and the absolute, human imperfection and divine perfection, the brawling chaos of historical experience and God's promise to fulfill a design in history. The biblical outlook is informed, I think, by a sense of stubborn contradiction, of a profound and ineradicable untidiness in the nature of things, and it is toward the expression of such a sense of moral and historical reality the composite artistry of the Bible is directed. (154)

21. Auerbach, *Mimesis*, 9.

22. Assmann, *Moses the Egyptian*, 1, 7.

23. The narrative problems of monotheism differ diametrically from the critical tradition of Renaissance syncretism, which emphasizes the integration of polytheism into Christianity. See, for example, Edgar Wind, *Pagan Mysteries in the Renaissance* (London: Faber & Faber, 1958); Jean Seznec, *The Survival of the Pagan Gods*, trans. Barbara Sessions (Princeton: Princeton University Press, 1981). John Mulryan, *Through a Glass Darkly: Milton's Reinvention of the Mythological Tradition*

(Pittsburgh: Duquesne University Press, 1996), makes the case for continued syncretism.

24. Assmann, *Moses the Egyptian*, 19, 55–143, discusses Cudworth and Toland, among others in the period, in terms of the Mosaic distinction.

25. Ibid., 1.

26. Lenn Evan Goodman, *Monotheism: A Philosophical Inquiry into the Foundations of Theology and Ethics* (Montclair, N.J.: Allanheld, Osmun, 1981), 23.

27. Meir Sternberg, *The Poetics of Biblical Narrative: Ideological Literature and the Drama of Reading* (Bloomington: Indiana University Press, 1985), 7, 84–128.

28. Assmann's *Moses the Egyptian* is the best of several recent books. Miltonists may know Regina Schwartz's *The Curse of Cain: The Violent Legacy of Monotheism* (Chicago: University of Chicago Press, 1997). Schwartz describes monotheism in terms of the logic of "scarcity"—there can be only one God and the rest must be denied. Assmann and Schwartz represent a trend in the theorization of monotheism that might be considered a liberalizing critique born of Freud's work. Also see Rosemary R. Ruether, *Sexism and God Talk: Toward a Feminist Theology* (Boston: Beacon Press, 1983), and Jonathan Kirsch, *God against the Gods: The History of the War between Monotheism and Polytheism* (New York: Viking Compass, 2004). These are responding to, one suspects, the overly sanguine "ethical monotheism" that celebrates how monotheism instantiates the universality of values. This is also a kind of liberalism, though older and less deconstructive. See especially Hermann Cohen, *Religion of Reason Out of the Sources of Judaism*, trans. Simon Kaplan (New York: Frederick Ungar, 1972), and Richard Niebhur, *Radical Monotheism and Western Culture* (New York: Harper and Row, 1960).

29. Challenges to the provenance of *De doctrina Christiana* failed to make a persuasive case. Gordon Campbell, Thomas N. Corns, John K. Hale, David I. Holmes, and Fiona J. Tweedie, *Milton and the Manuscript of* De Doctrina Christiana (Oxford: Oxford University Press, 2007), have concluded it "rightfully belongs in the Milton canon" (161). The strongest voice against doubting its provenance was John Rumrich, "Stylometry and the Provenance of *De Doctrina Christiana*," in *Milton and the Terms of Liberty*, ed. Graham Parry and Joad Raymond (Cambridge: Brewer, 2002), 125–36; and "The Provenance of *De doctrina Christiana*: A View of the Present State of the Controversy," in *Milton and the Grounds of Contention*, ed. Mark R. Kelley, Michael Lieb, and John T. Shawcross (Pittsburgh: Duquesne University Press, 2003), 214–33.

30. *The Complete Psychological Works of Sigmund Freud*, vol. 9, ed. James Strachey (London: The Hogarth Press, 1959), 245. Assmann, *Moses the Egyptian*, 5.

31. David Hume could also be included in this group for his *Natural History of Religion* (1757), ed. A. Wayne Colver (Oxford: Clarendon, 1976). He argues for a continual movement between polytheism and monotheism, which he calls "theism": "men have a natural tendency to rise from idolatry to theism, and to sink again from theism into idolatry" (56–57).

32. Although Ishmael Reed's Papa LaBas groups Milton and Freud together as pure Atonists, part of a worldwide, orthodox conspiracy to suppress the forces of voodoo. Milton, according to the hero of Reed's novel, is "Atonist apologist extraordinary"; see *Mumbo Jumbo* (New York: Scribner, 1972), 171.

33. Maurice Kelley's annotations to *De doctrina Christiana* in the *Complete Prose* persuasively make the case for Milton's heretical leanings. See also Christopher Hill, *Milton and the English Revolution* (New York: Penguin Books, 1979). Studies of Milton's heretical religion include Stephen Fallon, *Milton among the Philosophers: Poetry and Materialism in Seventeenth-Century England* (Ithaca, N.Y.: Cornell University Press, 1991); Dobranski and Rumrich, *Milton and Heresy*; Michael Lieb, *Theological Milton: Deity, Discourse, and Heresy in the Miltonic Canon* (Pittsburgh: Duquesne University Press, 2006). Questions about the provenance of *De doctrina Christiana* should be understood as part of this debate over Milton's heresy, for *De doctrina* is the clearest, although by no means the only, statement of Milton's Antitrinitarianism.

34. Botwinick, *Skepticism, Belief, and the Modern*, 7.

35. Botwinick's study makes no explicit historical claims for Maimonides's influence on Hobbes, concentrating on similarities in the structure of their thinking. But the influence of Maimonides on early modern theology is clear. See Aaron L. Katchen, *Christian Hebraists and Dutch Rabbis: Seventeenth Century Apologetics and the Study of Maimonides' Mishneh Torah* (Cambridge, Mass.: Harvard University Press, 1984). Selden regularly cites Maimonides, who is one of the main sources for *De diis Syris*. See Jonathan R. Ziskind's translation of Selden's *Uxor Hebraica* (Leiden: E. J. Brill, 1991), 191, and Jason P. Rosenblatt and Winfried Schleiner, "John Selden's Letter to Ben Jonson on Cross-Dressing and Bisexual Gods," *English Literary Renaissance* 29, no. 1 (1999). So does Samuel Purchas in the second edition of *His Pilgrimage* (London, 1614), 156, 169, 174, 181. Dionysius Vossius published a Latin translation out of Maimonides, *De idolotria*, which appeared in *De theologia Gentili*, by his father Gerardus Vossius (1641). Ralph Cudworth also cites Maimonides, in Hebrew, *The True Intellectual System of the Universe* (London: 1678), 467–71.

36. Botwinick, *Skepticism, Belief, and the Modern*, 25.

Notes to Chapter 1

1. *The Anchor Bible,* trans. John L. McKenzie (Garden City, N.Y.: Doubleday, 1967).

2. A. W. Verity, *Milton: Paradise Lost* (Cambridge: Cambridge University Press, 1910), 672–74. Verity points to Philo, *On the Giants,* trans. F. H. Colson and Rev. G. H. Whitaker (New York: Loeb Library, 1929): "It is Moses's custom to give the name of angels to those whom other philosophers call demons (or spirits)" (7). For an example from Milton's period, see Hugo Grotius, *True Religion* (1632; repr., New York: Da Capo Press, 1971), 105.

3. According to Lowell Handy, "The Appearance of Pantheon in Judah," in *The Triumph of Elohim: From Yahwisms to Judaisms,* ed. Diana V. Edelman (Kampen: Kok Pharos, 1995), 38, the angels that surround Yahweh in many of the Hebrew Bible's pantheons are vestiges of the polytheism of Ugaritic tradition. The Hebrew word *elohim,* Handy argues, simply underwent a semantic shift from "gods" to "angels" in, for example, Psalm 82. A mere shift in name is all that is needed to inscribe the Ugaritic gods within the monotheistic system. Milton translated Psalm 82, rendering *elohim* as "gods" (lines 3, 21). On *elohim* and Milton's councils, see Sister M. Christopher Pecheux, "The Council Scenes in *Paradise Lost,*" in *Milton and the Scriptural Tradition,* ed. James H. Sims and Leland Ryken (Columbia: University of Missouri Press, 1984), 82–103.

4. Compare John Leonard's discussion of the fallen angels' names in *Naming in Paradise: Milton and the Language of Adam and Eve* (Oxford: Clarendon Press, 1990), 50–85. Leonard points out that no fallen angel ever addresses another by name (69).

5. Milton's place among the tradition of Christian poetry is made obvious by his late poetry. In *The Reason of Church Government* he announces his interest: "That what the greatest and choicest wits of *Athens, Rome,* or modern *Italy,* and those Hebrews of old did for their country, I in my proportion with this over and above of being Christian, might doe for mine" (YP 1:812). Milton also argues that poetry is "of power beside the office of a pulpit, to imbreed and cherish in a great people the seeds of vertu...to celebrate in glorious and lofty Hymns the throne and equipage of Gods Almightinesse" (YP 1:816–17). The religious hostility he partially felt toward classical poetry and "their gods ridiculous" is most famously expressed in *Paradise Regained* 4.339–49.

6. *A Variorum Commentary on the Poems of John Milton,* ed. A. S. P. Woodhouse and Douglas Bush (New York: Columbia University Press, 1972), 2:100. Thomas Keightley, *The Poems of Milton* (London: Chapman and Hall, 1895), also cites *De diis* in his gloss of line 201.

7. Patrick Hume, *Annotations on Milton's* Paradise Lost (London, 1695), 21–31.

8. Edward Gibbon, *The Decline and Fall of the Roman Empire* (New York: Heritage Press, 1946), 349n4. This passage is quoted by Todd, *The Poetical Works of John Milton*, ed. Henry John Todd (London: Bye and Law, 1801), 47.

9. Jason Rosenblatt, *Torah and Law in* Paradise Lost (Princeton: Princeton University Press, 1994), 71–82. Rosenblatt, *Renaissance England's Chief Rabbi: John Selden* (Oxford: Oxford University Press, 2006), captures Selden's influence on Milton the poet as well as seventeenth century England as a whole.

10. Seymour Chatman, *Story and Discourse: Narrative Structure in Fiction and Film* (Ithaca, N.Y.: Cornell University Press, 1986), 96–145.

11. "Storyworld," according to the *Encyclopedia of Narrative Theory*, ed. David Herman, Manfred John, and Marie-Laure Ryan (New York: Routledge, 2005),

> captures what might be called the ecology of narrative interpretation. In trying to make sense of a narrative, interpreters attempt to reconstruct not just what happened but also the surrounding context or environment embedding the storyworld existents, their attributes, and the actions and events in which they are involved.... More than reconstructed timelines and inventories of existents, then, storyworlds are mentally and emotionally projected environments in which interpreters are called upon to live out complex blends of cognitive and imaginative response. (570)

Also see David Herman, *Story Logic: Problems and Possibilities of Narrative* (Lincoln: University of Nebraska Press, 2002), 1–24.

12. Regarding these issues, see Thomas Pavel, *Fictional Worlds* (Cambridge, Mass.: Harvard University Press, 1986), and George Steiner, *Real Presences* (Chicago: University of Chicago Press, 1989).

13. William Prynne, *Histrio-Mastix: The Player's Scourge or, Actor's Tragedy* (1633; repr., New York: Johnson Reprint Corporation, 1972), 79.

14. Ibid., 83–84.

15. Abraham Cowley, *Davideis*, in *Poems* (London, 1656), 5; hereafter cited parenthetically in the text by page number.

16. See Bernard Weinberg, *A History of Literary Criticism in the Italian Renaissance* (Chicago: University of Chicago Press, 1974), 173, 532, 562, 648–53, 774, 784, 1030, and throughout.

17. Torquato Tasso, *Discorsi dell'arte poetica*, trans. Lawrence F. Rhu, *The Genesis of Tasso's Narrative Theory* (Detroit: Wayne State University Press, 1993), 102.

18. Compare Tobias Gregory's discussion of Tasso in "Tasso's God: Divine Action in *Gerusalemme Liberata*," *Renaissance Quarterly* 55, no. 2 (2002): 559–95. Also see Gregory, *From Many Gods to One: Divine Action in Renaissance Epic* (Chicago: University of Chicago Press, 2006).

Gregory's excellent scholarship proceeded at the same time as this study.

19. Tasso, *Discorsi dell'arte poetica,* 104.
20. Weinberg, *A History,* 650.
21. Tasso, *Discorsi dell'arte poetica,* 105.
22. Mindele Anne Treip, *Allegorical Poetics and the Epic* (Lexington: University Press of Kentucky, 1994), 79.
23. Ibid., 67.
24. Henry Reynolds, *Mythomystes* (London, 1632), in *Critical Essays of the Seventeenth Century,* ed. J. E. Springarn (Oxford: Oxford University Press, 1908), 1:147.
25. *The Divine Weeks and Works of Guillaume de Saluste Sieur du Bartas,* trans. Josuah Sylvester, ed. Susan Snyder, (Oxford: Clarendon Press, 1979), 1.4.366–850, 1.2.343, 414, 433; hereafter cited parenthetically in the text.
26. Also Thomas Hobbes, *Leviathan,* ed. Michael Oakeshott (Oxford: Basil Blackwell, 1946), chap. 12, writing on "The absurd opinion of Gentilism": "They invoked also their own wit, by the name of Muses; their own ignorance, by the name of Fortune; their own lusts by the name of Cupid" (73–74).
27. "Sen verse did then in heaven first bud and blume / If ye be heavenly, how dar ye presume / A verse prophane and mocking for to sing / Gainst him that leads of starrie heavens the ring?" King James I, *The Uranie, or Heavenly Muse,* English Reprints, vol. 5, ed. Edward Arber (New York: Ames Press, 1906).
28. Lily B. Campbell, "The Christian Muse," *Huntington Library Bulletin* 8 (1935): 60. For some of the important elements of the movement for Christian poetry, see Douglas Bush, *Mythology and the Renaissance Tradition in English Poetry* (New York: Norton, 1963).
29. *The Works of Michael Drayton,* ed. J. William Hebel (Oxford: Shakespeare Head Press by Blackwell, 1961), 3:327.
30. Michael Drayton, *The Poly-Olbion* (1613; repr., London: The Spenser Society, 1889), 33.
31. William Camden, *Brittania,* trans. Philemon Holland (London, 1610), 6.
32. Drayton, *Poly-Olbion,* 243.
33. David Sandler Berkowitz, *John Selden's Formative Years: Politics and Society in Early Seventeenth Century England* (Washington, D.C.: Folger Books, 1988), 48.
34. *The Table Talk of John Selden,* ed. S. W. Singer (London: Reeves & Turner, 1890), 116.
35. Samuel Purchas, *Purchas His Pilgrimage* (London, 1613), 6r.
36. John Toland, preface to *Letters to Serena* (London, 1704), writes, "no woman on Earth (and very few men) can make any thing of Selden or Salmasius, without being tir'd and disgusted."

37. Anne Lake Prescott, "Marginal Discourse: Drayton's Muse and Selden's Story," *Studies in Philology* 88, no. 3 (1991): 317, 328.

38. Sir William Davenant, "Author's Preface," in *Gondibert*, ed. David F. Gladish (Oxford: Clarendon Press, 1971), 7; hereafter cited parenthetically in the text.

39. Thomas Hobbes, "The Answer of Mr. Hobbes to Sir Will. D'Avenant's Preface Before Gondibert," in Davenant, *Gondibert*, 51; hereafter cited parenthetically by page number in the text.

40. "When neither Religion (which is our art towards God) nor Nature (which is Gods first Law to Man, though by man least study'd), nor when Reason (which is Nature, and made art by Experience) can by the enemies of Poesy be sufficiently urg'd against it, then some, whose frowardnesse will not let them quitt an evil cause, plead written Authority" (Davenant, "Author's Preface," 42–43).

41. Sir Philip Sidney, *Astrophel and Stella*, in *Silver Poets of the Sixteenth Century*, ed. Gerald Bullet (London: Everyman's Library, 1966), 174.

42. George Williamson, *Milton and Others* (Chicago: University of Chicago Press, 1965), 106.

43. Samuel Johnson quotes Thomas Rymer as preferring the *Davideis* to Tasso's *Gerusalemme*. Johnson, who does not like the *Davideis*, responds, "I know not, indeed, why they should be compared; for the resemblance of Cowley's work to Tasso's is only that they both exhibit the agency of celestial and infernal spirits, in which however they differ widely: for Cowley supposes them commonly to operate upon the mind by suggestion; Tasso represents them as promoting or obstructing events by external agency." See "Life of Cowley," in *Lives of the English Poets*, ed. George Birkbeck Hill (Oxford: Clarendon Press, 1905), 1:55.

44. René Le Bossu, *Treatise of the Epick Poem*, trans. W. J. (London, 1695); reprinted as *Le Bossu and Voltaire on the Epic*, ed. Stuart Curran (Gainesville, Fla.: Scholars' Facsimiles & Reprints, 1970), 225.

45. John Dryden, "The Art of Poetry," 616–19, in *The Works of John Dryden*, ed. H. T. Swedenberg Jr. (Berkeley and Los Angeles: University of California Press, 1974), 2:143.

46. Selden is there quoting Joseph Scaliger, so Cowley's "some think" could refer to him rather than Selden. But Cowley follows Selden's argument exactly by immediately turning to the worship of Beelzebub at Ekron, and then to the specific example of Ahaziah's worship.

47. Thomas Fuller, *History of the Worthies of England* (1662; repr., New York: AMC Press, 1965), 3:259.

48. Gerard Genette, *Narrative Discourse: An Essay in Method*, trans. Jane E. Lewin (Ithaca, N.Y.: Cornell University Press, 1980), 161.

49. William Riley Parker, *Milton: A Biography* (Oxford: Clarendon Press, 1968), 584. In two of the most prominent discussions of poetry

and poetics in Milton's prose, in *The Reason of Church Government* and *Of Education,* Milton mentions Tasso as exemplary; see YP 1:814, 2:404–05.

50. As mythography, *De diis* follows in the path of the major Italian mythographers of the sixteenth century, Vincenzo Cartari, Lilio Gregorio Giraldi, and Natale Conti—especially Giraldi, whose *De deis gentium* includes a section on the Syrian deities, and who, John Mulryan, *Through a Glass Darkly: Milton's Reinvention of the Mythological Tradition* (Pittsburgh: Duquesne University Press, 1996), says, wrote "the first scholarly history of the gods" (209). Even so, Selden's historical method represents a significant step toward comparative religion. Jean Seznec, *The Survival of the Pagan Gods,* trans. Barbara Sessions (Princeton: Princeton University Press, 1981), describes the Italian mythographers as "even more lacking in historical sense than in critical faculty. They pay no attention to place or time. They mix together all the gods, regardless of their place of origin, the most ancient with those of later times" (241). For Seznec the mythographers laid a foundation "for a kind of comparative mythology, which was to produce its monuments in the following century in the works of Huet, Bochart, and Vossius" (250)—all thinkers whose comparative mythology Selden influenced. Cowley and Milton turn to Selden in place of the mythographers because Selden's scholarship offers a more rigorous attempt at historical truth.

51. For example, Milton includes the detail that the noise of the drums was used to cover up the cries of the children sacrificed to Moloch: "Though for the noise of drums and timbrels loud / Their children's cries unheard, that passed through fire / To his grim idol" (*PL* 1.394–96). Selden takes this from Paul Fagius, whom Milton uses as an important authority in the *Doctrine and Discipline of Divorce* (YP 2:239, 43, 46). Milton also could have found the same information in Thomas Fuller, *A Pisgah-Sight of Palestine* (London, 1650), book 4, p. 134, where Fagius is also cited.

52. John B. Broadbent, *Some Graver Subject: An Essay on* Paradise Lost (New York: Barnes and Noble, 1960), 88.

53. Rosenblatt, *Renaissance England's Chief Rabbi,* reads the catalog of gods differently, emphasizing Milton's divergence from Selden's inclusive attitudes: "Although Milton's zeal and intransigence of judgement have their own terrible beauty, one might wish that the poet had drawn less often on Maimonides' antagonistic depiction of pagan counter-religion and more often on Selden's calm and tolerant historicist approach to the potentially incendiary topic of idolatry" (80).

54. As Anthony Grafton, *The Footnote: A Curious History* (Cambridge, Mass.: Harvard University Press, 1997), describes them, footnotes "are the humanist's rough equivalent of the scientist's report on data: they offer the empirical support for stories told and arguments presented" (vii).

55. Jan Assmann, *Moses the Egyptian: The Memory of Egypt in Western Monotheism* (Cambridge, Mass.: Harvard University Press, 1997), 3.

56. "Capiti imposuisse sibi dicitur haec Dea, uti regni insigne, taurinum caput, orbeque tandem peragrato, invenisse *stellam ex aere* delapsam...quam postea in Tyro, insula sacra, dedicavit. Quaenam fuerit haec stella haud constat: committas licet quae de Remphan sive Ciunmox dicimus sed assumpto taurino capite, fronte curvatos imitabatur ignes, lunaeque speciem prae se ferebat" (Selden 2:347–48). All Latin translations, unless otherwise noted, are mine. This translation is partly based on the translation by W. A. Hauser. See John Selden, *The Fabulous Gods Denounced in the Bible*, trans. W. A. Hauser (Philadelphia: J. B. Lippincott, 1880). Hauser only translated parts of *De diis*, and none of the prolegomena. I thank John Fendrick for checking my translations.

57. Fuller, *A Pisgah-Sight of Palestine*, book 4, p. 130.

58. Assmann, *Moses the Egyptian*, 7.

59. See Geoffrey Hartman, "Milton's Counterplot," *English Literary History* 25 (1958): 1–12; reprinted in *Milton: Modern Essays in Criticism*, ed. Arthur E. Barker (Oxford: Oxford University Press, 1965), 386–97.

60. Stanley Fish, *Surprised by Sin: The Reader in* Paradise Lost (New York: St. Martin's Press, 1967).

Notes to Chapter 2

1. Thomas Fuller, *A Pisgah-Sight of Palestine* (London, 1650), 126.

2. David Sandler Berkowitz, *John Selden's Formative Years: Politics and Society in Early Seventeenth Century England* (Washington, D.C.: Folger Books, 1988), 29.

3. Selden and Purchas quarreled over the 1617 edition of *Purchas His Pilgrimage* when Purchas apparently mutilated an essay Selden wrote on the history of the Jews in England; see "Selden," in *Dictionary of National Biography*. There are a few places in the first two editions, 1613 and 1614, where Selden and Purchas contest each other's authority in a similar way. In 1613 Purchas cites Michael Drayton calling Joseph Scaliger "the Dictator of knowledge and great Prince of learnings state" in the *Poly-Olbion*; see *Purchas His Pilgrimage* (London, 1613), 56. In the next year's edition, however, the citation has been corrected to reflect that the quote actually came from "M. Selden Annet. on M. Drayton. Poly-Olb"; see *Purchas His Pilgrimage* (London, 1614), 67. Selden, however, also loses air time in the second edition. He had provided a 15-line commendatory poem to the 1613 edition which, in addition to praising Purchas, spun off in a footnote a page and a half of scholarship on the gods. Since much of the detail from this footnote is found in the text that follows, Selden's commendation can be read as a preemptory claim

on the intellectual property. The 1614 edition included the poem but no footnote. *Purchas His Pilgrimage* had seen three editions between the writing of *De diis* and its publication in 1617, and it is easy to imagine both Selden and Purchas being proprietary. Aside from such skirmishes, those parts of the *Pilgrimage* in which Purchas deals with polytheism have numerous points of resemblance with *De diis*.

4. "Polytheism," in *Oxford English Dictionary*. Origen and Athanasius use forms of the word (see "Polytheismus," in *Theologische Realenzyklopädie* [Berlin: Walter de Gruyter, 1994]), as did Philo and Procopius (see *A Greek English Lexicon* [Oxford: Clarendon Press, 1985]).

5. Purchas, *Purchas His Pilgrimage* (1613), 43. The 1613 edition will hereafter be cited.

6. Ibid., 55–85.

7. Ibid., 1.

8. Thomas Herbert, *A Relation of Some Years Travel* (London, 1638), 315.

9. Don Cameron Allen, *Mysteriously Meant* (Baltimore: The Johns Hopkins University Press, 1970), 69.

10. Gerardus Vossius, *De theologia gentili et physiologia Christiana* (Amsterdam, 1641), 326, 391, 414, 467, 499.

11. Fuller, *A Pisgah-Sight of Palestine*, book 2, p. 64; book 4, pp. 80, 128, 129, 131, 136.

12. While he acknowledges Selden as a source for Dagon, Cowley inserts a line from Horace, "Desinit in Piscem mulier formosa superne," which is not in *De diis*, but which Fuller had included in his treatment of Dagon in *Pisgah-Sight* (Cowley, *Davideis*, in *Poems* [London, 1656], 80n83). Fuller translates: "Upwards man-like he ascended, / Downwards like a fish he ended," (*A Pisgah-Sight of Palestine*, book 4, p. 220).

13. Mario M. Rossi, *La vita, le opere, i tempi di Edoardo Herbert Di Chirbury*, vol. 3, ed. G. C. Sansoni (Florence: G. C. Sansoni, 1947), 243.

14. Selden considers the sun to be the first object of fallen worship, associating it, through Job 31:26–28, with the practice of kissing one's hand and inclining one's head (Selden 2:226). Perhaps this passage lies behind Satan's worship of the sun, "at whose sight all the stars / Hide their diminished heads" (*PL* 4.34–35). Satan would therefore be performing the first act of transgressive worship and initiating the process of decline into idolatry and polytheism.

15. Bernhard Lang, *Monotheism and the Prophetic Minority* (Sheffield: The Almond Press, 1983), 13–59. Lang traces the idea of an ur-monotheism from Herbert of Cherbury. William Foxwell Albright's *From the Stone Age to Christianity: Monotheism and the Historical Process* (Garden City, N.Y.: Doubleday, 1957), is a modern example of the investigation into process.

16. Vossius, *Theologia gentili*, xx; *De religione*, 56–67; *Purchas His Pilgrimage*, 47. Fuller, *A Pisgah-Sight of Palestine*, book 4, p. 124.

17. See Allen, *Mysteriously Meant*, 61–82. And see Paolo Rossi, *The Dark Abyss of Time: The History of the Earth and the History of Nations from Hooke to Vico*, trans. Lydia G Cochrane (Chicago: University of Chicago Press, 1984), 152–87, on Vico and his responses to Vossius, Toland, and others.

18. His argument begins with the assertion that "polytheism and idolatry was, and necessarily must have been, the first and most antient religion of mankind"; see David Hume, *The Natural History of Religion*, ed. A. Wayne Colver (Oxford: Clarendon, 1976), 26.

19. "For when the Gentiles, which have not the law, do by nature the things contained in the law, these, having not the law, are a law unto themselves: Which shew the work of the law written in their hearts, their conscience also bearing witness, and their thoughts the mean while accusing or else excusing one another" (Rom 2:14–15). D. P. Walker, *The Ancient Theology* (Ithaca, N.Y.: Cornell University Press, 1972), 22–41, identifies a concern for an underlying monotheism in paganism within the Neoplatonic writings of Ficino and others. Also see Allen, *Mysteriously Meant*, 21–51.

20. Jean Calvin, *Institutes of the Christian Religion*, vol. 1, ed. John T. McNeill, trans. Ford Lewis Battles (Philadelphia: The Westminster Press, 1960), 47; see book 1, chaps. 3–4.

21. *Purchas His Pilgrimage*, 2; Vossius, *Theologia gentili*, 8–32; Fuller, *A Pisgah-Sight of Palestine*, 126; Alexander Ross, *Pansebia; or, A View of All Religions in the World*, 2nd ed. (London: 1658), 71–72, 126–27, 527–29.

22. "Caeterum ex ante dictis tandem satis constat Graecorum, Latinorum, & AEgyptiorum, qui nempe omnes longe ante alias gentes arcanorum naturae studiis incumbebant, abditiorem & quam in vulgus edere non immerito abhorrebant, theologiam non tam plures quam unum supremum Deum agnovisse" (Selden 2:251).

23. See John Anthony Butler's introduction to *De religione*, 37–38, and throughout in the footnotes. Rossi, *La Vita*, claims that "every citation, every allusion" comes from Vossius (3:110).

24. Vossius, *Theologia gentili*, 29.

25. Butler, introduction to *De religione*, 39. Also see J. A. I. Champion, *The Pillars of Priestcraft Shaken: The Church of England and Its Enemies, 1660–1730* (Cambridge: Cambridge University Press, 1992), 141.

26. *Purchas His Pilgrimage*, 48. In *De diis*, Selden explains how Egyptian priests led worship of a sphere that they alone, secretly, thought represented the one God. This is repeated at More's coining of the word monotheism, as discussed later in this chapter, with both authors implying a conspiracy of priests. Selden is largely objective concerning the

priesthood in his study of polytheism, but then this same historical objectivity later proved to be a devastating political weapon against the clergy in the *History of Tythes*.

27. Charles Blount, *Religio laici* (London, 1683), 18–29. Also see John Locke, *The Reasonableness of Christianity* (London, 1695), 257–58.

28. See especially the fourth and fifth chapters of Champion, *The Pillars of Priestcraft Shaken*, 99–169. Speaking of the Catholic hierarchy, Milton tells the same story: "Wolves shall succeed for teachers, grievous wolves, / Who all the sacred mysteries of heaven / To their own vile advantages shall turn / Of lucre and ambition" (*PL* 12.508–11).

29. What I term "occult monotheism," Frank Manuel, *The Changing of the Gods* (Hanover, N.H.: University Press of New England, 1983), 27–51, calls "primitive monotheism" while discussing its importance to deism.

30. Ross, *Pansebia*, 4v.

31. David Masson, *Life of John Milton*, 2 vols. (Gloucester, Mass.: Peter Smith, 1965), 2:608, suggests that Selden "was at heart a kind of Latitudinarian or Freethinker" who hated the clergy and believed in "more than Erastianism; but he was long-headed enough to pass for the nonce as only the chief of the Erastians."

32. Jason Rosenblatt, *Renaissance England's Chief Rabbi: John Selden* (Oxford: Oxford University Press, 2006), 71.

33. Basil Willey, *The Seventeenth Century Background* (New York: Columbia University Press, 1934), 123.

34. The other Religious Common Notions are ethical: (3) virtue and piety are essential features of religion; (4) sin must be expiated by repentance; (5) there is life after death.

35. Aryeh Botwinick, *Skepticism, Belief, and the Modern: Maimonides to Nietzsche* (Ithaca, N.Y.: Cornell University Press, 1997), 53.

36. Richard Tuck, "The 'Christian Atheism' of Thomas Hobbes," in *Atheism from the Reformation to the Enlightenment*, ed. Michael Hunter and David Wooton (Oxford: Oxford University Press, 1992), 128. Hobbes greatly admired *De veritate*, calling it a "high point" in a letter to William Cavendish dated 13/23 June 1636; see *Thomas Hobbes: The Correspondence*, ed. Noel Malcolm (Oxford: Oxford University Press, 1994), 1: 32. For a competing view of Hobbes's religion, which argues against reading Hobbes as anticipating the deist God, see Richard Sherlock, "The Theology of Leviathan: Hobbes on Religion," *Interpretation* 10 (1982): 43–60.

37. Ralph Cudworth, *The True Intellectual System of the Universe*, 3 vols. (London: T. Tegg, 1845), xliii. Cudworth engages specifically with Cherbury's *De religione* (2:1). See J. L. Mosheim's note, translated into English in the 1845 edition.

38. Henry More, *An Antidote against Atheism*, in *A Collection of Several Philosophical Writings*, 4th ed. (London, 1712), 144–45. See Sterling P. Lamprecht, "Innate Ideas in the Cambridge Platonists," *Philosophical Review* 35 (1926): 553–73.

39. So the God of occult monotheism is without the proper attributes: "But not only this obvious Attribute of *Unity* is wanting to this Pagan Deity, but several others also that are as necessarily included in the Notion of a God: such as are *Spirituality, Immensity, Omnipotency, Omnisciency* and the like" (*GMG* 60).

40. "Reconditam & vero proximantem theologiam neque evulgabant, neque omnino sibi retinebant; sed in iis quae vulgo in uso erant sacris, mysteria instituebant solennia, unde ansam occultae veritatis eruendae non ita difficile erat sanioribus arripere. Non ita, ut opinor, AEgyptiorum prophetae. Sed tamen & iis unitatis erat reconditissimum symbolum" (Selden 2:249).

41. "Nam ridiculas figuras, innumeras ac portentosas profano hominum coetui ostentantes, atque inde inprimis imperitorum & foventes & ludentes superstitionem, alia sibi inclusa sacris scriniolis servabant mysteria, hoc est, quasdam sphaeras (si recepta Synesii lectio vera sit, de qua statim) quarum singulae in singulis sanis a profanorum conspectu abditissimae, symbola, ut videtur, universi orbis moderatoris unici erant" (Selden 2:249–50).

42. More, *Collection of Several Philosophical Writings*, iv.

43. Marjorie Nicolson, "The Spirit World of Milton and More," *Studies in Philology* 22, no. 4 (1925): 435, first pointed out that More's "sensuous afterworld" shows a "remarkable correspondence" to Milton. C. S. Lewis, *A Preface to Paradise Lost* (London: Oxford University Press), 1960, 109–11, draws a parallel to More as an example of the period's Neoplatonic interest in the details of angelic life. Stephen Fallon, *Milton Among the Philosophers: Poetry and Materialism in Seventeenth-Century England* (Ithaca, N.Y.: Cornell University Press, 1991), compares them in the context of Cartesian and Hobbesian philosophies of matter, although he argues that material monism separates Milton from the duality of More's Platonism.

44. James Henry Breasted, *The Dawn of Conscience* (New York: Scribner, 1950), 275.

45. David Norbrook, *Writing the English Republic: Poetry, Rhetoric, and Politics, 1627–1660* (Cambridge: Cambridge University Press, 1999). Joan Bennett, *Reviving Liberty: Radical Christian Humanism in Milton's Great Poems* (Cambridge, Mass.: Harvard University Press, 1989), 27–28, argues that Milton rejects the equation of the one omnipotent God with monarchy. Also see Michael Bryson, *The Tyranny of Heaven: Milton's Rejection of God as King* (Newark: University of Delaware Press, 2004).

46. Lenn Evan Goodman, Monotheism: A Philosophical Inquiry into the Foundations of Theology and Ethics (Totowa, N.J.: Allanheld, Osmun, 1981), 24–25.

Notes to Chapter 3

1. Irene Samuel, "The Dialogue in Heaven: A Reconsideration of *Paradise Lost*, III, 1–417," in *Milton: Modern Essays in Criticism*, ed. Arthur E. Barker (Oxford: Oxford University Press, 1965), 233. For a contrary opinion, see, for example, William Empson, *Milton's God*, rev. ed. (London: Chatto & Windus, 1965); J. B. Broadbent, *Some Graver Subject: An Essay on* Paradise Lost (London: Chatto & Windus, 1960), 144–57. For recent discussions of Empson, see Michael Bryson, *The Tyranny of Heaven: Milton's Rejection of God as King* (Newark: University of Delaware Press, 2004), and Peter Herman, Paradise Lost *and the Poetics of Incertitude* (New York: Palgrave MacMillan, 2005). Alexander Pope, *The First Epistle of the Second Book of Horace Imitated*, 101–02, in *Poetry and Prose of Alexander Pope*, ed. Aubrey Williams (Boston: Houghton Mifflin, 1969).

2. Douglas Bush, *Paradise Lost in Our Time: Some Comments* (Gloucester, Mass.: Peter Smith, 1957), 43; C. S. Lewis, *A Preface to* Paradise Lost. (London: Oxford University Press, 1960), 130–31; quotation at 130.

3. Broadbent, *Some Graver Subject*, 146, 143. Roland M. Frye, "The Father," in *A Milton Encyclopedia*, vol. 3, ed. William B. Hunter Jr. et al. (Lewisburg, Pa.: Bucknell University Press, 1978), describes Milton's God as "pure intellect, pure reason, unmixed with passion or uncertainty, so that He simply and instantaneously knows what is right, correct, or wise" (98). This is also like the God that Denis Saurat, *Milton, Man and Thinker* (London: J. M. Dent, 1944), emphasizes, the God that is "identical with the Absolute of nineteenth-century philosophy" (93).

4. Lenn Evan Goodman, *Monotheism: A Philosophical Inquiry into the Foundations of Theology and Ethics* (Totowa, N.J.: Allanheld, Osmun, 1981), 11.

5. This argument is typical of the tradition of ethical monotheism. Hermann Cohen, *Religion of Reason Out of the Sources of Judaism*, trans. Simon Kaplan (New York: Frederick Ungar, 1972), argues that in polytheism,

> the religious and hence absolute difference between good and bad cannot arise. The gods favor men in accordance with their own discretion, even in accordance with their caprice. Because of this Homer is the Bible of freethinkers. The gods cannot be united in

their government, for then they could not be different individuals. Monotheism is based on a uniform comprehension of the distinction of good and bad, and thus on a uniform attitude of God to man, as well as of man to God. (130)

Cohen provides a reading of Genesis 18:25 that is similar to Goodman's, ibid., 118–19.

6. Compare Catherine Gimelli Martin, *The Ruins of Allegory: Paradise Lost and the Metamorphosis of Epic Convention* (Durham, N.C.: Duke University Press, 1998), and her argument for a baroque God: "In contrast to both the deistic First Cause and the revealed deity, Milton's God baroquely multiplies his images" (9).

7. Maimonides, *The Guide for the Perplexed*, trans. M. Friedlander (New York: Hebrew Publishing, 1881), 2:197–98.

8. John H. Sailhamer, *The Pentateuch as Narrative* (Grand Rapids, Mich.: Zondervan, 1992), 160, 162.

9. John E. Parish, "Milton and the Anthropomorphic God," *Studies in Philology* 56 (1959): 619–25, discusses Genesis 18:25. Merritt Hughes, "The Filiations of Milton's Celestial Dialogue," *Ten Perspectives on Milton* (New Haven, Conn.: Yale University Press, 1965), 104–35, picks up Parish's discussion. James H. Sims, *The Bible in Milton's Epics* (Gainesville: University of Florida Press, 1962), 202–04, 210, discusses the first half, Genesis 18:1–16. Jason Rosenblatt, "Celestial Entertainment in Eden: Book V of *Paradise Lost*," *Harvard Theological Review* 62, no. 4 (1969): 411–27, provides the most extensive treatment of Genesis 18. Bryson, *The Tyranny of Heaven*, 67, 117, considers the second half of Genesis 18.

10. Thomas Newton, *Paradise Lost: A Poem in Twelve Books* (London, 1749).

11. On the freedom of Milton's God, see Stephen Fallon, "'To Act or Not': Milton's Conception of Divine Freedom," *Journal of the History of Ideas* 49 (1988): 425–52.

12. Goodman, *Monotheism*, 24–25. See also chapter 2 above.

13. Hugo Grotius, *The Rights of War and Peace*, trans. J. Barbeyrac (London, 1738), 11, 12.

14. Both Milton and Grotius appeal to the near universality of the knowledge of justice. Grotius argues that the Law of Nature can be known "with very great probability" if it is "generally believed to be so by all, or at least, the most civilized, Nations" (ibid., 13–14). For Milton the laws, which control even God, are to be extolled "not onely as they are his, but as they are just and good to every wise and sober understanding." This assertion of universality sets up natural law as authoritative precisely because it is outside of revelation, and available to pagans. In Milton's reading of Genesis 18:25 universality does not replace revelation—"but

in the delivery and execution of his Law, especially in the managing of a duty so daily and so familiar as this is whereof we reason, has plain anough reveal'd himself"—but does assist in his project of undoing the authority of the New Testament revelation over the Old. Milton is arguing against accepting Rivetus in his claim that dispensation has negated the clear Law of Deuteronomy regarding divorce. The universality of law demonstrated by 18:25 thus serves to diminish the exclusiveness of the Christian revelation, forming a key moment in the inclusive argument of *The Doctrine and Discipline of Divorce*. On Milton's God's adherence to natural law, see Joan Bennett, *Reviving Liberty: Radical Christian Humanism in Milton's Great Poems* (Cambridge, Mass.: Harvard University Press, 1989), 59–93.

15. Grotius, *Rights of War and Peace*, 16. Grotius's placement of natural law before a God of personality contributes to what Richard Tuck, *Natural Rights Theories: Their Origin and Development* (Cambridge: Cambridge University Press, 1979), 76, calls the "untheistic character" of *De iure belli*.

16. Richard Tuck, *Hobbes* (Oxford: Oxford University Press, 1989), 82–84, 78. Tuck says of Hobbes's God: "Modern astrophysicists' 'Big Bang' might have played the same role as 'God' for him. The crucial point is that all the conventional attributes of God such as benevolence and omnipotence were excluded from the *philosophical* concept of God"; see Richard Tuck, *Hobbes: A Very Short Introduction* (Oxford: Oxford University Press, 2002), 89.

17. For example, John Calvin, *Commentaries on the First Book of Moses Called Genesis*, trans. Rev. John King (Edinburgh: The Calvin Translation Society, 1847): "Seeing that God here takes counsel, as if concerning a doubtful matter, he does it for the sake of men; for he had already determined what he would do" (1:478).

18. Calvin, *Commentaries on Genesis*, 1:489. David Pareus, *In Genesin Mosis commentarius* (Geneva, 1614), 1261, similarly argues against Abraham being impious in questioning God. Martin Luther, *Lectures on Genesis*, in *Luther's Works*, ed. Jaroslav Pelikan (St. Louis: Concordia, 1961), 235, dwells on Abraham in the exchange, calling his prayer "foolish" and "impulsive," although also praiseworthy, reflecting the problem with human discipline of God.

19. Parish, "Milton and the Anthropomorphic God," 619.

20. Jeffrey Shoulson, *Milton and the Rabbis: Hebraism, Hellenism, and Christianity* (New York: Columbia University Press, 2001), argues that "The figure of the Son serves as a typological paradigm for all work of scriptural accommodation. That is, just as the Son must descend to the realm of flesh so as to effect the redemption and translation of all fallen humanity back to its divine originary substance, so, too, accommodated language condescends to the fleshly realm, insisting on its materiality

precisely so that it may point to a spiritual conception of the godhead" (102).

21. Hughes, "Filiations," 115; Parish, "Milton and the Anthropomorphic God"; and Rosenblatt, "Celestial Entertainment in Eden," all point out the allusion to Numbers 14.

22. For example, Jonathan Culler's description of the deconstructed subject in *The Pursuit of Signs: Semiotics, Literature, Deconstruction* (Ithaca, N.Y.: Cornell University Press, 1981): "As the self is broken down into component systems, deprived of its status as source and master of meaning, it comes to seem more and more like a construct: a result of systems of convention. Even the idea of personal identity emerges through the discourse of a culture: the 'I' is not something given but comes to exist as that which is addressed by and relates to others" (22).

23. Empson, *Milton's God*, 120. Empson also stresses God's omniscience (42) and his "contemptuous omnipotence" (110).

24. Dennis Danielson, *Milton's Good God* (Cambridge: Cambridge University Press, 1982), finds "no disharmony" in the Son's "That be far from thee" (108). And he views "Die he or justice must" as a "theological compatibilism," which is in opposition to voluntarism (154). Similarly, Dennis Burden, *The Logical Epic: A Study in the Argument of* Paradise Lost (Cambridge, Mass.: Harvard University Press, 1967), responds to Empson by stressing God's conformity to principles of logic. Michael Bryson, *The Tyranny of Heaven*, 13–15, argues in support of Empson, and he, in turn, reemphasizes God's personality, in particular recognizing its relationship to monotheism.

25. Compare Victoria Silver, *Imperfect Sense: The Predicament of Milton's Irony* (Princeton: Princeton University Press, 2001): "When God's hiddenness is understood in the reformers' sense, there can be no stable 'object,' whether perceptible or metaphysical, to which our ideas of the divine can refer" (57).

26. Calvin, *Commentaries on Genesis*, for example, comments on the actions of Abraham and Sarah: "Here is the sweet concord of a well-conducted family" (1:471). See also Gervase Babington, *Certaine Plaine and Comfortable Notes upon Genesis* (London, 1592), fol. 65, and James Kugel, *Traditions of the Bible* (Cambridge, Mass.: Harvard University Press, 1998), 334–36.

27. For example, Justin Martyr argues, "I should say that the word ate is intended in the same way as we ourselves might say of fire that it devoured everything, and that we ought not at all to understand this to mean that they ate by (actually) chewing with teeth and jaws." Quoted in Kugel, *Traditions of the Bible*, 344.

28. Babington, *Notes upon Genesis*, fol. 65.

29. Sarah goes on to laugh within herself at the idea that she will bear a child (Gen. 18:12), demonstrating, as many exegetes say, a degree of

disbelief in God's power. Eve does not laugh, but the allusion to Sarah raises the possibility that she is somehow laughing inside. Eve may not be taking the warning about Satan seriously, but the possibilities are numerous and interesting to consider. For Sarah's laughter, see Luther, *Lectures on Genesis*, 207.

30. Ibid., 197.

31. Samuel Johnson, *Lives of the English Poets*, ed. George Birkbeck Hill (Oxford: Clarendon Press, 1905), 1:184.

32. Stephen Fallon, *Milton among the Philosophers: Poetry and Materialism in Seventeenth-Century England* (Ithaca, N.Y.: Cornell University Press, 1991), 80. Also see John Rogers, *The Matter of Revolution: Science, Poetry, and Politics in the Age of Milton* (Ithaca, N.Y.: Cornell University Press, 1996).

33. On matter and the creation *ex nihilo*, see Saurat, *Milton, Man and Thinker*, 102–08, and Gordon Teskey, *Delirious Milton: The Fate of the Poet in Modernity* (Cambridge, Mass.: Harvard University Press, 2006), 86–106.

34. Jacques Lezra, *Unspeakable Subjects: The Genealogy of the Event in Early Modern Europe* (Palo Alto, Calif.: Stanford University Press, 1997):

> The rule of the *unpredictability* of *declinatio* would make conditional a division (between properties and accidents) that first presents itself as ontological, and on which the discursive pairs of form and matter, of *essentia* and *materia*, soul and body, are made to depend.... Lucretius's care that the swerve in originary matter be merely *momen mutatem*, not too pronounced...is not only a way of sticking to what facts tell him about falling bodies, but of introducing the swerve as a minimum, an *exiguum clinamen* that makes all the difference but *is in itself* in no defining, material or ontological sense a difference. (17)

35. Ibid., 133.

36. D. Bentley Hart, "Matter, Monism and Narrative: An Essay on the Metaphysics of *Paradise Lost*," *Milton Quarterly* 30, no. 1 (1996): 25. That Milton's material angels serve an important narratological function may explain why in *De doctrina* Milton abjures the microscopic consideration of matter in angels that is so prominent in *Paradise Lost*. Milton lists several angelic qualities, but does not speak of their materiality, and concludes, "Those who tried to say more about the nature of angels earned the apostle's rebuke, Col. ii.18: *intruding into those things which he has not seen, rashly puffed up by his fleshly intelligence*" (YP 6:315). Materiality is necessary to narrative, but less so to doctrine.

37. John Guillory, *Poetic Authority: Spenser, Milton, and Literary History* (New York: Columbia University Press, 1983), 148.

38. See Kugel, *Traditions of the Bible*, 341–42; Calvin, *Commentaries on Genesis*, 1:495; Andrew Willet, *Hexapla in Genesin* (London, 1608), 198.

39. See E. A. Speiser's notes to Genesis 18:3 in *The Anchor Bible* (New York: Doubleday, 1964). Speiser settles on the human "My Lord." Ibn Ezra advocates letting the textual variations in pointing dictate the meaning. Luther, *Lectures on Genesis*, 186, takes the ambiguity as evidence of Abraham's hospitality and humility. But Henry Ainsworth, *Annotations upon the First Book of Moses, Called Genesis* (London, 1621), 93, interprets it as a direct statement to God.

40. Calvin, *Commentaries on Genesis*, 1:470.

41. Willet, *Hexapla in Genesin*, 198–99.

42. The ontological instability of Genesis 18 is a signal example of a tendency throughout the Hebrew Bible to blur the distinctions between angels and God, as well as angels and humans. The Hebrew vocabulary has inscribed within it the ontological negotiations of monotheism, so that words such as *elohim* and *malach* demand that the reader attempt to distinguish between divine beings. Milton discusses this blurring in his explanation of the Hebrew words *elohim* and *malach* in *De doctrina Christiana* (YP 6:233–39, 250–55). The Hebrew Bible, in fact, never develops a specific notion of angels—*malach* remains relatively undefined prior to Christianity. The beginning of the Samson story, Judges 13, particularly expands upon this need to make ontological distinctions between angel and man, as will be discussed in chapter 7.

43. Jonathan Richardson, *Explanatory Notes and Remarks on Milton's* Paradise Lost (London, 1734).

44. Michael Lieb, "Reading God: Milton and the Anthropopathetic Tradition," in *Milton Studies*, vol. 25, ed. James D. Simmonds (Pittsburgh: University of Pittsburgh Press, 1989), 213–37. Lieb revisits the argument in *Theological Milton: Deity, Discourse, and Heresy in the Miltonic Canon* (Pittsburgh: Duquesne University Press, 2006), 127–62, where he suggests calling Milton's God a "theopathetic God."

45. Lieb, *Theological Milton:* "Milton appears initially to dismiss the notion of divine passibility, only afterward to reintroduce it in another form. He dismisses it as a trope through which theologians presume to come to terms with God's unknowableness, and he reintroduces it as a fact through which God's unknowableness is manifested in accommodated form to one's limited capacities" (145).

46. C. A. Patrides, "*Paradise Lost* and the Theory of Accommodation," in *Bright Essence: Studies in Milton's Theology*, ed. W. B. Hunter, C. A. Patrides, and J. H. Adamson (Salt Lake City: University of Utah Press, 1971), 163, claims that accommodation "applies" to the deity. Roland M. Frye, *God, Man, and Satan: Patterns of Christian Thought and Life in* Paradise Lost, Pilgrim's Progress, *and the Great Theologians*

(Princeton: Princeton University Press, 1960), says that "Milton makes clear that the method of accommodation as operative in Scripture is also the basic mode of development in *Paradise Lost*" (14). Lieb, *Theological Milton,* 159–61, also argues for accommodation's applicability, through a process by which the author is identified with divine accommodation, and so authorized to make adjustments.

47. William G. Madsen, *From Shadowy Types to Truth: Studies in Milton's Symbolism* (New Haven, Conn.: Yale University Press, 1968), 74. Also see Guillory's discussion of Madsen and accommodation in *Poetic Authority,* 46–71.

48. James Holly Hanford, "That Shepherd Who First Taught the Chosen Seed: A Note on Milton's Mosaic Inspiration," *University of Toronto Quarterly* 8 (1939): 403–19. Also see William Kerrigan, *The Prophetic Milton* (Charlottesville: University of Virginia Press, 1974).

49. Hanford, "That Shepherd," 415.

50. Shlomith Rimmon-Kenan, *A Glance Beyond Doubt: Narration, Representation, Subjectivity* (Columbus: Ohio State University Press, 1996), 12.

51. *The Works of John Milton,* 18 vols. in 21, ed. Frank Allen Patterson et al. (New York: Columbia University Press, 1931–42), 14:51. Maurice Kelley uses God's words in *Paradise Lost* to gloss this passage in his edition of *De doctrina* in YP and connects the two phrases as well in *This Great Argument: A Study of Milton's* De Doctrina Christiana *as a Gloss upon* Paradise Lost (Princeton: Princeton University Press, 1941), 75.

52. Aryeh Botwinick, *Skepticism, Belief, and the Modern: Maimonides to Nietzsche* (Ithaca, N.Y.: Cornell University Press, 1997), 53. The classic examples of negative theology are Pseudo-Dionysius, *On the Divine Names,* and *Mystical Theology.* Also see Aquinas, *Expositio super Dionysium de divinis nominibus* and *Summa theologica,* part 1, Q. 3; preface, part 1, Q. 13.

53. Milton connects these two verses in his discussion of accommodation (YP 6:135–36).

54. As Calvin, *Commentaries on Genesis,* puts it, discussing Genesis 1:26, before the "infection of sin" in Adam's mind, "perfect intelligence flourished and reigned, uprightness attended as its companion, and all the senses were prepared and moulded for due obedience to reason" (1:95).

55. Botwinick, *Skepticism,* 48. Miltonists may be familiar with Thomas Merrill's description of God-talk, which is a linguistic response to negative theology: "the language of the 'physical world' placed under logical stress because it is put to special use. Some describe it as ordinary language that has been 'stretched' to include realities beyond the reach of conventional grammar." See Thomas Merrill, *Epic God-Talk:* Paradise Lost *and the Grammar of Religious Language* (Jefferson, N.C.: McFarland, 1986), 12. Catherine Gimelli Martin's baroque God describes

similar qualities: "The God of *Paradise Lost* offers an on-going negotiation with his self-authorizing subjects, a constant realignment of covenantal accords that represent him, not as a static 'one,' but as an infinitely multiplicative zero, a variable vanishing point located everywhere and nowhere in the universe" (*Ruins of Allegory,* 112).

Notes to Chapter 4

1. Patrick Hume, *Annotations on Milton's* Paradise Lost (London, 1695), 193. Stanley Fish, *Surprised by Sin: The Reader in* Paradise Lost (New York: St. Martin's Press, 1967), 185, also notices the contradiction.

2. As Regina Schwartz, *Remembering and Repeating: Biblical Creation in* Paradise Lost (Cambridge: Cambridge University Press), puts it, Milton runs the risk of making it appear that "God plays with himself" (35).

3. According to S. H. Butcher's translation of Aristotle, *Poetics,* trans. S. H. Butcher, ed. Richard Koss (Mineola, N.Y.: Dover, 1977), 14.

4. E. M. Forster, *Aspects of the Novel* (New York: Harcourt, Brace, 1927), 130; Gérard Genette, *Narrative Discourse: An Essay in Method,* trans. Jane E. Lewin (Ithaca, N.Y.: Cornell University Press, 1980), 30; Gérard Genette, *Narrative Discourse Revisited,* trans. Jane E. Lewin (Ithaca, N.Y.: Cornell University Press, 1988), 18–19. For a clear summary of minimal plots, see Suzanne Keen, *Narrative Form* (New York: Palgrave, 2003), 75.

5. That God brought the Israelites out of Egypt prefaces the first commandment: "I am the LORD thy God, which have brought thee out of the land of Egypt, out of the house of bondage. Thou shalt have no other gods before me" (Exod. 20:2–3); also see Deut. 5:6–7. The reminder echoes throughout the Bible and the Jewish liturgy.

6. Analyzing Abdiel's "noble stroke"—another instance of the action of the angelic arm—William Kolbrenner, *Milton's Warring Angels* (Cambridge: Cambridge University Press, 1997), recognizes Milton's strategic inclusion of both the timeless and the temporal, and reads it as an example of "the narrativity and non-narrativity of providence" (144).

7. Compare Fish, *Surprised by Sin,* 177–80.

8. S. B. [Samuel Barrow], "In Paradisum Amissam summi poetae Johannis Miltoni," in *The Riverside Milton,* ed. Roy Flannagan (Boston: Houghton Mifflin, 1998), 349; Earl of Roscommon, *Milton: The Critical Heritage,* ed. John T. Shawcross (London: Routledge and Kegan Paul, 1970), 92–93; Dennis quotation from the preface to *The Passion of Byblis,* in Shawcross, 99; Addison quotation from *Notes upon the Twelve Books of* Paradise Lost, in Shawcross, 156.

9. Edward Le Comte, "Dubious Battle: Saving the Appearances," *English Language Notes* 19 (1982): 183; Alexander Pope, *Rape of the Lock*, 3.147–52, in *Poetry and Prose of Alexander Pope*, ed. Aubrey Williams (Boston: Houghton Mifflin, 1969).

10. Alexander Pope, *Peri Bathous*, in *Poetry and Prose*, 434: "If you have need of Devils, draw them out of *Milton's Paradise*, and extract your *spirits* from Tasso." On Milton's polemical humor in book 6 and throughout the poem, see John King, *Milton and Religious Controversy: Satire and Polemic in* Paradise Lost (Cambridge: Cambridge University Press, 2000).

11. Samuel Johnson, *Life of Milton*, in *Lives of the English Poets*, vol. 1, ed. George Birkbeck Hill (Oxford: Clarendon Press, 1905), 185. Robert H. West, *Milton and the Angels* (Athens, Ga.: University of Georgia Press, 1955), 108–12, discusses Johnson's critique.

12. Arnold Stein, *Answerable Style: Essays on* Paradise Lost (Minneapolis: The University of Minnesota Press, 1953), 22.

13. Le Comte, "Dubious Battle," summarizes Stein's influential perspective, with some cynicism: "The great modern literary virtue is irony, and now Milton turns out to have it, along with a sense of humor previously denied" (187).

14. Addison, quoted in Shawcross, *Critical Heritage*, 191.

15. Shaftesbury, Anthony Ashley Cooper, *Characteristics of Men, Manners, Opinions, Times*, ed. Lawrence E. Klein (Cambridge: Cambridge University Press, 1999), 59.

16. James A. Herrick, *The Radical Rhetoric of the English Deists: The Discourse of Skepticism, 1680–1750* (Columbia: University of South Carolina Press, 1997), 54. Also see John Redwood, *Reason, Ridicule, and Religion: The Age of Enlightenment in England, 1660–1750* (London: Thames & Hudson, 1976).

17. John Leland, *A View of the Principal Deistic Writers*, 2 vols. (London: Longmans, Hurst, Reese, and Orme, 1807), devotes a large portion of his monumental study of deism to Bolingbroke: "Any one that reads Lord Bolingbroke's work with attention, must be convinced, that one principal design he had in view, was to destroy the authority of the divine revelation in general, and of the Jewish and Christian in particular" (2:46).

18. Charles Leslie, *The History of Sin and Heresie* (London, 1697), A2v; hereafter cited parenthetically in the text.

19. John Toland, *Life of Milton*, in *The Early Lives of Milton*, ed. Helen Darbishire (London: Constable, 1932), 178–79.

20. Ibid., 195.

21. Henning Graf Reventlow, *The Authority of the Bible and the Rise of the Modern World*, trans. John Bowden (Philadelphia: Fortress Press, 1985): "Though he does not raise any objections against parts of the

canon itself, Toland's references are still effective in the way in which they radically question the certainty with which all parties felt that they could refer to the New Testament as a fixed entity. This, however, is to attack at a central point the scriptural faith dominant in Humanist Protestantism of a Calvinist stamp, above all among the Puritans" (308).

22. Sharon Achinstein, "Milton's Spectre in the Restoration: Marvell, Dryden and Literary Enthusiasm," *Huntington Library Quarterly* 59 (1997): 1–29. For Milton's heretical opinions, see Christopher Hill, *Milton and the English Revolution* (New York: Penguin Books, 1979), and *Milton and Heresy*, ed. Stephen B. Dobranski and John P. Rumrich (Cambridge: Cambridge University Press, 1998).

23. Anthony Collins, *A Discourse of Free-Thinking* (London, 1713), 177. "Father Paul" is Paolo Sarpi.

24. David Hume, *The Natural History of Religion*, ed. A. Wayne Colver (Oxford: Clarendon, 1976), 28.

25. Shawcross, *Milton: The Critical Heritage, 1732–1801* (London: Routledge & Kegan Paul, 1972), 89.

26. Joseph Frank, "Milton's Movement toward Deism," *Journal of British Studies* 1, no. 1 (1961): 38–51. William Haller, "Milton and the Protestant Ethic," *Journal of British Studies* 1, no. 1 (1961): 52–57, argues against Frank, also in very general terms.

27. J. B. Broadbent, *Some Graver Subject: An Essay on* Paradise Lost (New York: Barnes & Noble, 1960), 143; Kolbrenner, *Milton's Warring Angels*, 118.

28. Catherine Gimelli Martin, "Unediting Milton: Historical Myth and Editorial Misconstruction in the Yale Prose Edition," in *Milton, Rights and Liberites*, ed. Christophe Tournu and Neil Forsyth (Bern: Peter Lang, 2007), 113–30.

29. Leland, *A View*, 1:ii.

30. Maximillian E. Novak, "Defoe, the Occult, and the Deist Offensive during the Reign of George I," in *Deism, Masonry, and the Enlightenment: Essays Honoring Alfred Owen Aldridge*, ed. J. A. Leo Lemay (Newark: University of Delaware Press, 1987), 93–94.

31. Daniel Defoe, *The Political History of the Devil* (London, 1726), 73; hereafter cited parenthetically.

32. Charles Leslie, *A Short and Easie Method with the Deists* (London, 1697), 16.

33. Collins, *A Discourse of Free-Thinking*, 123–24.

34. Richard Bentley, *Remarks upon a Late Discourse of Free-Thinking, Part the Second*, 6th ed. (Cambridge, 1725), 31–32.

35. Kolbrenner, *Milton's Warring Angels*, 122.

36. Dennis's clear opposition to deism in *The Advancement* is interestingly complicated by his own anticlerical statements a year later in *The Danger of Priestcraft to Religion and Government* (London, 1702),

which occasioned a response by Charles Leslie, *The New Association* (London, 1702).

37. René Le Bossu, *Treatise of the Epick Poem*, trans. W. J. (London, 1695); reprinted in *Le Bossu and Voltaire on the Epic*, ed. Stuart Curran (Gainesville, Fla.: Scholars' Facsimiles & Reprints, 1970), 225–26, 9, 216.

38. John Dryden, *Discourse Concerning the Original and Progress of Satire*, in *The Works of John Dryden*, vol. 4, ed. A. B. Chambers and William Frost (Berkeley and Los Angeles: University of California Press, 1974), 19.

39. Dryden, "Absalom and Achitophel," in ibid., vol. 2, ed. H. T. Swedenberg, 36: "He said. Th'Almighty, nodding, gave Consent; / And Peals of Thunder shook the Firmament" (1025–26). Given Dryden's opposition to deism in *Religio laici*, this is a divine intervention curiously in sympathy with natural religion. Compare the revelation Herbert of Cherbury reports as he wonders whether to publish *De veritate*, in *The Autobiography of Edward, Lord Herbert of Cherbury*, ed. Sidney Lee (London: Routledge, 1906), 133–34.

40. Nicolas Boileau-Despréaux, *L'Art poétique*, canto 3, lines 199–204. *Dryden* also translates these famous lines in "The Art of Poetry," in *Works*, 2:626–29. Dryden's pronouncements on the matter of Christian machinery are not consistent—his endorsement of Boileau's skeptical pronouncement shows that his seemingly commonsensical allowance of machinery from the Old Testament is not a position held with ease.

41. Dennis apparently considered his digression against deism to be important: he reprinted these pages in his *Vice and Luxury Publick Mischiefs* (London, 1724), as Hooker observes (1:480).

42. *The Rape of the Lock and other Poems*, ed. Geoffrey Tillotson (New Haven, Conn.: Yale University Press, 1962), 343.

43. David B. Morris, *The Religious Sublime: Christian Poetry and Critical Tradition in Eighteenth-Century England* (Lexington: University Press of Kentucky, 1972), 47.

44. Isaac Watts, preface to *Horae lyricae*, in *The Works of The Rev. Isaac Watts*, vol. 9 (London, 1813), 222; qtd. in A. F. B. Clark, *Boileau and the French Classical Critics in England* (New York: Russell & Russell, 1965), 314.

45. *Essay on Man*, 1.17, in Pope, *Poetry and Prose*.

Notes to Chapter 5

1. "Monotheismus," *Theologische realenzyklopädia* (Berlin: Walter de Gruyter, 1994).

2. Ralph Cudworth, *The True Intellectual System of the Universe* (London, 1678), 233, challenges More quite directly when he argues that

an inscription at the temple at Sais indicates that the Egyptians worshipped "some *One thing* which was *All*" (341). This is the same inscription, taken from Selden's *De diis Syris*, that More cites as evidence of the pure materiality of Egyptian worship, and hence polytheism, when he coins the word "monotheisme." More later credits Cudworth and Edward Stillingfleet with changing his mind on occult monotheism, in the Scholia added to *An Antidote against Atheism*. Henry More, *Opera omnia* (London, 1679), 49.

3. Latitudinarians would not go so far. Cudworth and More both seek to contain the spread of Antitrinitarianism, More by arguing for mystery in *The Grand Mystery of Godliness*, and Cudworth using the increasingly persuasive argument for occult monotheism to fend off doubts about the Trinity by arguing that a Platonic Trinity demonstrates the universality of the tripartite godhead:

> This Parallelism, betwixt the Ancient or Genuine Platonick, and the Christian Trinity, might be of some use to satisfy those amongst us, who Boggle so much at the Trinity, and look upon it as the Choak-Pear of Christianity; when they shall find, that the Freest Wits amongst the Pagans, and the Best Philosophers, who had nothing of Superstition, to Determine them that way, were so far from being shy of such an Hypothesis, as that they were even Fond thereof. (Cudworth, *True Intellectual System*, A8v)

4. Again, latitudinarians resisted such an extreme. In *Origines sacrae*, subtitled *A Rational Account of the Grounds of Christian Faith* (London, 1662), Stillingfleet deduces "by clear and evident reason the necessity of some particular Divine revelation" (362). Locke's *Reasonableness of Christianity* exemplifies best the way latitudinarians celebrate rational religion, but ultimately insist on the necessity of miracle and revelation.

5. Gerald R. Cragg, *From Puritanism to the Age of Reason* (Cambridge: Cambridge University Press, 1950), locates this resistance at the point of mystery:

> In the later seventeenth century the trend of religious thought was steadily toward rationalism and enlightenment. At certain points the Cambridge Platonists fostered this tendency and contributed to it, but in one respect they stood aside from the main current of contemporary thought. As the seventeenth century drew to a close, the growing trust in reason led increasingly to a veneration of clear and distinct ideas. But the Cambridge Platonists were all, in some degree, mystics. (51)

W. M. Spellman discusses the "limits of reason in religious experience" in *The English Latitudinarians and the Church of England, 1660–1700*

(Athens: University of Georgia Press, 1993), 6. Spellman appropriately cautions against Whiggish readings of the latitudinarians as clear precursors to deism (1–10).

6. As Regina Schwartz, *The Curse of Cain: The Violent Legacy of Monotheism* (Chicago: The University of Chicago Press, 1997), suggests, "A stubborn emphasis on oneness asserts itself in preoccupations with purity. Whether as singleness (this God against the others) or totality (this is all the God there is), monotheism abhors, reviles, rejects, and ejects whatever it defines as outside its compass" (63).

7. Charles Blount and Charles Gildon, *The Oracles of Reason* (London, 1693), 91.

8. This is to place Milton within the extremes of the period's rational religion, a context that has been largely ignored by Miltonists—perhaps due to an overemphasis on Milton's poetry and prose as prophetic. Despite close ties with Quakers, Milton's statements about inspiration by the Spirit are ambivalent, while his rational biblical hermeneutics are clear. On this rational context, especially see Herbert McLachlan, *The Religious Opinions of Milton, Locke, and Newton* (Manchester: Manchester University Press, 1941), and George Newton Conklin, *Biblical Criticism and Heresy in Milton* (New York: Octagon Books, 1972).

9. See J. N. D. Kelly, *Early Christian Doctrines*, 5th ed. (New York: Continuum, 2000). On Arianism, see Maurice Wiles, *Archetypal Heresy: Arianism through the Centuries* (New York: Clarendon Press, 1996); and Michael Bauman, *Milton's Arianism* (Frankfurt am Main: Verlag Peter Lang, 1986).

10. On the history of Socinianism, see Earl Morse Wilbur, *A History of Unitarianism: Socinianism and Its Antecedents*, 2 vols. (Cambridge, Mass.: Harvard University Press, 1945); H. John McLachlan, *Socinianism in Seventeenth-Century England* (Oxford: Oxford University Press, 1951). Maurice Kelley's summary in the Yale Prose edition of *De doctrina Christiana* is very useful (YP 6:47–73).

11. McLachlan, *Socinianism in Seventeenth-Century England*, 63–89.

12. John Biddle, *A Confession of Faith Touching the Holy Trinity, According to the Scripture* (London, 1648), and *A Twofold Catechism: The One Simply Called a Scripture-catechism; The Other, A Brief Scripture-catechism for Children* (London, 1654); both texts are hereafter cited parenthetically in the text. A life of Biddle appears in the important Unitarian collection, *The Faith of One God* (London, 1691). Also see McLachlan, *Socinianism in Seventeenth-Century England*, 163–217.

13. The continuity of this monotheistic argument is one major indication, along with the emphasis on *sola scriptura*, that Antitrinitarianism represents a logical progression of the Reformation. McLachlan, *Socinianism in Seventeenth-Century England*, calls Socinianism a "further stage in the Reformation" (4).

14. Also see Biddle, *Twofold Catechism*, 21; *Racovian* 16–17; and *The Acts of Great Athanasius* (London, 1690), 4, where the Trinity is compared to "idolatry and polytheism."

15. Francis Cheynell, *The Rise, Growth and Danger of Socinianisme* (London, 1643), 24.

16. Henry More, *Apocalypsis apocalypseos* (London, 1680), 84; cited in the *Oxford English Dictionary*, s.v. "monotheist." Also see *Apocalypsis apocalypseos*, 80, 81.

17. Dennis 1:345; Daniel Defoe, *The Political History of the Devil* (London, 1726), 75; Jonathan Richardson, *Explanatory Notes and Remarks on Milton's* Paradise Lost (1734), in *Milton 1732–1801: The Critical Heritage*, ed. John T. Shawcross (London: Routledge and Kegan Paul, 1972), 84. Also see John Rumrich, "Milton's Arianism: Why It Matters," in *Milton and Heresy*, ed. Stephen B. Dobranski and John P. Rumrich (Cambridge: Cambridge University Press, 1998), 75–92.

18. Joseph Wittreich, "Milton's Transgressive Maneuvers: Receptions (Then and Now) and the Sexual Politics of *Paradise Lost*," in Dobranski and Rumrich, *Milton and Heresy*, 244–66.

19. *Bright Essence: Studies in Milton's Theology*, ed. William B. Hunter, C. A. Patrides, and J. H. Adamson (Salt Lake City: University of Utah Press, 1971), especially "Milton's Arianism Reconsidered" (29–51) and "Milton and Arianism" (63–70). Hugh MacCallum, *Milton and the Sons of God: The Divine Image in Milton's Epic Poetry* (Toronto: University of Toronto Press, 1986), describes the clear affinity between *De doctrina* and Socinian writing: "Passing from Milton's *De Doctrina Christiana* to the *Racovian Catechism* of the Socinians, one experiences a shock of recognition" (54).

20. The study of Antitrinitarian Milton is not entirely new: see Maurice Kelley, *This Great Argument* (Princeton: Princeton University Press, 1941), 72–130, and his frequent citations of Socinian and anti-Socinian arguments in the notes to *De doctrina*; Christopher Hill, *Milton and the English Revolution* (New York: Penguin Books, 1979), 285–306; Bauman, *Milton's Arianism*; MacCallum, *Milton and the Sons of God*, 50–58. More recently, see Dobranski and Rumrich, *Milton and Heresy*; Michael Lieb, *Theological Milton: Deity, Discourse, and Heresy in the Miltonic Canon* (Pittsburgh: Duquesne University Press, 2006), 213–78; and John Rogers, "Milton's Circumcision," in *Milton and the Ground of Contention*, ed. Mark R. Kelley, Michael Lieb, and John T. Shawcross (Pittsburgh: Duquesne University Press, 2003), 188–213.

21. Bauman, *Milton's Arianism*, 2–4.

22. Kelley, *This Great Argument*, 122. Hunter and Patrides, in *Bright Essence*, assert orthodoxy by arguing against Arianism, while Bauman's important account of Milton's Antitrinitarianism is a defense of the Arian label.

23. Although "Arian" is itself a loosely defined term, and not very useful as a label, as Michael Lieb argues in *Theological Milton*, 261–78.

24. McLachlan, *Socinianism in Seventeenth-Century England*, 187–90; Hill, *Milton and the English Revolution*, 292; Stephen B. Dobranski, "Licensing Milton's Heresy," in Dobranski and Rumrich, *Milton and Heresy*, 141–44. Socinians, in turn, took notice of Milton. A. S. P Woodhouse, *The Heavenly Muse* (Toronto: University of Toronto Press, 1972), 167, notes a Socinian publication of 1659 that cites *Of Civil Power in Ecclesiastical Causes* as a supporting authority.

25. Hill, *Milton and the English Revolution*, 285.

26. The young Milton held fairly regular views on the Trinity. In *On the Morning of Christ's Nativity* (1629), the Father sits "midst of trinal unity" (11). And in *Of Reformation* (1641), Milton refers to "one Tripersonal godhead" (YP 1:613–14). Kelley, however, concludes that soon after, between 1645 and 1655, "Milton began his progress toward heterodoxy" (YP 6:22). This coincides with the explosion of Socinian controversy, spearheaded by Biddle, in the 1640s and 1650s. And it prepares Milton for his mature writing.

27. The 1560 Geneva Bible glosses "God is manifested in the flesh" with "he was not onely a man, but God."

28. Later, Stephen Nye, *A Brief History of the Unitarians, Called Also Socinians* (London, 1687), 137–38, also argues that this passage is corrupt; *The Acts of Great Athanasius* (London, 1690), 9. Also see *An Impartial Account of the Word Mystery*, in *Faith of One God*, 9–11.

29. In the same preface Biddle adopts Herbert of Cherbury's vocabulary for the authoritative functioning of reason in religion: "This assertion of Three Persons in God thwarteth the Common Notion that all men have of God." Anyone holding the Athanasian position would "deny the dictate of his reason" (*A Confession of Faith*, E1r). Cherbury, in turn, expresses great respect for the Socinian Johann Crell (*De religione* 54).

30. Klaus Scholder, *The Birth of Modern Critical Theology: Origins and Problems of Biblical Criticism in the Seventeenth Century*, trans. John Bowden (Philadelphia: Trinity Press, 1985), 42–43. Also see Paul Best, *Mysteries Discovered* (London, 1647). This emphasis on reason clearly led Nye, *History of the Unitarians*, to call Grotius "a socinian all over" (31). Douglas Bush, *English Literature in the Earlier Seventeenth Century* (Oxford: Clarendon Press, 1945), comments that "the epithet 'Socinian' was readily flung at anyone who tried to link reason with religion" (321).

31. McLachlan, *Socinianism in Seventeenth-Century England*, 12. As McLachlan points out, the Unitarian Stephen Nye was fond of quoting Chillingworth's motto, "The Bible, the Bible, the Bible only is the religion of the Protestants." See Nye, *History of the Unitarians*, 171, and *Doctor Wallis's Letter Touching the Doctrine of the Blessed Trinity*

Answered by His Friend, in *Faith of One God*, 6. Their liberal Protestant insistence on *sola scriptura* is a primary reason why McLachlan includes the Circle at Great Tew; see McLachlan, 63–89. Cheynell, *The Rise, Growth and Danger of Socinianisme*, 28–35, speaks of Chillingworth at length, arguing against calling him a Socinian. According to George Newton Conklin, *Biblical Criticism and Heresy in Milton* (New York: Octagon, 1972), Socinianism is "less a corpus of doctrine than an attitude toward religious enquiry" (37).

32. Scholder, *Birth of Modern Critical Theology:* "It is an event of extraordinary significance for the history of theology that the Socininan approach was so convincingly supported by scripture at the central point which it attacked, namely the doctrine of the Trinity" (41).

33. 1 John 5:7: "For there are three that bear record in heaven, the Father, the Word, and the Holy Ghost: and these three are one." See Joseph M. Levine, "Erasmus and the Problem of the Johannine Comma," *Journal of the History of Ideas* 58 (1997): 573–96.

34. See McLachlan, *Socinianism in Seventeenth-Century England*, 5, and Scholder, *Birth of Modern Critical Theology*, 41.

35. MacCallum, *Milton and the Sons of God*, finds More taking a stand "in opposition to the kind of rationalism and biblicism represented by the Socinians" (52).

36. Henry More, *Conjectura cabbalistica* (London, 1653), 122.

37. Biddle, *Twofold Catechism:* "They set so high a rate on the sublime indeed, but uncertain notions of the Platonists, and in the mean time slight the plain, but certain letter of the sacred Writers, as being far below the Divine Majesty, and written only to comply with the rude apprehensions of the vulgar, unless by a mystical Interpretation they be scrued up to Platonism" (A8v [mispaginated]).

38. John Crell, *The Two Books of John Crellius Francus, Touching One God the Father* (Kosmoburg, 1665), 248.

39. Also see Biddle's logical analysis in *Twelve Arguments Drawn Out of the Scripture* (London, 1647), 7.

40. Bauman, *Milton's Arianism*, notes: "In contrast to the orthodox or organic conception of the Godhead, Milton's view is rigorously mathematical. That is, while they conceive of the Trinity in light of its natural wholeness and its inherent indivisibility, Milton prefers to formulate his views according to the laws of numerical reason. The orthodox view, he believed, was an affront to monotheism and to the laws of mathematics" (136).

41. Cited in *De doctrina* (YP 6:216). Also see Hill, *Milton and the English Revolution*, 286.

42. Lenn Evan Goodman, *Monotheism: A Philosophical Inquiry into the Foundations of Theology and Ethics* (Totowa, N.J.: Allanheld, Osmun, 1981), 5.

43. Maurice Kelley summarizes the relationship in his introduction to *De doctrina Christiana:* "From Judaism, Christianity inherited an unreserved monotheism.... But also asserted in the New Testament is the divinity of Jesus Christ. He is called God. He performs functions usually reserved to God. And he is the object of prayer. Thus, to avoid the charge of ditheism, Christianity had to formulate a doctrine of God that would harmonize its monotheistic heritage with its new belief in the deity of Christ" (YP 6:48). Freud, expressing a fundamentally Jewish perspective, says that Christianity "was no longer strictly monotheistic; it took over from the surrounding peoples numerous symbolical rites, reestablished the great mother goddess, and found room for many deities of polytheism in an easily recognizable disguise, though in subordinate positions" (*MM* 112).

44. Also in the same volume, see Biddle's *A brief Scripture-Catechism for Children,* 5.

45. John Owen, *Vindiciae evangelicae* (London, 1655), 61–72.

46. Nye, *History of the Unitarians,* 159. According to McLachlan, *Socinianism in Seventeenth-Century England,* 315, Thomas Firmin, who probably edited the compendium of Biddle's writings, *The Faith of One God* (1691), under Nye's influence did not reprint the *Twofold Catechism* because of its anthropomorphism. On the other side of the debate, Edmund Porter's anti-Socinian treatise, *Theos anthropophoros; or, God Incarnate* (London, 1655), spends considerable time dwelling on the same problem of personality and visibility, asserting the mysterious ways in which God is both invisible and visible. Porter dwells particularly on Genesis 18 and accounts for the many appearances of anthropomorphic descriptions in the Bible by claiming that these either are the Son or typological foreshadowings of the Son's Incarnation (book 3, pp. 1–16).

47. Michael Lieb, "Reading God: Milton and the Anthropopathetic Tradition," in *Milton Studies,* vol. 25, ed. James D. Simmonds (Pittsburgh: University of Pittsburgh Press, 1989), 224–25. Also see Lieb, *Theological Milton,* 127–62. See a discussion of anthropopathy and accommodation in chapter 3 above. Biddle also rejects anthropopathy in *A Confession* (D6v).

48. Patrides, *Bright Essence,* asks, "Was Milton aware that in rejecting the triune God of orthodoxy as well as the incommunicable God of Arius, he had in fact espoused three Gods?" (70).

49. Thomas Edwards, *Gangraena* (1646) (Exeter: The Rota and the University of Exeter, 1977), 2:149.

50. Andrew Marvell, *The Rehearsal Transpros'd* (London, 1672), 172; qtd. in McLachlan, *Socinianism in Seventeenth-Century England,* 140.

51. Robert E. Sullivan, *John Toland and the Deist Controversy: A Study in Adaptations* (Cambridge, Mass.: Harvard University Press,

1982), 82–108, illustrates the convergence of Socinianism and deism in great detail. Among many examples, he quotes Robert Jenkin from *The Reasonableness and Certainty of the Christian Religion* (1696), on the Socinians: "and it is but too plain, that there is a combined Design carried on between them and the Deists, who are contented to pass for Christians, with a Distinction, and without a Mystery: *Anti-Trinitarian* is a milder word than *Anti-Christian*, and Unitarian is but a different Name for Deist" (106).

52. Edward Stillingfleet, *Discourse in Vindication of the Doctrine of the Trinity* (London, 1697), xlvii. Stillingfleet names four major points of contact, all of which quite accurately describe how Socinianism and deism must be seen as deeply intertwined. Both groups, he says, seek the lessening of the authority of Scripture; both represent clergy as dissembling practitioners of "Priest Craft"; both object to mysteries of faith and "absurd notions taken up from the Schools"; and both support natural religion (xlviii–l).

53. Ibid., lxii.

54. Ibid., 230–76.

55. Gerard Reedy, "Socinians, John Toland, and the Anglican Rationalists," *Harvard Theological Review* 70 (1977): 285–304, associates this reception with the Socinian controversies issuing from *Faith of One God* and argues that Toland resembles the Socinians both in his aversion to mystery and his rational methods of reading Scripture. Also see Sullivan, *John Toland*, 109–14.

56. Stephen Nye, *The Agreement of the Unitarians with the Catholick Church* (London, 1697), 55; qtd. in Sullivan, *John Toland*, 10.

57. Stephen Nye, *A Discourse Concerning Natural and Revealed Religion* (London, 1696), A2r.

58. John Toland, *Christianity Not Mysterious* (London, 1696), 24; *Impartial Account*, 23.

59. See Sullivan, *John Toland*, 75–79. According to Wilbur, *History of Unitarianism*, "the rationalistic tendencies springing from Locke's philosophy were creating a new atmosphere; and most of all, symptoms of Deism charged to him were beginning to appear and to attract alarmed attention as a more serious danger than Socinianism or Unitarianism" (1:234–35).

60. Toland, *Christianity Not Mysterious*, 24.

61. *Impartial Account*, 19.

62. Toland, *Christianity Not Mysterious*, 25.

63. Richard Baxter, *More Reasons for the Christian Religion* (London, 1672), 79–168. Also see *De religione* 53 and John Anthony Butler's note.

64. For example, Thomas Woolston, *Six Discourses on the Miracles of Our Saviour* (London, 1727–29).

65. Charles Blount, *The First Two Books of Philostratus concerning the Life of Apollonius Tyaneus* (London, 1680), addresses a reader "who would indifferently judge between both (Apollonius and Christ)" (5). In the preface, Blount takes notice of More's comparison as a means of defending himself against the criticism he anticipates (A2v).

66. Charles Blount, *Religio laici* (London, 1683), 69.

67. Blount and Gildon, *The Oracles of Reason*, 89. Also see Spellman, *English Latitudinarians*, 149.

68. William Stephens, *An Account of the Growth of Deism in England* (London, 1696), iv.

69. Scholder, *Birth of Modern Critical Theology*, 43–44.

70. John Locke, *The Reasonableness of Christianity* (London, 1695), 258.

71. Toland, *Christianity Not Mysterious*, 80.

72. On reason and revelation in latitudinarianism and deism, see Spellman, *English Latitudinarians*, 72–88, and Sullivan, *John Toland*, 63–73. Locke also discusses reason and revelation in *An Essay Concerning Human Understanding*, 4.18–19, ed. Peter Nidditch (Oxford: Clarendon Press, 1979), 688–706.

73. Toland, *Christianity Not Mysterious*, 151–52. Similarly, Blount, *Religio laici*, describes how his skepticism toward superstition "brought me at last to be more sparing in the Belief of Miraculous Narrations" (34). For Toland's equivocal position on miracles, see Sullivan, *John Toland*, 127–28.

74. Also see Blount, *Religio laici*, 14, 32; Blount, *Miracles No Violations of the Laws of Nature* (London, 1683) 21; and Toland, *Christianity Not Mysterious*, 38. Thomas Hobbes, *Leviathan*, ed. Michael Oakeshott (Oxford: Basil Blackwell, 1946), is similarly skeptical about the authority of one who witnesses a miracle: "So that though God Almighty can speak to a man by dreams, visions, voice, and inspiration; yet he obliges no man to believe he hath so done to him that pretends it; who, being a man, may err, and, which is more, may lie" (244).

75. For example, see *De veritate* 309–10; Blount, *Religio laici*, 18–32; and Toland, *Christianity Not Mysterious*, 168. Also see J. A. I. Champion, *The Pillars of Priestcraft Shaken* (Cambridge: Cambridge University Press, 1992); James A. Herrick, *The Radical Rhetoric of the English Deists: The Discourse of Skepticism, 1680–1750* (Columbia: University of South Carolina Press, 1997), 32–34.

76. Locke, *Reasonableness*, 55–56. Also see book 2, chapter 10 of Edward Stillingfleet, *Origines sacrae* (London, 1662), 334–59.

77. Hobbes, *Leviathan*, 261.

78. Locke, *Reasonableness*, 257–58.

79. Ibid., 258.

80. Jan Assmann, *Moses the Egyptian: The Memory of Egypt in Western Monotheism* (Cambridge, Mass.: Harvard University Press, 1997): "The agenda of the Moses/Egypt discourse was to deconstruct 'counter-religion' and its implications of intolerance by blurring the basic distinctions as they were symbolized by the antagonistic constellation of Israel and Egypt" (147). In *Moses and Monotheism*, a fascination with Egyptian monotheism is what makes Freud, according to Assmann, "the most outspoken destroyer of the Mosaic distinction" (5).

81. Assmann describes Freud's Aton as congruent with the God of deism: "With this sublime idea of a Supreme Being, we are back to the God of the Enlightenment. This is the God Strabo attributed to Moses, the God of Cudworth and of Schiller, of the Deists, the free-thinkers, and the Freemasons, the God whose gospel forms the subtext of the Moses/Egypt discourse" (ibid., 157).

82. Dennis, *The Grounds of Criticism*, 259.

83. Hill, *Milton and the English Revolution*, 248.

Notes to Chapter 6

1. Francis Cheynell, *The Divine Triunity of the Father, Son and Holy Spirit* (London, 1650), 21–22; qtd. by Kelley (YP 6:273n179). Also see Johan Crell, *The Two Books of John Crellius Francus* (Kosmoburg, 1665), 170.

2. Maurice Kelley, *This Great Argument* (Princeton: Princeton University Press, 1941), 86; Michael Bauman, *Milton's Arianism* (Frankfurt am Main: Verlag Peter Lang, 1986), 262–67.

3. Also see John Biddle, *A Briefe Scripture-catechism for Children*, in *A Twofold Catechism: The One Simply Called a Scripture-catechism; The Other, A Brief Scripture-catechism for Children* (London, 1654), 4; hereafter cited parenthetically in the text. Compare the Athanasian Creed, "The Son is from the Father alone, not made nor created but begotten," quoted by Kelley (YP 6:51).

4. Compare YP 6:209, where Kelley connects the claim that God "stands in not need of propagation" to "No need that thou shouldst propagate." Also see Kelley's discussion in the introduction to *De doctrina* (YP 6:110). Fowler disagrees with Kelley (418n).

5. Augustine, *The City of God against the Pagans*, trans. R. W. Dyson (Cambridge: Cambridge University Press, 1998), 741–43 (book 16, chap. 29); Augustine, *The Trinity*, trans. Stephen McKenna (Washington, D.C.: The Catholic University of America Press, 1970), 76 (book 2, chap. 11); Martin Luther, *Lectures on Genesis*, in *Luther's Works*, ed. Jaroslav Pelikan (St. Louis: Concordia, 1961), 177.

6. John Calvin, *Commentaries on the First Book of Moses Called Genesis*, trans. John King (Edinburgh: The Calvin Translation Society, 1847), 1:472. Also see David Pareus, *In genesin Mosis commentarius* (Geneva, 1614), 1239–40, who names Socinus as an opponent in his commentary on Genesis, argues against rabbinical skepticism toward the Trinitarian reading, and insists that the Son and two angels visit Abraham.

7. Johan Crell, *The Expiation of a Sinner*, trans. Thomas Lushington (London, 1646), 330. John Biddle, *The Testimonies of Irenaus* (London, 1653), 27–39, translates and comments on selections from the early church fathers that undermine Trinitarian claims. The excerpts from Justin Martyr, *Dialogue with Trypho* deal extensively with Mamre and the identity of the visitors.

8. Daniel Defoe, *The Political History of the Devil* (London, 1726), 69.

9. Also see John Biddle, *A Confession of Faith Touching the Holy Trinity, According to the Scripture* (London, 1648), 42–43; hereafter cited parenthetically in the text. The Antitrinitarian debate over whether the Son provides satisfaction for human sins similarly revolves around the Resurrection. Socinians find an enormous difference between the Son before the Resurrection, when he is a mere man, and the Son after his ascent to heaven, when he has a far more divine function in interceding for human sin. Biddle says that satisfaction is not to be found in the event of Christ's death, but in his intercession after the Resurrection: "neither did Christ offer his sacrifice for our sins upon the Cross, but when after his Resurrection, being clothed with Robes of Glory and Immortality, he entered into Heaven, the true Sanctuary, and presented himself to God" (38). On satisfaction and Socinians, see Hugh MacCallum, *Milton and the Sons of God: The Divine Image in Milton's Epic Poetry* (Toronto: University of Toronto Press, 1986), 54–55.

10. See, for example, Biddle, *A Scripture-catechism*, 30; Biddle, *Confession of Faith*, 2; Crell, *Two Books*, 272–78. For Arians, according to Bauman, *Milton's Arianism*, "There was an unbridgeable chasm which stood between a being who is begotten and the one who is not—a chasm so great as to preclude any communication of either attribute to the one who was without it. If a line were drawn between the creator God and the created world, the Son would need to be aligned on the side of the creatures" (41).

11. Acts 13:33 reads, "God hath fulfilled the same unto us their children, in that he hath raised up Jesus again; as it is also written in the second psalm, Thou art my Son, this day have I begotten thee." Also regularly cited is Hebrews 5:5, which quotes Psalm 2:7 and interprets it as the moment when the Son was exalted as "high priest." For example, see Biddle, *Scripture-catechism*, 63, 30, and Crell, *Two Books*, 134, 152.

12. Kelley, *This Great Argument*, 94–101.

13. William Hunter, "The War in Heaven: The Exaltation of the Son," in *Bright Essence: Studies in Milton's Theology*, ed. W. B. Hunter, C. A. Patrides, and J. H. Adamson (Salt Lake City: University of Utah Press, 1971), 124.

14. This pattern of distinguishing his Christology from both orthodoxy and Socinianism continues in Milton's treatment of Christ's satisfaction: "Those who maintain that Christ sought death not in our place and for the sake of redemption, but only for our good and in order to set an example, try in vain to evade the evidence of these texts. Moreover I confess that I cannot see how those who hold that the Son is of the same essence as the Father manage to explain either his incarnation or his satisfaction" (YP 6:444).

15. Kelley, *This Great Argument*, 100.

16. Ibid., 105.

17. Hunter, "The War in Heaven," 118. Although, as Bauman, *Milton's Arianism*, 260, points out, Milton had associated the begetting with rebellion in his translation of Psalm 2, made in 1653. To the second psalm Milton adds the parenthetical statement:

> but I saith he
> Anointed have my king (though ye rebel)
> On Sion my holy hill. A firm decree
> I will declare; the Lord to me hath said
> Thou art my Son I have begotten thee
> This day.   (11–16)

18. Kelley, *This Great Argument*, 105; MacCallum, *Milton and the Sons of God*, 79.

19. Defoe, *Political History*, 74.

20. Ibid., 74; Irene Samuel, "The Dialogue in Heaven: A Reconsideration of *Paradise Lost*, III, 1–417," in *Milton: Modern Essays in Criticism*, ed. Arthur E. Barker (Oxford: Oxford University Press, 1965), 242; William Empson, *Milton's God*, rev. ed. (London: Chatto & Windus, 1965), 278. Hunter, "The War in Heaven," however, argues that Milton's "artistry was handmaiden to his theology, not the other way around" (117).

21. In a typically monotheistic negotiation just before the expedition, Raphael inserts another disclaimer for his accommodated language, explaining the exact problem of narrating God's creation: "Immediate are the acts of God, more swift / Than time or motion, but to human ears / Cannot without process of speech be told, / So told as earthly notion can receive" (*PL* 7.176–79).

22. For example, *Paradise Lost* 7.243, 249, 261, 263, 282, 304, 331, 336, 337, 345, 352, 387, 391, 450, 515, with the exception of "the almighty" (7.339) and "the spirit of God" (7.235).

23. C. A. Patrides, "Milton on the Trinity: The Use of Antecedents," in Hunter, Patrides, and Adamson, *Bright Essence*, 12.

24. Calvin, *Commentaries*, 1:92. On *elohim*, see my introduction.

25. So while MacCallum, *Milton and the Sons of God*, initially registers shock at the disjunction between Son and God, he ultimately sees "a seamless continuity, so that one figure dissolves insensibly into another" (97). MacCallum first says, "one might almost be tempted to argue that this middle section represents a different stage of composition, and that the change of manner marks the joints" (93). This sounds remarkably like modern biblical criticism, which often recognizes narrative discontinuities in the Bible as stemming from different sources. *Paradise Lost* does indeed resemble biblical narrative in its visible suppression of "joints." So, I will argue below, does *Paradise Regained*.

26. Hebrews 1:3 reads, "Who being the brightness of his glory, and the express image of his person, and upholding all things by the word of his power, when he had by himself purged our sins, sat down on the right hand of the Majesty on high." Crell, *Two Books*, argues: "no Image is of the same Essence in number with that whereof it is the Image, otherwise it would be the Image of itself. Wherefore since Christ is the Image of God, he cannot be the same Substance in number with God, and consequently not be God, namely, the most high God" (139). Also see Crell, *Expiation of a Sinner*, 3; Biddle, *Confession of Faith*, 39; and *Racovian* 63. Milton makes the same Antitrinitarian argument in *De doctrina* (YP 6:211–12).

27. On the Son's visibility, also see "Effulgence of my glory, Son beloved, / Son in whose face invisible is beheld / Visibly, what by deity I am" (*PL* 6.680–82). Adam is made "in the image of God / Express," (*PL* 7.527–28). Because Milton's Antitrinitarian Son is created, he is an image and an expression similar to Adam. Also see *PL* 11.354, which seems to refer to the Son. Raphael is explicit about visible bodies in his defense of his accommodated language: "what surmounts the reach / Of human sense, I shall delineate so, / By likening spiritual to corporal forms, / As may express them best" (*PL* 5.571–74).

28. *Milton: The Critical Heritage*, ed. John T. Shawcross (London: Routledge and Kegan Paul, 1970), 104, 146.

29. Alan Fisher, "Why Is *Paradise Regained* So Cold?" in *Milton Studies*, vol. 14, ed. James D. Simmonds (Pittsburgh: University of Pittsburgh Press, 1980), 195–217; Stanley Fish, "Things and Actions Indifferent: The Temptation of Plot in *Paradise Regained*," in *Milton Studies*, vol. 17, *Composite Orders: The Genres of Milton's Last Poems*, ed. Richard Ide and Joseph Wittreich (Pittsburgh: University of Pittsburgh Press, 1983), 163–85. Fish's article is hereafter cited parenthetically in the text.

30. Don Cameron Allen, *Harmonious Vision: Studies in Milton's Poetry* (Baltimore: The Johns Hopkins Press, 1970), writes, "We do well

to forget the existence of *Paradise Lost*, for if we remember the Christ of Book Three, we are unlikely to see the temptation as anything more than a formalized set piece. We must, consequently, think of the 'exalted man' as forgetful of his divinity" (117).

31. René Girard, *Job, the Victim of His People* (Palo Alto: Stanford University Press, 1987). See also Horace Meyer Kallan, *The Book of Job as a Greek Tragedy* (New York: Moffat, Yard, 1918).

32. John Rogers, "Family Heresies in *Paradise Regained*" (paper presented at MLA convention, Chicago, December 27, 1999). MacCallum, *Milton and the Sons of God*, emphasizes the poem's appeal to the Socinian position:

> For almost the entire poem, the divinity of the Son is connected not with his previous existence as the only-begotten in heaven, but with his generation by the Father from the seed of the woman. Indeed, what is remarkable about the Father's first speech in heaven (1.130–67), as well as the angel song which immediately follows it, is the absence of reference to the Son's pre-existence. This introduction might appeal to a Socinian who held that the Son of God first came into existence at the Nativity. (239)

33. Barbara K. Lewalski, *Milton's Brief Epic: The Genre, Meaning, and Art of* Paradise Regained (Providence: Brown University Press, 1966), 133; hereafter cited parenthetically in the text. For an argument against the identity motif as crux, see Regina Schwartz, "Redemption and Paradise Regained," in *Milton Studies*, vol. 42, Paradise Regained *in Context: Genre, Politics, Religion*, guest ed. David Loewenstein (Pittsburgh: University of Pittsburgh Press, 2002), 26–49.

34. D. C. Allen, *Harmonious Vision*, for example, argues that Satan "pretends to doubt who Christ is in order to establish a mood of self-distrust in the mind of the 'exalted man'" (111).

35. MacCallum, *Milton and the Sons of God*, argues that "His final speech of self-justification and analysis (4.500–540) is extraordinarily interesting, and we do Satan an injustice to think of it as a mere rhetorical strategy. Satan is meditating aloud, and the history of his preoccupation with Jesus displays a parallel with the soliloquy in which Jesus first meditates on his life" (254).

36. Christopher Hill, *Milton and the English Revolution* (New York: Penguin Books, 1979), 416.

37. Ibid., 422; MacCallum, *Milton and the Sons of God*, 242.

38. Allen, *Harmonious Vision*, 118.

39. Ibid., 159. Also see Crell, *Expiation of a Sinner*, 6; Biddle, *A Scripture-catechism*, 30, 60; *Confession of Faith*, 43.

40. On orthodox conceptions of mediation, see MacCallum, *Milton and the Sons of God*, 32–39, who shows that in his "uncompromising

monotheism," Milton's assertion that the mediatorial office is possible without a Trinitarian sharing of essence departs from Calvin and standard Protestant theology. Milton's arguments against mediation coexisting with the Trinity are identifiably Socinian; compare Crell, *Two Books,* 31, 130; Biddle, *Confession of Faith,* 19–21; *Racovian* 27.

41. See Crell, *Two Books,* 74–79, and Stephen Nye, *A Brief History of the Unitarians, Called Also Socinians,* in *Faith in One God* (London, 1691), 5.

42. Milton further discusses *theanthropos* in *De doctrina,* YP 6:427, 438–43. Also see John Rumrich, "Milton's Theanthropos: The Body of Christ in *Paradise Regained,*" in *Milton Studies,* vol. 42, Paradise Regained *in Context: Genre, Politics, Religion,* guest ed. David Loewenstein (Pittsburgh: University of Pittsburgh Press, 2002), 50–67.

43. Allen, *Harmonious Vision,* develops this sense of fractured subjectivity at length. But he argues for a conclusion on the pinnacle in which the Son ceases his fluctuation between God and man, in which "the full concept of God-in-man is rounded out" (121). The fractured subject eventually, and redemptively, becomes, in E. M. Forster's terminology, a rounded character. Leaving behind the partiality of an allegorical figure, the Son is said to gain a depth that is described by a vocabulary normally applied to the novel.

44. Fish, "Things and Actions Indifferent," aligns his indifferent narrative with a general Protestant emphasis on inward spirituality over external event, but things indifferent, or *adiaphora,* more specifically mark what is neither positively commanded nor forbidden by Scripture. Fish acknowledges the theological version, quoting from William Bradshaw, *A Treatise of the Nature and Use of Things Indifferent* (London, 1605), and Francis Mason, *The Authoritie of the Church in making Canons and Constitutions concerning things Indifferent* (London, 1607). Nearer to Milton is Lord Brooke, *A Discourse Opening the Nature of That Episcopacie, Which is Exercised in England* (London, 1641). Nearer to the writing of *Paradise Regained* is Edward Stillingfleet, *Irenicum: A Salve for the Churches Wounds* (London, 1661). Milton describes *adiaphora* in *Areopagitica:* "What else is all that rank of things indifferent, wherein Truth may be on this side, or on the other, without being unlike her self" (YP 2:563). On indifference and Milton's conception of Christian liberty, see Arthur Barker, *Milton and the Puritan Dilemma, 1641–1660* (Toronto: University of Toronto Press, 1942), 93–112.

45. So in *The Grounds of Criticism* Dennis says that Milton happened upon a proper use of religion in *Paradise Lost* because he uses machinery, but "he has err'd very widely from it in his *Paradise Regain'd.*" See Dennis 1:369.

46. Hill, *Milton and the English Revolution,* 286.

47. E. M. W. Tillyard and Maurice Kelley disagree over the issue of miracles in Maurice Kelley, "Milton and Miracles," *Modern Language Notes* 53 (1938): 170–72. Joseph Frank, "Milton's Movement toward Deism," *Journal of British Studies* 1 (1961), argues that Milton's "discomfort when he has to describe miracles rather than morality, when, if only briefly, his poem has become supernatural, seems obvious" (48).

48. Hill, *Milton and the English Revolution*, 422n5.

49. Irene Samuel, "The Regaining of Paradise," in *The Prison and the Pinnacle*, ed. Balachandra Rajan (Toronto: University of Toronto Press, 1973), 118, answers her question: "Something, I surmise, like what he said to the multipliers of Biblical mysteries: 'no inferences from the text are to be admitted but such as follow necessarily and plainly from the words themselves'" (119).

50. Samuel, ibid., 115, shows that "Tempt not the Lord thy God" refers to Deuteronomy 6:6, which in turn refers to Exodus 17, where the Israelites request miracles from God. The temptation on the pinnacle is a temptation to perform miraculous action.

51. H. John McLachlan, *Socinianism in Seventeenth-Century England* (Oxford: Oxford University Press, 1951), 9.

52. This account is largely taken from Kelley's introduction to *De doctrina* (YP 6:53–68).

53. Charles D. O'Malley, introduction to Jacobus Acontius, *Satanae strategamata*, trans. Charles D. O'Malley (San Francisco: Sutro Branch, California State Library Occasional Papers, 1940), xi–xvi.

54. McLachlan, *Socinianism*, 57–58. An Italian exile, Aconcio wrote *Satanae strategamata* in England and, according to W. K. Jordan, *The Development of Religious Toleration in England* (Cambridge, Mass.: Harvard University Press, 1932), is "the first man in England to enunciate a systematic and philosophical defense of religious toleration" (303). Also see William Haller, *The Rise of Puritanism* (New York: Columbia University Press, 1938), 195–99.

55. Acontius, *Satanae strategamata*, 27. For a similar plea for toleration, see Crell's letter to the reader in *Two Books*.

56. William Chillingworth, *The Religion of the Protestants: A Safe Way to Salvation* (London, 1638), arguing for a basic creed against "Deifying our own Interpretations, and Tyrannous inforcing them upon others," declares he has learned this position from Book Seven of Acontius (198).

57. Acontius, *Satanae strategamata:* "In my judgement it would be better to draw up one watchword of the faith in precise terms and to do away with all other confession of faith. For undoubtedly such an accord of the churches would allay much talk among men, and remove many great stumbling-blocks, which retard the progress of the Gospel to a remarkable extent" (197). In a similar vein, Biddle says on the title page

to *A Twofold Catechism* that it is "Composed for their sakes that would fain be meer Christians, and not of this or that sect, inasmuch as all the sects of Christians, by what names soever distinguised, have either moer or less departed from the simplicity and truth of the Scripture."

58. Acontius, *Satanae strategamata*, 201–02. Also see the critical edition, *Jacobi Acontii Satanae strategamatum libri octo*, ed. Gualtherus Koehler (London: David Nutt, 1927), 182n.

59. M. D. H., "The Nonconformist No. xxi," *The Monthly Repository of Theology and General Literature* 16 (1821): 458.

60. Acontius, *Satanae strategamata*, 186. Similarly, John Goodwin writes in the letter "To the Reader" in his translation of Acontius, *Satan's Stratagems; or, The Devil's Cabinet-Council Discovered* (London, 1648), "Among the many strains of that unreasonableness in men, which renders the days we live in so calamitous and sad, there is scarce any more deplorable or comporting with our misery, then for men to have their mouths wide open in declaiming against what they are pleased to call errors and heresies."

61. Acontius, *Satanae strategamata*, 29.

62. Ibid., 11.

Notes to Chapter 7

1. "Nowadays the external authority of our faith, in other words, the scriptures, is of very considerable importance, and generally speaking, it is the authority of which we first have experience. The pre-eminent and supreme authority, however, is the authority of the Spirit, which is internal, and the individual possession of each man" (YP 6:587). This passage suggests that the Spirit is even capable at times of superseding the Bible. However, in *A Treatise of Civil Power* Milton draws limits to the Spirit's authority by stressing how often it is unavailable, and how it is incommunicable from one person to another: Divine illumination, "no man can know at all times to be in himself, much less to be at any time for certain in any other" (YP 7:242).

2. Joseph Wittreich, *Interpreting Samson Agonistes* (Princeton: Princeton University Press, 1986), 136–38.

3. Geoffrey Nuttall, *Holy Spirit in Puritan Faith and Experience* (Oxford: Basil Blackwell, 1947), 34. In the classroom, *Samson Agonistes* can be interestingly read next to John Locke's "Of Enthusiasm," *An Essay on Human Understanding*, book 4, chap. 19.

4. Christian exegesis investigates, and exacerbates, the problem of ontological calculation. The Geneva Bible glosses "man" in Judges 13:11 with: "He calleth him man, because he so seemed, but he was Christ the eternal word."

5. Although monotheistic ambiguity does continue in the Hebrew vocabulary. In Judges 13:21 the narrator tells us that Manoa knew he was seeing an angel (*malach*). But in 13:22 Manoa fears for his life "because we have seen God" (*elohim*). Manoa's wife reassures him, but the language resists ontological certainty. Milton lists Judges 13:21–22 in *De doctrina* as his first example of the complexity of *elohim* (YP 6:234). Francis Quarles, *The Historie of Samson* (London, 1631), captures the skeptical dynamics of Judges 13.

6. John M. Steadman, "Faithful Champion: The Theological Basis of Milton's Hero of Faith," *Anglia* 77 (1959):

> Dr. Johnson's observation is not altogether unjust, for Milton has patently substituted the development of character for that of the plot of fable.... According to the Protestant conception of the relation of faith to works, the spiritual regeneration of the inward man, rather than a concatenation of external events, was the really significant factor in heroic activity. The true causes of good works were to be found in a pattern of internal events—a spiritual "plot"—rather than in a sequence of causes entirely outside the mind and will of the agent. (27–28)

For readings of the inward plot, also see Anthony Low, *The Blaze of Noon: A Reading of* Samson Agonistes (New York: Columbia University Press, 1974), and Mary Ann Radzinowicz, *Toward* Samson Agonistes: *The Growth of Milton's Mind* (Princeton: Princeton University Press, 1978).

7. For a survey of critical responses to the rousing motions, see Derek N. C. Wood, *"Exiled from Light": Divine Law, Morality, and Violence in Milton's* Samson Agonistes (Toronto: University of Toronto Press, 2001), 129–39. For a recent discussion of what "rousing motions" are, see Richard DuRocher, "Samson's 'Rousing Motions': What They Are, How They Work, and Why They Matter," *Literature Compass* 3 (2006): 453–69; available at http://www.blackwell-compass.com.

8. Stanley Fish, "Question and Answer in *Samson Agonistes*," *Critical Quarterly* 9 (1969): 237–64, and "Spectacle and Evidence in *Samson Agonistes*," *Critical Inquiry* 15 (1989): 556–86.

9. Mario Rossi, *La vita, le opere, i tempi di Edoardo Herbert Di Chirbury* (Florence: G. C. Sansoni, 1947), 1:582; qtd. in Eugene Hill, *Edward, Lord Herbert of Cherbury* (Boston: Twayne, 1987), 29. As Hill describes the relationship between the common notions and Cherbury's radical theological agenda, "Overt epistemology or psychology is, in fact, covert religious polemic" (28).

10. Nathaniel Culverwell, *Discourse of the Light of Nature* (London, 1652), 4, makes direct reference to Cherbury's common notions. Henry More, *Antidote against Atheism*, in *A Collection of Several Philosophi-*

cal Writings (London, 1712), follows Cherbury's insistence that the soul of man is not "abrasa tabula," but rather has "innate ideas" (17).

11. Richard Baxter, *More Reasons for the Christian Religion* (London, 1672); Charles Blount, "Epistle Dedicatory," *Religio laici: Written in a Letter to John Dryden, Esq.* (London, 1683).

12. See John Locke, *An Essay Concerning Human Understanding*, book 1, chap. 3, sec. 15–19, where Locke, who usually does not cite other writers, argues at length against Cherbury's *De veritate* and the Common Notions.

13. Jason Rosenblatt, *Torah and Law in* Paradise Lost (Princeton: Princeton University Press, 1994), 71–137.

14. Rossi, *La vita*, 236–37.

15. David Masson, *The Life of John Milton* (Gloucester, Mass.: Peter Smith, 1965), 3:68.

16. Edward, Lord Herbert of Cherbury, *The Autobiography of Edward, Lord Herbert of Cherbury*, ed. Sidney Lee (London: Routledge, 1906), 133–34. Both Cherbury and Milton are echoing Paul's experience on the road to Damascus (Acts 9:3–6).

17. Sidney Lee, ibid., remarks, "This testimony to a special divine revelation strangely contrasts with the advanced views that Lord Herbert elsewhere advocates respecting the subject of Revelation" (134n1). This episode has been used to show that Cherbury should not be called a deist, although the humor in it, once recognized, feels very much in keeping with deist raillery.

18. "The true Catholic Church is not supported on the inextricable confusion of oral and written tradition to which men have given their allegiance. Still less is it that which fights beneath any one particular standard, or is comprised in one organisation so as to embrace only a restricted portion of the earth, or a single period of history. The only catholic and uniform church is the doctrine of Common Notions which comprehends all places and all men" (*De veritate* 303).

19. "The rousing motions are usually taken to be the sign of God's intervention.... But while this is surely true on a higher level of generality (it could hardly be otherwise) the reader who remembers the history of Samson's 'rousing motions' may be wary of labelling these new motions 'of God'" (Fish, "Question and Answer," 255). On the extensive debate over regenerationist readings of *Samson Agonistes*, see Alan Rudrum, "Milton Scholarship and the Agon over *Samson Agonistes*," *Huntington Library Quarterly* 65 (2002): 465–88.

20. An impulse could be a "Force or influence exerted on the mind by some external stimulus...a strong suggestion supposed to come from a good or evil spirit," or it could be an "Incitement or stimulus to action arising from some state of mind or feeling." See "Impulse," *Oxford English Dictionary*, 2nd ed. (1989).

21. John Guillory, "The Father's House: *Samson Agonistes* in Its Historical Moment," in *John Milton*, ed. Annabel Patterson (New York: Longman, 1992), 214.

22. "Discursive thought is superfluous when a Common Notion is at hand or when the inner or outer forms of experience are the judges of events" (*De veritate* 232).

23. Eric J. Sharpe, *Comparative Religion: A History* (London: Duckworth, 1975), 17.

24. Jan Assmann, *Moses the Egyptian: The Memory of Egypt in Western Monotheism* (Cambridge, Mass.: Harvard University Press, 1997), 7.

25. Ibid., 3.

26. Ibid., 1.

27. Sharon Achinstein, "Samson Agonistes and the Politics of Memory," in *Altering Eyes: New Perspectives on Samson Agonistes*, ed. Mark R. Kelley and Joseph Wittreich (Newark: University of Delaware Press, 2002), argues that

> It is the trick of his genius that Dalila's bid for feminist heroism is consistent and plausible; indeed, he summons the fights for women's public voice in the seventeenth century that were fought over the very biblical example of Jael. There is nothing in the text itself that could adjudicate these two versions of history: the only clear difference in the two stories is not in their exposition, but in the knowledge of on whose behalf the true God is working, not in epistemology, but in ethics. (175)

28. Assmann, *Moses the Egyptian*, 55.

29. See Fish, "Question and Answer": "For his purpose is not to deny the reality of a just and benevolent God, but to suggest that we cannot infer his benevolence or validate his justice from the known facts" (263).

30. Samuel Johnson, *Rambler* 139, in *Johnson as Critic*, ed. John Wain (London: Routledge & Kegan Paul, 1973), 116. According to John Rumrich, "Samson and the Excluded Middle," in Kelley and Wittreich, *Altering Eyes*, "the middle is the category of dramatic analysis that would seem to align best with the project of theodicy: it is in the indeterminate transition from beginning to end that the ways of a God of history manifest themselves" (315).

31. Joost van den Vondel, *Samson or Holy Revenge*, trans. Watson Kirkconnel, in *That Invincible Samson: The Theme of* Samson Agonistes *in World Literature with Translations of the Major Analogues* (Toronto: University of Toronto Press, 1964), 120, 141.

Notes to Afterword

1. Samuel Monk, *The Sublime in Sixteenth Century England* (New York: Modern Language Association, 1935), 45–52, considers Dennis to be an important innovator of the sublime because he adds the psychological dimension of terror to the earlier neoclassical sense of mere elevation.

2. David B. Morris, *The Religious Sublime: Christian Poetry and Critical Tradition in Eighteenth-Century England* (Lexington: University Press of Kentucky, 1972), 71; Edmund Burke, *A Philosophical Enquiry into the Origin of Our Ideas of the Sublime and Beautiful*, ed. J. T. Boulton (London: Routledge and Kegan Paul, 1958), 63.

3. Monk, *The Sublime*, 7.

4. Burke, *Philosophical Enquiry*, 62.

5. Aryeh Botwinick, *Skepticism, Belief, and the Modern: Maimonides to Nietzsche* (Ithaca, N.Y.: Cornell University Press, 1997), 53, 22.

6. Immanuel Kant, *Critique of Judgment*, trans. Werner S. Pluhar (Indianapolis: Hackett, 1987), 114, 116, 135.

7. Longinus, *On the Sublime*, trans. W. Rhys Roberts (Cambridge: Cambridge University Press, 1899), 65 (sec. 9). Morris, *Religious Sublime*, 37, describes how Boileau's celebration of the *fiat lux* in the preface to his translation of Longinus helped to make it a touchstone of the eighteenth century sublime. A. F. B. Clark, *Boileau and the French Classical Critics in England (1660–1830)* (New York: Russell & Russell, 1965), concludes that the controversy surrounding Boileau's use of the *fiat lux* "had forced upon Englishmen the view that 'the sublime' means the grandest thought expressed in the simplest language" (379).

8. Burke, *Philosophical Enquiry*, 59.

9. Ibid., 59.

10. Henry Reynolds, *Mythomystes* (London, 1632), in *Critical Essays of the Seventeenth Century*, ed. J. E. Springarn (Oxford: Oxford University Press, 1908), 1:147.

11. Edmund Spenser, *The Faerie Queene: Book Five*, ed. Abraham Stoll (Indianapolis: Hackett, 2006), 5.7.2.1–2. Spenser also adds a reminder of his allegorical method, which enables the inclusion of gods: worshippers of Osyris, and Spenser too, are "With fayned colours shading a true case" (5.7.2.7).

12. Gordon Teskey, *Allegory and Violence* (Ithaca, N.Y.: Cornell University Press, 1996), 55. On Duessa's journey to the underworld, see 53–55. Elsewhere, Teskey says that in Spenser "The power of a decaying polytheism, even as it gave impetus to narrative, was exploited to lend a certain numinous terror to static allegorical figures." But these figures

were still "clearly subordinate to a higher, more comprehensive power," that is, to the Christian God (38).

13. Edmund Spenser, *The Faerie Queene: Book Six, and the Mutabilitie Cantos*, ed. Andrew Hadfield and Abraham Stoll (Indianapolis: Hackett, 2007), 7.8.2.8–9.

14. Michael Murrin, *The Allegorical Epic: Essays in Its Rise and Decline* (Chicago: University of Chicago Press, 1980), suggests that "Linguistically, iconoclasm cut Milton off from the traditional language of analogy. An older poet could have represented heaven through allegory, a method rarely used in *Paradise Lost*" (169). Catherine Gimelli Martin's *The Ruins of Allegory:* Paradise Lost *and the Metamorphosis of Epic Convention* (Raleigh, N.C.: Duke University Press, 1998), argues for a baroque and ruined allegory in *Paradise Lost*, which has numerous points of contact with this reading of allegory and monotheistic narrative.

15. Edmund Spenser, *The Faerie Queene: Book One*, ed. Carol Kaske (Indianapolis: Hackett, 2006), 1.1.14.9, 1.1.16.3.

16. Ibid., 1.1.18.9–10.

17. Victoria Kahn, "Allegory and the Sublime in *Paradise Lost*," in *John Milton*, ed. Annabel Patterson (New York: Longman, 1992), 185–98.

18. Steven Knapp, *Personification and the Sublime: Milton to Coleridge* (Cambridge, Mass.: Harvard University Press, 1985): "With its individuality utterly absorbed by the ideal it embodies, the personification is the perfect fanatic" (83). Also see James Noggle, *The Skeptical Sublime: Aesthetic Ideology in Pope and the Tory Satirists* (Oxford: Oxford University Press, 2001).

Index

Abraham, 15
abstract godhead: Bolingbroke and, 205; criticisms of, 91–93; Hobbes and, 337n16; monotheism and, 11–15, 74, 100, 102, 107, 141, 278–79; rational religion and, 91–93, 110; representation and, 13–14, 85, 96, 107, 125, 141. *See also* aniconism
accommodation, doctrine of, 125–31, 138, 141, 337n20, 340n46
Acontius, Giacomo, 186, 256–58, 261–63, 360n56, 360n57
Acts 13:33, 222, 355n11
Adam, in *Paradise Lost*, 132–42, 196, 229
Adamson, J. H., 188, 340n46
Addison, Joseph, 156, 158–59, 177, 181, 309
Ainsworth, Henry, 340n39
Albright, William Foxwell, 331n15
allegory, 38, 170, 314–19, 366n14
Allen, D. C., 76, 232, 238, 358n34, 359n43
Alter, Robert, 14–15, 322n20
angels: Christian poetry likened to, 175; in *De doctrina Christiana*, 339n36; deist rejection of, 208–09; eating of food by, 115–16, 118, 120; in Genesis 18, 106–07, 115–17, 121–23; gods vs., 3–4, 29–31, 71, 325n3; in Hebrew Bible, 208, 340n42; in Judges 13, 267–72; as machinery, 170; materiality of, 117–21; mystery and, 96; narrative and, 117–18; in *Paradise Lost*, 115–24, 144–68; in *Samson Agonistes*, 267–72; subjectivity of, 120; in van den Vondel's *Samson*, 307

aniconism: Davenant and, 51; deism and, 9–10, 213; Freud on abstraction of deity, 11–12; Milton and, 308; monotheism and, 9–10, 12–14, 57, 308; second commandment and, 9, 13, 16, 40, 49, 51, 84, 100, 171, 312; and the sublime, 312
animal life, 89–90
An Impartial Account of the Word Mystery, 202
anthropomorphism, 192, 197, 351n46
anthropopathy, 126–27, 129, 198
anticlericalism, 81, 277, 333n26, 333n28, 344n36
Antitrinitarianism: latitudinarians and, 346n3; mathematics and, 192–93; Milton's, 4, 188–90, 193–96, 216–18, 222–23, 226, 228, 230, 246, 258, 260–61, 324n33, 349n26, 350n40, 351n48; monotheism and, 187–88, 196; origins of, 256; *Paradise Lost* and, 112; *Paradise Regained* and, 22; rational religion and, 190–91, 199–200; Reformation and, 347n13; *Samson Agonistes* and, 22; scriptural interpretation and, 191, 350n32; Socinianism and, 8–9, 184–99, 257–58, 350n32; and the Son, 198–99, 219–20, 222, 240–41, 244; and toleration, 257–58, 260–61. *See also* Trinity
Apollonius Tyaneus, 203
Areopagitica (Milton), 33, 108, 163, 258, 359n44
Arianism, 162, 186, 188, 203, 217, 222, 226, 355n10
Aristotle, 267
Arminianism, 108
Assmann, Jan, 17, 19–21, 28, 66, 68, 188, 198, 295–96, 299–301, 306,

367

322n16, 323n28, 354n81; *Moses the Egyptian*, 212, 354n80
Athanasian Creed, 193–94, 354n3
Athanasianism, 191–94
atheism, 87, 93, 293
atomic science, 119–20
Aton, 11–14, 21, 97–98, 102, 196, 212–13, 324n32, 354n81
Auerbach, Erich, 14–15, 71, 117
Augustine, Saint, 217
Austin, Samuel, 40

Babington, Gervase, 116
Bacchae (Euripides), 270
Bailey, Nathan, 321n8
Barrow, Samuel, 156
Bauman, Michael, 189, 217, 348n22, 350n40
Baxter, Richard, 203, 276–77
Beardslee, John W., III, 321n11
Beelzebub, 58
Bennett, Joan, 334n45
Bentley, Richard, 163, 166–67
Berkowitz, David Sandler, 43
Best, Paul, 199
Bible, literal interpretation of, 127, 191–92, 205, 257, 259–60, 343n21, 347n13, 349n31, 350n32
Biddle, John, 186–87, 191–93, 195, 197–98, 200–201, 220, 257, 258, 261, 350n37; *A Confession of Faith Touching the Holy Trinity*, 186, 187, 355n9; *The Faith of One God*, 200–201, 351n46; *The Testimonies of Irenaus*, 355n7; *A Twofold Catechism*, 186, 192, 197–98, 351n46, 360n57
Blackmore, Richard, 172
Blount, Charles, 9, 163, 203; *Anima mundi*, 201; *Oracles of Reason*, 185, 201, 204; *Religio laici*, 81, 201, 204, 277, 353n73
Boileau, Nicolas, 55–56, 169, 171–73, 312, 365n7
Bolingbroke, Henry St. John, Lord, 78, 86, 159–60, 164, 180, 182, 204–05, 207–13, 343n17; "Farther Reflections on the Rise and Progress of Monotheism," 6–7, 183
Botwinick, Aryeh, 13, 22–23, 85, 139–41, 311, 324n35
Breasted, James Henry, 98
Broadbent, J. B., 64, 69, 102, 114, 163
Brown, George Spencer, 19

Brute, 42
Bryson, Michael, 338n24
Budick, Sanford, 322n15
Burden, Dennis, 338n24
Burke, Edmund, 310–14, 319
Bush, Douglas, 32, 101–02, 105
Butler, John Anthony, 81

Calvin, John, 79, 111, 116, 122, 126, 140, 228, 256, 337n17, 337n18, 338n26, 341n54
Cambridge Platonists, 88, 276, 346n5
Camden, William, 42
Campbell, Gordon, 323n29
Campbell, Lily, 40
Cartari, Vincenzo, 329n50
Castellio, Sebastien, 256
Catechesis ecclesiarum quae in Regno Poloniae, 186, 189
Catholicism, 51, 75, 83, 259–61, 333n28
Certain Verses Written by Several of the Author's Friends; to Be Reprinted with the Second Edition of Gondibert, 56–57
Champion, J. A. I., 81
Charles II, King of England, 99
Chatman, Seymour, 34
Cherbury, Edward, Lord Herbert of, 7, 77–86, 88–89, 110, 201, 203–04, 207, 208, 210, 253, 275–87, 294–95, 297, 301, 362n9, 362n10, 363n12; *De religione gentilium*, 74, 77, 79, 81, 83, 88, 277, 294–95, 297; *De veritate*, 83, 85–86, 88, 203, 275–87, 294, 333n35, 363n12
Cheynell, Francis, 187, 216, 350n31
chiasmus, 133
Chillingworth, William, 110, 257, 350n31, 360n56
Christ: and accommodation, 337n20; Antitrinitarianism and, 198–99, 219–20, 222, 240–41, 244; Apollonius Tyaneus and, 203–04; begetting of, 220–26; and Creation, 220, 227–29; in *De doctrina Christiana*, 193, 196, 221–27, 229, 239–45, 256; deism and, 203–04; divinity of, 192, 239–48; as expression of God, 230; human capacity to understand, 234–38, 245, 256, 262–63; manifestation of, 151; as mediator, 240–45, 248, 358n40; Milton's conception of, 199;

miracles of, 208, 209; monotheism and, 199, 204; and narrative, 112, 226–27, 231–32; ontology of, 219, 228–56, 263; in *Paradise Lost*, 112, 199, 221–31; in *Paradise Regained*, 199, 231–56; preincarnate, 220, 222–27, 229–33; and Resurrection, 220, 355n9; and satisfaction, 355n9, 356n14; Socinian view of, 187, 192, 219–22, 230, 233, 239–40, 246–47, 249, 355n9; subjectivity of, 219, 242, 247–48, 359n43; and the Trinity, 216–21, 351n43. *See also* Antitrinitarianism; Trinity

Christianity. *See* Catholicism; Protestantism; revealed religion

Christian poetry: vs. classical poetry, 168–70, 173–76; historical perspective on, 42–45; machinery in, 170–77; Milton's place in, 325n5; passion and, 174–76; and polytheism, 31–41, 52–58, 65; rational, 46–51

Circle at Great Tew, 350n31

classical gods, 70–71

Cohen, Hermann, 335n5

Collins, Anthony, 159, 162, 164, 166–67

commandments. *See* first commandment; second commandment

Common Notions, 88–89, 280–92, 362n9, 362n10, 363n12. *See also* Religious Common Notions

comparative religion: Cherbury and, 295; concept of development central to, 78; mythography vs., 329n50; occult monotheism and, 79–94; poetry and, 32–33; polytheism and, 18–19, 64–73; revelation put in question by, 82–83; Selden and, 32–33, 64–73; Selden's influence on, 74–77

Conklin, George Newton, 350n31

Conti, Natale, 329n50

Corns, Thomas N., 323n29

councils of gods, 3, 25–26, 29–31, 37–38, 49, 54, 62–72

counter-religion, 18, 68, 299

Cowley, Abraham, 32, 46, 98; "Author's Preface," 52–53; *Davideis*, 35–36, 45–46, 52–63, 69, 77, 328n43, 331n12

Cragg, Gerald R., 346n5

Creation, 220, 227–29

Crell, Johan, 186, 192, 217–18, 239–40, 244, 357n26

Cudworth, Ralph, 88, 184, 324n35, 345n2

Culler, Jonathan, 338n22

cultus proprius, 80

cultus symbolicus, 81

Culverwell, Nathaniel, 362n10

Cupid, 49–50

Dagon, 59, 302–05

Dalila, in *Samson Agonistes*, 297–300

Danielson, Dennis, 114, 338n24

Davenant, William, 32, 98; "Author's Preface," 46–50, 55; *Gondibert*, 45–51, 56–57, 68, 72, 164

Death, in *Paradise Lost*, 312–13, 318–19

De doctrina Christiana (Milton): and accommodation, 125–29, 198; on angels, 339n36; and Arianism, 189; authorship of, 188, 323n29, 324n33; *elohim* in, 3, 30; and first commandment, 187; on God's characteristics, 198; on *imago dei*, 140; and literal interpretation of Bible, 214; on miracles, 250, 256; monotheism in, 5, 9, 134–35; *Paradise Lost* in relation to, 21; on revelation, 164, 277–78; and Socinianism, 189–90, 348n19; on the Son, 193, 196, 221–27, 229, 239–45, 256; on spirit, 273–74; on toleration, 260–62, 294; on the Trinity, 190–91, 193–95, 216–18, 258, 264

Defoe, Daniel, 164–65, 188, 219, 226, 231

deism: angels rejected by, 208–09; and aniconism, 9–10, 213; Bolingbroke and, 183, 204–05, 208, 213, 343n17; comparative religion and, 295; criticisms of, 96, 174–75, 213, 293–94; Dennis on, 169, 174–75, 180–81, 344n36, 345n41; emergence of, 7, 51, 201; freethinking and, 162; Freud and, 354n81; *Gondibert* and, 50; and idolatry, 185, 203; Locke and, 352n59; Milton and, 162–64, 266, 279; miracles rejected by, 203, 207–08, 250, 353n74; and monotheism, 9–10, 183–85; mystery rejected by, 202–03; occult

370 Index

monotheism and, 79, 81–82, 86;
Paradise Lost and, 22, 102, 144,
159–68; vs. revealed religion, 9,
163, 204–15, 343n17; Scripture
rejected by, 205–06; skepticism
and, 84–85; Socinianism and,
200–203, 205, 352n51; and the Son,
203–04; strategies of, 159, 165–66;
supernatural rejected by, 203,
206–09. See also rational religion
Dennis, John, 39–40, 55, 96, 156,
168–82, 188, 213, 249, 309–12,
344n36, 345n41, 359n45, 365n1;
*The Advancement and Reformation
of Modern Poetry*, 168–69, 171, 173,
176, 180; *The Grounds of Criticism
in Poetry*, 177; *Letters on Milton
and Wycherley*, 177, 181; *Remarks
upon a Book Entituled Prince
Arthur*, 172; *Remarks upon
Mr. Pope's Rape of the Lock*, 180
Descartes, René, 22, 120
Deutero-Isaiah, 25–26
discursive thought, 281, 288–92,
364n22
divine instinct, 281–82
divine life, 89–90, 95
*Doctrine and Discipline of Divorce,
The* (Milton), 103, 108, 109, 134–35,
337n14
Drayton, Michael, 39, 40, 41–43, 62,
69, 330n3
Drummond of Hawthornden, William,
40
Dryden, John, 52, 55–56, 169–71,
345n39
Du Bartas, Guillaume, 38–39, 40
Dury, John, 258

Edwards, Thomas, 199–200
Egyptian religion, 90–91, 93–94,
211–13, 303, 354n80
Eikon Basilica, 99
elohim, 3, 30, 228, 320n2, 320n3,
321n5, 325n3, 362n5
emotion, 126–27, 174–76, 197–98
Empson, William, 114, 226, 338n23
epic poetry, 36–37, 46–58, 169–72
Erasmus, Desiderius, 190, 191
Erastianism, 333n31
essence, 193–95, 216, 239
Euripides, *Bacchae*, 270
Exodus, Book of, 149–50
Ezra, Ibn, 340n39

Fall, the, 140
Fallon, Stephen, 118–19, 334n43
Ficino, Marsilio, 79
Firmin, Thomas, 200, 351n46
first commandment, 5–6, 134–35, 187,
193, 219–20
Fish, Stanley, 16, 248, 250, 263, 273,
280, 359n44, 363n19, 364n29
Fletcher, Phineas, 38
footnotes, 41–45, 58–62, 65, 329n54
Forster, E. M., 148
Fowler, Alastair, 147, 317
Frank, Joseph, 163, 360n47
freethinking, 162, 166
free will, 108, 118–19, 291–92
Freud, Sigmund, 11–15, 21–22,
97–98, 102, 196, 212–13, 285,
302–03, 324n32, 351n43, 354n80,
354n81; *Moses and Monotheism*,
11–15
Frye, Roland M., 335n3, 340n46
Fuller, Thomas, 39, 59, 60, 67, 74,
76–77, 78–79, 331n12

Gale, Theophilus, 77
Genesis 1:26, 228–29
Genesis 2, 141
Genesis 18, 103–24, 132–37, 141–42,
217–18
Genette, Gerard, 62, 64, 148–49
Gibbon, Edward, 33, 63
Gildon, Charles, 9, 185, 201, 203,
204
Giraldi, Lilio Gregorio, 329n50
Girard, René, 232
Gladish, David, 50
God: debates with, 106–13, 133–37,
226–27; dualistic conception
of, 11–12, 14–15; and emotion,
126–27, 197–98; human capacity to
understand, 134–38, 140–42, 291–92,
364n29; justice of, 291–93 (*see also*
theodicy); narrative and, 99–100,
113–14, 126, 143–58, 196; negative
theology and, 138–42, 196, 341n52;
and objective morality, 103–05,
108–13, 134; omnipotence of, 13–14,
146, 148–54, 158; omniscience
of, 13–14, 109–11, 145–54, 158;
in *Paradise Lost*, 98–99, 101–42,
335n3, 336n6; personality of,
99–102, 105, 109–10, 141, 143,
197–98; of revealed religion,
211–13; skepticism toward, 85;

and theophany, 105–07, 115, 132–33, 143; visible body of, 197, 351n46. *See also* abstract godhead; aniconism; Antitrinitarianism; deism; monotheism; representation of divinity; Trinity
God-man, 245–48
Goodman, Lenn Evan, 20, 99, 102–03, 109–10, 134, 196
Goodwin, John, 186, 258, 361n60
Gosse, Edmund, 55
Grafton, Anthony, 329n54
Grierson, Herbert, 321n7
Grotius, Hugo, 109–14, 278, 336n14, 337n15, 349n30
Guillory, John, 121, 285

Hale, John K., 323n29
Hales, John, 257
Handy, Lowell, 325n3
Hanford, James Holly, 129–30
Hart, D. Bentley, 120
Hartlib, Samuel, 258
Hebrew Bible: deism and, 205; Genesis 18, 103–24, 132–37, 141–42; monotheism and polytheism in, 3, 25–26, 320n3; ontology in, 340n42; Socinianism and, 187
Hebrews 1:3, 230, 357n26
Hebrews 5:5, 355n11
Herbert, Thomas, 76
Herbert of Cherbury. *See* Cherbury, Edward, Lord Herbert of
Hill, Christopher, 189, 214, 236, 237, 250, 251, 362n9
Hobbes, Thomas, 22, 85, 98, 110, 208, 324n35, 327n26, 333n35, 337n16, 353n74; "The Answer of Mr. Hobbes to Sir Will D'Avenant's Preface Before Gondibert," 46–47, 50, 55
Holmes, David I., 323n29
Holy Spirit, 264
Homer, 49, 54, 72, 177
Hooker, Richard, 259, 286
Hopton, Arthur, 44
Hughes, Merritt, 113
human knowledge: of Christ, 234–38, 245, 256, 262–63; of God, 134–38, 140–42, 291–92, 364n29
Hume, David, 78, 162–63, 324n31
Hume, Patrick, 32–33, 145
Hunter, W. B., 188, 223, 226, 348n22, 356n20
hypostases (persons), 193–95

iconoclasm, 9
idolatry: deism and, 185, 187, 203. *See also* aniconism; polytheism
imago dei, 139–40
impulses, 282–85, 363n19
Incarnation, 220–26, 245–46
indifference, 248–50, 254–63, 294, 359n44
internal apprehension, 281, 283–87
invocations, 39–43, 48–49, 53–54, 76, 129–30, 327n26
Isaiah, Book of, 25–26

Jahve, 11–14, 21, 97, 196, 212–13
Jenkin, Robert, 352n51
Jesuits, 75
Jesus. *See* Christ
Job, Book of, 232–33, 272
Johannine Comma, 191–92
John 1, 220, 223, 224
John 10, 239
1 John 5:7, 191
Johnson, Samuel, 4–5, 23, 117, 157, 248, 307, 328n43
Judeo-Christian revelation. *See* revealed religion
Judges 13, 267–74, 307, 362n5
justice, 291–93
Justin Martyr, 338n27, 355n7

Kahn, Victoria, 318–19
Kant, Immanuel, 310–12
Kelley, Maurice, 189, 194, 217, 223, 225–26, 261, 321n11, 324n33, 341n51, 351n43, 354n4
kingship, 98–99
Kirsch, Jonathan, 323n28
Knapp, Steven, 319
knowledge. *See* human knowledge
Kolbrenner, William, 163, 167, 342n6
Koran, 77

Lang, Bernhard, 78, 331n15
language, and the sublime, 310–13
latitudinarians, 184, 200, 205, 346n3, 346n4
Le Bossu, René, 54, 169–70
Le Comte, Edward, 156, 343n13
Lee, Sidney, 363n17
Leland, John, 163, 343n17
Leonard, John, 325n4
Leslie, Charles, 160–61, 164–66, 169, 345n36
Lewalski, Barbara, 234, 251

372 Index

Lewis, C. S., 97, 101–02, 105, 114, 334n43
Lezra, Jacques, 119–21, 339n34
Lieb, Michael, 126–27, 198, 340n44, 340n45, 341n46
local forgetting, 151–56, 158
Locke, John, 201–02, 206–11, 352n59, 363n12; *An Essay Concerning Human Understanding*, 201, 210, 277; *The Reasonableness of Christianity*, 184, 206–07, 209–11, 346n4
logic, 192–94
Longinus, 312, 365n7
Lucretius, 119
Lushington, Thomas, 186, 218
Luther, Martin, 117, 217, 337n18, 340n39

MacCallum, Hugh, 226, 237, 348n19, 350n35, 357n25, 358n32, 358n35, 358n40
machinery, Christian, 144, 159–60, 164, 167–76, 249
Macrobius, 88
Madsen, William, 129
Maimonides, Moses, 13, 22, 106, 139, 324n35
malach, 340n42
Manuel, Frank, 333n29
Martin, Catherine Gimelli, 163, 336n6, 366n14
Marvell, Andrew, 200
marvelous, the, 36–38, 55, 249. *See also* miracles; supernatural
Masson, David, 277, 333n31
materiality of divine beings, 115–21, 164–67, 197
mathematics, 192–94, 350n40
Matthew, Gospel of, 240–44
McLachlan, John, 186, 191, 256, 349n31, 351n46
Merrill, Thomas, 341n55
middle life, 88–91, 95
Milton, John: Antitrinitarianism of, 4, 188–90, 193–96, 216–18, 222–23, 226, 228, 230, 246, 258, 260–61, 324n33, 349n26, 350n40, 351n48; and Cherbury, 276–77; and Christian poetry, 325n5; Cowley and, 62–63; and deism, 162–64, 266, 279; general religious views of, 21–22, 161, 347n8; on God and morality, 103–04; and heresy, 4,

22, 162, 188–89, 259–60, 324n33; and literal interpretation of Bible, 191–92, 214, 259; and monotheism, 68, 189–90, 195–96, 198, 246–47, 265–66, 308; polytheism in works of, 31; and prophecy, 129–30; and rational religion, 347n8; on revelation, 163–64, 214, 259, 361n1; and Selden, 63–72; and Socinianism, 162, 186, 189–90, 223, 233, 260, 348n19, 349n24, 359n40; and toleration, 258–63, 294. *See also individual works*
mimesis, 62, 64
Minor Reformed Church of Poland, 186
miracles: in *De doctrina Christiana*, 250, 256; deist rejection of, 203, 207–08, 250, 353n74; Locke's defense of, 208, 209; in *Paradise Regained*, 248–56; truth and, 36–37. *See also* marvelous, in narrative; supernatural
Moloch, 58
monism, 118–21
Monk, Samuel, 310, 365n1
monotheism: abstraction and, 11–13, 85, 91–93, 100, 102, 141, 278–79; and aniconism, 9–10, 12–14, 57, 308; Antitrinitarianism and, 187–88, 196; anxiety over, 26–28, 32, 72, 102, 111, 220, 271, 314; Bolingbroke and, 183, 210–11; Cherbury and, 77–86; coining of term, 6, 8, 77, 90, 93, 96–97, 321n8; comparative religion and, 18–19, 32–33, 66, 78, 295; in *De doctrina Christiana*, 5, 9, 134–35; deism and, 9–10, 183–85; duality in, 11–13; Egypt and, 212–13, 303, 354n80; ethical, 335n5; Freud on, 11–15; inward religiosity and, 50; kingship and, 98–99; Milton and, 68, 189–90, 195–96, 198, 246–47, 265–66, 308; Milton's contemporaries and, 6–10; and morality, 103, 336n5; More and, 87–97; Mosaic distinction and, 296; narrative and, 13–23, 42, 57, 143–44, 148–49, 152, 158, 196–97, 214, 311; occult, 74, 79–94, 169, 184, 210–11, 279, 295, 333n29, 346n2, 346n3; in *Paradise Lost*, 1, 25–28, 134–37, 168; in *Paradise Regained*, 9; personality and, 99–100; vs. polytheism, 1, 4,

6–8, 17–18, 28, 68, 73–74, 77–79, 93, 296, 299–306; and purity, 184–85, 196, 347n6; rational religion and, 184; representation and, 13–23; revelation and, 296, 301; in *Samson Agonistes*, 299–306; Selden and, 6–8, 32, 73, 79, 93; skepticism and, 18, 22, 84; Socinianism and, 184, 187, 193, 196; and the Son, 199, 204; in Spenser's *Faerie Queene*, 315–16; supernatural rejected by, 17, 84; and theophany, 105; Trinitarianism and, 8; universalizing tendency of, 134; and violence, 299–300, 302, 305–06. *See also* monotheistic narrative; Mosaic distinction
monotheistic narrative: by Adam in *Paradise Lost*, 132–33, 138, 142; ambiguity of, 15–21, 68–69, 97, 113–14, 142, 158, 168, 228–29, 247; Christ's place in, 218–19; defined, 16–17; Milton and, 316, 318–19; problem of, 36, 156, 179, 314; revelation and, 266; Selden's influence on, 63, 68; Spenser and, 315; and the sublime, 311–12
morality: deism and, 204; God and, 103–05, 108–13, 134; monotheism and, 336n5; polytheism and, 335n5; universality of, 336n14
More, Henry, 6, 8, 87–98, 102, 107, 110, 184, 188, 278, 295, 334n43, 345n2, 350n35, 362n10; *Antidote to Atheism*, 88; *Conjectura cabbalistica*, 192; *An Explanation of the Grand Mystery of Godliness*, 74, 77, 87, 117, 190, 192–93, 203, 246, 346n3
Morris, David, 310, 365n7
mortalism, 162
Mosaic distinction, 17, 19, 21–22, 28, 31, 67–69, 71–72, 188, 198–99, 212, 295–97, 299–303, 306, 314–16, 319, 354n80
Moses, 11–12, 303
Mosley, Humphrey, 63
Mulciber, 71–72
Mulryan, John, 329n50
Murrin, Michael, 366n14
mystery: allegory and, 170; Incarnation as, 190, 246–47; justice vs., 109; rational religion vs., 89–97, 165–66, 190–92, 202
mythography, 329n50

narrative: angels and, 117–18; Christ and, 112, 226–27, 231–32; God and, 99–100, 113–14, 126, 143–58, 196; minimal requirements of, 148; monotheism and, 13–23, 42, 57, 143–44, 148–49, 152, 158, 196–97, 214, 311; ontology of, 33–35, 65; in *Paradise Regained*, 248–49, 255, 263; polytheism and, 36, 55–57, 59, 68–69; in *Samson Agonistes*, 248, 362n6; theology and, 19–21; war in heaven and, 144–58. *See also* monotheistic narrative
narrative presence, 33–35, 65
natural instinct, 280
natural law, 109–10, 336n14
natural religion: Cherbury's, 89–93, 275–76; criticisms of, 162–63, 205; Milton and, 109; and miracles, 208; rationalism of, 172, 185, 205; receptivity of masses to, 207–08, 210; and Scripture, 205; as universal religion, 295. *See also* deism; rational religion
nature, 39
negative theology, 138–42, 196, 341n52
neoclassical criticism, 36
neoclassical sublime, 310, 312, 365n1
neoclassicism, 53–55
Newton, Thomas, 108
Nicolson, Marjorie, 334n43
Norbrook, David, 99
Novak, Maximillian, 164
Nuttall, Geoffrey, 268
Nye, Stephen, 197, 200–02, 349n30, 349n31

occult monotheism, 74, 79–94, 169, 184, 210–11, 279, 295, 333n29, 346n2, 346n3
Ochino, Bernardino, 189
Of Civil Power in Ecclesiastical Causes (Milton), 349n24
Of Education (Milton), 329n49
Of True Religion, Haeresie, Schism, Toleration (Milton), 258–60, 263, 294
omnipotence, 13–14, 146, 148–54, 158
omniscience, 13–14, 109–11, 145–54, 158
On the Morning of Christ's Nativity (Milton), 32, 63

ontology: of Christ, 219, 228–56, 263; Christian poetry and, 33–46; in Genesis 18, 121–23; in Hebrew Bible, 340n42; monotheism and, 17; in *Paradise Lost*, 4–5, 28–30, 64, 122–25; of storyworld, 33–35
ousia (essence), 193–95
Ovid, 56
Owen, John, 187, 197

paganism: Christianity continuous with, 77, 83, 86, 301; Christian poetry vs. poetry of, 168–70, 173–76; and monotheism, 8, 78–87; rejection of, 87–88. *See also* polytheism
Paradise Lost (Milton): accommodation in, 125–31, 138, 340n46; Adam in, 132–42, 196, 229; allegory in, 316–19, 366n14; angels in, 115–24, 144–68; anticlericalism in, 333n28; bathos in, 145–46, 151–52, 156–60, 167, 176–82; Christ in, 199, 221–31; Creation in, 227–28; Death in, 312–13, 318–19; *De doctrina Christiana* in relation to, 21; deism and, 22, 102, 144, 159–68, 181–82; Dennis on, 168–82, 309–11; Freud and, 21; Genesis 18 and, 105–24, 132–37, 141–42, 217–18; God in, 98–99, 101–42, 335n3, 336n6; historical perspective in narrative of, 64–65, 72; machinery in, 144, 159–60, 164, 167–68, 172–79; monotheism in, 1, 25–28, 134–37, 168; More and, 97–98, 107, 334n43; narrative in, 130–32; ontology in, 4–5, 28–30, 64, 122–25; polytheism in, 1–4, 16–17, 25–33, 63–72, 313–14; Raphael in, 115–16, 118–20, 122–29, 131; reception of, 156–82; *Samson Agonistes* and, 308; Selden's influence on, 63–72; Sin in, 317–19; and Socinianism, 190; Spenser's *Faerie Queene* and, 316–18; the sublime in, 151, 153, 156, 158–60, 167, 176–81, 309–14, 319; the Trinity in, 216–18; Urania in, 40; war in heaven in, 144–68, 177–78, 227
Paradise Regained (Milton): Antitrinitarianism and, 22; Christ in, 199, 231–56; human vs. divine perspective of, 232–33; identity motif in, 234–54; indifference in,

248–50, 254–63, 294; miracles in, 248–56; monotheism in, 9; narrative in, 248–49, 255, 263; polytheism in, 32; reception of, 231; and revelation, 272; and Socinianism, 190, 233–34, 239, 358n32
Pareus, David, 355n6
Parish, John E., 112
Patrides, C. A., 188, 228, 348n22, 351n48
Paul, Saint, 79, 222, 224
Pecheux, Sister M. Christopher, 4, 320n4
Phillips, Edward, 231
Philo, 29, 126
philosophy, 19–21, 173
Philostratus, 88, 203
Platonism, 205, 346n3
plot, 148–49. *See also* narrative
poetry. *See* Christian poetry; epic poetry
polytheism: allegory and, 314–15; as atheism, 87, 93; Christian poetry and, 31–41, 52–58, 65; classical gods, 70–71; classical poetry and, 168–69; comparative religion and, 18–19, 32–33, 64–73, 78; English language appearance of, 75; history of, 77–78; interrelatedness in, 66–67, 296–97; Milton's contemporaries and, 31–46, 49–62; monotheism vs., 1, 4, 6–8, 17–18, 28, 68, 73–74, 77–79, 93, 296, 299–306; and morality, 335n5; narrative and, 36, 55–57, 59, 68–69; neoclassicism and, 55; and occult monotheism, 74, 79–94, 169, 295; in *Paradise Lost*, 1–4, 16–17, 25–33, 63–72, 313–14; in *Paradise Regained*, 32; priestcraft and, 81, 90, 93–94, 332n26; Purchas and, 74–76; in *Samson Agonistes*, 32, 297–305; Selden and, 32–33, 60, 62–80, 331n14; in Spenser's *Faerie Queene*, 314–16; studies of, 74–77
Pope, Alexander, 101, 159; *Essay on Man*, 182; *Peri Bathous*, 157; *The Rape of the Lock*, 156–57, 159–60, 180
Porter, Edmund, 187, 351n46
Prescott, Anne Lake, 45
priestcraft, 81, 90, 93–94, 208, 332n26
Protestantism, 51, 75
Prynne, William, *Histriomastix*, 35
Psalm 2, 221, 224, 355n11, 356n17

Pseudo-Dionysius, 341n52
Purchas, Samuel, 6–8, 79, 81, 87;
  Purchas His Pilgrimage, 6, 44,
  74–76, 93, 324n35, 330n3
Puritans, 274

Quakers, 274, 347n8

Racovian Catechism, The, 186,
  189–91, 195, 219–22
Radzinowicz, Mary Ann, 308
Ramus, Pater, 258
Raphael, in *Paradise Lost*, 115–16,
  118–20, 122–29, 131
Rashi, 320n3
rational religion: and
  Antitrinitarianism, 190–91,
  199–200; criticisms of, 88–92,
  95–96, 174–75; latitudinarians and,
  184, 346n4; Milton and, 347n8; and
  monotheism, 184; and personality
  of God, 109–14; revealed vs., 7–8,
  23, 82, 84, 86, 282; Socinianism
  and, 187, 190–92, 349n30. *See also*
  deism; natural religion
Reason of Church Government, The
  (Milton), 325n5, 329n49
Reed, Ishmael, 324n32
Reedy, Gerard, 352n55
relativism, 296–302
Religious Common Notions, 83–84,
  88–89, 110, 204, 207, 208, 210,
  275–76, 278, 282, 294, 297, 301,
  333n34. *See also* Common Notions
religious toleration, 256–63, 294–95,
  297
representation of divinity: biblical,
  125–26; difficulties in, 148;
  dualistic, 11–12, 14–15; linguistic,
  13–23; narrative and, 99–100,
  113–14; negative theology and,
  138–42, 341n52; *Paradise Lost*
  and, 124, 136–42. *See also* abstract
  godhead; aniconism; theophany
republicanism, 99
Resurrection, 220, 355n9
revealed religion: communicability of,
  95–97; in *De doctrina Christiana*,
  164, 277–78; defense of, 89–97;
  deism vs., 9, 163, 204–15, 343n17;
  God of, 211–13; latitudinarians and,
  346n4; Locke and, 206; machinery
  and, 172, 175–76; Milton and,
  163–64, 214, 259, 361n1;

monotheism and, 296, 301; *Paradise
  Regained* and, 272; questioning of,
  74, 78, 82, 167, 209, 268–71, 275–78,
  294, 301, 337n14; rational vs., 7–8,
  23, 82, 84, 86, 282; receptivity to,
  174–75; ridicule of, 159; *Samson
  Agonistes* and, 265–308; and truth,
  296; witnesses to, 253, 269–70, 275
Revelation 12:7, 165–67
Reynolds, Henry, 38, 314
Richardson, Jonathan, 124, 188
ridicule, 159
Rimmon-Kenan, Shlomith, 131
Rivetus, Andreas, 103
Rogers, John, 233
Roscommon, Wentworth Dillon, Earl
  of, 156
Rosenblatt, Jason, 33, 82, 329n53
Ross, Alexander, 77, 79, 82
Rossi, Mario M., 275, 332n23
rousing motions, 286–87, 290–91, 305,
  363n19
Ruether, Rosemary R., 323n28
Rumrich, John, 323n29, 364n30
Rymer, Thomas, 328n43

Sailhamer, John, 107
Samson Agonistes (Milton): angel in,
  267–72; Antitrinitarianism in,
  22; Dagon in, 302–05; Dalila in,
  297–300; divine instinct in, 281–82;
  impulses in, 282–85, 363n19; inward
  events in, 265–66, 272–87, 362n6;
  monotheism in, 299–306; narrative
  in, 248, 362n6; naturalism of, 267;
  Paradise Lost and, 308; polytheism
  in, 32, 297–305; regenerationist
  readings of, 280, 286; and revelation,
  265–308; rousing motions in,
  286–87, 290–91, 305, 363n19;
  Selden's influence on, 277; and
  theodicy, 293, 297; theodicy in,
  306–08, 364n29; thought in, 288–93;
  and toleration, 294, 297
Samuel, Irene, 101, 226, 254, 360n49,
  360n50
Satan, 25–28, 234–36, 262
Saurat, Denis, 335n3
scala natura, 119–20, 125
Scaliger, Joseph, 328n46, 330n3
Scholder, Klaus, 191, 205–06, 350n32
Schwartz, Regina, 323n28, 347n6
scripturalism. *See* Bible, literal
  interpretation of

second commandment, 9, 13, 16, 40, 49, 51, 84, 100, 171, 312
Selden, John, 313; anti-invocation of, 41–45; beliefs of, 333n31; and comparative religion, 32–33, 64–73, 82, 329n50; Cowley's *Davideis* and, 58–65, 328n46, 329n50, 331n12; *De diis Syris syntagmata*, 6, 32–33, 58, 63–66, 69–70, 73–75, 77, 93–94, 98, 277, 324n35, 329n50, 332n26; historical perspective on poetry, 42–45, 68; *History of Tythes*, 82, 333n26; "Illustrations" to *Poly-Olbion*, 41–45, 62, 64, 69; influence of, 74–77, 80, 82, 87, 93–94; and Maimonides, 324n35; Milton's poetics and, 32–33, 63–73, 329n50; and monotheism, 6–8, 32, 73, 79, 93; and occult monotheism, 82; poetry of, 44–45; and polytheism, 32–33, 60, 62–80, 331n14; Purchas and, 74, 330n3; *Table Talk*, 44
Servetus, Michael, 186, 189, 256
Seznec, Jean, 329n50
Shaftesbury, Anthony Ashley Cooper, Earl of, 159
Sharpe, Eric, 295
Shawcross, John, 163
Sherlock, Richard, 333n35
Shoulson, Jeffrey, 337n20
Sidney, Philip, 50
Silver, Victoria, 338n25
Sin, in *Paradise Lost*, 317–19
skeptical extreme, 10, 51, 57–58, 68, 84–85, 93, 265–66, 308
skepticism: Antitrinitarianism and, 199–200; Davenant and, 46–51; deism and, 84–85; faith and, 22–23; history of, 22; monotheism and, 18, 22, 84; polytheism as subject of, 72; rational religion and, 7, 9; about revelation, 268–71, 275–78, 294, 301; ridicule and, 159; Selden and, 32. *See also* skeptical extreme
Smith, John, 102
Socinianism: deism and, 200–203, 205, 352n51; emergence of, 186–87; expansion of, 200; and Hebrew Bible, 187; and idolatry, 185, 187; and literal interpretation of Bible, 191, 205–06, 257, 260; and mathematical logic, 192–93; Milton and, 162, 186, 189–90, 223, 233–34, 260, 348n19, 349n24, 359n40; and monotheism, 184, 187, 193; mystery rejected by, 202–03; *Paradise Lost* and, 190; *Paradise Regained* and, 190, 233–34, 239, 358n32; and personality of God, 197; and rational religion, 187, 190–92, 349n30; and the Son, 187, 192, 219–22, 230, 233–34, 239–40, 246–47, 249, 355n9; Toland and, 352n55; and toleration, 256–58, 260; and the Trinity, 8–9, 184–99, 257–58, 350n32. *See also* Unitarianism
Socrates, 166
sola scriptura, 191–92, 205, 259–60, 347n13, 349n31. *See also* Bible, literal interpretation of
Son of God. *See* Christ
source criticism, 14, 214
Sozzini, Fausto, 186
Speiser, E. A., 340n39
Spellman, W. M., 346n5
Spenser, Edmund, 38, 46–47, 314–18
spirit, 273–74, 361n1. *See also* revealed religion
Stavely, Keith W. F., 259
Steadman, John, 273, 362n6
Stein, Arnold, 157–58, 343n13
Stephens, William, 205
Sternberg, Meir, 20
Stillingfleet, Edward, 200, 346n2; *Discourse in Vindication of the Doctrine of the Trinity*, 201, 352n52; *Irenicum*, 259; *Origines Sacrae*, 184, 346n4
storyworld, 34–35, 38, 96, 118, 326n11
subjectivity, 119–20, 219, 242, 247–48, 359n43. *See also* God, personality of
subjunctive mood, 62, 64
sublime: aniconism and, 312; Dennis and, 309–12, 365n1; eighteenth-century conceptions of, 310–13; language and, 310–13; monotheistic narrative and, 311–12; neoclassical, 310, 312, 365n1; in *Paradise Lost*, 151, 153, 156, 158–60, 167, 176–81, 309–14, 319
subordinationism, 189
substance, 194
Sullivan, Robert E., 351n51
supernatural, the: belief in, 37; Christian poetry and, 39–40, 49–58; deism and, 206; in Milton's works, 266–67; monotheism and, 17, 84; mystery and, 92; in *Paradise Lost*,

164, 175. *See also* marvelous, in narrative; miracles
superstition, 48, 81, 87, 94, 159–60, 165, 166, 203, 208–11
Sylvester, Joshua, 38
syncretism, 29, 322n23

Tasso, Torquato, 32, 36–38, 54–55, 62, 249, 329n49; *Discorsi dell'arte poetica*, 36; *Discorsi del poema eroico*, 38; *Gerusalemme liberata*, 37–38, 47, 328n43
Teskey, Gordon, 315, 365n12
theodicy, 104, 266, 293, 297, 306–08, 364n29
theology, 19–21
theophany, 105–07, 115, 126, 132–33, 143. *See also* representation of divinity
things indifferent, 255–63, 294, 359n44
Tillotson, Geoffrey, 180
Tillotson, John, 200
1 Timothy 2:5, 241
1 Timothy 3:16, 190, 191, 246
Toland, John, 161–62, 164, 206–08, 327n36, 343n21, 352n55; *Amyntor*, 162; *Christianity Not Mysterious*, 201–02, 207; *Life of Milton*, 161, 169
toleration. *See* religious toleration
translation, polytheistic, 66–67, 296–97
Treatise of Civil Power, A (Milton), 361n1
Treip, Mindele Anne, 38
Trinity: Christ and, 216–21, 351n43; in *De doctrina Christiana*, 190–91, 193–95, 216–18, 258, 264; *elohim* and, 320n2; Genesis 18 and, 217–18; as idolatrous, 187; More's defense of, 190; mystery and, 96. *See also* Antitrinitarianism; Christ; God

truth: historical, 42–46, 59–61, 65; miracles and, 36–37; Mosaic distinction and, 17; poetic vs. historical, 42, 44, 68, 76; poetry and Christian, 33–38, 47, 51, 55; revelation and, 296; storyworld and, 34–35, 38. *See also* skepticism; verisimilitude
Tuck, Richard, 85, 110, 337n15, 337n16
Tweedie, Fiona J., 323n29

Unitarianism, 189, 197, 200–202. *See also* Socinianism
Urania, 40

Va-yera, 105–07
verisimilitude, 36–38, 47, 56–57. *See also* truth
Verity, A. W., 29
Virgil, 49, 54, 177
Vondel, Joost van den, 307–08
Vossius, Dionysius, 324n35
Vossius, Gerardus, 7, 59, 76–82, 332n23
Vossius, Isaac, 77

Walker, D. P., 332n19
Waller, Edmund, 46
war in heaven, 144–68, 177–78, 227
Watts, Isaac, 181
Weber, Max, 285
Weinberg, Bernard, 37
Westminster Assembly, 258
Wilbur, Earl Morse, 352n59
Willet, Andrew, 123
Willey, Basil, 82–83
Wittreich, Joseph, 188, 268
Wollebius, 321n11
Woolston, Thomas, 159, 250
worship, 7